LUCIEN GREGOIRE'S

MURDER IN THE VATICAN

THE REVOLUTIONARY LIFE OF JOHN PAUL I

". . . Like a shimmering white light, he rose up out of the mud in the street and left no one untouched.

For those of us at the top - from heads of churches, to leaders of nations, to those of great scientific achievement - he was the Enlightener - the Imitation of the Holy Ghost.

For those of us at the bottom - from the poor, to the homeless, to the handicapped, to the oppressed - he was the Redeemer - the Imitation of Christ.

*But, above all - he was the best of men."**

* Il Messaggero 4 Oct 78 Vatican, Cardinal Suenens, Archbishop of Brussels, eulogizes his friend
translation: 'Albino Luciani' = 'White Light'

ISBN: 1-4033-4805-7 (e)
ISBN: 1-4033-4806-5 (sc)
ISBN: 1-4033-4807-3 (dj)

Library of Congress Control Number: 2002092871

Printed in the United States of America
Bloomington, Indiana

This book is printed on acid-free paper.

Part I His Life - a Philadelphia bookstore owner,

"Many people come into our shop and pick up your book, and although not all of them buy it, each one of them leaves here thinking things they never thought before."

Part II The Investigation Into His Death - Michael Malak, critic,

"A conspiracy buff's delight."

Signed copies can be purchased at selective bookstores listed on www.murderinthevatican.com or by contacting the author @ vatican@att.net or 410 625 9741

MURDER IN THE VATICAN and other books by this author including the sequel to this book "The Reincarnation of Albino Luciani" also published as "A God for Lions" are previewed and available on www.authorhouse.com and www.murderinthevatican.com. Lucien Gregoire's books are also available on all major Internet booksellers' sites.

1stBooks - rev. 04/08/05

FOREWORD

On the evening of September 23, 1978, the newly appointed Pope called together the twenty-one Vatican cardinals who hated what he stood for so much that they had refused to vote for him on the recount that had been taken to render his election unanimous. He talked of the problems of the world, -that the Church's ban on contraception was the driving force behind the spread of disease, poverty and starvation in third world countries, and abortions in first world countries. He told them it was morally wrong for 'holy' men to stand in the way of long term loving relationships between any of God's children, whether it be a matter of race, creed, remarriage or homosexuality. He told them it was morally wrong for 'holy' men to stand in the way of a woman's right to minister the will of Christ. He told them many other things. And then he told them one thing more. He told them that the following week he would go to the podium and tell the world,

"Mother Church will cease to be the cause of many of the world's problems and rather will begin to be the answer to them."

A WEEK LATER HE WAS DEAD

Except for the names of *Guy Beene, Jack Champney, Tom Jones and Piccolo,* which names are nicknames or have been used to protect the privacy of families, all names discussed in this book are actual.

The author's appreciation to those who helped him gain access to records held by certain Italian dioceses and libraries, the Vatican Apostolic Library, the British National Museum, the Cairo Museum and other sources that contribute to the factual nature of this book.

Special recognition to,

the angel Victoria and the angel of the spring of 2004

translations – *Morena Ciringione, Maria Cristina Tolomeo*

caricature on the cover – *Ben Vogelsang*

consultations Italy: *Carlo Benelli, Roberto Buontempo. John Calvi, Jorge Ceschin, Giovanni Luciani, Guiseppe Luciani, Anna Montini, Nina Moro, Teresa Roncalli, Mario Signoracci.* Europe other: *Marcel Leusink, Hans Lubbers, Bouwien Rutten, Mark Tyminski, Linda Suenens, Hans Willebrands.* United States: *Pascal Cantona, Kevin Herron, Randall Reade, Archbishop Bruce Simpson, Harry Vedder. Some important contributors to this book including active priests and bishops of the Church have asked that their names not be printed in this book.*

the nun who so graciously let me back into the bishop's castle in Vittorio Veneto after so many years, in the winter of 2004

many references to the press herein were widely published and can be found in the world's major newspapers at the times indicated. For those events reported locally, the specific publication is footnoted in the text. Other sources include the parliamentary and judicial records of nations.

this book is dedicated to John Paul I

CONTENTS

PREFACE

In the crypt beneath St. Peter's altar is a plain slab of granite,

IOANNES PAVLUS P. P. I

Like its counterpart partway around the world in Arlington, it too marks an unknown tomb, "*The Tomb of the Unknown Pope.*" Unlike the tombs of the other popes that are interred in magnificent sculptures of marble and gold and tell of their lives, there is no inscription other than his name. Not even the period of his reign appears to mark his time in history, for the Church would rather his life remain a secret, *The Secret Life of John Paul.*

author's collection

birthplace of Albino Luciani in Canale d'Agordo

Although a few other Popes have been born into less than well-to-do means, Albino Luciani was the only one to have been born into dire poverty, -one who came within a whisker of having starved to death as a child, -one who overcame obstacles that most us can barely fathom and yet eventually rose to the papacy. One would think that such a story would have been the subject of motion pictures and Broadway plays much less than a simple book. Go out onto the Internet and into the history books in the libraries and seek him out, and you won't find him there. Yes, much about his death, and the one page résumés here and there, *"he was born on . . . became a priest on . . . etc.,"* but not much of his life.

Murder in the Vatican is the only existing biography of John Paul and despite its title you will find that it is much more the record of his life than it is of his death. And although this protects me from possible accusation of plagiarism, it has on the other hand made the task much more difficult, particularly in that we are talking not of tales, but of history. And insofar that this book is a matter of history, does not mean that I am in possession of all of the pieces of the puzzle in this thing that I often refer to as the *"Secret Life of John Paul."* Yet I do, as you will see, have almost every other piece, and when one has almost every other piece of a puzzle, one fairly well knows what almost all of the other pieces look like. Yet, there are some pieces that will remain missing for all time.

The dialogue herein is in both *italicized* and unitalicized text. The latter, although representative of what was actually said by real people, is not supported by public record or documentation.

For purposes of consolidation, I relate my time with Albino Luciani as if it were a single encounter in 1969, whereas there were actually a dozen or so sessions ranging from an hour or two to as much as six or seven hours each and they took place on my visits to Vittorio Veneto in 1968 and 1969.

In writing about a man's life, particularly one who has been dead for many years and where there is very little existing record of his life; it is not prudent to rely on witnesses, particularly when one records history as in the case of a pope. This is because a witness is very often a person of motive and is usually one of poor and confused memory in recalling events that happened decades ago. I should note that except for two of the Pope's distant cousins, the Luciani family has refused to help me in my effort for it, like the Church, would rather that there be no record of his life, as many of the things that he said and did would block his chance at sainthood in a conservative Church, which is his family's objective. They would prefer that the world remember him as a man who ignored the issues of his day and rather spent his life on his knees.

Yet, nothing could be more short of the truth. For, as a matter of fact, he had spent much of his life pulling others up off of their knees and putting them to work caring for the immense orphan population of his time. And concerning the issues, he was one of the most outspoken men in the history of the Church, the reason why he had risen to the papacy.

Yet, one does have a few reliable witnesses, a few of which were in the Vatican the night the Pope died. There is also the press, the written records of the man himself, the forty four orphanages he built and the potter's pine box in which he is entombed. And then there is a collection of drafts of his sermons through the years that I was fortunate enough to have picked up for a couple of dinners and two hundred bucks from a diocese clerk in Vittorio Veneto. There is a pair of cut-glass cruets that had been given to him by his mother which I won at auction. In addition, there is the sometimes light and often heavy theology that permeates Luciani's own best sellers, *Illustrissimi* and *Catechism in Crumbs,* which authenticates the underlying ideology which permeates this book.

Yet, much of what is set forth here recounts my personal encounters with the man and I recall every moment of each of them as if it were yesterday. And I relished those moments as I witnessed this good man Luciani smiling, grinning, laughing, teasing, joking and then smiling some more. As much as I would have wanted, although this man has been the most powerful force in my life, I was not a personal acquaintance of Albino Luciani. On the other hand, I was for the last years of his life the closest friend of one of his closest confidants, the reason why I had the good fortune to have met the man on those memorable occasions. A great deal of what I talk about here is the record of my friend *Jack's* correspondence and the many conversations he had with me.

The stories that pertain to his childhood and young life as a teenager and as a priest, including the story of *the golden cross in the window* and *his walk along the railroad tracks* and the story of *the strange little boy in the playground* and many other heartwarming stories set forth herein are recollections of these sessions and I often refer to them as his memoirs.

Some of my personal experiences with the bishop of Vittorio Veneto are abridged in this book. For example, the story of '*The Boy on the Fence',* which I confine to a paragraph or two, actually ignited a discussion that lasted an afternoon.

We were enjoying the afternoon sun, the three of us, Albino, Jack and I, when the local newspaper boy delivered a week old copy of the New York Times and there was the picture of a boy on a fence. A gay Hispanic teenager had been arrested in Washington Square Park and had been brought into the Tenth Precinct Station for booking. Later that night he was found impaled face down on the heavy iron fence that enclosed the station, with six of its blood tipped spikes protruding upwards through his body from his neck to his thigh. It was only then that I learned that this smiling, grinning, laughing, teasing, joking Albino Luciani, could cry.

Associated Press Photo

"What is important, is not how many babies are born - but that every child that is born has an equal chance at a good and healthy life!"

In July 1978, just a month before his election, when just about every cardinal and bishop in the world had condemned Louise Brown, the world's first artificially inseminated child, as being "*a child of the devil;*" Luciani, reached to the *left* and took up his pen and wrote her parents, *"My very personal congratulations to you on the birth of your little girl. I (the Church) have no right to condemn you for what you wanted and asked the doctors to carry out. I want you to be assured that there is reserved for both you and your child a high place in Heaven."* Above, as Pontiff, he is asked by a reporter why he had done such a thing. "W*hat is important is not how many babies are born, but that every child that is born has an equal chance at a good and healthy life. Genetic science will eventually take us there."*

Dear Mr. Gregoire

My name is Tommy. I read Murder in the Vatican..

I was born with one eye and had a wrinkled face so nobody wanted me. I think I scared them. Then one day when I was five years old my father showed up and took me home. I remember the kids used to laugh at me in the playground. Then my fathers sold everything they had including the house and I spent a long time in the hospital and the doctors and nurses made me look good. We have still many bills to pay. But now I am quite a ladies man at school. I hit my first home run last summer and this year I am going to hit forty more.

My parents love me. That is, they used to love me. Now only one of them loves me. Because the other one is dead. He gave his life trying to win freedom for Iraq. He died on my fourteenth birthday. I noticed in your book that General Patton said some words over the grave of another soldier who like my father was gay and gave his life to save some Italian school children, "Freedom without equality is not what it pretends to be. For the diamond would be made of paste."

As you know I won't be getting any benefits from the army or from social security to pay for my education or my medical bills because my parents did not have the freedom to marry and I was adopted by the father that is still with me. I didn't even get his purple heart or bronze star. The army gave them to his parents who hated him and sold them in a tag sale. I would have liked to have them.

My father tells me not to feel bitter because according to the last census there are more than a million children in gay families and they are in the same boat. But, of course, I am not listed with them because of the don't ask don't tell policy. My father says that there are also over fifteen million other children in single parent families, many like me who are of gay parents who are not counted in the census because they are fearful of losing their jobs too. So we are talking about a lot of children here, million s of them, not just me.

Both my father and I are sure that your book will be a best seller. I want to ask you a favor. I want to ask you when you are on Larry King Live, could you please read my letter. I think it might help people to understand our problem.

I was planning on being a baseball player. But your book has made me change my mind. Instead I am going to study hard and I am going to become president. Well, maybe not president, but I am going to help other people. Like me.

Tommy

In MURDER IN THE VATICAN find out why General Patton objected to a Don't ask, Don't tell policy. Why our forefathers, the American Psychological Association, the United States Supreme Court and John Paul I all agree that marriage is an individual right and cannot be imposed upon by the majority. There are an estimated four million* like Tommy who can only be helped by gay marriage.

* *United States Census 2000/Statistical Abstracts of the United States 2000*

United Press International Photo

Although he shuddered at the word 'divorce' he did believe fervently in remarriage. After the war, he sent a letter to the Vatican requesting that Hitler and Mussolini be excommunicated on a post-mortem basis. Pius saw it as an opportunity to silence the young rebel from the foothills of Belluno once and for all. He answered Luciani's request in the press, "*We must learn to forgive our enemies as Christ has taught us.*" Alluding to the Church's ban on remarriage, Luciani responded, "*I am greatly tormented that Mother Church would see it as her duty to close the Gates of Heaven to so many young innocent people who have at last found true love and yet on the other hand see it as her duty to leave the Gates of Heaven open to the likes of Hitler and Mussolini.*" The largest tabloid in Italy, capitalizing on Luciani's expertise in the game of chess, gave the incident front-page coverage with the bold headline, *"ACACCO-MOTTO!" "CHECKMATE!"*

As residing bishop, he concluded his remarks on *falling-in-love* at commencement services of the seminary at Vittorio Veneto in Northern Italy 23 Jun 61,

"... and therefore, we must hold most hallowed this epitome of God's creation - this perfect balance of mental energy that exists between two people when they fall-in-love - this perfect union of minds that can only be made by God. We must find the great courage within us to set aside the many prejudices that have been built into us by our Christian forefathers and we must hold this holy union in sacred trust before Almighty God whenever it exists between any of God's children whether, it be between man and woman, or black and white, or royalty and commoner, or German and Russian, or Christian and Jew, or virgin and divorcee, or man and man, or woman and woman or eunuch and hermaphrodite, or what have you. The rest of this thing we call 'love' is simply the animal in us. To think differently, that it pertains to physical parts of the body, is to say that the Holy Sacrament of Matrimony pertains equally to apes in the forests as it does to human beings."

Associated Press Photo

Just a few months before his election to the papacy, John Paul criticized an American bishop for having paid off an alleged victim of a pedophile priest. ***"It would be better that we try our accused fellow servants in a court of law so that they can be cleared of any wrongdoing and if found guilty they should pay their debt to society. It is not Mother Church's business to pay their debt in cash, particularly to pay it with money that was intended for the poor. Besides, if we take no action to get at the truth, we may very well be endangering countless children in the future."****

John Paul, at the time Archbishop Albino Luciani of Venice, was particularly concerned with what went on within the Vatican walls. The Pope is pictured here just a few months later with one of the Maltese altar boys, whom his policy was intended to protect from predator priests, bishops and cardinals inside and outside the Vatican, a policy that was later reversed by his successor's policy, *"Avoid scandal at any cost."* (dollars or children)

* *Messaggero Mestre 17 Mar '78*

Agenzia Ansa Photo

"Never be afraid to stand up for what is right whether your adversary be your parent, your teacher, your peer, your politician, your preacher, your constitution, or even your God." [1]

[1] Cardinal Albino Luciani speaks to a youth organization in Venice. He pays homage to Lincoln for defying the written word of God, the Tenth Commandment, *"Thou shalt not covet (desire to take from) thy neighbor his property, including his house, his wife, his slaves, his ox and his ass."* Moses intent was clearly to protect the right of one man to enslave another and this is explicit in all Bibles produced prior to the nineteenth century. In the twentieth century, some editions have changed the word from *slaves* to *servants.* The Ten Commandments are the most credible testimony in the Old Testament, as they are the only written word of God. Catholic and Jewish versions remain unchanged today - *slaves.*

Above, the nonconformist Albino Luciani is shown at age eleven attending the minor seminary at Feltre. He peruses the pages of the Old Testament. When he questioned that the earth was created by a God that did not know the earth was round and He created vegetation the day before He created the sun, when vegetation cannot exist without photosynthesis which is a product of the sun, it brought the child prodigy poor grades. When, as Editor of the school newspaper, he suggested that the government should place a warning on the Old Testament, *"This book is a work of fiction,"* it came within a whisker of bringing him expulsion.[2]

[1] *Messaggero Mestre 21 Apr 73*

[2] *Parish Bulletin Feltre,* 16 May '21

MAIN CHARACTERS

Cardinal Giovanni Benelli, Archbishop of Florence. As Undersecretary of State under Paul VI he was the most powerful man in the Church. In 1982, though in guarded condition in a Florence hospital, an order came from the Vatican to remove him from life support equipment and return him to the cardinal's mansion where he died two hours later. When doctors criticized the order, the Vatican claimed that Benelli himself had requested that he be moved. His personal physician told the press "*that would have been quite a trick as although the cardinal was expected to recover he was comatose at the time he was moved.*" Benelli had been the most outspoken cardinal calling for an autopsy in the death of John Paul I. Just a month before his death he had made a remark to the press that insinuated Vatican involvement in Roberto Calvi's murder..

Roberto Calvi, President of the Banco Ambrosiano. He was engaged by John Paul II to mastermind what came to be known as the *Great Vatican Bank Scandal*. He was found hanging from Blackfriar's Bridge in London a week after he had made a statement to the press that inferred that he was being blackmailed by someone high up in the Vatican.

Bishop Giuseppe Caprio, Undersecretary of State during the last two years of Paul VI's reign.

Bishop Agostino Casaroli, Vatican Foreign Minister under Paul VI. He spent much of his time in Eastern Europe and in North Africa fighting Communism. In December 1973, he was one of two dozen survivors when a French Caravelle jet crashed in the Moroccan Desert killing over a hundred people.

Reverend John Champney, an instructor in the seminary at Vittorio Veneto and for a time secretary to Albino Luciani who presided as bishop there. He was the author's closest friend and at the same time one of John Paul's closest confidants. He was killed by a hit-run driver outside the Vatican walls the day following the Pope's death. The driver of the car has never been apprehended.

Cardinal Carlo Confalonieri, Dean of the College of Cardinals. He was the oldest of the cardinals under Paul VI and John Paul I. An influential member of the *curia*, he was an ultraconservative and a close confidant of Cardinal Siri and Bishop Casaroli, co-leaders of the *far right* in the Church. He was of the Mafia family of the same name.

Teresa Corrocher, Roberto Calvi's secretary and closest confidant. She was found hanging in a closet in Milan on the same day that Roberto Calvi was found hanging under Blackfriar's Bridge in London. Both 'suicides' were later determined to be homicides.

Albert Einstein, John XXIII often referred to Albino Luciani as the *"Albert Einstein of the Roman Catholic Church."* and Einstein, himself, once said of him, *"Luciani thinks of things today, as the rest of us will think of them a thousand years from now."*

Albino Luciani, Bishop of Vittorio Veneto. He was the first bishop appointed by John XXIII and a close advisor of this Pope during his reign. It was Luciani's influence on John XXIII that caused this Pope to shed his conservative cloak of eighty years and bring change to the Church. Luciani developed the seminary at Vittorio Veneto from utter obscurity to one of the most recognized schools of theology in the world. He was named Patriarch of Venice in December 1969 and became John Paul I on August 26 1978. A revolutionary prelate, whose pontificate spanned only thirty-three days, it was that the Vatican was caught by the press in a series of lies concerning the circumstances of his death that gave rise to rumors of foul play.

Monsignor John Magee, secretary to Paul VI. He was transitional secretary under John Paul I. At the time of the Pope's death he was on notice that he would be replaced by the secretary who had served John Paul I in his previous assignment as Archbishop of Venice. He was the primary spokesman for the Vatican in matters concerning the death of John Paul I.

Bishop Paul Marcinkus, President of the Vatican Bank under Paul VI and John Paul I. An unexplained deficit of a few million dollars occurred during his watch and was uncovered by an audit that had been ordered by John Paul I. In his first organizational move upon becoming Pope, John Paul II elevated Marcinkus, a common bishop, to the rank of archbishop and made him President of the Vatican State, the Pope's civil office previously held only by pontiffs. Marcinkus eventually became the fall guy for much of the collapse of Banco Ambrosiano, which brought Italy to financial ruin under John Paul II when the Pope loaned $1.3 billion that had been deposited by that bank in the Vatican Bank to a conglomerate in Panama. The money disappeared and despite years of Italian court proceedings and investigations no one ever found out what happened to it. A leading candidate for the *red hat*, Marcinkus was suddenly forced into exile when he made the statement to the press, "*I keep telling John Paul (II) that if we keep sweeping things under the rug we will eventually trip over it.*" Shortly after the incident the Pope paid $241million in cash to European investors and swept the scandal under the rug once and for all.

Cardinal Giovanni Montini, Archbishop of Milan. He was the first cardinal appointed by John XXIII and was John's handpicked successor. When elected to the papacy in 1963, he took the name of Paul VI. Anxiety for those around him reduced him to being a simple spokesman for the *Vatican Curia.* His fear of those who shared the Vatican with him is quite apparent from his memoirs, "*My weakness for life has resulted in poor leadership for my flock!*" He died at the Castel Gandolfo in August 1978 under even more mysterious and conflicting circumstances than did his successor John Paul. The press widely criticized the strange circumstances of his death but foul play was never suspected because of his advanced age.

Aldo Moro, leader of the Christian Democratic Party during the reign of Paul VI. His liberal philosophies dominated much of the thinking of the Italian population, which at the time was entirely Roman Catholic. For this reason he was a bitter enemy of *right wing extremists* in the Catholic Church, particularly those clustered in the Vatican. He was a lifelong acquaintance and the closest friend and ally of Paul VI and was murdered by extremists in May of 1978, just a short time before the sudden and unexpected deaths of Paul VI and John Paul I.

Metropolitan Nicodim, Archbishop of Leningrad. A *left wing* Russian prelate who believed that Christ's dictate of *a redistribution of wealth society* could be successfully incorporated into modern civilization despite the fact that the attempt to do so in Russia had failed. Midway through the thirty-three day pontificate of John Paul, he fell dead at the Pope's feet. Rumors surfaced that he had been poisoned by coffee that had been intended for the Pope.

Cardinal Giuseppe Siri, Archbishop of Genoa. Under John XXIII and Paul VI, he was the leader of *right wing* extremists in the field. It was he who made the remark upon the passing of John XXIII, "*It will take the Church four hundred years to recover from John's pontificate.*" Siri's comment was sound as a Pope's major decisions are irrevocable in the short term. This is one of the great problems in managing the Church, that a successor Pope cannot easily reverse the decisions of his predecessors for the credibility of the Church rests on the infallibility of its leader. Siri was twice the runner-up in papal elections, being defeated by Paul VI in 1963 and by John Paul I in 1978.

Cardinal Leon Joseph Suenens, Archbishop of Brussels. He was the backbone of liberalism in the Church during the last half of the twentieth century. He led the lobbying in the election conclaves that won the papacy for both Paul VI and John Paul I. He was the genius and main force behind *Vatican II*, the council that brought change to the Church in 1963. In 1979, he criticized John Paul II for having used monies deposited by Mother Teresa in the Vatican Bank to build a luxurious swimming pool for his personal pleasure. Almost immediately, he was removed by the Pope as Primate of Belgium and exiled. He died unexpectedly and under identical circumstances as those that surrounded the death of John Paul, *"sitting up reading a book, which book was still clutched upright in his hands."*

Cardinal Jean Villot, Secretary of State under Paul VI. Paul named the French cardinal to the post when midway in his pontificate the conservative he had inherited upon his election died. Being a *liberal,* Villot was undermined by the members of the *curia* and as a result his undersecretary Benelli emerged as the informal leader of the *Vatican Curia* and thereby the Roman Catholic Church during the latter part of Paul's reign. Jean Villot died unexpectedly a short time after the death of John Paul I of symptoms identical to those of Paul VI's death a month earlier.

Cardinal Karol Wojtyla, Archbishop of Krakow. He became John Paul II in the second conclave of 1978, an ultraconservative who brought an end to change in the Church that had been begun by John XXIII in 1959.

Cardinal Yu Pin, Archbishop of Taiwan. In his last official act as Pope, Paul VI elevated Yu Pin to the rank of Grand Chancellor of Eastern Affairs on August 5, 1978. A few days later Yu Pin keeled over at Paul's funeral. The Vatican issued an official statement that *'the cardinal had suffered a heart attack.'* Several newspapers called for an autopsy, but one was never performed. On August 16, 1978 his body was returned in a sealed coffin to Taipei for interment.

PART I

PAUPER WHO WOULD BE POPE

his life, his philosophies, his ambitions and his mysterious death

Albino Luciani was born into abject poverty in a small village in the Italian Alps to a scullery maid and a migrant worker. His mother was a devout Catholic who prayed before crucifixes made of bits of wood. She told him that Christ was his God. His father was a social revolutionary activist who often burned his mother's crucifixes in the stove. He told him that Christ was a Santa Claus for grownups.

After he became Pope his brother Eduordo was interviewed,

"*It was terrible; we even went without shoes most of the year as to save them for the wintertime.*"

One day in the Italian Alps, when he was just six years old, his grandfather told him the bad news, *"Today, you believe in both Jesus and Santa Claus. Well,"* he apologized, *"there is no Santa Claus. We've been kidding you."* He remembers crying himself to sleep that night. How could they take Santa away from him? In his dreams he *waved* goodbye to Santa, but he still had his Jesus and he pleaded, *"Please don't take my Jesus from me!"*

The next day he trudged along the railroad tracks in the knee-deep snow. His shoes were tattered and torn and worn and they did not match and his feet were frozen and they tormented him with each step. Yet he continued on pausing here and there, filling his pail with pieces of what had fallen from the rumbling coal cars and he thought of the day before when he had gazed through the glass store window at the golden crucifix. At three hundred lire a pail he needed three more pails full and he would have enough to buy this splendid treasure for the very best mama in the world. A smirk of a leer tinged his lips as he imagined his father's frustration when he would try to burn this one, and it quickly broadened into a smile as he imagined the look of surprise and wonderment that his mother would have when she would open the gift on Christmas morn. He pictured her puzzled expression when she would read the card,

You gave him life, I gave him hope.
Together, for a time, we gave him paradise.
Now my quest must end, but for you the work goes on.
The struggle must endure, for the challenge remains.
For the hope is still there, and his dream must never die.

Santa

Although his mother had won the first round, it was his father who would give him his commission in life. It was he who in the end would cause Albino to take his place on the *left,* who would mold him into the revolutionary that he would become.

On October 1, 1923, eleven year old Albino Luciani climbed into the carriage that was to take him to the minor seminary at Feltre. His father, reconciled to his son's wish that he wanted to become a priest, told the boy, *"Piccolo, unlike those hypocrites who prance about in the Vatican palaces in their magnificent robes of silk and satin with jeweled chalices and rings of diamonds and rubies and gold, you must promise me that you will live your life in imitation of Christ. For Christ would not approve of this masquerade on the part of His earthly representatives. You must play your cards carefully and work hard until that day when at the helm of their ranks you will tear them down."*

Shortly after he became Pope, rumors surfaced that the first woman would be ordained. A young journalist challenged the new Pope on doctrine. John Paul told the reporter, *"When I was a teenager my father made me promise that I would live my life in imitation of Christ, and I have kept that solemn promise. Each time that the fork in the road has come up, often only minutes apart, I have asked myself, 'Now, what would Jesus have done in this case?' And I have often pondered the possibility as to how much better the world would be if everyone were to do this."* He then asked the reporter, *"Now, what do you think Jesus would do in this case?"* When the young man remained silent, the Pope told him, *"It makes no difference what was written by self-serving men for yesterday, all that counts is what Jesus would do today."* Then reaching for a microphone the Pope raised his voice and told the crowd, *"Never forget that God is more our Mother than She is our Father!"** Cardinal Carlo Confalonieri, the aging Dean of the *College of Cardinals*, passed out. The next day the Pope was dead.

This is the testament and fate of John Paul I

* *IL Messaggero Rome September 27, 1978. Note: the Vatican Curia edited most of what John Paul actually said before it was released to newspapers; some papers reported the word "He' vs. "She"*

Chapter 1

HIS LIFE

his ideology,

For those of us who knew him, who remember him, I bring nothing new. But for those of us who have allowed the Church's misrepresentations of what he was all about, who have allowed Rome's falsehoods to distort his legacy, I bring a treasure trove of yesterday.

Let me begin by telling you of *Piccolo*, better known as Albino Luciani and perhaps best remembered as Pope John Paul I.

First of all, concerning ecclesiastical matters, Luciani was a moderate conservative. As long as doctrine did not treat people unfairly he conformed to decisions that had been made. Concerning some issues he appeared to be an ultraconservative; but whenever he took such positions his motive was to preserve his ability to accomplish his major objectives, which were entirely progressive.

For example, he opposed the efforts of ultraliberals who wanted to relax the dress of women in the Church. His objective concerning women was a much greater one as he intended to bring about equality of women in the Church. He believed that the already established respect for the habit would make it easier for the clergy and the congregation to accept the transformation of aspiring nuns into the priesthood. To him, if nuns were to start wearing street clothes it would be a step in the wrong direction. He would extend this requirement of dress to official functions only, permitting even priests to wear casual clothes when not on official duty.

Luciani also believed in priest celibacy and he would extend this requirement to all those women of the Church to whom he would one day grant the privilege to create the Eucharist. He felt that in exchange for the great power of being able to give birth to the Eucharist one must make this great sacrifice; otherwise, in his words, "*one would have his cake and eat it too.*" On the other hand, it was his intent to lift the requirements of celibacy and dress for those nuns and monks who did not aspire to the priesthood; so that in the end only priests, whether they are men or women, would be restricted by celibacy and dress.

So yes, for those who would want to think that way, Luciani was a moderate conservative. And if one were to read his official biographical briefs as they have been released by the Vatican, he was an ultraconservative. But the underlying purpose of any conservatism he may have displayed was to bring his liberal objectives to fruition. One might consider what follows as being the first independent biography of John Paul ever published, that is based on the facts as they have survived today and not altered or edited out by the Vatican. As a matter of fact, *Murder in the Vatican* is the only complete record of this good man's life that exists today, - of his struggles as an impoverished child - as a promising teenager - as a young revolutionary priest - as a compassionate bishop - as an outspoken cardinal, and as a beloved pope. And concerning his unwitnessed death, *Murder in the Vatican* is the only book to have investigated his unwitnessed death that has been written by someone who actually met the man; and I recount my time with him in these pages.

As a common priest in a remote mountain village of Northern Italy, it was Luciani's outspoken stance against several papal decrees that attracted the attention of John XXIII and made him into the protégée of this first liberal Pope of the twentieth century. Albino at one time possessed an intense fear of public speaking and, as set forth herein, John XXIII tricked him into taking his place at the podium. Although Luciani was never to become what one might call a great orator, the action was enough to make it possible for him to accept his rank and make his mark in life.

On that particular occasion, as a village priest, he addressed the Vatican cardinals in the Sistine Chapel. It was way back then that he set the stage for what one day would be his papacy, "*Our great enemy is the bigot. He lives in each and every one of us,*" he told them, "*His ally is scripture. Our ally is conscience. His ally is Moses. Our ally is Christ.*"

These words more than any others describe Luciani as the man he truly was; the way he lived his life, the way he wanted others to live their lives. For his purpose in life above all else was to rid the world of the bigot. As he so profoundly stated on that occasion, "*As long as he exists no man is truly free. Not even he, the bigot himself, is free. If one is to be successful in bringing down an enemy, one must know who he is, know where he is coming from, know his armament, know his mental embattlement, how he thinks. And believe me, all the bigot has are words, flimsy words, - flimsy arrows. Flimsy arrows that he believes will win for him. Flimsy arrows built in an ancient factory.*"*

Luciani was referring to the sparse and ambiguous testimony of the Old Testament which serves as ammunition for the bigot in his war against blacks, women, homosexuals and certain ethnic peoples, - that most of what it had to say could be taken to mean whatever the bigoted preacher wanted it to say. And he made it clear to his audience, the great

* *L'Osservatore Romano December 19, 1958*

majority of which at the time were the very enemies he spoke of, that the war he was about to wage would be fought on all fronts.

his writings,

His comment concerning Moses was well founded and was consistent with his debut onto the public stage thirty years earlier, when a paper he had written as a secondary school student reached a local socialist revolutionary newspaper. "*I cannot accept,*" he wrote, "*that Moses was the holy man the Church and the motion pictures make him out to be. After all, Moses introduced the concept of FASCISM to the western world, that ideology based on a rich and poor society, one in which children are born without equal opportunity, many of them born into poverty and starvation. Moses stressed God the Father's dream in which the white Aryan male rules at His side and woman is to be held in servitude to man and all others who are different are to be either subordinated, annihilated or cast into slavery. Specifically, Moses in his book 'Leviticus' subordinates those he refers to as 'those with flat noses' (Negroes) and 'those who are of physical blemish' (the handicapped). I am quite dismayed that in all of my life I have never seen a black person as black people are not allowed in Italy. We are an entirely white Catholic country because the minds of the voters are controlled by a Vatican that wants to preserve the purity of our Aryan race.*

"*I am equally dismayed that many steps must be mounted to enter most churches. It is almost as if their architects had in mind Moses' command, 'those who are lame, blind and are of other deformity are not to approach the altar of the Lord.' Or perhaps it is that Rome had this in mind when it had ordered them built. And if that is not enough there is Moses' horrific taking of the Promised Land in which he puts to the sword all men, women, children and even infants who worshipped gods other than his god. Moses gave birth to what has been more than three thousand years of ethnic cleansing wars which continue to go on even today. The mainstay of Moses' religion is hatred of others who appear to be different.*

"*Yet, on the other side,*" he continues, "*we have Christ. He introduces COMMUNISM to the western world, that ideology based on the premise that all God's wealth is to be divided equally among all of His children and a world in which every child has an equal opportunity at a good life; a far different world than we live in today. Christ introduces a single commandment, 'Love thy neighbor as thyself.' In all of His life Christ commits only one sin, the grave sin of anger. He so hated the republicans, the money makers, that in a fit of rage He upturns their money tables and throws them out of His Father's house. Christ's most basic requirement in the New Testament is that one gives up one's material wealth and come follow Him. The mainstay of Christ's religion is love of others no matter how different*."

And his paper goes on, "*There are no other philosophies of life, one either believes in the equality of all of God's children or one doesn't. One must choose between COMMUNISM, which is the extreme form of socialism on the left; and FASCISM, which is the extreme form of conservatism on the right. These are the pillars of society, Communism and Fascism. They stand at either end of this rope called Humanity. And the job of the people is to make certain that neither one of these extremes wins the tug-of-war. For that would result in a one-party system and dictatorship. And if that were to happen, either the Anarchy of Communism or the Anarchy of Fascism would emerge as an enemy of the people. So it is important that we work out something in-between or we will all end up in the drink. Yet, one can choose to be closer to Christ or closer to Moses. Although you would never get either one of them to admit it, - a good democrat strives toward COMMUNISM and a good republican strives toward FASCISM. That is, the democrat strives toward Christ and the republican strives toward Moses. And despite Christ's overwhelming testimony two thousand years ago, Christianity remains deeply steeped in FASCISM today. It is quite obvious that Mother Church in its support of a fascist state has chosen the word of Moses over the word of Jesus Christ Himself.*"[1]

Albino's editorial, written when he was just fourteen years old, was undoubtedly influenced by his father, who was a social revolutionary activist; the reason it was published. His father did not believe that Christ ever lived, yet he did believe in the philosophy of Christ as was set forth in the New Testament and he also believed that good men had written the New Testament. His letter was undoubtedly in response to an order of Pius XI two weeks earlier requiring that all of Italy's children under sixteen be enrolled in the new *Fascist Youth Organization,* which later served as the kindling wood for World War II. So, as I have said before, although his mother's influence had made him into a devout Catholic, it was his father's influence that would dominate his life; that would cause Albino Luciani to take his place on the *left*.

[1] *Povera Tigre Belluno December 23, 1926*

Interspersed between the lines of the often heavy theology that permeates Luciani's own best sellers, *Illustrissimi* and *Catechism in Crumbs,* can be found his basic ideology concerning women, "*True, God made men stronger physically, but He made women stronger spiritually.*" [2] and, "*God is more our Mother than She is our Father.*" [3] It is quite apparent from these remarks published as a cardinal and repeated verbally during his brief pontificate, that he intended to establish the equality of women in the Church early in his papacy.

And then there is his famous letter to that little mischievous boy that the great Master Geppetto had once created,

"Dear Pinocchio,

I was seven years old when I first read your Adventures. I can't tell you how much I liked them. In you, I recognized myself as a boy, and in your surroundings I saw my own.

My dear Pinocchio, there are two famous remarks about the young.
I commend the first by Lacordaire, to your attention: 'Have an opinion and assert it!' This is one of reason. It is the lion. It will win for you. The second is by Clemenceau, and I do not recommend it to you at all, 'He has no ideas of his own, but he defends them with ardor!' This is one of belief. It is the sheep. It will lose for you.

Think of this, as you go through life, as you run through the woods with the Cat and the Fox and the poodle Medoro,

Your magical friend,
Piccolo"

Luciani was obviously spelling out the difference between *Lacordaire* the progressive socialist on the *left*, and *Clemenceau* the conservative republican on the *right*. This letter was republished from his best seller *Illustrissimi* in just about every major newspaper of the world when John Paul first wrote it as a cardinal in 1976. Yet, if one were to read any of the biographical briefs released by the Vatican, he is painted to be a conservative, actually an ultraconservative. And there is a good reason for

[2] *Illustrissimi 1976*
[3] *Illustrissimi 1976*

this misrepresentation, for had Luciani been a conservative there would have been no ecclesiastical motive for murder. Great men do not kill great men for personal gain; they kill them to prevent the assimilation of their philosophical ideologies into society. And this is fundamental to the question that we will answer in Part II of this book: Did Albino Luciani's struggle for equal human rights for the poor, for unparented children, for women, for homosexuals, for the remarried and for others, cost him his life?

One need not go further than to read his letter to his dear friend Pinocchio, one of his most famous, to determine on which side of the aisle he stood. So take your choice, those biographies, which published by Rome, are designed to cover up the ecclesiastical motive for murder and depend entirely upon the blind faith or credulity of the reader, or this rendition which relies entirely upon the facts.

And then among the great prelate's other writings, "*The two greatest sins of mankind have been Original Sin and bigotry. The Bible reads that Original Sin was man's doing, but it also reads that bigotry was God the Father's doing. One could ask, if the Old Testament is the word of God, why did He do this? Why did He tell us to hate and persecute our brothers? He knew that He had put into each of us a part of Him, this thing we have come to know as our conscience. He wanted each of us to make the effort, to make the judgment, ourselves, when what we read or heard from another was right or wrong.*"

And then, again, in his *Illustrissimi*, he points again toward the socialist and away from the republican in his expedition beyond the great wall,

"Dear Casella,

I have had the good fortune to have visited those places which, as we all know, lie beyond the wall. And for each of us, I have found that the Father provides that we will live beyond the wall as we have chosen to live on this side of the wall.

First, I was granted the privilege of seeing Hell. As I peered in through the gates, I saw an immense room with many long tables. On these were so many bowls of cooked rice and gourmet delicacies as one could imagine, properly spiced, aromatic, inviting. The diners were all seated there, filled with hunger, two at each bowl, one facing the other. And then what?

To carry the food to their mouths they had - in oriental fashion - two chopsticks affixed to their hands, but so long that no matter how great their efforts, not a single grain of delicacy could reach their mouths. Although starving, they could not take of these things.

And then, I was able to peer into Heaven. And, here again, I saw a great room with the same tables, same gourmet delicacies, same long chopsticks. But here the people were happy, smiling and quite satisfied. Why?

Because each, having picked up the food with the chopsticks, raised it to the mouth of the companion that sat opposite, and all was right.

So my dear Casella, we must learn here, as we make our way toward the great wall, how to use the chopsticks, else we will not know how to use them when we are on the other side of the wall.

Your magical friend,
Piccolo"

And again in his *Illustrissimi,* his condemnation of the critics of those who happen to be born different, even going so far as to reach out to those outside the heterosexual mainstream,

"Dear Figaro,

Well then, who and what are you my dear Figaro? A variety of dress? A mixture of feminine and masculine? Of Orient and Occident?

Poor Figaro, against all these nobles with their coats of arms, these bewigged bourgeois, who themselves do every trespass. They are no better, perhaps worse, than you. Barber, marriage broker, adviser of pseudo diplomats, yes, ladies and gentlemen, whatever you like.

They demand that you alone be honest in this world of cheats and rogues. Do not accept what they say, my dear Figaro, for you, too, are a citizen.

But, sadly, perhaps, your only solution is in revolution!

Your magical friend,
Piccolo"

note: letters on page 7, 8 & 9 have been reprinted from Luciani's best seller Illustrissimi 1976

Luciani was referring to the scant evidence condemning homosexuality and transsexuality in the scriptures. No mention of either of these in the Ten Commandments or for that matter in all of Christ's testimony in the Gospels and only a single explicit condemnation and less than a half-dozen ambiguous mentions of it elsewhere in the Bible. This, as compared to more than eighty explicit condemnations of heterosexual sexual activities in the Bible, several of which call for the death penalty and permanent exclusion of heaven for fornication and adultery.

As a matter of fact, Luciani did not believe in the Ten Commandments, the *rule of law* as prescribed by Moses, the *rule of law* of which republican congressmen speak. And this is quite apparent from the strong stance he took in defending the rights of women.

In particular he had a great problem with the all-inclusive tenth commandment that protects man's property, "*Thou shalt not covet* (desire to take from) *thy neighbor his property including his house, nor his wife, nor his slaves, nor his ox, nor his ass*." He opposed those who wanted to place the Ten Commandments in public buildings in Italy, for he knew their evil motive; they wanted to remind the public that society was straying too far from this and some of the other commandments. For example, the third commandment goes even one step further and subordinates women to slaves in that it requires only the wife to work on the Sabbath, "*The seventh day is the Sabbath of the Lord thy God, in it thou shalt not do any work, thou, nor thy son, nor thy daughter, nor thy slave, nor thy cattle, not thy stranger that is within thy gates*." Here God the Father specifically excludes the words, *nor thy wife*. In part, the United States Constitution, which was put together entirely by Christian men, was based on these commandments insofar as they recognized both Negroes and women to be man's *property* and therefore not citizens. And although we all recall the horrific record of Negroes in America, most of us today are unaware that women too, were not only subordinated, but many were persecuted until the likes of Elizabeth Cady Stanton and Susan B. Anthony came along in the middle of the nineteenth century.

Women, being *property*, were often sold by parents for considerable sums and being *property* themselves they had no right to own property, not even through inheritance. Women were generally perceived as being house servants and in the bedroom they were often sex slaves. A man could legally rape his wife in the eyes of the law. When children were born they became the property of the man. In the event of separation or divorce the woman had no rights, not even visitation rights, to the children. And women being *property*, as decreed by Moses, had no right to higher education prior to the nineteenth century, the reason why men dominate American history.

But today, because of the work of Luciani and others like him, most Christians totally ignore both these commandments, and some others, as if they were not there at all. They just don't believe in God the Father's most sacred message as related to Moses in the Old Testament. They no longer believe in slavery and the subordination of women. And most feel free to work whenever they choose to work.

How can one believe in Christ and yet not accept the only known written word of God the Father in the Old Testament? It certainly made no sense to Luciani that society would reject the only known written word of God the Father as passed on through the years in the tablets; that society would ignore God the Father's sacred instructions, - that slavery was to be a way of life, - that woman was no more than a piece of man's property, - that one is to do no work on the Sabbath; yet still accept other tales of the Old Testament that were passed on down through the centuries, subject to change and embellishment to satisfy the self-serving interests of thousands of preachers and storytellers for a millennium or so, until papyrus had been developed to a point that permitted at least some of them to be reduced to writing.

Although he had these problems with God the Father as He is described by Moses in the *Old Testament*, he did believe fervently in Christ and it was his ecclesiastical goal in life to separate the *love* that permeates the *New Testament* from the *hate* that permeates the *Old Testament*, to somehow separate Christ from Moses; to put it more pointedly, to somehow separate Christ from His Father.

Although Luciani was not what one would call a great speaker, he was certainly a most eloquent one. It was common practice for the newspapers to publish quotes from his sermons. Among the most widely published of these was one he gave to a youth organization in Venice in which he paid homage to Lincoln for having had the great courage to defy the written word of his God, the tenth commandment, *"Thou shalt not take from thy neighbor his . . . slaves . . ."*

*"Never be afraid to stand up for what is right, whether your adversary be your parent, your teacher, your peer, your politician, your preacher, your constitution, or even your God!"**

* *Messaggero Mestre, Albino Luciani in Venice, 19 Apr '73*

Here, he also warns against the fourth commandment, *"Honour and obey thy father and thy mother."* As a child he often wondered why it was there at all. After all, if one wanted to survive in the early years it was not an option. And he knew why Moses had put it there. Because Moses knew that *the hatred of people who appear to be different* he had built into his religion could best be perpetuated and passed on from parent to child.

The Ten Commandments can probably best be described as the *Bill of Rights and Wrongs of Christianity*. Yet, it would not take a mind of genius proportions to recognize that they were put together by a person of less than average intelligence and organization, much less a Supreme Being. From a point of view of *right versus wrong*, although they do include murder and theft, they don't include rape, child molestation, kidnapping and a host of other transgressions that then and now are considered serious crimes. Also, at the time, fornication was the most damned sin in the Bible and it is not mentioned at all. And the tablets include some commandments that are not considered transgressions at all today like *"thou shalt do no work on the Sabbath. . ."* And then there is the commandment, "*thou shalt have no graven images before thee"* which is ignored by all Christians today who think there is something holy about a crucifix, the image of a near naked man nailed to a tree. And the tenth commandment, as we all know today, is an absolute abomination. Although Moses claimed that it was *right,* every man and woman of good conscience today knows that it is *wrong.* And then there is the most glaring inconsistency of all, the Ten Commandments omit the most fundamental commandment of a good and just society, Christ's commandment: *"Love thy neighbor as thyself."*

the unborn,

Six months after the chat with the author as related herein Albino Luciani was named Archbishop of Venice and five years later became a cardinal of the Roman Catholic Church. Still holding to moderate views on most issues, he moved radically to the *left* on those doctrines which placed undue hardship on the everyday lives of people. He became particularly outspoken on women's equality, birth control and human sexuality.

Luciani proposed radical views concerning abortion and was convinced that removing the stigma associated with out of wedlock pregnancies would eliminate what was then the cause of the greatest share of abortions, -family disgrace and embarrassment.

He recalled his childhood in his memoirs, "*I could hear my mother and aunt and sister talking in low tones and every time I entered the room there was a hush-hush of some kind. Then one day my sister took a short holiday. I was told that she had gone to a neighboring village to rest for awhile. But they didn't fool me at all, for I knew exactly what was going on. And as I fell on my knees that night I vowed that I would someday bring an end to it all. And believe me, I will!* "

It was for this reason that he supported much of what has brought about this thing we know today as the "sexual revolution" including his personal contribution of having introduced *sexual education* into schools. His primary objective was to remove what was at the time the major cause of abortions – family disgrace and embarrassment.

As he once explained to the press, "*My part in this thing one calls sexual education is to bring about a day when the young girl would no longer think that she has gotten herself into trouble as the preacher might lead her to believe, but rather that she would realize that she had, indeed, gotten herself into paradise.*" And one now knows that he was right, for today very few abortions are owed to embarrassment. It is much to the credit of Luciani and the many other fathers and mothers of the sexual revolution that millions of children who might have otherwise been aborted now see the light of day.

Unlike other members of the clergy who simply complained about the problem of abortion, he did something about it. Shortly after being named Bishop of Vittorio Veneto he received a letter from a wealthy man who was terminally ill. Lacking heirs, the man offered to leave his entire fortune to build a large church dedicated to *Christ the Savior*. Luciani went to visit the man the very next day and asked him to leave the money to build an orphanage rather than a church. The man held his ground and demanded that the great church be built. Having exhausted every possible alternative, Luciani finally reached into his hip pocket and played his trump card, one that he often used to get his way. *"When I was a teenager,"* he told the man, *"my father made me promise that I would live my life in imitation of Christ, and I have kept that solemn promise. Each time that the fork in the road has come up, often only minutes apart, I have asked myself, 'Now, what would Jesus have done in this case?' And I have often pondered the possibility as to how much better the world would be if everyone were to do this."* He then asked the man, *"Now, what do you think Jesus would do in this case?"* Two weeks later, the man took up a shovel and broke ground for the new orphanage, one that was designed for infants who otherwise would have been aborted. He was buried a month later in a small nearby cemetery. A simple granite marker was placed on his grave by Luciani himself, *"Each day he breathes new life into the world."*

Some years later, shortly after becoming Archbishop of Venice, he addressed his congregation in the great Basilica of San Marco. Looking up toward its immense dome, he told them, *"We must learn to lower our ceiling height to make room for all of God's children."* What he meant by this confusing statement is that Mother Church must cease building great edifices to the glory of God in order to provide the funds necessary to put roofs over the heads of all of His children. In the twenty years that he served as a bishop and as a cardinal, Luciani never dedicated a single church, yet he built forty-four orphanages, many of them equipped with schools and clinics. A monk, one of an army of monks and nuns who had spent most of their lives in prayer, once spoke of him, *"He literally pulled us up off of our knees and put us to work, we monks building and maintaining orphanages and serving as youth counselors, and the nuns teaching class and others caring for those children too ill to come to class."* Most of these orphanages still remain today, one built by the dying man standing at the foot of the mountain just below the bishop's castle in Vittorio Veneto.

the bonding glue of unions,

While he withheld public comment on homosexuality, he did much to encourage single persons to adopt unparented children. In fact, it was his lobbying in the Italian parliament that made it legal for single persons to adopt children in Italy. When an opposition member of the assembly challenged his proposal, *"But, that would make it legal for homosexuals to adopt children,"* Luciani responded,

*"The need to parent children is a basic human need and until the day comes that we can guarantee basic human rights to the tiniest minority, we cannot truthfully call ourselves a democracy."**

But his adversary didn't give up, *"But homosexuals have a record of splitting up after the 'honeymoon' is over and this would subject children to lose either one or both parents."* Luciani closed the gap on his attacker, *"There are two major forces involved in making for long-term loving relationships and regardless of what Rome might believe, sex is not one of them. As a matter of fact, sex is most often a declining force in many relationships. It has very little to do with the long term survival of a union. The longevity of a relationship of two people who parent children that is so important to protecting the rights of children until they reach adulthood depends not on sex, but rather on the two major forces that create long-term relationships, love and companionship. And when one considers the latter, the homosexual has a great advantage. Two people of the same*

Albino Luciani, Italian Parliament, 16 Jan '67

sex who fall in love with each other make much better companions of each other because they are far more likely to share common interests and it is for this reason that children parented by homosexual couples are less likely to undergo the trauma of divorce." Needless to say Luciani's rebuttal silenced his opponents and the measure passed. Within two years, more than a quarter-million children, who had previously been confined to the streets, were provided loving and economic support by single parents. Some of these were homosexual couples in which case one of the parents had adopted the child, as it remained illegal for two people of the same sex to adopt the same child.

Although gay marriage or gay unions were not a matter of public debate in his time, as a matter of fact not even an issue, Luciani once responded to the question when raised by a member of a small homosexual group that had gathered in Venice, *"Time and tradition are your only real obstacles. Today, Mother Church doesn't even want to talk about this thing because she is convinced that sex and not love is the foundation of long term loving relationships. Thus, she defines marriage as being limited to being between two people of the opposite sex. This is because she believes fervently in what Moses had to say and we are coming to know today that most of what Moses had to say were lies. In time, as she becomes better educated in this thing that she claims to be the expert in - the psychology of loving relationships, she will come to realize that love and not sex is the foundation of long term loving relationships. So be tolerant of her, it's just that her mindset is frozen in time by Moses' hatred of people who are different and it will take her much longer to tell right from wrong.*

"But, nevertheless, it is more likely that society, as she has had to do so many times before, will raise her hand on this issue first. In a court of law, as you know, the court will analyze long term loving relationships as a basis for making its decision particularly since children are involved. If it is found that the Church is right, that long term loving relationships are built on sex, then you will be out of luck. But, if the jury decides that love and not sex is the foundation of long term loving relationships then you will have won your day in court, for society will replace the phrase 'between man and woman' with the phrase 'between any of God's children' in this thing called marriage. Mother Church won't have any say in the matter for God would have played His hand. Believe me, love is the only permanent glue that bonds relationships that will survive beyond the grave." A young man in the audience questioned him, *"But tradition . . ."*

Luciani quickly cut him off, *"Tradition doesn't have anything to do with it. A court of law does not base its decision on tradition. It bases its decision on what is right and what is wrong. The Church bases its decision* *on tradition, regardless of whether it is right or wrong. The bottom line in making this particular determination will be the answer to the question, 'Is sex or love the foundation of long term loving relationships?' That's the beginning and the end of it. Tradition will have nothing to do with it."**

Albino found in his experience that homosexual couples would take handicapped and less than healthy and attractive children. Most importantly, they would take bastards who were at the bottom of the barrel. Heterosexual couples, on the other hand, went for the cutest babies as if they were shopping for a puppy in a pet shop.

One might wonder why at that time Christian Europe had over twelve million orphans. The reason was that most of them were children born out-of-wedlock - bastards - and everyone looked on them with loathing and disgust - the reason why the word 'bastard' was considered a swear word. This was Church doctrine which was backed up by God the Father's 'holy' testimony in Deuteronomy 23, *'A bastard child shall not enter into the congregation of the Lord.'*

When he had been a child, Luciani had often found orphans frozen to death in the streets. The most common comment of passer-buyers, *"better off dead"* or *"It is God's will."* Precisely the reaction of today's *born again Christian* whose gay child commits suicide.

In 1973, when Paul VI motioned to make Luciani a cardinal, Albino sent a private message to the Pope that he would refuse the 'red hat' unless Paul changed the Church's doctrine condemning bastards. Needless to say Paul complied. Yet, today, the word 'bastard' still has its stigma much like a quarter century after medical science determined that homosexuality is a matter of instinct its stigma continues to persist. The minds of the populace continue to be controlled by the hatred of Moses, despite the proven fact that both of these kinds of children are clearly God's children. On the plus side, we have now put behind us hatred of children who are born out-of-wedlock; yet, society continues to look at homosexual children - those who can only *fall in love* with one of their own sex - with loathing and disgust. Moses' hated continues to take its toll on children today - millions of predominantly straight children in gay families are being denied social security survivor and other benefits because of opposition to gay marriage which is the only viable solution to their problem; and gay children are growing up as outcasts in an irresponsible society, many taking their own lives

* *Nostro Priviliegio – "Our Privilege"' an underground Venice gay newspaper, 16 Jun' 71.*

The great enemy of society remains today what it has been throughout history, "*the ability of the hatred of the Christian preachers to prey on the ignorance and weakness of the minds of men.*"

the strange little boy in the playground,

Albino realized the plight of the homosexual before he was old enough to receive his first communion. He recalled Giovanni in his memoirs, "*He was a frail little boy and he spoke with a lisp and waved his hands in a funny little way. All the kids laughed at him in the playground. Then one day he died. No mass was said for him and he was buried in unconsecrated ground. The day after his funeral the nun explained to the class that Giovanni had been born bad, so the devil had taken him back. But I knew that the nun was wrong for I knew that Giovanni, being one of God's children, had been born good. And I also knew why Giovanni had killed himself. He just couldn't take it anymore. And that afternoon as I stood over my friend's grave I vowed that I would never let anyone laugh at him again!*"

Just three months before his death, Pope Paul permitted Luciani to address the Vatican cardinals on the possibility that the Church might encourage homosexuals to enter into long-term loving relationships, -as they represented the only population group that was large enough and willing to provide economic and emotional support to millions of children who might otherwise be aborted by women too young or too poor to support them. Luciani argued that the Church's traditional position exiled homosexuals from society, forcing many of them into lives of despair. He emphasized the Church's position was one of prejudice, as Church doctrine acknowledged that sexual orientation cannot be changed.

And this is seen quite clearly in that homosexuality was at the time and is today recognized by the Church as grounds for annulment. Unlike the *born again* denominations of the *far right*, the Catholic Church does not recommend sexual orientation therapy, but rather it renders a simple statement of compassion to these unfortunate people in its Catechism. Very recently, American/European psychiatric associations issued stern warnings, threatening loss of membership to those members who capitalize on the whims of preachers and experiment in sexual orientation change therapy.

Unlike the general public, those at the top of both the Catholic Church and of the *born again Christian* movement know what the worldwide, psychiatric, psychological and medical communities have to say about homosexuality. And this is seen quite clearly in many of their public statements. For example, Belgium Cardinal Gustaaf's controversial remark to the press, *"most gays and lesbians are not really gay at all, they are perverts."** And this word *really* shows up time and again on television talk shows. For example, Pat Robertson has a standard question he asks in response to gay teenagers, who confused by preachers, call into his '700 club' talk show, *"Are you really a homosexual or are you simply someone who was molested as a child?"* And if one watches the Catholic talk shows one will find that the good monsignor uses the very same tactic, *"Are you really a homosexual or are you someone who has been molested as a child?"*

If these leaders recognize that homosexuality is a basic instinct as the psychiatric world tells them it is, one would ask why they continue to persecute homosexuals, especially gay children and teenagers. The only reason one can come up with is hatred and prejudice.

Nevertheless, Luciani reasoned that the Church could bring about a better balance in society by accepting homosexuals into its fold. Although nothing ever came of his appeal Luciani thanked the Pope for having allowed him to be heard.

the strategy of a strange war,

Forty years before the world's psychiatric and medical communities came to the same conclusion, Luciani reasoned that sexual orientation could not be changed by therapy, that the ability to *fall in love* is a basic instinct. He did not extend his protection to the bisexual population because its members have the natural ability to *fall in love* with a member of either sex. Unlike what most people think, bisexuals outnumber homosexuals by about two to one, one in every ten at the very most is an absolute homosexual, whereas one in every five at the very least is a bisexual. And also contrary to what the general public believes the great majority of bisexuals lead straight lives, not gay lives, as they grow up in a heterosexual world. This is readily seen in that one in every three incest cases is homosexual in nature indicating the high level of bisexuality among offending parents.

It was quite remarkable that Luciani realized that bisexuals comprised a significant part of the population, as at his time the Kinsey Report and other studies had placed it at less than one-half of one percent of the population. This was because these researchers assumed that all bisexuals were a part of the homosexual community and looked for them only in the homosexual population; not a very logical assumption as it

* *see Internet 2004*

would make no sense that if one had the freedom to choose, one would choose to be exiled from society and to be ridiculed by one's peers. It wasn't until studies on incest and other behavioral patterns came into conflict with the earlier reports that researchers came to realize that their overwhelming numbers were buried in the heterosexual population.

As the psychiatric community also tells us today, Luciani found that sexual *behavior* could be conditioned by therapy or other circumstances. He reasoned that there are only two forces that can drive a sexual act, *love* and *lust*. He knew when two people are in love, *love* tends to drive the sexual act and that when two people are not in love, then *lust* tends to drive the act. He understood then what we are coming to know now; that a homosexual male, for example, can be conditioned to have sex with a woman only by changing the motivating factor from one of *love* to one of *lust*. It is because he felt strongly that God's children not be products of *lust* that he opposed this type of experimentation.

Luciani's intermediate thesis *The Strategy of a Strange War,** was based on this subject. As a young seminarian he had done much work in prisons and knew that heterosexual men who were confined for long periods of time did engage in homosexual acts. But he also found *"no matter how long the practice went on a heterosexual male could never fall in love with another male, that lust and not love was the driving force behind such behavior, that when a heterosexual male would have a long-term intimate relationship with another male in prison he could never be made to fall in love with his partner, that he would never be able to share an intimate kiss with him. Yes, he might grow to like him and even develop great affection for him but he would never be able to fall in love with him."* Correspondingly, Luciani drew from his experience in the prisons that when one conditions a homosexual male to enter into a heterosexual relationship he can never truly *fall in love* with his mate of the opposite sex. "*Yes, he might grow to like her, even develop great affection for her, even parent children with her, but he will never be able to fall in love with her*." He concluded "*children sired in such marriages would be the product of lust and it is important to all men of good conscience that all of God's children be the product of love, not lust."*

Yet, Luciani did recognize that a bisexual who has been a part of the homosexual community could be conditioned by therapy since he already possesses the instinct that enables one to *fall in love* with a member of either sex. *"But even in the case of a bisexual,"* he wrote, *"therapy*

* *Vatican Apostolic Library. Not to be confused with his doctoral thesis, The Origin of the Human Soul.*

is not a viable solution as a bisexual who has followed his homosexual instinct is likely to eventually stray; this would put the children at risk of growing up without a father." Of course, as mentioned above, very few bisexuals, about one-half of one percent of the population, are a part of the homosexual community. This is the reason why most of those outside of the scientific community today believe there are relatively few of them, whereas in fact their overwhelming numbers are hidden in the heterosexual population. Today it is the bisexual who is in the closet, so to speak. Actually, the bisexual doesn't even know where he or she is.

And it is for this reason he felt the ministry, both within and without the Church, was primarily bisexual, and that bisexuals confused of their sexual uncertainty sought refuge in faith.

"Our natural instincts cannot be changed by artificial therapy," he wrote. *"We are born with two basic instincts, -the instinct of survival and its enemy, the instinct of compassion. Unlike all our other impulses only these two are felt as if coming from the heart. The instinct of survival is reserved exclusively for our work for ourselves. It is why God the Father requires that in order to be saved that we spend our life in adoration of Him. It drives selfishness and material gain in most of us, and in some of us it inspires lying, cheating, stealing, raping, molesting, murder and so forth. In its epitome it expresses itself as hatred, specifically hatred of others.*

"The instinct of compassion, on the other hand, is reserved for our work for others. It is this instinct of Christ who tells us not to adore Him, but rather that salvation can only be achieved through helping others. Affection is a good example of an expression of the basic instinct of compassion. The instinct that causes us to laugh and cry also comes from this same basic instinct of compassion. We don't teach babies what to laugh at or what to cry about, they are born with this instinct, and all babies will laugh at the same things and cry about the same things. And what's more they will laugh and cry about these same things for all the remaining days of their lives.

"Whom one falls-in-love with is the greatest manifestation of the basic instinct of compassion. It is best defined as the creation of a perfect balance of mental energy between two people. At its epitome it totally neutralizes the instinct of survival, that is, either one of the parties would readily give their life for the other without so much as a second thought, so one knows that such a union can only be made by God. And our instinct that controls who we are able to fall in love with will never change. It would be like trying to condition a person to laugh whenever something bad or terrible happens, and cry whenever something wonderful happens.

"To see this more clearly, one can consider one's own experiences. How many times in one's life has one met a person to whom he or she is physically attracted, a person of unusual beauty and personality, yet one finds, time and again, that one cannot fall in love with that person. Falling in love is not an accident, but rather it is clearly an act of nature, an act of God. Unlike the preacher might want one to believe, it is not a learning process, it is a union that can only be made by God. "

Luciani concluded his thesis, ". . . *the preacher, so confused by sex himself, believes that whom one has sex with defines one's sexual orientation.*" And he knew that nothing could be further from the truth, for he knew that one could have sex with an animal or a banana or even a chicken skin. "*It is quite obvious to me*," he concluded, "*that whom one has the natural instinct to fall in love with is what determines sexual orientation. Not whom one has sex with.*" Luciani felt so strongly about his conclusion that in addition to underlining it, he repeated it four times in his thesis.

Today we are coming to know what was obvious to Luciani fifty years ago, -a straight person could never be conditioned to share an intimate kiss with a member of the same sex. And it is equally obvious to a gay person today that he or she can never be conditioned to share an intimate kiss with a member of the opposite sex. One can no more make a straight person out of a gay person, than one can make a gay person out of a straight person. But only the heterosexual and homosexual can understand this. The bisexual, the preacher, so confused by his own sexual orientation, totally ignores what the worldwide psychiatric and medical communities are telling him and believes that sexual orientation, much like a light bulb, can be changed. As Luciani surmised, "*The preacher thinks that he is dealing with a bowl of soup whereas in reality he is dealing with the complexities of the human mind, the very manifestation of God Himself on earth.*"

It is for this reason that Luciani never placed the *persecution of homosexuals* issue very high on his agenda, for he felt the issue would eventually resolve itself, and true heterosexuals would eventually realize there is no power on earth that can cause them to have an intimate loving relationship with one of the same sex. And likewise, true homosexuals would eventually realize there is no power on earth that could cause them to have an intimate loving relationship with one of the opposite sex. So only the bisexual would remain confused about his or her sexual orientation and it is this confusion which allows the preacher to shepherd most of them into his flock. It has been the influence of the preacher or bisexual on the vast heterosexual population that has kept the gay in his or her place so to speak. So the enemy of gay rights is the substantial bisexual population, not the larger heterosexual population. As Luciani once told the Vatican cardinals in the Sistine Chapel, ". . . *If one is to be successful in bringing down an enemy, one must know who he is, know where he is coming from, know his armament, know his mental embattlement, how he thinks. . .*"

trauma of a strange teenager,

Whenever the Church's policies were harsh or inhumane, he stepped in. During the ten years he was a bishop every hospital in Italy was Catholic. It was in Italy that hospital policies first barred visitation rights to other than family members. The objective was to keep lifelong partners of homosexuals from being present thereby allowing the priest to demand that the dying partner renounce his or her loved one. "Otherwise," the priest would heartlessly tell the dying partner, "you will certainly go to hell!" This is one reason why Christian churches oppose legal recognition of gay unions today, as it would deprive them of the opportunity to coerce the dying gay into disavowing his or her beloved partner of many years. The original source of this *sick* policy was a papal decree issued by Pius IX in the nineteenth century which has been adopted through the years by most Christian churches.

As a bishop, Luciani is known to have interceded on behalf of homosexuals who had shared long-term loving relationships, in at least six specific cases that were reported in the press. In these cases, and perhaps several others not reported in the press, he ordered hospitals within his jurisdiction to admit longtime partners of homosexuals into critical care units. Despite the fact that his actions defied a papal decree, the Vatican never challenged them probably because of the strong following of his congregation or perhaps it feared reaction from the press, which at the time was a great ally of the bishop from Vittorio Veneto.

In the early sixties, when the *Christian right* waged its war against equal rights for blacks, he issued a statement of great praise for President Johnson and his followers ". . . *whose great courage have allowed their conscience to override what is wrong in their scriptures*."

When civil rights legislation was enacted in 1964, the *Christian right* in the United States, having lost its quest to keep the black in his corner, turned its hatred and its persecution efforts toward homosexuals. By the end of the decade almost two million homosexuals had been arrested and incarcerated; those in northern states for relatively short sentences and those in southern states for long terms. Two states, Louisiana and Alabama, came within one legislative vote of requiring the death penalty for a single homosexual act.

In the spring of 1967, acting on a tip from a neighbor, police broke into the home of Robert Wise and Timothy Wilson, both 22, just outside

Augusta Georgia. Armed with cameras, they caught the couple in their bedroom. The two were tried and convicted of committing a homosexual act and sentenced to twenty years under Georgia law. Timothy Wilson served only four days of his term. He cut his wrists, and bled to death in his cell on his twenty-third birthday.

Bishop Luciani addressed his congregation in Vittorio Veneto a week later, *"The United States is a great nation, but it is a young one. This rings of the Inquisition and of Salem witch hunts and of slavery, -things that we have already put behind us. How many more must suffer and die before we too put this one behind us. How many more must suffer and die before men and women of good conscience rise up and say, 'it makes no difference how much of Moses' evilness has crept into the laws and constitutions of nations. All that counts is what is right and what is wrong.' And this action is clearly wrong. It is clearly wrong to any man or woman of good conscience."*

Twenty years after the conviction of Wilson and Wise, the United States Supreme Court upheld the constitutionality of the Georgia law. In August of 1987, Chief Justice Rehnquist led the Court in a 5 to 4 decision that upheld the Georgia law as providing fair and equitable justice for homosexual acts committed between consenting adults in private. Justice Stevens, who had led the opposition, spoke of the decision, *"It strikes against everything that is good and decent and mostly it is a strike against the most basic of freedoms, the right to be left alone."*[1]

Ironically, just twenty years after John Paul I had condemned the Georgia court's action, his successor John Paul II led the American cardinals in applauding the higher court's decision as being fair and equal justice for homosexual acts and with them stood Pat Robertson, Jerry Falwell, Billy Graham and a host of other Christian leaders.

Timothy Wilson did not stand alone in his demise for during this same twenty year period homosexuality surfaced as the leading cause of suicides among children and teenagers in Bible-belt states. In all, tens of thousands of American children and teens who had been born to parents whose minds had been deranged by the hatred of Christian preachers took their own lives.[2]

[1] *the court reversed its decision in November 2003*

[2] *Statistical Abstracts of the United States 1960-1979. Although greatly curtailed, this problem still persists to this day. In 2001, following a rash of teenage suicides caused by sexual orientation change therapy, the American Psychiatric Association issued a stern warning to its members who prey on mentally deranged parents threatening loss of membership to those who driven by greed capitalize on the whims of preachers and engage in this kind of dangerous experimentation of defenseless children*

In the spring of 1969, the local newspaper boy delivered a copy of the *New York Times* to the Bishop of Vittorio Veneto. The bishop opened the paper and his eye caught a headline which read something like this, "*Police Murder Young Gay*." Just below the heading was a photo, a view looking down toward a dark alleyway, there impaled atop a heavy iron picket fence was a small framed boy. Although the picture had been taken at night, as it was dark and quite fuzzy, one could see that four or five of the spikes had completely penetrated his body from his right thigh to his neck and that the tips of the spikes were wet with blood.

As Luciani read the article, he came realize the caption was wrong, -that the boy, a thirteen year old Hispanic youth, although in critical condition, was still alive. It took several hours for the fence to be cut with blow torches to free the boy and the young teen was removed to St. Agnes, a Greenwich Village hospital, with the spikes still embedded in his body.

The boy had been arrested by an undercover cop in Washington Square Park and had been brought into the Tenth Precinct Station for booking. Fearing disclosure to his parents, the boy sobbing relentlessly pleaded for them to let him go. The boy asked to use the restroom where two officers were allegedly overheard threatening to force themselves on the youngster and the boy was either thrown from or leaped out of a window into the dark night and landed atop the fence. The officers involved were placed under suspension pending an investigation of the incident and were eventually returned to active duty when the witness who occupied a booth testified that he had seen nothing; he had only heard the confrontation and the most he could come up with is that of the officers used the term, *"little faggot."*

Whereas others blamed the police, Luciani sent a telegram that placed the blame elsewhere. " . . . *It is quite obvious that the motive of these preachers is not one of morality, as they would want one to believe, it is clearly one of hate and prejudice and in the case of this boy it is murder. Cold blooded murder. Yes, it is not so much these officers of the American Gestapo that are responsible, although they are the direct instrument of this dreadful deed, but rather it is the preachers and politicians, who falsely claim to be representatives of God, who in perpetuating this type of hatred, are the real killers, the real killers of the boy on the fence*."

A few weeks later the boy died and the following week homosexuals in New York City, infuriated by the boy's death, for the first time stood their ground and fought off the police in what became known as the *Stonewall* incident. The Gay Revolution had begun, the prediction Luciani had made in his famous letter to Figaro had become a reality.

Four years later when the American Psychiatric Association adopted the resolution that homosexuality is a matter of instinct and is not a matter of mental illness Luciani got himself into trouble with his congregation when he made the remark, *"I wonder how long it will take for the sheep to understand this one."* He was referring to the fact that even after Galileo proved through his *Falling Bodies Law* that the earth was round, that the mass of Christianity continued to believe that it was flat until years later when Magellan sailed off into the west and returned from the east. And more than half of them even refused to believe it then.

It was his position on homosexuality that gave rise to rumors that he himself was a homosexual. Specific allegations had arisen in 1976 when the French physician-priest, Marc Oraison, made public his homosexuality and citing the fact that medical science had proved that sexual orientation was a matter of natural instinct declared that homosexual love was the will of God. In a statement to the press Cardinal Luciani warned Oraison that *"if a priest preaches as he does, everything is ruined."*[1] Although somewhat confusing on the surface, the remark obviously meant that Oraison should have kept his sexual identity private, that one can best help an oppressed group by appearing to be an outsider, that one is far less effective if he appears to be trying to help himself.

It is interesting to note that although Luciani spent much of his lifetime studying, explaining and defending homosexuality, including having written his intermediate thesis on it, there is only a single mention of homosexuality in all of his biographical briefs issued by the Vatican since the time of his death. Ironically, that single mention attempts to capitalize on this very same phrase, *"if a priest preaches as he does, everything is ruined."*[1] This Vatican biographical brief of John Paul's life claims that this criticism of Oraison was a condemnation of homosexuality by the Pope, yet one knows that nothing could be further from the truth.

Luciani's statement gave rise to a rumor that he himself was keeping his own sexual identity a secret, although this was most likely not the case as if this were true he certainly would have been a fool to have made such a comment publicly. Nevertheless, the rumor persisted.

Some of the tabloids took this a step further and suggested that he was a practicing homosexual. They reported that the cardinal frequented a square that was notorious for homosexual activity and they backed it up with pictures of him walking through the park. The photos were obviously of him performing his morning office in the small plaza Piazetta

[1] *IL Gazzettino Venezia, 14 Jul '76*

dei Leoncini that fronted the cardinal's palace in Venice. By coincidence the tabloids were right in that the park was a haven for homosexuals.

And there was the added fact that he had moved his secretary Lorenzi into his relatively small apartment in the Patriarch's Palace to make room for unwed mothers. Lorenzi was an extremely attractive almost angelic looking young man, enough so as to give the tabloids added fuel for their fire. But because Luciani was so well liked by the legitimate press, it never pursued the allegations and eventually the rumors tapered off.

Regardless, for Luciani to have spoken his piece on the world's stage must have taken immense courage. He never for an instant thought of himself, of what people might think of him, he thought only of others.

A couple of days after the Oraison incident he was asked why he helped "*those kinds of people.*" Citing the fact that a quarter-million homosexuals had been murdered in concentration camps, he replied, *"If we are ever to be truly free, we must stamp out what Hitler stood for, once and for all."*[2]

the world's problems,

And concerning what he considered to be a much more important issue, as a cardinal, Luciani became particularly outspoken about the population explosion, that the Church's position on birth control was aggravating the problem, that the unprecedented population growth rate was creating massive poverty and starvation at its fringes, particularly in the poorer countries of Latin America and Africa. And then there was the fact that the Church's position on birth control was resulting in untimely pregnancies that forced abortions in the United States and Europe, that the Church's policy on birth control was in direct conflict with its policy on abortion, that the Church was, itself, in many areas of the world, the underlying cause of more than half of abortions. As he once published as a bishop and repeated verbally as a Pope,

"Mother Church has a responsibility to the world to cease to be the cause of many of its problems and rather must begin to be the answer to them." *

What Luciani meant by this statement is seen quite clearly today in the AIDS crisis. At the time of his election to the papacy, he

[2] *IL Gazzettino Venezia, 17 Jul '76*
**Veneto Nostro, Jul '66*

was particularly concerned about the emergence of a new killer disease that had surfaced in Africa. He suspected that the Church's policy on unprotected sex could be the driving force behind the rapid spread of the disease. And in retrospect it is quite clear to the most casual of observers that it has been his successor's ban on contraceptives which has resulted in many millions of deaths and many millions more yet to come; which in the end will number much greater than the fifty-million killed by Hitler in World War II. It has been the Church's irresponsible ban on protected sex which has resulted in the births of hundreds of thousands of AIDS babies who will never see their sixth birthday; that an increasingly alarming number of the half-billion Catholics in Africa and Latin America are being infected each day. The accelerating rate of AIDS births is so serious in some heavily Catholic populated countries today that some governments are considering banning natural reproduction in favor of artificial means. The risk of AIDS in a child born by natural conception in these countries is becoming too great.

Exactly what changes Luciani would have made had he lived will perhaps never be known. But what one does know as a matter of fact is that he died on the very eve of that time that he was about to announce to the world a change in the Church's ban on protected sex, something that horrified many of those cardinals with whom he shared the Vatican.

Incredibly, even after it was determined by medical science in 1982 that unprotected sex was the driving force behind the AIDS epidemic, his successor John Paul II continued to forbid his followers to use condoms to protect themselves against disease. Had he made a more rational and compassionate judgment at that time, millions might be alive today, including Ryan White and hundreds of thousands of other children.

Luciani's positions on birth control and homosexuality were particularly dangerous to the *Vatican Curia*, that cluster of twenty or so cardinals in Rome that controlled the *far right* in the Church and had traditionally held a stranglehold on the papacy. Not so much in that his positions constituted departure from scripture, as the instruction of the Bible in these cases was quite flimsy and ambiguous anyway, but rather because they struck at the very survival of the Church as the largest in the world. For the Roman Catholic Church, like most other churches, depends primarily on large families for its membership since it depends largely on the indoctrination of children before they reach the age of reason. Encouraging smaller families and recognizing homosexuality as an acceptable lifestyle would result in a dwindling Catholic population that would eventually reduce its influence in the world. Also if it were to abandon its persecution of homosexuals it would influence the substantial bisexual population, which comprises as much as a quarter of its membership. It is quite obvious that if it were to lift its ban on protective sex that hundreds of millions of children would no longer be born into poverty and starvation in third world countries. Furthermore, it is obvious that if it were to lift its ban on protective sex that millions of children would no longer be born of AIDS only to suffer unspeakable deaths.

In general, concerning matters of personal intimacy, Luciani could never understand how a group of old men in Rome, who had never been in the bedroom, could take it upon themselves to tell others what they can or cannot do in the bedroom.

his revolutionary ideas,

As Archbishop of Venice, Luciani was faced by an abortion toll of two million a year in Italy, -a country one fifth the population of the United States. He initiated the concept of *Planned Parenthood,* which has since been referred as the number one enemy of the Roman Catholic Church. When word reached Rome that he was preaching this kind of thinking he was summoned to the Vatican and although no one knows what he was told, it can generally be assumed that he was instructed to cease preaching this message from the pulpit.

On his return to Venice, perhaps because he felt so strongly about this issue, he was greeted by tabloid headlines that suggested that he was planning a schism. A schism occurs when a ranking prelate separates from the Church and takes a sizable part of the congregation with him. Schism is an incumbent pope's greatest nightmare.

There is nothing in the legitimate press that says that Albino Luciani ever considered a schism. On returning from Rome he ceased to preach *Planned Parenthood* in public but very obviously continued to encourage it among his congregation in private. And one knows this because when he completed his reign as Patriarch of Venice it had the lowest birth and abortion rates of any metropolitan area in all of Europe. Today, of course, *Planned Parenthood* is the way of life in all first world countries.

Luciani made another radical departure from Church doctrine when he supported Cardinal Suenens' proposal to remove the papal elections from the *College of Cardinals* to the Worldwide Conference of Bishops. This was one of his more dangerous positions to the very conservative core of cardinals who shared the Vatican with him, for the closer one gets to the congregation the more liberal is the thinking. Like his good friend Cardinal Suenens, Luciani felt strongly that by bringing the election of successor Popes closer to the pastoral level that the Church could more readily respond to the needs of its congregation, something that they felt was necessary to bring it into rapid reconciliation with the emerging scientific and technical revolution.

But, perhaps, most dangerous of all was that he recognized Moses to be the monster that he was. That it had been Moses who had first spelled out the difference between man and woman and black and white and normal and handicapped and straight and gay four thousand years ago. That it had been Moses who had first inspired hate among the different peoples of the world which in turn has inspired all of the ethnic cleansing atrocities in the Western Hemisphere including the horrific taking of the Promised Land, the heartless slaughter of the Crusades, and in more modern times, World War II and the Holocaust.

make-believe children,

In July of 1978, Pope Paul was in seclusion at the Castel Gandolfo when Karol Wojtyla of Poland in support of the decree of Pius XII prohibiting genetic research of any kind, condemned Louise Brown the world's first artificially inseminated child as being "*a child of the devil.*" Luciani, on the other hand reached to the *left* and took up his pen and sent the following letter to the parents of the new born child,

"My very personal congratulations to you on the birth of your little girl. I want you to be assured that there is reserved for you and your child a high place in Heaven..."

Albino Luciani, Patriarch of Venice

Concurrent with the sending of this private message, he released the following statement to the Italian press,

"I have sent my most heartfelt congratulations to the English baby girl whose conception took place artificially. As far as her parents are concerned, I (the Church) have no right to condemn them. If they acted with honest intentions and in good faith, they will be deserving of merit before God for what they wanted and asked the doctors to carry out." *

The message was viewed as the most defiant rebuttal of a formal papal decree in modern history by a ranking prelate of the Church. Rumors

* *IL Gazzettino Venezia Jul '78; subsequently published in major world newspapers*

surfaced both in Venice and in the Vatican that when his reconfirmation came due later that year, it would not be forthcoming. Most people believe that a cardinal, once appointed, is forever a cardinal. This is not so. Cardinals are appointed for five-year terms and require the reconfirmation of the reigning pontiff when their terms lapse.

One might wonder why Luciani came out in defense of artificial insemination when it would obviously aggravate the possible attainment of one of his greatest objectives – to provide loving and economic support for the then two million orphans in Italy; the reason why he had lobbied in parliament to make it legal for single persons to adopt children; the reason why he had petitioned the Vatican cardinals to encourage long-term loving relationships between homosexuals; the reason why he objected to the Church's ban on remarriage. For all of these would provide parents for unparented children. And, of course, there was the sizable sterile population, also a reservoir of parents for orphans.

Artificial insemination would make it possible for both sterile and homosexual couples to have their own children, and would rob Italy of the two largest population groups that would otherwise be available to parent the nation's growing orphan population. One could say that compassion was a part of his reasoning in his defense of Louise Brown, but it was more likely Luciani's vision for the future.

A week after giving his statement to the press he was challenged by a reporter of a small newspaper on this very point, that artificial insemination would aggravate the orphan problem in Italy. Luciani responded, *"My good friend Einstein once told me that he could not accept the existence of God because he could not accept that God would play dice with His children, that there is something horrific about how God goes about making children, that millions of fertilized eggs are cast into the sewer in everyday sexual intercourse, and many others are destined only to live and die unspeakable deaths.*

"Here on the realization of this great event in genetic research, from a practical point of view, certainly from a humanitarian point of view, it makes no sense for man to allow God to continue to have His way in this thing. The question I have to ask myself is: is it right? Is it right for the child to suffer because of this selfish or insane desire of the preacher? Or is it better that every child have an equal chance at a healthy life? The answer is clear to me, that what is important is not how many children are born, but is that every child that is born has an equal chance at a healthy life.

"I believe that artificial insemination will eventually lead to man's greatest achievement, the creation of a perfectly healthy child every

time. The day is not too far off when all children will be born of artificial insemination and that natural conception will go by the wayside. This does not mean that the child will not be God's child. And this I see as the bottom line. Not that it is my child, or your child, or his child, or her child, but all that counts is that it is God's child. We are now only decades away from the time that doctors will be able to test the sperm and the egg before conception to weed out genetic impairments, disease and other birth defects to make possible a perfectly healthy child every time. Responsible parents-to-be will choose artificial insemination over natural conception to guarantee the health of their offspring. Irresponsible parents-to-be will continue to have children of natural conception and risk having children born only to suffer abbreviated lives and die unspeakable deaths. Eventually men and women of good conscience will step in and natural conception, being cruel and irresponsible, will become illegal.

"And this will, of course, remove intercourse as the acceptable method of having children. Sexual acts will be sexual acts, a means of intimate communication between people who love or are attracted to each other. When sexual lovemaking is the objective one will resort to contraception, when bearing children is the objective one will see one's doctor.

"One can probably best understand this if one considers the case of diseases that are transmitted through natural conception. We are presently aware of a new killer disease that is spreading across Africa. If it were determined that the chance of a child being born of this kind of fatal disease through natural conception becomes too great, then the state will step in and make natural conception illegal. The preacher won't have anything to say in the matter. Society will do what it must do to protect the unborn.

"The heterosexual, the homosexual, the transsexual, the bisexual and all the other sexuals will all be on the same playing field. They would all be able to parent children. The problems of sexual orientation and sexual identity and what have you will have resolved themselves once and for all. The Holy Sacrament of Matrimony would no longer sanctify the union of the penis and the vagina as Church doctrine has claimed in the past, but rather would sanctify the sacred mental union of the parties that can only be made by God.

"Science will be able to remove a healthy sperm from the father and a healthy egg from the mother and all children will have an equal opportunity at a healthy life, not just those who God has chosen in the past. And my good friend Einstein will at last be able to accept his Creator. It is as if the Creator has commissioned science, man, to perfect His work,

*to kind of finish off the rough edges of His creation so to speak."** Albert Einstein, himself, had once said of Luciani, *"Luciani is one who thinks of things today, as the rest of us will think of them in centuries to come."*

the embers of war,

In speaking of Pius XII, Luciani had always had a problem accepting this Pope for he knew that he had allied himself with the fascist movement before the war and that he had done nothing to stop the persecution of the Jews. Yes, there are those who today argue that it would have taken immense courage on the part of this Pope to have so acted. But Luciani knew that it would not have taken any courage at all on the part of this Pope to have interceded on the part of these oppressed people. After all, Italy at the time was entirely Catholic; there wasn't a Muslim or a Hindu or a Buddhist or for that matter a Protestant in all of Italy. The only exception was a handful of Jews scattered throughout the country, some living in Rome who had been required for some time by Italian law to attend and listen to sermons in the Catholic Church of Sant'Angelo which was located in the Jewish ghetto.

One hundred percent of the Italian Army, Hitler's major ally, was Catholic. Pius XII controlled the thinking of every single one of them. After all he was the representative of their God on earth. He was their Pharaoh. They would have done anything he would have asked of them.

Throughout the ages the Pope has many times made peace between Catholic nations simply by saying the word. And this is seen quite readily even today. For example, when Chile and Argentina, two Catholic countries, were in dispute over the Beagle Channel and were mobilizing on either side of the Andes and war seemed eminent, President Carter called on the Pope to intervene and the matter was settled overnight.

The power of the Pope to control the populace is perhaps best demonstrated by what happened in Central America where there exists a polarization of immense wealth and immense poverty. In 1983, when it appeared that the revolution that might have brought about a more equitable society was taking hold, the Pope, at the request of the wealthy families upon which the Church depended for its revenues, toured these countries and told the people to stop supporting the revolution. Despite the fact that it meant returning to a life of dire poverty and starvation, the people abandoned the revolution and it failed. Shortly after his visit, John Paul II replaced more than twenty bishops who had supported the revolutionaries

* *Messaggero Mestre 12 Aug '78*

and, of course, poverty and starvation remain the way of life in most of these countries today, modified only by what America has put there.

Pius XII very clearly controlled the minds of the entire Italian army during World War II. All he would have had to say was "stop." And the reason he did nothing was because he and Hitler and Mussolini shared the very same fascist ideology. Had the Nazis won the war we would today be living in a world of white Aryan male superiority rather than in this world in which we find ourselves, -this world of equal human rights for everyone including Jews, Negroes and women, -this anti-Christian, this anti-Fascist philosophy of human equality, which even today threatens to be extended to homosexuals.

why Italy was Hitler's only major ally,

One might ask why Italy was Hitler's only major ally in the war. Being Christian, the overwhelming part of the population believed fervently in the superiority of the Aryan race. If one were to read many of Pius XII's writings prior to the war, one would find that his major objective was to make God the Father's promise of rule by the Aryan race as told in the Old Testament a reality. It was for this reason that blacks were not allowed in all of Italy or for that matter other heavily populated Catholic countries of Europe, -the reason why so few of them died in concentration camps.

Yet, of course, there remained the Jews who were believed to be of the Aryan race. In 1937, Pius XI commissioned Hitler to conduct the largest investigation ever undertaken to search out the origin of the Aryan race. The objective was to determine that the Jews were not of the Aryan race. Hitler financed the expedition and employed half of his SS guard to conduct the search, which spanned half of the globe, but no reasonable conclusion was ever reached. Nevertheless, Hitler hated them so much that even though he could not prove that they were not of the Aryan race, he tried to annihilate them anyway.

So at the time, Pius and Mussolini and Hitler shared the same ideology, the Aryan race ideology. As a matter of fact Hitler could not have succeeded without the other two. It was this triad of men who were the architects of the fascist movement in Europe, which eventually culminated in World War II. Specifically in Italy's case was the black-white issue. In 1936, Italy invaded Ethiopia, a country made up of about fifty-million blacks. Mussolini, like most Italians at the time, was a racist.

Realizing that Italians who were stationed in Ethiopia might integrate themselves with the blacks, Mussolini imposed heavy penalties for sexual intercourse between Italians and the natives. The minimum penalty for an Italian was five years in prison and for the Ethiopian the penalty could range all the way up to death. In any event the pregnancy no matter how progressed was always aborted. The objective, consistent with that of the Vatican at the time was to maintain the purity of the Aryan race. He also imposed strict segregation guidelines, going so far as to restrict the places the blacks could go. For example, it was illegal for a black to use a paved road or modern toilets.

Although the United States was no angel itself concerning the treatment of Negroes, the atrocities were so great in Ethiopia that it joined together with its allies and placed sanctions on both Italy and Ethiopia. And it was these sanctions which remained in place at the start of the war in 1939 combined with its Aryan race philosophy that made Italy the great ally of Germany. Actually, its persecution of blacks was the mainstay of its Aryan race philosophy.

Fascism, of course, had been implanted in Italy several years earlier. When one plans to take over the world at sometime in the future, one starts with the young who will carry out the plan in the future. Up until that time the Catholic Church used the *Catholic Scouts of Italy* to indoctrinate or brainwash the youth of Italy into its fascist fold; much as in the United States, where the Mormon Church and many *born again* denominations require all children to belong to the *Boy/Girl Scouts of America* today, to indoctrinate or brainwash the youth of America into their fascist folds.

The *Christian Scouts* grew out of Mormon Sunday schools in the latter part of the nineteenth century. After the turn of the century when the scouts were nationally organized, its founders discarded the name *Christian Scouts* in favor of the name *Boy Scouts of America.* The objective of this name change was originally to attract Jewish children and indoctrinate them into *Christianity* or what at the time was commonly referred to as *Fascism.* Today, one knows that *Boy Scouts of America* is about as un-American an organization as one can get, as it excludes homosexual, transsexual, atheist and other teens who do not conform to its basic fascist ideology. One might note that the great majority of racial and ethnic slurs like the words *kike, spook, faggot, spic* and *chink* all originated in the scouts; scoutmasters often used these slurs to discipline scouts when they got out of hand by referring to them as *freaks* of society.* The word *nigger*, on the other hand did not originate in the boy scouts. To the best that history has recorded, the word first appeared in the latter part of the

** see History of Boy Scouts of America or Christian Scouts of America or similar books.*

seventeenth century and the culprit was alleged to have been a preacher in Charlestown who used the term in referring to Negroes being unloaded from vessels as being animal dung.

As early as 1925, Pope Pius XI and Mussolini began graduating Italy's youth, both girls and boys, from the scout organization into a new fascist organization. These would be the same boys and girls who fifteen years later would join Hitler and Mussolini in their struggle to establish the superiority of the Aryan race. In April of 1926, the fascist youth movement was given official legal status in Italy and in January of the following year a law was passed in Italy which forbade the formation of any new youth movement and dissolved most branches of the *Catholic Scouts*. That both Mussolini and Pius XI were grooming these children for war is clearly demonstrated in that they dispensed with the almost angelic dress of the *Catholic Scouts* in favor of military uniforms for the scouts of the new *Fascist Youth Organization*. In December of the same year, the Pope issued an order to all elementary schools in Italy to enroll all children under sixteen years of age in the new *Fascist Youth Organization,* and as has already been mentioned, this action prompted Albino Luciani to make his debut onto the public stage.

In February of 1929, Pius and Mussolini entered into an agreement that united the Catholic Church with the Italian fascist movement. There began a campaign by the Catholic Church to preach *Fascism* from the pulpit and the following year a special election was held in Italy that invited the populace to vote **Yes** or **No** to the question of whether they supported the new fascist government. Pius XI issued a letter to his congregation, which comprised 99.9% of the population and it was read from every pulpit throughout the country and published in every newspaper telling them to vote **Yes** on the issue. The voters went to the polling stations on March 24, 1929 and the score was 8,519,539 **Yes** and 155,761 **No**. It demonstrates quite conclusively the power that the infallibility of the Pope had upon the Italian population at the time. Although he would never waiver from the mission his people had given him, they would string Mussolini up in Milan just fifteen years later.[1]

Five years later Chancellor Hitler set before the German Parliament his *Enabling Act* the intention of which was to make him dictator of Germany. The problem he faced was that such an act required a two-thirds majority and his Nazi Party was a minority party. So like Mussolini before him he appealed to the Vatican. Pius XI issued a letter to the two Catholic

[1] *can be found in any history book of the time; look for Italian and German Concordants.*

parties of Germany instructing them to vote **Yes** for the *Enabling Act* and the next week Hitler became dictator of Germany. [1]

So one is on solid ground when one says that the success of the fascist movement in Europe which was to cost fifty-million war lives depended entirely upon papal decisions, for neither the Italian nor German referendums would have passed without their support as it was the papacy and not Hitler or Mussolini that controlled the votes. It was clearly the Pontiff who was the puppeteer who held the strings of fate that would eventually cost fifty-million lives. Without the support of the Pope *Fascism* would have been defeated by a 100% margin in Italy and Mussolini would have never become dictator and Hitler would have never gotten past the year nineteen hundred and thirty four in his quest to rule the world, for he would have never become dictator of Germany.

But getting back to the scouts, those young men and women who would actually fight the war; by 1935 the process had been completed and Italy's youth like that of Germany had been indoctrinated, or if one might use a more appropriate term, brainwashed. *Fascism*, as has already been pointed out, is synonymous with the Aryan race, emphasizing the subordination of women and particularly prejudice against blacks, Jews and homosexuals.

Keep in mind that during the thirties the word *Fascism,* like the word *Communism,* did not have the connotation that it has today. Actually, before the war it was a good word as it was synonymous with the word *Christianity.** To Christian Italians and Germans the ideology of the superiority of the Aryan male and the subordination of women and the persecution of blacks, Jews, homosexuals and certain ethnic was something that was basic to their beliefs. So it is only natural that Catholicism and its allies in the evangelical movement, which have their roots in *Fascism,* continue to preach the remnants of *Fascism* today. They continue to cling to those parts of *Fascism* which society has not yet completely taken from them - bigotry against women and gays and others who appear to be different.

Luciani knew that it had been this same view of Christianity that had inspired the Boxer Rebellion in China in 1900 that attempted to drive Christians out of China. The Chinese had never known racial strife despite the fact that three of the world's four major race groups were native to China.

* *recent polls in the free world countries of Europe today show that most see Christianity (not Christ) as a bad word today; it refers to those who spread hatred of others.*

Until that time ethnic strife had only been a problem in the West, in those Christian and Muslim countries where culture was driven by the *Old Testament* and by what Moses had to say, "*And the Lord said unto Joshua, See, I have given into thine hand the Promised Land. And take for thyself all the silver, and gold, and vessels of brass and iron, and treasure thereof. Take all ye men of war and go around the cities . . . and ye are to enter and take to the sword all of the non-believers and those who are different thereof, every man and woman and child. Let none remain!*"

Luciani knew the Boxers realized that all Christian and Muslim wars had been driven by this instruction of God the Father in the *Old Testament.* They didn't want this kind of influence in the East. Although China had a long history of wars of aggression it had never thought there to be differences among races and this extended to other people who appeared to be different including various religions, ethnic groups and even homosexuals. Until Christian preachers started to preach bigotry and hatred of people who appear to be different the Chinese people never knew what the word bigotry meant as all people were considered to be equal, for they were all seen to be children of the same God.

The Boxers, who were Caucasoids themselves, knew that the United States, being a Christian nation, held other than Caucasoid races as subordinate peoples at the time. Those of the black, yellow and red races and other ethnic groups living in the United States were made to live as inferior peoples, -they were not permitted in white neighborhoods or schools, blacks were imprisoned if caught using a 'white' toilet or riding in the fronts of trolleys or even sitting in the ground floor pews of churches, and many of these peoples were persecuted, tortured and even killed in hate crimes. And they knew that it was the white Christian preacher who was inspiring hatred.

Luciani knew that the Civil War in the United States had also had its roots in what Moses had to say. He had learned from his history books that the reformation of the sixteenth century had moved the Protestants toward the *left* away from the ways of Moses and in 1626 Roger Williams founded the Baptist Church in Rhode Island which intent was to return them back to literal belief in the word of Moses. His history books also told him that in 1841 the Baptist Church split into the Southern Baptist Church and the Northern Baptist Church, the former believing in the tenth commandment as had been allegedly handed down from God to Moses on Mount Sinai which dictated slavery as a way of life, "*Thou shalt not covet* (desire or take from) *thy neighbor his . . . slaves . . .*" and the latter no longer believing in the tenth commandment and he knew that it had been this difference that had set the stage for the Civil War. Whereas most saw Grant as the commanding general of the north and Lee as the commanding general of the south, Luciani saw something else. Luciani saw Christ leading those in the north and Moses leading those in the south, northern men and women of good conscience who took from their southern neighbors their slaves, once and for all. They didn't give a damn for what Moses' commandment had to say.

So Luciani saw this happening all over again when he witnessed the first glowing embers that would eventually fire the world war. He knew that the Pope clearly controlled the Italian army in 1943 when the great atrocities committed against the Jews were first becoming known. He also knew that the Pope believed literally in the directives of God the Father of the *Old Testament*. At that time, Hitler found himself to be struggling on two fronts, the Russians on the east and the Americans and British on the west. He was protected only on the south by the Italian army, which was the only thing that stood between him and the allied forces that had stormed their way across North Africa into Sicily. Pius XII had only to say the word and the entire Italian army would have stood still.

Luciani knew that Pius XII didn't even have to do that. For Pius could have simply threatened Mussolini or Hitler with excommunication. But he did nothing. And Pius XII knew exactly what was going on. He was faced with it firsthand when, in September of 1943, five hundred Jews showed up on a boat in Naples begging for asylum in the Vatican and he sent them back to their deaths. Luciani had never forgiven Pius for that. For it was Albino Luciani himself, who had pleaded with the Vatican to give refuge to those on the boat, two hundred and seventy five of which were children.

It was then as a simple priest that Luciani had come to realize that the Pope is not truly infallible, that all of a pope's major decisions are not made by Christ as the doctrine reads. For this had been one of the most important decisions this pontiff was to make in all of his papacy and it was quite obvious that it had not come from Christ. For Christ was a God of love and compassion. Rather, to him, it was quite obvious that it had come from Moses or, perhaps, from the devil, himself. As a matter of fact the most important decision of his predecessor's pontificate had also come from Moses, as it had indoctrinated German and Italian youth into the fascist movement that ultimately resulted in the loss of fifty-million lives.

Just a month later another thousand Jews were deported to Germany during the SS raid of October 16, 1943 in Rome. Although the Jewish Ghetto annexed the Vatican, Pius sealed the Vatican gates preventing their gaining asylum. He then issued a warning through intermediaries to Luciani who had engaged the press to pressure the Pope into a more compassionate action.

After the war, Albino came to realize that according to Church doctrine both Hitler and Mussolini were in heaven as not having been excommunicated, both died as Catholics and both had considerable time before their demise to repent for any misdeeds. It also troubled him immensely that this very same Church doctrine condemned the Jews who had been turned back at Naples and those who had been herded from the ghetto to the everlasting fires of Hell.

a simple game of chess,

It was this experience that caused him to mold his cause for life, to rid the world of the bigot. A few years before becoming a bishop he wrote an editorial directed at Rome that suggested that both Hitler and Mussolini be excommunicated on a post mortem basis. Pius saw this as an opportunity to silence the young rebel from the foothills of Belluno once and for all and he answered Luciani's editorial in his own comment to the press, "*We must learn to forgive our enemies as Christ has taught us.*"

It has been said of Luciani that he was a poor strategist. As a matter of fact, on several occasions he said so himself. But in reality he was a brilliant strategist. He had acquired his ability when he was confined as a child to a sanatorium for a year and a half with tuberculosis. He developed a liking to chess and later in three successive years during his secondary school days, he placed third, then second and finally first in European competition.

One can see quite clearly in his actions that his sole goal was to win the game. He had learned that in order to win the game that he often had to sacrifice many *pawns*, sometimes his *rooks* and on occasion even his *queen*. This was quite evident in his strategy to bring about equal rights for women in the Church. His sole goal was *checkmate,* -to bring about equality of women in the Church. He knew that he could only bring this about by sacrificing some of his *pawns*, like priest celibacy and relaxation of dress for women in the Church. He knew that if he were to try to save these *pawns* he would risk losing the game.

In this case it seemed on the surface that the Pope had won the game. Bishop Giuseppe Siri, later to rise to become a cardinal and leader of the *conservative right* in the Church, belittled Luciani, telling the press that "*this young and inexperienced whippersnapper of a common priest from Belluno is absolutely no match for his Holiness. The two men are quite obviously on completely different levels of intellect. Luciani very obviously is dealing in matters that are beyond his ability to comprehend.*" In retrospect one can clearly see that Luciani had set a trap for Pius XII. He had chosen to sacrifice his *queen* in order to win the game.

Contrary to what Bishop Siri may have been trying to suggest, one must keep in mind that during the twenty years that he served as a bishop and as a cardinal, Albino Luciani was considered to be one of the most brilliant men in the Church, perhaps in the history of the Church. John XXIII once called him, *"the Einstein of the Roman Catholic Church,"* and Luciani often referred to Einstein as *"my patron saint."* Einstein himself reciprocated, -as on more than one occasion he had claimed to be *"of the school of Luciani."*

marriage and remarriage,

But getting back to Church doctrine, one of his greatest problems was with its definition of *marriage:* the *Sacrament of Matrimony* emphasized the sanctification of the union of a penis and vagina and that it applied to these genitalia whether or not they worked, as in the case of paraplegics, sterile couples or the elderly. Luciani, being a disciple of Einstein, knew that the most fundamental unit of all of God's creation was *energy* and the greatest manifestation of God's creation was *mental energy,* -that is, the exchange of mental energy between human beings. He knew that every day people were exchanging mental energy with each other and that there were some people who were mostly energy thieves, while others were mostly energy givers.

For example, when one would tell new and interesting stories, one was an energy giver, whereas when one told repetitive and boring stories, one was an energy thief. When one said nice things to another, one was an energy giver and the receipt of that energy could be profoundly felt by the receiver. Yet, on the other hand, when one yelled at or argued with another, one became an energy thief and the loss of that energy could be profoundly felt by the receiver.

Luciani found that there was only one circumstance in which the mental energy exchange could be perfectly even between two adults, and that occurred when two people *fell in love*. He believed that this union of two minds could only be made by God and that Christ was referring to this union when He said, *"What God has joined together let no man put asunder."* And he felt strongly that it applied to anyone who happened to be a part of it.

Prompted by the struggle in America in the early sixties to make marriage between blacks and whites legal, he made his position on the *Holy*

Sacrament of Matrimony quite clear on a balmy afternoon in the summer of 1961. As presiding bishop, he was the keynote speaker at commencement services of the seminary located at Vittorio Veneto in Northern Italy. He summed up his lengthy address, in which he at times had gone into great detail as to how mental energy is exchanged between people,

". . . and therefore, we must hold most hallowed this solemn personification of God's creation – this perfect balance of mental energy that exists between two people when they fall in love – this perfect union of minds that can only be made by God. We must find the great courage within us to set aside the prejudice and hatred that has been implanted in us by our Christian forefathers and we must hold this kind of holy union in sanctified trust before Almighty God whenever it exists between any of God's children, whether it be between man and woman, or black and white, or Christian and Jew, or believer and unbeliever, or German and Russian, or royalty and commoner, or virgin and divorcee, or man and man, or woman and woman, or hermaphrodite and eunuch, or what have you. The rest of this thing we call 'love' is simply the animal in us. To think differently – that it somehow pertains to physical parts of the body - is to say that the Holy Sacrament of Matrimony pertains equally to the apes in the wild as it does to human beings."[1]

One must realize that when John Paul said this the movie "*Guess Who's Coming to Dinner*" had not yet been thought of and that most of the other possibilities that he spoke of were being condemned by Christian preachers as being against the will of God. Again, he felt strongly that the Church was in violation of Christ's will; the Church deeply steeped in prejudice and hatred in many cases was *"putting asunder what God had joined together."*

Afterwards, a local reporter who had covered the event asked the bishop how he had been able to voice his opinion with such great conviction. How did he know that the phenomenon of *falling in love* could only be made by God? *"My father was the village trouble maker, -particularly outspoken against the Church,"* he told the reporter, *"The only Catholic part of him was the fact that he had been born and baptized a Catholic. When my mother, who was of an extremely devout family, fell in love with him and they approached the village priest he refused to marry them. In fact, my mother told me that they had to travel two hundred miles south to a small village on the Adriatic Sea where my father was unknown before they found a priest who was willing to marry them. She lost half of*

[1] *Albino Luciani at commencement services of the seminary at Vittorio Veneto 23 June '61*

her family for having married a renegade, her brother never talked to her again. So this is why I know that this kind of holy union that is so powerful that it is able to bury centuries of prejudice and hatred of men can only be made by God." [2]

Of course, the *falling-in-love* phenomenon, of which Lucian spoke, had little to do with traditional marriage. Regardless of what the motion pictures would want one to believe, marriage in the pre-nineteenth century, with some exceptions in regency, was a contract between two men - the father of the bride and the husband to be. It was a matter of business and was a covenant of two men and not a covenant of a man and a woman. The woman was the merchandise. Nowhere does the Bible talk of this *falling-in-love* phenomenon as existing between a man and a woman. In fact, the only time the Bible mentions what Luciani referred to as '*the perfect balance of energy between two people that can only be made by God.*' it occurs between two men: 1 Samuel 18, *'And it came to pass, when he had made an end of speaking unto Saul, that the soul of Jonathan was knit with the soul of David. Then Jonathan made a covenant with David, because he loved him as his own soul.'* Only the union of souls can survive beyond the grave. Unions of bodies end in death.

In the ensuing months, civil rights advocates in the United States, faced by population polls that were overwhelmingly against integration, continued their struggle state-by-state in their efforts to make interracial marriage legal. Luciani, who after the war had led the same effort in Italy all the way to its Supreme Court, *"The state cannot tell its citizens who they can or cannot marry, less we cease to be a free society. Marriage is an individual right and not the decision of the majority. There is no issue more basic to freedom than is the right to marry whomever God deems one fall in love with. There is no more fundamental issue that divides democracy from hypocriscy."* [1]

Luciani objected to the American process in that it wrongly assumed that the right of marriage was not a basic human right and therefore was a state's prerogative. Even as late as 1967, when the Supreme Court finally rendered its decision on *Loving vs. Virginia*, there remained sixteen, mostly southern states, that did not permit marriages between blacks and whites.

He criticized the American process in his address to the Christian Democratic Party Convention in 1963, *"In a free society, the most sacred duty of the federal government is to protect certain basic human rights for all of its citizens regardless of race or religious background and it should*

[2] *Messaggero Veneto 24 Jun '61*
[1] *Bishop Luciani, Italian Supreme Court 22 Aug '59*

*not be an option of any of its states or tributaries to abuse these basic rights. The right to fall in love with whomever God deems one fall in love with is one of these basic human rights. And these basic human rights are individual rights and therefore cannot be imposed upon by the state or for that matter by the majority. Democracy, which finds its strength in rule by the people, can only find its purpose, its sacred duty to society, in preserving the basic human rights of its loneliest individual."**

He followed up on his declaration in a series of seminary lectures, *"If the Constitution of the United States had declared it to be a Christian nation, which it does not, then interracial marriage would clearly be an abuse of its basic truths, as intermarriage, particularly between blacks and whites, would be a gross violation of the Bible's definition of marriage - 'the union of a man and woman solely of the Aryan race.' One must keep in mind that so overpowering is God the Father's instruction in the Old Testament to preserve the purity of the Aryan race, the reason why the laws of Christian nations have enforced segregation of blacks and whites for centuries, that it would be in closer adherence to Church doctrine and the Bible's definition of 'marriage' to change the wording 'woman and man' to 'man and man' than if one were to abandon its link to the Aryan race.*

"In recent history, both America and Mother Church have been challenged concerning the traditional definition of marriage, which for centuries has been based on the Tenth Commandment - that woman is property and marriage is a contract that conveys that piece of property from one man to another man. We are now coming to know that this is wrong. We are undergoing a transformation that will take much time, as the preacher cannot give up his conviction that marriage is a pledge of sexual submission of a woman to her new owner. In time, we will no longer think as animals do, but we will honor only that covenant that could possibly survive beyond the grave - the mental and spiritual exchange between two people, that falling-in-love phenomenon, 'that the soul of Jonathan was knit with the soul of David. And Jonathan made a covenant with David, because he loved him as his own soul.' Marriage is love - sex has very little to do with it.

"So we are faced here with the very same problem with which Lincoln and his followers in the nineteenth century were faced. And like them we must find the great courage within us to stand up to our God and tell Him that He was wrong in His dictate of the superiority of the Aryan race. Just as Lincoln and his followers found the great courage within themselves that caused them to stand up to their God and tell Him,

* *Bishop Albino Luciani, Christian Democratic Party 22 August '59*

'We don't give a damn for what your tenth commandment has to say, for slavery is wrong, it is an abomination of mankind and we won't put up with it anymore!' Once more America, like Mother Church before her, must see it as her duty to change with the times. For if she does not she will be a hypocrite among nations when she claims to be free.

"Insofar as the Constitution of the United States does not define it as being a Christian nation; that is, it clearly provides for freedom of religion, the right of its citizens to believe or not to believe, the Bible's definition of marriage does not apply. But, nevertheless, one has this word 'marriage' which has crept from scripture into everyday life. So let us look at how it crept into doctrine to begin with.

"The function pertaining to the word 'marriage' is quite different, religion versus the state. From a doctrinal point of view, marriage is the sanctification of fornication, the most damned sin in the Bible; a physical union. The Sacrament of Matrimony was originally incorporated into Church doctrine in the fifth century as a technical measure to get around the Bible's overwhelming condemnation of fornication, in order to permit people to engage in procreation without committing sin. At the time, the sacrament sanctified only the physical union (of a penis and a vagina) of two people of the Aryan race. This doctrine has since been adopted by all Christian churches and in turn has been the driving force behind segregation for centuries. Keep in mind that for centuries most Christian preachers including Mother Church required the aborting of fetuses and even newborns when it was known that conception involved interracial couples.

"For centuries, marriage was limited to only this,-sanctification of fornication. And it was for this reason that for more than a millennium marriage was limited to those who were of childbearing age. It was extended in more recent times to include the mental union of the parties when society raised its hand and forced it to recognize those mental unions between the elderly, handicapped and others who, because of emotional and physical limitations, could not procreate children, some of whom like paraplegics and others could not even engage in sex. And these changes, of course, removed procreation as a requirement of marriage.

"Marriage has been an evolutionary process through the years. From being in the fifth century a sexual union between a man and a 'slave' (woman) both not having been previously married and both being of the same race in which the 'slave', having no freedom of choice in the matter, was forced to pledge to live in dire servitude to the man; and on top of all of this both parties had to have been of the same religion. And we all know that in the seventeenth century some Protestant religions deleted the

phrase 'not having been previously married' from the equation. Recently, here in twentieth century, courageous men and women have removed the phrase, 'must be of the same religion.'

"So what are we left with today? Marriage is the sanctification of a mutual mental union between a man and woman of the same race that no longer requires fornication and procreation as a required part of the union. And now the time has come for America to remove the phrase 'of the same race' from the definition of marriage.

author's note: *The Evolution of Marriage*
Christianity only

Changing times	*century*
Sacrament of Matrimony is added to Church doctrine marriage is sanctified fornication and requires the woman to be in servitude (slavery) to her husband in all things particularly his sexual desires	*5th*
for first time one is able to marry outside of one's social status	*14th*
for first time a commoner is able to marry into royal blood	*15th*
for the first time a Christian church sanctifies remarriage	*16th*
fornication and procreation is no longer a requirement – elderly	*17th*
fornication and procreation is no longer a requirement – handicapped	*18th*
marriage evolves from a woman's commitment into a mutual contract	*19th*
for first time state/church recognizes the mental union between the parties	*19th*
state/church eliminates common religion as a requirement	*20th*
state/church eliminates common race as a requirement	*20th*
woman is taken out of the home into the workplace	*20th*
at age three children are parented in day care centers	*20th*
state/church artificial insemination makes procreation possible for everyone	*20th*
state/church postoperative transsexuals born of the same sex can marry	*20th*
artificial insemination replaces natural conception in third world countries	*21st?*
genetic blueprint completed - fornication is no longer an acceptable means of procreation. Natural conception is replaced by artificial insemination.	*21st?*

Note: Christianity only. In some religions many of these things and a wide variety of other things remain requirements today within specific religions. For example, some Islamic countries don't 'recognize mixed marriages and sanctification within most sects of the Islamic religion requires that both parties be Muslims.

Note: state/church. The word 'church' refers to Christianity and is not restricted to the Roman Catholic Church, although prior to the sixteenth century it is synonymous with the Roman Church but not necessarily with the Eastern Church. State is listed first as the state is always the driving force behind change in religion. This is because it is not the job of the preacher to determine what is right and what is wrong. His sole job is to impose scripture on the populace whether or not it is right or wrong. There is often a gap of decades between acceptance by the state and acceptance by the church. Yet, there has never been a change instituted by the state that eventually has not also been accepted by the church, for the church cannot exist outside of society. For example, marriage between postoperative transsexuals was accepted by the state shortly after Christine Jorgenson's transformation into a woman. It wasn't until the end of the 20th century that most of Christianity would recognize her marriage to a man."

"Nevertheless, this word sanctification needs some attention. The word 'sanctification' pertains only to the soul and has nothing at all to do with the body; as a matter of fact it has nothing to do with the mind; it has only to do with the soul. One can no more sanctify a mortal body than one can sanctify an animal. Sanctity of marriage in the Church today continues to emphasize the union of two animals as Church doctrine explicitly denies the possibility that marriage is a union of two souls in that it does not extend beyond the grave. And this same doctrine has been adopted by all Christian churches today, -that marriage is between two animals and not two human beings, otherwise it would be between two souls and would extend beyond the grave. For all Christian marriage ceremonies are required by doctrine to end with the phrase, 'Until death due us part' or its equivalent.

Note: today, some Christian denominations use variations, for example "until one meets Christ." This is consistent with the fundamental definition of the Christian afterlife in the Book pf revelation that in the afterlife, 'one will be as the bride of Christ and that all of one's love will be for Christ alone;' the only definition of the afterlife on which both the New Testament and the Old Testament agree. Regardless of the wording used, Catholic marriages are more bonding than are Protestant marriages in that they commit the couple for life, that is until one of the parties dies at which time the surviving partner is free to choose another mate, again testifying to the fact that the marriage is not of two souls but of two bodies. Protestant ceremonies generally bind the parties until death with the additional option of separation upon divorce. Nevertheless, all Christian practices and ceremonies conform to the fact that one will not be rejoined in the Christian heaven with one's loved one, as the provisions of remarriage upon death and/or divorce would mean that in the Christian heaven one would have many wives (polygamy). And one knows that would never hold up in a Christian court of law. One must keep in mind that unlike the Muslim Koran and eastern scriptures, nowhere in either the New Testament or the Old Testament is there provision for one's spouse to accompany one into heaven. As a matter of fact, God the Father in the book of Jeremiah makes it quite explicit, "Thou shalt not take thee a wife, and neither shalt thou have sons nor daughters in this place"'

*"And this can probably be seen more clearly when one considers that no marriage ceremony outside of Christianity ends in the phrase, 'Until death do us part.' And this includes not only those of eastern religions but those unions whose parties are suffering under unfair restraint placed upon them by scriptures and doctrines of the western world. * And this is because, except for Christianity, fornication is not considered to be sinful by most other religions. That in the eastern world, for example, it is considered to be a great gift from God, a good and wonderful thing, and not the evil and wicked thing that Moses conditioned the western world to believe that it is.*

"Today, much of the confusion concerning the definition of 'marriage' lies in the fact that what the Church considers as sin is not considered as sin at all by the state. Today, Christian doctrine considers all sex outside of marriage as being sinful. On the other hand, the state does not consider sex with oneself or with another outside of marriage a sin (a crime) at all, provided one doesn't cross the lines of rape or statutory rape; to consider an extreme, there is no law against two twelve year olds engaging in sex.

"Unlike the Church, the state in its definition of marriage is not concerned with sin. Its duty is a legal one; its duty is solely to protect the equal rights of the parties under law. As the American president Thomas Jefferson so eloquently put it, 'All men and women are endowed by their Creator with certain inalienable rights, that among these are Life, Liberty and the Pursuit of Happiness,' And today we all know that there can be only be one definition as to what Jefferson meant by 'the Pursuit of Happiness.'

** this phrase, which was repeated by Luciani in his papal acceptance speech in the Sistine Chapel several years later, is the only evidence that the author has been able to uncover that hints that Luciani may have at sometime officiated at or at least attended a ceremony uniting homosexual couples, that homosexuals, not restricted by the Church doctrine, at the time tended not to end their ceremonies with the words, "until death do us part." – a union of two souls – a sanctified union – one that would last forever. A union explicitly supported by the marriage of the souls of Jonathan and David. The gospels tell us that David was the Patriarch of Jesus. "Thou art Son of David."*
And likewise, Luciani, when asked to perform a marriage ceremony as a priest, as a bishop and as a cardinal, never ended the ceremony with the words, "until death do us part," emphasizing his conviction that the union he was blessing was a mental one - a sacred one - and not the physical one that both the state and the Church considered marriage to be.

"The Pursuit of Happiness is the most precious and fundamental human right in a free society. It is the inalienable right of each of its citizens to be free to grow up and fall in love with whomever God deems one fall in love with, and to be free to enter into a long-term loving relationship and to parent children and to provide for the economic and loving support of those children in order to enable them to grow up and likewise enjoy this most precious of freedoms, the Pursuit of Happiness.

"Because the United States recognizes freedom of religion, it must recognize all religions, and as one knows the requirement that both parties be of the Aryan race is not a requirement of marriage in religions other than Christianity. As a matter of fact, no two of the world's major religions are in agreement as to just what this word 'marriage' means. For example, there is no required separation of races, black versus white, in the Hindu, the Shinto or the Buddhist sects. And yet in the Middle East are those Muslim nations which recognize marriage only if both parties are Muslim.

"America has one of two choices: it can declare itself a Christian state and abandon its role as a free state, or it must recognize this kind of holy union between any two people of any races regardless of what any individual scripture has to say. 'Marriage' is synonymous with 'Pursuit of Happiness.' There is no room here for middle ground. The majority cannot compromise this basic human right of the individual, less the nation cease to be free.

*"Nevertheless, the important thing here is to separate church from state so that the state, in its solemn duty, is free to protect this most hallowed of human rights, the right to fall in love with whomever God deems one fall in love with and at the same time to protect America's status as a free state. For if the state permits a religion, any religion, to impose its beliefs upon its populace, it would no longer be free. America would no longer be what Lincoln and Jefferson intended it to be, it would no longer be what those who fought and died on the great battlefields of war wanted it to be, 'this nation is one nation under God, conceived in Liberty, and dedicated to the proposition that all men are created equal . . . and that they are endowed with certain inalienable rights including Life, Liberty and the Pursuit of Happiness!'**

"The great problem that America faces today in these things is that its Constitution ignores its most basic founding ideology. These words of Jefferson -"Pursuit of Happiness"- should preface its Constitution, but, rather they have never made it into the fine print. One must remember that

* *Lincoln's Gettysburg Address . . . Jefferson's Declaration of Independence.*

America was founded as a Christian nation and although it has developed today into a nation of many, it has not yet been able to break free of its Christian roots as Christian preachers and politicians have successfully kept these solemn words out of its Constitution for more than two hundred years.

"America is a caught up in a struggle between two kinds of people, those who have had the great courage to have put their religious convictions aside and place their God and country first and those who have been unable to find this kind of courage and continue to place their religion first. To put it more bluntly, the struggle is between Americans and Christians. Keep in mind that religion is not synonymous with God. Each one of us by nature has a direct and personal relationship with God. Religion is no more than a greedy middleman between a man and his God. Don't ever be so foolish to think that it is anything more than this."

In one session a student questioned the words, *'one nation under God,'* in America's founding documents, *"This means that the United States does not accommodate agnostics and atheists."*

"You are confusing religion with God" Luciani corrected the student, *"'God is the infinite energy force from which we all came from and to which we will all eventually return.'* All believers and unbelievers are in agreement with this definition that the scientific community tells us is a basic fact. God is the source of all of our physical energy and all of our mental energy and this includes that treasured manifestation of one of our most basic instincts, compassion - whom one is able to fall in love with.*

"Where the doubters differ from the believers is that they don't believe in religion – stories that different men of motivation made up through the ages; we know that the prophets of the Old Testament were driven by greed. To the doubters it is inconceivable that the infinite energy source from which we all come from is a super man of some kind who is going about keeping track of each of our daily lives from the time of our conceptions until we lay on our death beds and that our record will someday determine whether or not we will continue to be a part of the universal flow of energy that created us after we die - the fundamental premise of all religions.

"Every agnostic and atheist accepts the universal definition of God as the Creator as I've just described it. They know that Something created us – this thing Einstein referred to as energy – the fundamental unit of God's creation. What they do not believe in are the endless definitions of God that are peddled by religions, by various men; that this Something

**Albert Einstein 12 Feb 1918. Luciani often referred to Einstein as being the only true prophet*

is Someone. All religions personify God and the reason they do this is because it is the only way to prey on the imagination of their customers and make the bucks.

"Although the definition of God, religion versus religion, appears to be quite different on the surface they all boil down to this universal definition. For example, there are hundreds of millions of Buddhists who believe that man is an extension of God, that God as He exists today is mankind itself, that we are all a part of God, or better put,-we are God; that it is the composition of mankind that is the Supreme Being.

"And this certainly makes a lot of sense, that God is actually a part of each of us and not an individual being separate from humanity. Certainly, being a part of each of us would make the immense volume of paperwork required in keeping a full and complete record of each our lives much easier for Him.

"And likewise, although you would never get a single preacher to agree with it, Christianity in its basic theology is similar to that of Buddha. For all Christians accept the fact that they have a soul, that part of them that is infinite, that part of them that is immortal, that part of them that is a part of God; the only part of them that will survive beyond death intact. That upon death the soul returns to Christ to be in adoration of Christ for all time. And this in a nutshell defines the Christian heaven, perpetual adoration of Christ for all time, for in the Christian afterlife every day will be Sunday.

"Although the Christian world claims that the body will rise again, it also knows that it will not be the same biological body that one has enjoyed in this life. For example, it won't have to go to the bathroom, or clip its nails, or brush its teeth, or clean its ears, or even attend football games. And likewise, according to Christian doctrine, the human mind won't survive as it has been in this life. That is, it won't be able to make independent decisions or accomplish invention as it will no longer be faced with alternatives. For example, it won't be able to think anything bad, for in heaven everything will be good. And, perhaps worst of all it won't be able to grow up and fall in love and procreate children. As a matter of fact, Christianity is the only religion in the world that accepts the fact that what one has been in this life will not survive into the next life.

"Of all the practitioners of the faiths in the world, only the Christian accepts his mortality. Only the Christian accepts the fact that when he is dead, he is dead; only this thing we know as a soul bearing his name will live on forever in total adoration of Christ; that even one's freewill will not survive beyond the grave; the reason why of all the faiths of the world only the Christian prays for miracles. It is why one prays for a

miracle for the child on his deathbed despite the fact that as a child Christ guarantees him heaven, 'Blessed are the little children for theirs is the Kingdom of Heaven.' That if the same child was to survive to adulthood, his chances would be seriously diminished, 'Many are called, but few are chosen.'

"Nevertheless, when one removes the imaginative aspects of religions, the great cathedrals, the golden crucifixes, the horrific retelling of passion plays, the endless array of artwork and images that the preacher uses to advertise his product, that the preacher uses to exaggerate and prey on men's minds, we all believe in the same God as does the atheist, ***God is the infinite energy force from which we all came from and to which we will all eventually return.***

"For us, this infinite energy source is the Sun. The nonbeliever - like the ancient Egyptians - thinks that the Sun is God; whereas the believer thinks that the Sun is only the Hand of God - that there is a conscious man with a penis that doesn't work behind it. Yet, both non-believers and believers agree that the Sun is either God or is God's vehicle controlling all life - animate or inanimate - in our solar system. The believer and the non-believer are not very far apart.

"Atheists, like Buddhists, just can't accept that God is a powerful 'man' of some sort garbed in princely robes and sitting on a golden throne or that He is a beautiful young man nailed to a cross as most of us imagine Him to be. Or should I say as the prophets imagined Him to be. They just can't believe in the definition provided by Moses that God is a Supreme Being who did not know that the earth was round when He created it and that He created vegetation on the day before He hung the sun it the heavens, the only thing that could give life to it. Nevertheless, the basic difference between the believer and a nonbeliever is not so much one of faith, but that the latter lacks the imagination, or should I say the gullibility of the other.

"Ironically atheists, agnostics and those of eastern religions as a rule live their lives in much closer adherence to Christ's instruction than do their Christian counterparts who like fools pay their preacher for their salvation. Preachers, who for few bucks, fool their greedy followers into thinking that they can ignore the overwhelming message of Christ' testimony, 'sell all that thou hast and give to the poor,' dictating a redistribution of wealth society." It was quite evident from this and other remarks that he made in my presence, that Luciani agreed with his counterpart Gandhi in the east, who had once said, *"I love Christ, but I hate Christians."*

"Keep in mind that separation of church and state does not mean separation of God from state. Contrary to what one might be led to believe

'church' and 'God' are not synonymous. Church is organized religion, it is a hundred billion dollar business, and it has nothing to do with belief in God, for as I have just said all men believe in God by nature, it's just that they have various definitions as to what God is, and these various definitions are due to the various convictions of men, and mostly to the greed of men. The business of a church is to prey on the imagination of men and provide its customers with a description of God and the possibility of an afterlife in exchange for dollars. So the founding principle of America, 'one nation under God,' does accommodate all people."

Note: forgoing is a summary of notes by the author on his visit to Vittorio Veneto in 1968. The lectures took place at the Seminary of Vittorio Veneto and the Gregorian University of Theology in Rome.

As a matter a fact, the definition of marriage when Luciani had been growing up had been even more restrictive, "*Marriage is a physical union between a penis and a vagina that are of the same faith, that are of the same race, that are of the same Aryan blood lines, that are of the same social level, that are of the same nationality, that are not of congenital handicaps, that have not previously been married, etc. etc. etc."* Educated men and women of today are coming to know that marriage is something much more, they are beginning to see it as *the sanctification of a perfect mental union that can only be made by God between any two people who fall in love, a sanctified trust,"* precisely Luciani's definition of a half-century ago.

That the Christian definition of marriage sanctifies only body parts is seen more clearly when one considers what modern day doctrine has to say about transsexuals. If Christine Jorgenson (a man) were to *fall in love* with another man today then Christianity would recognize the marriage, because he now has the right body parts. But if he were to *fall in love* with a woman, then Christianity would not approve the marriage because he no longer has the right body parts. But had he *fallen in love* with a woman before he had his penis amputated then Christianity would have recognized the marriage. In short, if two males *fall in love* and want recognition of their marriage Christianity requires surgery. It makes no difference if the resulting parts work or not as long as they look the part. And this is also true of the state.

checkmate,

But getting back to Luciani's confrontation with Pius XII and Bishop Siri, of all the exclusions that he had talked of in his profound address at the commencement seminary exercises in Vittorio Veneto, it was perhaps the Church's position on remarriage that tormented him the most. He just could not accept that the Church could take it upon itself to refuse sanctification of the mental union of two people who, having had made a mistake in choosing a lifelong partner at the age of twenty, at thirty had fallen truly in love. This issue troubled him deeply, as the record clearly shows.

He was a priest for less than a month when he was sent by his bishop to visit the bishop's sister who was terminally ill. The woman had remarried and her first husband was still alive. He was told that he had to convince the woman that she must renounce her husband or else she would not be buried in consecrated ground and therefore would be forever barred from entering the Kingdom of Heaven. When he arrived at the hospital he was assigned still another job. The woman's doctor met him outside of her room and told him that the woman had only a few hours to live and asked him if he would tell her this. One must keep in mind that although he would be dealing with a woman who had remarried, she was nevertheless a devout Catholic.

He entered the room and taking up her hand he told her the bad news. And then he reminded her that it was Church doctrine that unless she were to renounce her husband before she died, she would certainly go to hell. Much to his astonishment she answered him with a question, *"What do you think I should do?"* Realizing that he was caught up between doctrine and conscience, he asked her, *"Do you love him?"* And without hesitation yet with great emotion that caused a tear to roll down her cheek she told him, *"With all my heart."* Albino, still holding her hand in his, fell silent for a moment or two wondering what he should do. Then, suddenly, his eye caught a small standup crucifix that sat on the table beside her bed and he had his answer, *"Now, I wonder what Jesus would have done in this case?"*

Without any further hesitation, other than to attempt to roll a tear back into the corner of his eye, he told her, *"Then cling to it, your love for your husband. Don't ever give it up. Not for your brother, not for Pius XII or for the matter all the popes that have reigned before him and will reign after him. For your love for your husband was not given to you by men, but rather it was given to you by God, and He would not be happy with you if you were to give it back to Him to satisfy the whims of common men. And I promise you, if you have the courage to do this thing for me, that there will be reserved for both you and your husband a high place in heaven. And believe me, if it takes me all the remaining of days of my life, I will make this possible for you."* Then reaching over and passing by the small standup crucifix he picked up a small framed picture of her husband and placed it in her hands. He stayed with her until she died four hours later, still clutching the picture in her hands.

When he returned to the bishop's mansion and told him the news, the bishop was livid. He blamed the young priest for having failed in his duty. And after calming down he asked Luciani if at least he would falsely attest to the fact that she had renounced her husband in order that she could be buried in the Church. But Albino refused. Fortunately, for our hero the bishop was transferred just a few weeks later for otherwise Albino would have probably suffered a fate worse than death.

The woman was buried in a remote cemetery reserved for outcasts. Her brother and her family didn't show up. Only a few loyal friends and her husband were there for the interment; and one more, Albino Luciani who, in defiance of a papal decree, said the prayers and gave the eulogy.

So Luciani had a personal motive in what was to be one of his most publicized and certainly his most perilous attack on Pius XII; his suggestion that both Hitler and Mussolini be excommunicated on a post mortem basis.. He answered the Pope and Bishop Siri with a second editorial in which he challenged the Church's authority to excommunicate and thereby condemn to eternal damnation millions of young people who, having made a single mistake in their initial choice of a lifelong mate, had remarried. In his article he suggested that the authority to grant annulments be removed from Rome to the local bishop level, "*I am greatly tormented that Mother Church would see it as her duty to close the Gates of Heaven forever to so many young innocent people who have at last found true love and yet on the other hand see it as its duty to leave the Gates of Heaven open to the likes of Hitler and Mussolini.*" The largest tabloid in Italy, capitalizing on Luciani's fondness for the game of chess, gave the incident front-page coverage with the bold headline, *"ACACCO-MOTTO!" In English, CHECKMATE!*

The Vatican refused to comment to the press concerning Luciani's response. Instead, the day after the editorial appeared Albino was summoned to Rome and chastised by Pius XII in the presence of the ranking Vatican cardinals of the time. He was told that aside from insulting the Vicar of Christ on earth that his action bordered on heresy and was issued an official letter requiring him to clear all future comments he had concerning ecclesiastical doctrine with the Vatican before releasing them to the press. The letter was structured in such a way that if he were to violate its provisions he would automatically excommunicate himself. And the record shows that Luciani did abide by this order as there is no further mention of him in the press for several years following the incident. He disappeared from the scene almost as if he had died.

the sexual revolution,

But he was not entirely dead. He turned back to the work of establishing sexual education in parochial schools and finally public pressure forced Pius XII to permit some measure of sexual education in Catholic schools on a worldwide basis, -which practice was almost immediately adopted by public schools. His primary objective had been to eliminate what was at the time the major cause of abortions, family embarrassment. He wanted to bring about a day when sex would be discussed openly between parents and children. Up until his time "sex" was something that was not to be talked about within the family. He looked forward to a time when children would be brought up in a world where *"sex is seen as being good and beautiful but there is a time and place for everything, rather than in one in which sex was seen to shameful and sinful.*" He knew that Christianity's position that sex was sinful caused many young people to grow up in a state of considerable trauma, resulting in guilt complexes which led to less than healthy sex lives. One knows to a certain extent this is still true today.

One should keep in mind that until the last half of the twentieth century all Christians believed sex to be sinful and evil, the reason why 'sex' was not a household word when our grandfathers were growing up. The reason for this, of course, was that until recent history the lion's share of Christians believed in the Bible. Today, of course, only those with a bargain-basement IQ believe in what most of what the Old Testament has to say, particularly in what it has to say about sex. One could ask why the Christian preacher continues today to use the Bible to perpetuate his hatred of different kinds of people. And the answer is simple, he capitalizes on the fact that few people will take the time to read and analyze what the Bible actually has to say. As a matter of fact, as has already been pointed out, few people in their lifetimes ever take the time to analyze what the Ten Commandments themselves actually have to say. And it is a rare Christian who follows Christ's most prolific testimony, *"sell all that thou hast, and give to the poor."*

the anatomy of sin,

In the case of Luciani, being an analytical genius, analysis was a way of life. As a teenager, he did take the time to analyze the Bible; not that he didn't trust the preacher, but just that he wanted to know for himself what the Bible had to say. He classified the severity of the condemnations of various kinds of sin in the Bible as follows,

misdemeanor (venial sin)
punishable by death (forgivable mortal sin)
exclusion from heaven (unforgivable mortal sin)

As already mentioned, Moses calls homosexuality an *abomination* in the Old Testament. Luciani classified this as a misdemeanor, as nowhere in the Old Testament did any condemnation of homosexuality call for the death penalty, or for that matter - the ultimate penalty of permanent exclusion from heaven. So, as a matter of fact, contrary to what the preacher might claim, Luciani found that the Old Testament was relatively tolerant of homosexuality, particularly as compared to heterosexual sexual acts. The enemy of *gay rights* is not so much the Bible, as it is the ignorance and weakness of the minds of men.

There were, of course, Paul's condemnations in *Corinthians* and *Romans* in the New Testament in which Paul excludes from the Kingdom of Heaven just about everything under the kitchen sink, -including *effeminates* (transsexuals in the King James Bible) and what are referred to as *boy harlots* (boy prostitutes in the Catholic Bible). Luciani knew, unlike the preacher might want one to believe, that the word *effeminates* referred to transsexuals, not to homosexuals, as most homosexual men were not effeminate by nature, the reason why most of them have been able to hide in the *closet* all these years. The quick Luciani noticed that Paul had left out the lesbians in both of these verses, which led him to conclude that God had nothing to do in drafting Paul's condemnation, as God would certainly not have made such a blunder as to leave out half of the *offenders*. But what really drove the nail into the coffin for the young Luciani concerning Paul's alleged condemnation of homosexuality was that he was unable to trace either one of these phrases - *effeminates* or *boy harlots* - back to the oldest known surviving text of the New Testament (375AD) held by the British Museum in London.

On the other hand, Luciani found twenty-seven condemnations of fornication in the Bible; eighteen prescribing the death penalty and/or permanent exclusion from heaven – two of which are included in Paul's letters to the Corinthians and Romans, as set forth above. As a matter of fact, he found that fornication was the most damned sin in the Bible. *"This,"* concluded Luciani, *"is why one has the Immaculate Conception in the case of Christ, why He was born free of the filthy sin of fornication."* At the time that he did his analysis, Luciani was unaware that modern science would eventually make a mockery of the doctrine of the *Immaculate Conception*, as artificial insemination would one day make it possible for millions of children to be born free of what the Bible told him was the *filthy sin of fornication*. As already mentioned, it also puzzled him that fornication, being the most damned sin in the Old Testament, had also been left out of the Ten Commandments.

To put the Bible's condemnation of fornication in clearer perspective he analyzed the Bible's condemnations of murder, which today is recognized as the most reprehensible crime in the modern world. In all, he found that there were eleven condemnations of murder in the Bible and most of them did carry the death penalty as is set forth in Moses' condemnation in *Genesis*, "an *eye for an eye"* and God's condemnation of Cain also in *Genesis*, *"And the Lord set a mark upon Cain, lest any finding him shall kill him."* But he found that not a single one of them called for the ultimate penalty of permanent exclusion from heaven. He took note that even Paul in *Corinthians* and *Romans* in the New Testament (in which he condemns everything under the kitchen sink as mentioned above) did not include murderers, *"Be ye not deceived, neither fornicators, nor idolators, nor adulterers, nor effeminates, nor abusers of themselves, nor thieves, nor greedy, nor covetous, nor drunkards, nor revilers, nor extortioners, shall inherit the Kingdom of God."* Luciani concluded *"the death penalty is not much of a penalty at all as it normally affords one time to repent and therefore go to live happily ever after in heaven. Yes, one might say it is a slap on the wrist, but in the world of Christian theology it is not a punishment at all. As a matter of fact it is a reward. The Bible quite clearly lets one get away with murder."* he concluded, *"But, of course, most Christians don't really believe in heaven; don't really believe in the Bible."*

Luciani observed that through the years men had changed various wordings in the Bible to satisfy whatever happened to be acceptable to their particular niche in society. For example, in the verse from *Corinthians* above, the word *greedy, grabbers, those who lust for material wealth* or similar wordings appear in the *Catholic, English, Eastern* and virtually every other version of the New Testament today including the oldest surviving substantial copy . . . except the *King James Version*. He knew the *King James Version* was the predominant Bible in the United States, and he also knew that Americans were by nature some of the most greedy people on earth, the reason why a single *two-hundred-million-dollar* lottery sells many more tickets than does two hundred *one-million* dollar lotteries, -tickets that are bought mostly by people who feed their children rice and beans for Sunday dinner. So somewhere along the line preachers had dropped the word *'greedy'* out of the *King James Version* since greediness was a fundamental necessity to American capitalism. As a matter of fact greed is the vehicle to the great American dream. Referring to this drive of Americans to accumulate great personal wealth, he once told an American business group, "*. . . Man never knows when he has enough . . . one might call the first hundred thousand dollars or so responsibility, but after that, it is simply greed.*" It was one the very few times he spoke without applause.

Nevertheless, it was this experience more than any other that led Luciani to conclude that other than the four gospels – the testimony of Christ Himself – the Bible was a product of man's self-serving interests and not the word of God. That it was indeed the work of fiction that he once as an eleven year old had proclaimed it to be. And this left him with the only other alternative available to guide his life, the testimony of Christ Himself, the only part of the Bible that had no conflict with that part of God that was a part of him - his conscience.

As the child prodigy Luciani had once published in his article in the newspaper of the Feltre School, *"The problems of the world will only come to an end when the state in accordance with its copyright laws requires that all copies of the Old Testament be prefaced,* **THIS IS A WORK OF FICTION**, *. . . and a dangerous one it is, as most people are using it to guide the way they live their lives, and this is costing many others their lives. . . . The state is derelict in its duty in failing to declare this book a fake. There is not a single word in the Old Testament that has been proven to be true. As a matter of fact all of the major claims set forth in that terrible book have been proven to be false, for after all every one of us knows today, the earth is round. Let us not be so foolish as to believe this man Moses who talked to a God who thought that it was flat."*[1]

This is still true today. For one purpose of copyright laws is to protect the public from what might not be true. Yet, the Old Testament, which many people are foolishly using to guide their lives and enforcing on others, would stand no chance at all before a tribunal; it continues to go on unquestioned, despite the fact, as we speak, it is costing thousands of children their lives.

Luciani's conclusion, reached when he was only eleven years old, is even more so substantiated today, -not a single one of the books of the Old Testament and many of the books of the New Testament would pass the test of truth in a court of law today. Yet, the testimony of Christ Himself remains unchallenged, -although one could not prove Christ to be

[1] *L'Osservatore del Feltre, 16 May '21*

a matter of historical fact, there is no proof that Christ is not a matter of historical fact.

ship of fools,

Today, sadly, the man in the street depends on the preacher for his salvation, the man he pays. Being the fool that he is, he is too lazy to do the job himself. And the man he pays knows no more about it than he does.

In June 1961, Albino Luciani, the presiding bishop of Vittorio Veneto and the great seminary there, told a graduation class, ". . . *The preacher is unique among entrepreneurs, -for all businessmen know immensely more about their products and services than do their customers - the reason they are able to sell their wares. But you as preachers know no more about the existence of a God, or for that matter which God is the true God, than do your customers. As a matter of fact you will know nothing about the possibility of an afterlife until after you are dead. And then, again, you may never know. All you have is your faith - and the conviction with which you speak. You came here with one of these - and we gave you the other. Now take them with you - feed them - nourish them - train them - cherish them - protect them - for they are the horses of your carriage that will one day take you to your destiny.*"[2] Luciani had a great problem not only with what the Bible said, but what self-serving men might convince the populace it said.

And the conviction with which a preacher speaks can be quite dangerous. Pat Robertson, in spreading his hatred of Islamism once referred to the taking of the Promised Land in which hundreds of thousands of men, women and children who had traditionally lived there were murdered, "*We must continue to support Israel in its suppression of the Palestinians because God gave that land to the Jews.*" One wonders how Pat Robertson *knows* that God gave that land to the Jews, for it is quite obvious that if God had wanted the Jews to have the Promised Land then God would have given it to them in the first place. There is the added phenomenon of conviction Falwell and Robertson and other *fascist preachers* have in that they are able to confuse their victims as to what the Bible actually has to say about them. For example, they are able to fool the gays into thinking that the Bible condemns them, whereas in fact, if one goes by what the Bible has to say, one would be condemning heterosexuals, not homosexuals.

[2] *author's collection*

Nevertheless, today only an imbecile would believe much of what the Bible has to say, and even less of what the preacher has to say. We no longer believe in the Ten Commandments and except for these *fascist preachers* we no longer think the way that Hitler thought. We no longer think that certain kinds of people, particularly children and teenagers, [1] should be deprived of equal human rights just because they appear to be different. We no longer think of fornication as dirty and ugly, but rather as a great gift from God that makes possible His greatest work of creation - a newborn child. And the reason we think this way is largely because of Albino Luciani, -who more than a half-century ago first fired the embers for what we have since come to know as the sexual revolution.

priest vs. nun pedophilia

There was another reason for his struggle for sex education. His concern was the pedophile. He wanted to bring him out in the open where society could better keep an eye on him. He knew that if sex could be discussed openly within the family, abused children could better expose a transgressor and bring such abuse to an end.

He knew that, consistent with the general population, a certain percentage of priests, monks and nuns had to be pedophiles. While studying for the priesthood he had done a paper[2] that addressed the question as to why the rate of pedophilia among priests seemed to be much higher than that of the general population and also why it appeared to be primarily homosexual while the preponderance of pedophilia was primarily heterosexual among the general population. *"I am particularly puzzled as to why there is practically zero incidence of pedophilia among nuns and monks who outnumber priests four to one and who in their respective roles as teachers and counselors of youth programs have immensely greater access to children than do priests. Certainly,"* he wrote, *"all three professions would attract the same mix of people as they offer one a life of celibacy, one dedicated to God. I wondered what could be the difference between a priest and a monk or a nun that could result in such a high rate of pedophilia among priests."*

He researched those who had gone before him, -those who had looked into the problem in the past. He found one researcher who believed that to a certain extent the cause of the problem was in the vestments

[1] *today an estimated four million children and teens are denied social security survivor, military and other benefits because they are in gay families. In 9/11, more than two dozen children of gay families did not share in survivor funds, three of them were children of firemen who gave their lives.*
[2] *Vatican Apostolic Library*

themselves, because they were attractive to the transgender population, those women who happened to be born into men's bodies. Certainly a monk's brown robe would not suffice, as everyone else would be wearing the same *dress*. And certainly the reverse transgender population - men born into women's bodies - would have no interest in the convent, as it required that they spend the rest of their lives in a black dress. This segment of the transgender population wanted to wear pants, not dresses. The researcher had concluded that this could result in a very significant transgender population among priests and zero transgender population among monks and nuns.

And this conclusion could have some meaning today. Although the transgender population is relatively small, it is relatively large when compared to the priest population. For example, there are over five million transsexuals in the United States and there are less than fifty thousand priests. So it is reasonable to believe that, attracted by the vestments themselves, there could be a significant percentage of transsexuals among priests. And when a transsexual priest has sex with a male child it is in fact a heterosexual act as the transgressor is in fact a woman trapped in a man's body.

And this is quite visual in the Church today, as a substantial number of priests are effeminate in their manner. Effeminate males, as mentioned above are rarely homosexuals; they are much more likely to be transsexuals.

Nevertheless, Luciani reasoned that it made some sense that there existed an abnormally high number of transgender people among priests, women in men's bodies, and he concluded that this could result in a high rate of homosexual pedophilia activity when one considers that the only significant contact priests have with children is with altar boys in the sacristy. Actually, because the general public assumes that a transsexual is a homosexual, this would be heterosexual activity that would be perceived to be homosexual activity as it would involve women who were trapped in men's bodies.

Most people view transsexuals as homosexuals. As a matter of fact most transsexuals mistakenly believe that they are homosexuals, particularly in the early years. In actuality, the great majority of transsexuals are heterosexual, -the reason they never marry, as believing they are of the opposite sex they can only *fall in love* with one of their own sex. The few transsexuals that do marry are homosexuals. A woman born into a man's body, for example, who is a homosexual, can *fall in love* with another women, and since 'she' has a man's biological body 'she' can father children. *"This could explain a part of the problem, why priest pedophilia appeared to be primarily homosexual in nature. But not good enough,*" Luciani concluded, "*there must be something else?*"

He knew that the only known *cure* of pedophilia at the time, which is still true today, was to keep the pedophile away from situations in which he or she is alone with a child. He knew that a priest was largely limited to altar boys, whereas a nun had unlimited access to all children. This is still true today as the altar girls of today are usually under the supervision of nuns. He also knew that an innocent act on the part of the child usually excited or aroused the pedophilia instinct in the adult and that this combined with access to the child resulted in the transgression.

Luciani traced much of the problem to the confessional box. He knew that eight, nine, ten and eleven year old children often talked about their 'sins of the flesh' to the priest in the confessional. "*After all masturbation is a sin,*" he wrote, "*actually by doctrine a mortal sin in the eyes of the Church. Children, lacking a vocabulary to otherwise explain their actions, often go to great detail in discussing what they do with their sexual bodies. And this is a very dangerous thing. I find that the record shows that pedophile priests who otherwise would remain dormant are often aroused by these children's stories. In addition I find that the pedophile priest often uses the confessional box to sort out those children or teens that were more likely to be receptive to his advances, which make easier prey of them so to speak.*" He concluded that the confessional box was a great weapon in the arsenal of the pedophile priest and he intended to take it from him, to eliminate to a great extent the CAUSE of the problem.

He further concluded that if his previously reached supposition were correct, -that an unusually high percentage of priests were bisexual, then such pedophilia would manifest itself primarily as a homosexual activity since all pedophilia activity depends on opportunity, and a priest's most significant opportunity was with altar boys. At Luciani's time there were no altar girls.

He discounted the notion that doing away with celibacy requirements would solve the problem, as he knew the vast majority of known pedophile cases involved incest, again pointing to the main cause of pedophilia activity – *opportunity*. The scant studies available to him at the time told him, as scientific studies based on tried criminal cases tell us today, that a married person is twice as likely to engage in pedophilia activity as a single person. This did not mean to him that there were twice as many pedophiles among married people but merely that they had greater *opportunity*. He knew that people who believed that lifting the celibacy requirements of the priesthood would solve the problem did not really understand this rather complex issue. This would obviously aggravate the problem rather than solve it, as it would give the pedophile priest greater private access to children.

He reasoned that it was the vow of chastity in the convent that was responsible for the almost nonexistent incidence of pedophilia activity among nuns, whereas their counterparts in the non-parochial teaching world had the highest level of pedophilia activity of any profession, - again pointing to *opportunity*. He concluded that the only way to prevent pedophilia activity was to remove the cause – *opportunity* or private access to children; still true today.

He resolved that no child short of puberty should be subjected to the confessional, -that they be permitted access to the Eucharist until the age of fourteen without the requirement of confession. He also concluded that some modifications should be made to the vestments themselves to give them a masculine rather than a feminine appearance, -that the priest should wear pants and not 'dresses' on the altar. A few years later as a common priest he appealed his cause directly to Rome, but all that it brought him was the chastisement of his bishop for having broken protocol. Once again, his voice had gone unheard. He would store this one up with all the others for that day on which he would someday be *infallible*.

Today, tried criminal cases substantiate Luciani's contention that the confessional booth is at the core of the problem. The combination of the Church's position that all sex outside of marriage including masturbation is sinful, together with the requirement of confession, has played a role in most of them. As a matter of fact, the Church considers most acts of normally acceptable foreplay within marriage as being sinful. Regardless of what individual priests might tell their congregations, any kind of sex outside of marriage is a mortal sin according to both the Bible and Church doctrine.

The following is representative testimony taken from one of these cases in which fourteen boys and two girls ages eight through thirteen were molested. All of these transgressions in this case actually took place in the confessional box itself. Here the victim was a ten year old boy,

victim stammering – *"I committed adultery."**
priest – *"How many times?"*
victim – *"Four times."*
where – *"In the bathroom."*
priest – *"No, where on the body?"*
victim – *"Below the belly button."*
priest - *"What happened?"*

**children often lack an adequate vocabulary in explaining their actions. Glennon - Melbourne 1991*

victim – *"It grew. It grew hard."*
priest – *"Is it hard now?"*

In another case an eight year old boy, who had confessed to having performed felatio on an older boy, was ordered to come into the priest's section of the confessional booth to do his *penance.* There, the priest forced the boy to perform felatio on him while he slid the window open to the adjoining booth and listened to a young girl confess her sexual exploitations. (Griffin vs. Illinois 1998) And in still another case, a priest molested an eight year old brother together with his nine year old sister in a confessional booth. And this same priest on another occasion had one boy masturbate him just ten minutes before he said mass. (McCardle - Rockhampton 2002). And there are literally hundreds of cases in which the accused priest has confessed to having used the confessional box to sort out children and teens who would be most receptive to his advances.

Today many responsible adults tell their children the truth, that sex is not sinful, and in which case the child, knowing that it is not sinful, does not bring sex up in the confessional box. But the parents of such children should not feel too comfortable in this, as there are dozens of cases in the record books in which the priest has probed a child as to what the child has been doing with his or her sexual body.

One must keep in mind that the confessional box is a cesspool of sexual perversion in that every Catholic adult and most children know that unless he or she confesses his or her sexual transgressions to a priest they will never get into heaven. The typical priest is also bombarded by adults week-in and week-out with endless tales of a range of sexual transgressions and perverted practices, from sadistic and masochistic rituals and rape and incest and even sexual murders. One must keep in mind that the great preponderance of sins confessed not only by children but also by adults are sexual in nature, as relatively few people steal, murder or commit adultery.

My friend Jack once told me that although the vow of chastity is a challenge to all those who take it, a priest, a monk and a nun, it is often an insurmountable one to a priest, particularly a young priest. *"To begin with,"* he once told me, *"they brainwash you with the word PURITY throughout the seminary years and then they ordain you and put you inside the pressure cooker, the confessional box, and force you to listen to pornographic tales that stagger the imagination for four hours every Saturday afternoon. It is the equivalent of starving a man to the brink of death and then waving a mouthwatering porterhouse steak in front of him."*

So one can easily understand why so many priests, being constantly exposed to an ongoing parade of livid pornography of people's everyday lives, do themselves become perverted, some of them confining themselves to self-manipulation in the privacy of their booths, while others become aggressive perverted monsters of prey. Did you ever wonder why the priest's section of a confessional has a door that locks from the inside?

"The Old Testament not once refers to pedophilia. God the Father, by either intent or omission, left it out. Although 'legal age of consent' is a product of modern times, in Moses' time a girl's life was acutely threatened if she were to become pregnant at too early an age. Yet, knowing this, Moses left it out, for according to his God's definition, a girl was a thing - an expendable thing to put a penis in to hopefully bring forth a male child. Christ countermands His Father's order in Mark 10, 'But whoso shall offend one of these little ones, it is better for him that a millstone be hanged about his neck and that he were drowned in the depths of the sea.'"[1]

That it takes the word of God of Moses over that of Christ is perhaps no better demonstrated in that the Vatican has taken no responsible action in the wake of the massive pedophile scandal in the Church, other than to issue instructions to pay off alleged victims and render a formal statement to the press through its Secretary of State, *"The issue of priest pedophilia has been exaggerated by the American media and is not a serious problem in the Church."*[2]

And one might wonder why the Conference of Bishops, when it met in 2003 concerning the issue of priest pedophilia, never mentioned this obvious driving force behind priest pedophilia. This is because the Pope issues very strict guidelines as to what may be discussed and what cannot be discussed in these meetings. For example, the bishops are also prohibited from discussing priest celibacy in its possible connection to priest pedophilia. In short, not being able to consider alternatives, the huge cost in conducting these meetings is a needless drain on the poor box.

Also one would wonder why, with actual tried criminal cases pointing overwhelmingly to the confessional box, no judge has ever issued an injunction against the Church's practice of confession. And where most might think that this is a matter of separation of church and state, or respect for the papacy, it is most likely to be a matter of lack of *courage*. Society has the sacred responsibility to protect all of its children until they

1 *Vittorio Veneto 1965 author's collection*

2 *Vatican Secretary of State, Cardinal Sedona's February 2003 response to 4,500 cases of priest pedophilia under investigation in the United States*

reach adulthood even when the wrongdoer is the family. And we see this in everyday life where parents are tried and imprisoned for neglect or otherwise endangering the physical or mental health of their children.

And there are those cases in which religious practices have endangered the *physical* wellbeing of children where the state has many times stepped in. Christian Scientists and members of other fundamentalist groups and cults have often found themselves in court for having deprived their children of proper medical attention thereby endangering their *physical* wellbeing. It is also society's sacred responsibility to challenge these perverted practices of the Roman Catholic Church which today threaten the *mental* wellbeing of children.

That Luciani was correct in his conclusion that the confessional box is the main culprit in priest pedophilia can readily be seen today, that in tried cases of priest pedophilia the victims have been almost entirely concentrated in the ages of eight to puberty, the earlier confessional years. Whereas, on the other hand, pedophilia in the general population is spread evenly between ages five through puberty. Molestation of teenagers is not pedophilia. Yet, in more than eighty percent of tried cases involving teenagers the offender used the confessional box to sort out his prey.

Even more abhorrent to him as a priest was that on occasion a young child of seven or eight would confess to him of an incestuous affair with a parent. And in one case, on repeated occasions, a certain young priest had confessed to him that he was a serial pedophile. He knew that all over the world this must have been a tormenting thing for priests who, bound by the trust of the confessional box, were unable to bring an end to this kind of atrocity. He voiced the problem to Rome and called that some modifications be made to the strict guidelines of the confessional imposed by the Church. He argued that it was a mortal sin for a priest to conceal abuse of a young child and to permit such an abomination to go on. This time he received a formal response from the Vatican, "*God will take care of those things. The confessional box must remain sealed.*" But Luciani knew in his heart that God would not take care of those things; that it was up to him to take care of 'those things'. And he vowed in his memoirs, "*someday I will take care of 'those things', once and for all!*"

In 1958, Pope Pius died and Luciani, freed of the restrictions that this Pope had placed on him, once again *came out on all fours.* And John XXIII *sharpened his claws* by making him into a bishop, a prince of the Church.

As Bishop of Vittorio Veneto and the great seminary located there he became increasingly aware of the pedophile problem among priests and the problem the confessional box posed. Among his instructors, he hired a number of degreed psychiatrists whose additional duties included rendering psychiatric evaluations of aspiring priests. Even his personal secretary was a licensed psychiatrist. On the surface his objective was to ascertain that the candidates were of sound mind. After all they would spend a lifetime dealing with the minds of others. But beneath it all he wanted to weed out the pedophile. He shortly found out that it was not possible to detect pedophilia, although he was able to determine that more than half of the student body was either bisexual or transsexual. His only remaining solution to the priest pedophilia problem was to try and eliminate the CAUSE, which in his judgment this continued to be the confessional box.[1]

In the spring of 1978, just a few months before his election, Luciani was reprimanded by the Vatican for having criticized an American bishop who had paid off the alleged victim of a pedophile priest. He told a group of bishops that had gathered in Venice, "*It would be better that we try our accused fellow servants in a court of law so that they can be cleared of any wrong doing and if found guilty they should pay their debt to society. It is not Mother Church's business to pay their debt in cash, particularly to pay it with money that was intended for the poor. Besides, if we take no action to get at the truth, we may very well be endangering countless children in the future.*"

And Luciani had not stopped there, "*Whereas I have often affirmed that Mother Church has no business poking her head into the bedroom, she does have a responsibility in certain sexual matters. She has the sacred duty to protect the rights of those who cannot defend themselves, including women in the case of rape and children in the case of molestation. In paying off alleged victims of pedophile bishops and priests she is not only failing in that sacred duty but she is taking an active role in promoting the perpetuation of an abomination against the world's children. And that this is her conscious policy is seen most clearly in her irresponsible dictate that children and teens short of adulthood must continue to discuss their 'sexual sins' with potential predators in the confessional box.*"[2] Here, it should be noted that Luciani had changed his earlier conclusion and limited

[1] *in 2004, Cardinal Winning made a change in Scotland that would keep children from receiving their First Communion before they make their Confirmation; this defers their first confession to the ages of fourteen or fifteen. In order not to draw the wrath of Rome, the good cardinal used the excuse that he is simply returning of what centuries ago had been the practice of the Church. The courageous man is obviously protecting the children of Scotland from predator priests by eliminating the cause of priest pedophilia, the confessional.*

[2] *Messaggero Mestre, 17 Mar '78*

confession to adults, probably to prevent predatory priests from tracking teenagers who would be most likely to respond to their advances.

the scandal of the Vatican cardinals and the Maltese altar boys

The Church failed to adopt Luciani's recommendation that children be allowed access to the Eucharist without the requirement of confession until their fourteenth birthday. That the Vatican continues to require children to discuss what they do with their sexual bodies with predatory priests, bishops and cardinals certainly sheds some suspicions on what goes on in Vatican City itself. We have already pretty much put to bed the fact that an unusually large percentage of priests are pedophiles and it would therefore follow that an unusually large number of bishops, cardinals and even popes have also been pedophiles through the years.

The Maltese altar boys who serve the hierarchy in Rome are selected for their great beauty and are aged thirteen and younger. Historically these children had been sent to the Vatican for a period of one month and during this time they were traditionally allowed ongoing communication with families and friends. In the early nineties, a Sicilian tabloid reported alleged abuse of these boys by high ranking cardinals and there is some credence to this in that it is common knowledge that the confessions of these boys are usually performed by high ranking Vatican officials including on occasion the Pope himself. There is nothing in the legitimate press to substantiate these charges but one has to keep in mind that there is only one courtroom and one judge in Vatican City, so things of this nature can quickly be swept under the rug. Tabloid reporting of Vatican cardinal abuse of Maltese altar boys is not unusual, but in this particular case the tabloid reported that a substantial amount of money was paid to the victims to squash the story.

Regardless of the validity of these reports, John Paul II has since restricted the ability of Maltese altar boys to communicate outside of the Vatican, excepting emergencies, with their families and friends back in Malta. And the question one has to ask oneself is why did he make this change? And one could also ask oneself the question as to why John Paul II still requires children under the age of fourteen to discuss their sex lives with potential predator priest, bishops and cardinals.

archbishop by popular vote,

For the next few years the Bishop of Vittorio Veneto served as a leading advisor to both John XXIII and Paul VI, -the two popes of the twentieth century who brought change to the Church. John once said of him, "*The prince of the Veneto country is Lacordaire and Rossini in one. Today I follow in his footprints in order that someday he might follow in mine!*"

The Pope was referring to those who were recognized as two of the greatest theologians in the Church's history. One must realize that until he came under the influence of his *protégé* Luciani in 1958, John XXIII had spent the first seventy-eight years of his life as a steadfast conservative, -the reason why he had been elected. It was not until the year following his election that John started to move to the *left* and announced plans for *Vatican II.* The record is that he spent much of the first year of his pontificate with his *protégé* at Vittorio Veneto, -six visits in all.

In that John alluded to the possibility that Luciani might succeed him confused his audience as it was generally assumed that John had intended Giovanni Montini to follow him as Pope. After all, one of the first things he had done upon becoming Pope was to name Montini a cardinal. Since John himself had some years left and Montini seemed good for an additional twenty or so the papacy appeared to be locked up for more than a quarter of a century. That he had named a second successor could mean only one thing. He knew that Montini, who silently shared many of Luciani's liberal views, would be in danger in the Vatican; that Montini, elected Paul VI in 1963, might not live out his natural years.

In 1969, the Archbishop of Venice died. This post is the ranking field position in Italy because it is the only one that holds the coveted title of *Patriarch;* one of only two such positions in the Catholic world, the other being the *Patriarch of Lisbon.* Historically, for this reason, a ranking cardinal had normally been moved from the Vatican to fill a vacancy. Realizing that a Vatican cardinal would be chosen to fill the post, thousands of people of the Veneto country marched through the streets of Venice demanding that the little-known bishop of the remote mountain diocese of Vittorio Veneto be named to the post. When Luciani was elevated to the post, the press billed it as the first democratic election of an archbishop in the history of the Church. But as we shall see in Part II of this book, Paul VI had already chosen Albino Luciani for the job, as a matter of fact he had already chosen him to one day fill his own job.

the sideshow,

In 1973, Albino Luciani was named a cardinal and two years later in July of 1975 he launched his most vigorous attack in the media concerning any issue of his ministry. He severely criticized a South

American bishop for capitalizing on a comatose twelve year old girl who was alleged to have the stigmata. The girl had been injured when she was nine in a farming accident and had never regained her faculties. The local bishop and the parents of the girl put her on public display through a one-way window set into the wall of her bedroom. In a circus-like atmosphere they paraded literally thousands of pilgrims past her room for a substantial fee, -enough so that the bishop was able to build a new mansion for himself and the parents themselves became millionaires.

*"I can understand why Rome might turn her head the other way when greedy people capitalize on defenseless children in this way, for after all She is at the source of this kind of satanic ritual. But what bothers me most is that men and women of good conscience of the state stand aside and do nothing about it."** Luciani, like most educated people today, knew that stigmata had been a fraudulent money-making scheme in the Church ever since the thirteenth century when St. Francis had first displayed wounds on the palms of his hands. Strangely, there is no record of a claim of stigmata before St Francis, so he is rightfully credited with having come up with this perverted idea. All popes since his time have capitalized on this *Sideshow of the Roman Catholic Church.*

Luciani knew that crucifixions involved the driving of spikes into a plank of wood that had been placed over the outstretched arm and then through the upper-arms and forearms just beneath the bone-line of the victim and into the cross. It wouldn't take a Roman historian to tell one that; and it would not take a PhD in Structural Engineering of the Anatomy to tell one that nails, particularly sharp-edged first century nails, if driven through the palms of the hands, would never support the weight of a hanging human body. Try it sometime.

This had been well publicized a short time before, when a photograph of the *Shroud of Turin* disclosed that the blood stains on the shroud evidenced that the blood was coming from the wrists and not from the palms, which would indicate that Christ was crucified through the wrists and not through the palms. Of course, one knows that Christ could not have been crucified through the wrists for if that were true He would have bled to death in a few minutes as the main arteries located there would have ruptured under the weight of His body upon hanging.

One must keep in mind that the official position of the Church concerning the shroud is that it is a fake. At the time that it first appeared Pope Innocent VI ordered the local bishop to investigate it, and after a

* *Messaggero Mestre, 17 Aug '75*

three year look into the matter the bishop concluded that it was a hoax. The Pope declared the shroud a fraud and ordered it removed from display. However, after Innocent died in 1362, the shroud resurfaced, appearing in churches across Europe. His successor Urban V, realizing that it was good for business, allowed the practice to go on.

As Luciani once told me directly, *"Scrupulous men continue to prey on the greatest weakness of man, -his mortality. Particularly vulnerable are those that would grasp at any straw that could possibly be connected to their hope for immortality. Take a peek at Jewish custom, as to how the Jews buried their dead at the time. While the body was customarily wrapped in white linen shroud as the Bible explicitly states in the Gospel of John, 'Then they took the body of Jesus, and wound it in linen clothes, as the manner of the Jews is to bury,' the face was first wrapped in a linen napkin as told in the same Gospel, 'Then cometh Simon Peter into the sepulcher, and seeing the linen clothes lie, And the napkin that was wrapped about his head, not lying with the linen clothes, but wrapped together in one place by itself' So where our thirteenth century hoaxers went wrong is that they failed to check out the Bible, which tells us explicitly that if the image of the face of Jesus survived today, it would be on the napkin, and not on the shroud."*

Likewise, Luciani never believed in stigmata despite the fact that sixty people had achieved sainthood principally because they had claimed this *affliction*. He knew that Christ had in fact been crucified through the arms as both the history books and common sense tell us. He also knew that when artists, several hundred years after Christ's death, painted the earliest renditions of the crucifixion they had placed the nails in the palms because it was more artistic and it was this that resulted in the public's misconception ever since. And furthermore, he knew that the Church knew this.

It was obvious to Luciani that if stigmata were truly a miracle - as the Church claimed it was - the wounds would appear in the upper-arms and forearms. Otherwise, one would have to conclude that God the Father had a short memory of what had actually happened at the event and has to depend on more recent artists renditions. He knew that every day thousands of the billions of people in the world developed cancerous and bleeding sores and ulcers in various parts of the body, sometimes in the toes, sometimes in the genitalia, sometimes in the buttocks, sometimes in the knees, sometimes in the neck, sometimes on the face, and so forth. Also, stigmata can also be a manifestation of hysteria and other mental disorders. So if stigmata were in fact an act of God, then the Church should have been granting sainthood to those afflicted in the upper arms and forearms. Of course, the Church has itself found the vast majority of stigmata to have been self-inflicted, and in the case of the comatose girl, it was found to be torture.

The situation was handled as quietly as possible behind closed doors in the Vatican, as Luciani's harsh criticism rippled across Latin America. Paul VI ordered the local bishop to stop the 'circus' and for all intents and purposes that was the end of it. And what's more, Paul VI took measures to bring an end to several similar atrocities that were taking place elsewhere.. Normally this would have been a milestone event in the Church's history as it would have marked the beginning of the end of mysticism in the Roman Catholic Church. However, when John Paul II rose to the papacy he gave a green light to these things provided they were under the supervision of the Vatican which meant that the Vatican would get the lion's share of the proceeds. One of the most famous of these involves Audrey Santos, -a comatose teenage girl in Worcester, Massachusetts, who has been displayed before thousands of people since she had a pool accident more than a decade ago. It is this kind of thing, together with the fact that they enjoy listening to seven and eight years olds discussing what they do with their sexual bodies, that proves that we are dealing with a *sick and perverted* group of old men in the Vatican today, -men who are in much need of professional help.

Albino Luciani, just a regular guy

It might be of interest to the reader to know that throughout his tenure as Archbishop of Venice Luciani lived as a common man rather than as the crown prince of the Church that he was. Except for official business he wore common street clothes wherever he went and this together with the fact that he came across as a 'regular guy' rather than a man of great rank and stature, on occasion got him into trouble. In one case he was stopped by police in an impoverished section of Venice and asked for his identification. When he failed to produce his papers and claimed to be the *Patriarch of Venice* they did not believe him and placed him under arrest.

On one occasion he entered into an extended conversation with a group of students in a pub and invited them to come and see him at home on the morrow. They asked him where he lived. *"On the Piazetta dei Leoncini,"* he replied. And they asked, *"You mean the Patriarch's Palace?"* *"Yes,"* he replied. *"And for whom should we ask?"* they queried. *"Just ask for Piccolo,"* he told them.

The next day when they arrived at the palace and asked for Piccolo they were directed to an elevator flanked by two Swiss guards who took them to the fifth floor where they were led to an office door, where two more Swiss guards stood at attention. When they entered the room they were astonished to find Piccolo sitting by the window chatting with Pope Paul who happened to be visiting him that day.

Luciani despised wearing vestments as he thought there to be something hypocritical about them. One day in the park that fronted the Patriarch's Palace in Venice, dressed in shorts and sandals, he was asked by a severely handicapped boy to pose with him for a photograph. When he knelt down beside the boy, the boy looked up at him and asked, *"Could you put on your beautiful clothes?"* Luciani got up and disappeared into the building and shortly returned wearing his cardinal's robe and miter. *"There are times,"* he told the boy's father, *"that we must shed our humility and put on our hypocrisy, and this is one of them."*

✝

two very different kinds of popes,

In these pages I have put before you and what is yet to come I have and I will often refer to John Paul II, as he was the successor of my patron John Paul I. In the event that you have not already picked it up, these were two different kinds of men, one an ultraliberal and the other an ultraconservative. How is it possible that the very same *College of Cardinals* elected these two very different popes just a month apart? I will answer that question quite conclusively later in Part II of this book, but for now I will outline just how far apart these two were in their basic ideologies and why they thought so very differently.

First, one must consider their upbringing. Karol Wojtyla was born into money so, unlike Albino Luciani, he never knew what it was to nearly starve to death as a child. He was born to two extremely devout parents who were steadfast believers in the Church. From the age of six through the time he entered college, Karol was educated in expensive prep schools, -something that even today is reserved for the very, very rich.

Laski Italfoto

Above, eight year old Karol Wojtyla, shown with his mother, wears the military uniform of the Wadowice Military Academy, a prep school that brainwashed its students in *Fascism*, that ideology which preached the superiority of the white Aryan male and the subordination of women, Jews blacks, homosexuals and certain ethnic groups. While he was growing up, in the interests of preserving the purity of the Aryan race, blacks were not allowed in Poland, as was true of other predominately Catholic countries in Europe.

John Paul II has sometimes been unfairly criticized in television documentaries because he refused to join the underground resistance during the war and instead went to work under the Nazis. It was extremely rare for anyone in their teens or twenties of either sex in any of the occupied countries, who did not have a family to support, not to escape to the forests and join the underground resistance. In Krakow, sixty-thousand courageous youths escaped to the sewers, Karol Wojtyla was not among them. His paid biographers have tried to cover up for this by claiming that during the occupation of Poland by the Nazis he was a member of an underground resistance theater group -which obviously had nothing at all to do with resistance. One must realize that at the time Karol Wojtyla, like Pius XII, shared the very same ideologies as did Hitler – the superiority of the white Aryan male; the subordination of women and blacks; and the persecution of homosexuals, Jews, Muslims and other ethnic peoples. The difference between these two kinds of men was the method by which they would attain their objectives, -Hitler through annihilation and Pius XII and Karol Wojtyla through political means. And the result can be equally devastating, millions dead in the World War and millions more dead of AIDS and gay child and teenage suicides which continue to go on today.

Sipa Italfoto

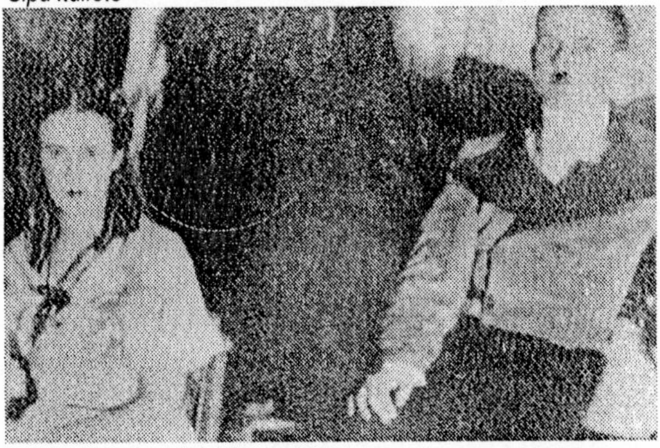

Karol Wojtyla in the leading role of a romantic satire of Adolph Hitler's young life (1942)

It may have been during his theater years - 1939 through 1943 - that he acquired the intense homophobic character that he has been unable to shed these many years. His own biographers will tell you that he wanted to be an actor or a journalist. In 1943, the atrocities of the Jews became known and peer pressure forcing him to join the resistance became unbearable. He escaped into a seminary and soon realized that he could use his acting abilities in the priesthood. And this is why he has been the best imaged pope in history; what the public sees is the epitome of a great actor on the world stage backed by a multi-million dollar public relations effort.

It was in Poland that the atrocities first became known. He lived only a short distance from Auschwitz where villagers could peer through the barbed wire fence and witness the smell of burning human flesh. In all, more than a million people died there, three quarters of them Jews and the others mostly homosexuals.

Corbis photo

Auschwitz where 800,000 Jews and 140,000 homosexuals were murdered

Although the Jews took the brunt of Hitler's massacre, a quarter-million homosexuals died in the concentration camps mostly at Auschwitz. Most of these were in their teens and twenties as youths were much more likely to reveal their identity in prewar Germany than were adults. Had it not been for their ability to hide in *closets* many more homosexuals would have died in concentration camps than Jews, as the latter were unable to hide in *closets*.

Nevertheless, had Hitler won the war, everything Karol Wojtyla had ever dreamed of would have become a reality. However, when Hitler lost the war much of what he dreamed of was taken from him -as the door had been opened to move civilization away from *Fascism,* away from *Moses,* toward *Christ,* -the equality of all men and women. When Albino Luciani was raised to the papacy the rest of what Karol Wojtyla had hoped was also about to be taken from him, -deprivation of equal human rights for the unborn (AIDS babies), for the poor, for women, for orphans, for homosexuals, for children of gay parents, for divorcees and countless others.

Albino Luciani on the other hand, was born into dire poverty and nearly starved to death as a child. He was born to a very different kind of parents, a devout mother who gave him the *imagery* of Christ and a social revolutionary activist father who gave him the *reality* of Christ. As was the case in Poland, blacks were not allowed in Italy while he was growing up. His father, who objected to all discriminatory practices, taught him from an early age that all of God's children were created to be equal regardless of race, creed, sex, sexual orientation, physical or emotional impairment or what have you. He did not believe in what Hitler had to offer, so when

Hitler lost the war it was the beginning of the realization of all that he had ever dreamed of.

Religious News Photo

Albino Luciani wearing the soft cap of the Italian Resistance in 1942

Albino developed his knack for mountain climbing when he ministered the members of the Italian Resistance who were hiding in difficult to get at places in the Dolomite Mountains during the war. He once told me of the most difficult moment of his life; he felt the pulse of a young boy run out between his fingers. The boy had been shot trying to blowup a railroad trestle to cut off military supplies coming from Germany.

the ecclesiastical record of two popes

	John Paul I Albino Luciani	John Paul II Karol Wojtyla
vow of poverty (all clergy including Pope)	yes	no
protective sex to prevent spread of disease	yes	no
planned parenthood	yes	no
contraception to reduce abortions	yes	no
payoff victims of pedophile priests	no	yes
sex education (post world war)	yes	no
ordination of women	yes	no
acceptance of homosexuals	yes	no
acceptance of pre-operative transsexuals	yes	no
acceptance of post-operative transsexuals	yes	yes
marriage is sanctification of -	mental union	penis and vagina

love and commitment define marriage	yes	no
remarriage	yes	no
priest celibacy	yes	yes
nun-monk celibacy	no	yes
black-white integration (post world war)	yes	no
artificial insemination	yes	no
genetic research	yes	no
mysticism	no	yes
Church management	democracy[1]	anarchy[2]
drives basic ideology	conscience	scripture
mentor	Christ	Moses

In the twenty years that they were princes of the Church, Luciani and Wojtyla were two of the loudest voices on their respective sides of the aisle, one reason why they had both risen to the papacy. For example, Wojtyla was a leader in the effort to preserve segregation between blacks and whites within the Church after World War II, and on the other side Luciani was a leader of the movement in Europe to do away with segregation, not only within the Church but in society as well. One must keep in mind that at the time the population overwhelmingly favored segregation.

Most Catholics, in fact the general populace as a whole, are of the misconception that a pope is restricted by either scripture or doctrine in making changes to Church doctrine. Yet, nothing could be further from the truth, as a pope by *Canon Law,* has the absolute ecclesiastical power to unilaterally make any change he deems fit.

Just before John Paul I became Pope he had declared that Louise Brown, the world's first artificially inseminated child, *"was a child of God,"* which contradicted the papal decree made thirty years earlier by Pius XII, *"that such children if ever born would be children of the devil."*

Because Luciani had shortly risen to the papacy, Louise Brown was recognized by most Catholics as being a child of God. On the very day following his election, John Paul II clarified the confusion caused by his predecessor's action. He issued a decree reaffirming the decree of Pius XII and he did it in such a way as to question the possible ensoulment of artificially inseminated children. In 1984, public pressure forced John Paul II to reverse this doctrine - his own doctrine of just six years before - a change that today recognizes the ensoulment of all children, whether naturally or artificially conceived. So although one might think that popes

[1] *representative government - equal balance of men and women, conservatives and liberals; doctors, teachers, psychologists, psychiatrists, scientists, genetic research, etc.*
[2] *dictatorship - papacy dominated group of entirely conservative men*

are infallible, there have been times that popes have not only reversed doctrine made by a predecessor, but have often reversed doctrine made by themselves; and this is one of them.

When one believes that the Pope cannot ordain women, cannot accept homosexuals into the Church, cannot sanctify remarriage, and cannot take a vow of poverty - one does not know what one is talking about. For the Pope is an absolute dictator of not only the present, but of the past, and of the future.

When one wonders why the Pope continues to impose a ban on contraception, which is the driving force behind poverty, starvation and the spread of AIDS in third world countries, he is relying upon more than simply Church doctrine. The theological basis for the Church's position is that *'of the thousands of sperm and eggs that a man and a woman produce in their lifetimes, God has already pre-selected that particular sperm and egg that will become a human being.*' Contraception, stem-cell research and abortion of a fertilized egg interfere with this natural flow of creation and are therefore mortal sins. It is this thinking that causes the preacher to consider a fertilized egg to be a human being.

This ideology - *that God has pre-selected that particular sperm and egg that will be a human being* - is supported by Jeremiah 1, *"The Lord came unto me saying, Before I formed thee in the belly I knew thee; and before thou camest forth out of the womb I sanctified thee."* Take this line out of the Bible and Christianity has nothing at all in scripture to support its ban on contraception, stem-cell research and abortion of a fertilized egg. Moses' testimony - the Bible's only condemnation of abortion - explicitly contradicts Jeremiah. Exodus 21, *'If men strive and hurt a woman with child, so that her fruit depart from her, and yet no mischief follow; he shall be surely punished, according as the woman's husband will lay upon him; and he shall pay a fine as the judges determine. And if any mischief follow, that thou shalt give life for life, eye for eye, tooth for tooth, hand for hand, foot for foot.*' According to the 'God' Moses spoke to, abortion of a fertilized egg is a misdemeanor while abortion of a viable fetus is murder. According to the 'God' Jeremiah spoke to, abortion of a fertilized egg is murder. So it depends entirely on which prophet one thinks was telling the truth?

It is this concept that divides *pro-choice* from *pro-life: pro-choice* generally being against the destruction of a viable fetus, while *pro-life* being against the destruction of a fertilized egg which is not yet an embryo; despite the fact that billions of them are flushed down the sewer in everyday sex. In the United States, it is that the preacher thinks that a fertilized egg is a human being that causes him to ban the *morning after pill* which results in a million otherwise avoidable abortions (murders) of fetuses each year.

It is this same verse in Jeremiah that supports the premise that ensoulment takes place just before birth, the reason why no church baptizes before birth. This is the reason why preachers are against aborting malformed or brain-dead fetuses. It makes no difference to the preacher whether or not a child is born only to suffer and die an unspeakable death. All that is important to him is that the child reaches that point at which it acquires a soul and goes to heaven.

In 1984, when public pressure forced John Paul II to reverse his own doctrine of 1978, which had denied ensoulment to artificially inseminated children, he took exception to his own basic premise as, in the case of artificial insemination, man and not God selects which sperm and which egg will become a human being. This means that the Pope no longer believes consistently in this most fundamental dogma of his papacy. Otherwise, he would have stood his ground as artificial insemination clearly violates the very same basic concept that causes him to claim that contraception, stem-cell research and abortion of a fertilized egg are the equivalent of murder.

And this is true of all other Christian denominations. That, as a matter of consistency, they must hold to their conviction that artificially inseminated children are not children of God, less they have no basis in scripture that a fertilized egg is a human being.

One must keep in mind that according to the testimony in the Bible itself, Jeremiah, like Moses before him, in convincing his followers that he had talked to God, became the wealthiest man of his time. As the twelve year old child prodigy Albino Luciani of the Feltre Minor Seminary had once called them, *"These scoundrels, these bigots, were clearly prophets for profits. The great enemy of society is not so much these evil men and those preachers driven by greed and bigotry who mimic them, but it is the ignorance and the weakness of the minds of those who are fooled by them"* [1]

Luciani was to live to see his supposition proved true. In 1946, he told a reporter, *"It was not so much Hitler and Mussolini who were the culprits in this thing, as it was the ignorance and the weakness of the minds of the masses that believed in them"* [2]

Unfortunately, as we shall see in what is yet to come, the papacy remains in Rome today the last remnants of the *Anarchy of Fascism* that the teenager Albino Luciani once warned of in his editorial that criticized

[1] *Parish Bulletin Feltre,* 16 May '21 Albino Lucian's first editorial in his school newspaper.
[3] *Messaggero Mestre* 17 Apr 46

the dictate of Pius XI to enroll all children under the age of sixteen in the *Fascist Youth Organization* that eventually cost fifty-million lives, this very same *Anarchy of Fascism* that is about to cost fifty-million more.

During the twenty years they served as a bishop and as a cardinal both of their countries suffered from an immense orphan problem – about two million in each country. During this time Wojtyla built and dedicated fifty-three churches and not a single orphanage. Luciani, on the other hand, built and dedicated forty-four orphanages and not a single church. Each time that the fork in the road would come up, Wojtyla would ask himself, *"Now, what would God the Father do in this case?"* And each time that the fork in the road would come up, Luciani would ask himself, *"Now, what would Jesus do in this case?"*

So these were two very different kinds of men, driven by two very different kinds of Gods, Karol Wojtyla striving to preserve the last bits and pieces of *Fascism,* of *Christianity;* and Luciani striving to bring the *reality* of *Christ* into modern society, striving to stamp out what Hitler stood for, once and for all!

Associated Press

the face of freedom*

Kenneth Jarecke photo

the face of anarchism

*the struggle for the equality of all of God's children in the Church died with him

Chapter 2

HIS DEATH

a pauper rises to the world's stage,

Just two weeks after Luciani sent his widely published letter to Louise Brown that embarrassed many cardinals who had condemned the child; Pope Paul VI died. On August 12, 1978 *The London Times* published a listing of the leading candidates for the succession. In order of their promise were listed: Cardinals Benelli, Siri, Hume, Pignedoli, Baggio, Poletti, Lorscheider, Koenig and Cordeiro. Conspicuously absent was the name of Luciani.

Astonishingly, when the white smoke rose from the Vatican on August 26, 1978, it bore his name. He was elected with ninety of the one-hundred-eleven votes that were cast. On the fourth ballot the count was seventy-five for Luciani; a marginal vote, exactly the two-thirds majority plus one vote required to elect him. On the recount, in an effort to make the election unanimous, fifteen others went his way. Only the twenty-one supporters of the ultraconservative Cardinal Siri, the members of the *Vatican Curia*, remained cast against him. In their loss, they were determined to send a message in their dissenting votes, just as they had done in Paul's case fifteen years before; the only two popes in the thousand-year history in which cardinals have elected the Pope who failed to have carried a unanimous vote on the recount. So bitter was the hate of those opposition cardinals who would share the Vatican with the new Pope that they could not accept the fact that Christ had spoken.

Luciani's election was a remarkable occurrence, particularly since he was an outspoken liberal and it was known that less than a third of the cardinals had liberal tendencies; most surprising of all was that he had so recently defied a major papal decree, -an action that most thought would cost him his *red hat* let alone his chance at the papacy. It was his old friend, Cardinal Suenens who had led the lobbying, and had yielded up the block of votes he himself controlled on the fourth ballot that won for Luciani the papacy. Just as Suenens had fifteen years earlier yielded up the block of votes that he controlled at that time to elect Paul VI. What Suenens did not know at the time is that his concession may have very well saved his life.

In accepting his pontificate from the *College of Cardinal*s Luciani took the name of *John Paul* in honor of his patrons - John XXIII who had groomed him and made him a bishop and Paul VI who had made him a cardinal. He then made a simple and quite confusing statement to them. "*Moses*," he said, "*may never forgive you for what you have done today.*"*

This was his actual statement as reported in the local press. Later, foreign newspapers, and subsequently some authors who wrote about John Paul's remark, took literary license and changed the word 'Moses' to 'Christ' - interpreting the name 'Moses' to be synonymous with the name 'Christ'. But if one studies his life, Luciani very obviously did not mean Christ. John Paul quite obviously meant exactly what he said in this, the first and most confusing comment of his brief papacy, "*Moses may never forgive you for what you have done today.*"

The comment was meant as a forewarning to the *Vatican Curia*, that cluster of cardinals who surrounded him in Rome, -that their days were numbered and he intended to bring an end to the bigotry that Moses had led the world into these past four thousand years. And it hinted that the new Pope might make his move in the not too distant future . . . that he intended to lead the Church and the western world away from Moses and closer to Christ.

Avoiding the pomp and pageantry that traditionally accompanies the installation of a pontiff, he took his office in a small private setting witnessed by the minimum number of Church prelates required and by his family and close friends including *Jack* and the housekeeper who had served him so faithfully at Vittorio Veneto. Outside a huge crowd, which had filled St. Peter's Square, kept its eyes watchfully on the great papal balcony anxiously awaiting his first blessing as pontiff. But no one appeared; just a rustling, a kind of a murmuring of the crowd that started at its edges and eventually filled the square. Luciani had chosen not to display himself from the royal balcony as all the others had done before him. Rather, he had chosen to walk among them.

In taking his place as the leader of the Roman Catholic Church with far less ceremony than that which had accompanied his installation as a common bishop twenty years earlier, he had begun to demolish the majestic image of the papacy. He refused to be crowned with the gold and jewel encrusted *St. Stephen's Crown*[2], which had been the focal point of previous coronations. In fact, there was no coronation at all. Instead he allowed a simple pastoral stole, the symbol of a common priest, to be placed upon his shoulders to mark his assumption of his new responsibilities, for

* *L'Osservatore Romano, 13 Aug'78*

[2] *one of many Papal Tiaras*

he did not intend to rule from the throne. His peers, the cardinals, the crown princes of the Church, felt much of their own regency endangered.

Whereas the rank-and-file and the hierarchy of the Church saw in the St. Stephen crown a symbol of royalty, Luciani saw something much different. He saw in it the right to a good and healthy life for a thousand children who would otherwise starve to death, and that's exactly what he intended to do with it.

Actually Luciani had never been a man of formalities. As a bishop he had refused to be addressed as *Your Excellency*, the title reserved for bishops. As a cardinal he had refused to be addressed as *Your Eminence*, the title reserved for cardinals. And as a Pope he refused to be addressed as *Your Holiness*. He asked that everyone, from heads of state to little children, address him by the nickname he had acquired as a child, *Piccolo*.

He had been the first bishop installed by John XXIII and at the conclusion of the ceremony in St. Peter's his mother who headed up the congratulatory reception line, approached him and moved to bow to kiss his newly acquired bishop's ring. So horrified was he that this woman who had given him life and nurtured him and had brought him up in a difficult world would bow to him, that rather than extending his hand, he grasped her in his arms and held her in an embrace that spanned several minutes. The entire congregation was moved to tears. A group of Vatican cardinals, appalled at what they had just witnessed stood off to one side, frozen in hostile stares. Finally, on releasing her, this newest prince of the Church, realizing that he had broken Church protocol, turned toward the Pope and rather than apologizing for his action told him, "*A prince must never forget that his mother is the queen!*"

On one occasion at the conclusion of a conference of cardinals during which tempers had flared on both sides concerning certain Church doctrine, he hugged the leader of the opposition in an embrace that one normally reserves for one's father. When asked by one of those on his side of the aisle why he had done such a thing he replied, "*I am a poor strategist and negotiator so I must use the only weapon that Christ has given me - love!*"

He never donned the *Fisherman's Ring*, the ring of the papacy; nor was he ever known to extend his hand for the ceremonial kiss. He would have no man or woman bow to him. Rather he would embrace his visitor, not in a ceremonial way, but in a real way.

The positions of John Paul I concerning bigotry, birth control, abortion, contraception, remarriage and homosexuality were quite apparent in his formal acceptance speech in the Sistine Chapel on August 27, 1978,

*"A particular greeting to all who are now suffering throughout the world; to the sick, to prisoners, to exiles, to the persecuted, and particularly, to those upon whom restraints are unfairly placed by doctrine in their everyday life. We must encourage all young adults in our congregation, no matter how scorned, to seek out and enter into long-term loving relationships in order to provide for the economic and loving support of unparented children. We must take upon our shoulders responsibility to help control the world's population, to bring an end to poverty and starvation. Let our differences mold into one and together we shall rise to bring the world to a condition of greater justice. We call upon all of you, from the humblest who are the underpinnings of nations, to heads of state. We encourage you to build an efficacious and responsible structure for a new order, this one more just and honest."**

In his first executive action, he ordered a complete review of the Church's finances, including a tally of all of its worldwide liquid assets. In fact John Paul, who had a background in finance, participated in the internal audit of the Vatican Bank himself. After all, it was he, who twenty years before, had inherited the bankrupt mountain diocese of Vittorio Veneto and had brought it to solvency and eventually to prosperity. It is known that he spent much of the month of his pontificate in the Bank and he also walked around many of the other offices in Vatican City to see who was doing what. It was his personal involvement in the audit that led many authors, who subsequently wrote books that suggested foul play in his death, to point to bank officials, three of which, including the president of the Vatican's correspondent bank, eventually became victims of unexplained suicide or murder. Another disappeared and was never found.

About this same time Luciani invited a number of art dealers to Rome for the purpose of obtaining appraisals of some of the art treasures of the Vatican Museum and the Sistine Chapel. It is also known that during his short reign he permitted a large real estate firm from Milan to survey the sprawling papal estate at the Castel Gandolfo on the outskirts of Rome. The Castel Gandolfo housed not only the papal summer residence but included four other majestic palaces and gardens that were enjoyed by European cardinals and bishops when vacationing there. Actually it was a luxury resort city in itself. It was quite obvious from the beginning that he intended to make *Mother Church* heed Christ's most prolific testimony

* *world press*

in the *New Testament*, "*If thou be perfect, sell all that thou hast and give to the poor.*"

Luciani had grown up in abject poverty in a little town in the Italian Alps, the only Pope in history to be born into dire poverty. So much so that borderline starvation had made him into a frail child and ultimately resulted in his confinement to a sanatorium for more than a year for tuberculosis. He could not bring himself to accept the immense wealth of the Church; that he himself, as its leader would live in luxury surrounded by magnificent art and architecture and jewels and gold and feather pillows, while children in Africa and other parts of the world were literally starving to death. And it anguished him much that it was the Church's position on birth control that was the reason why they were starving to death.

When John Paul II became Pope he went the other way, making the Papal Palace and summer residence even more lavish then they were by pouring a small fortune into them, including adding a majestic swimming pool for the enjoyment of his majesty and the princes of the Church.

a vow of poverty for the princes of Rome,

In order to calm the fears of those very conservative cardinals who shared the Vatican with him, who hated what he stood for so much that they had refused to vote for him, he did something that no other newly appointed pontiff had ever done before. He immediately confirmed the appointments of all existing cardinals.

On the other hand he reduced in half the substantial bonus that Vatican cardinals receive upon the election of a new pope. This seemed a forewarning to his eventually reducing the salaries of Vatican cardinals, which at that time was the equivalent of what is a hundred and ten thousand pre-tax dollars today; spending money for the cardinals as all of their living expenses were paid for by the Church, most of them living in the lap of luxury. Something that Luciani's successor John Paul II believed in as he raised Vatican cardinal salaries by eighteen percent almost immediately after his election, which action drew the comment from a leftist cardinal, "*it is almost as if it had been part of the deal.*"

Also, it was well known throughout Europe that upon becoming Patriarch of Venice ten years earlier Luciani had reduced his living quarters to a small four room apartment in the rear of the fifth floor of the patriarch palace in Venice and had converted most of the remaining part of the building to quarters for unwed mothers. There was considerable apprehension among field cardinals that they might end up sharing their sprawling mansions and palaces with the homeless and the poor.

And worst of all there was an underlying dread among all of the cardinals and bishops of the Church that they might be soon taking a *vow of poverty.*

And then there was from the very start the likelihood that Luciani would appoint a new *cabinet*, that is replace those in the most powerful positions in the Roman Catholic Church.

a modern day Martin Luther,

Shortly after he became Pope, Bishop Casaroli, someone you will get to know quite well in Part II of this book, was reported by an Italian tabloid as having said of Luciani's election, *"It is as if Martin Luther has come back from the dead to take his revenge on all of us; first to take from us our bonuses; and soon our salaries; and then our rank; and possibly even our palaces; and perhaps eventually end in our excommunication."*

There was some truth to this, for Luciani had studied Luther's life and often talked of him. In fact, when he became bishop and overseer of the seminary at Vittorio Veneto he added a subject on the *Reformation* to the curriculum and he, himself, taught it.

Most people today think that Martin Luther's central purpose in his *Thesis 95* objected to the sale of indulgences and absolutions by the Church. But, in actuality, Martin Luther's basic premise was much broader than this, as Luciani pointed out in one of his lectures, *"Martin Luther believed that man's relationship with God was a private and direct one and that a middleman was not necessary to one's salvation, particularly, a middleman who was driven by hatred and greed. To put it pointedly, his goal was to do away with the idea of a church once and for all; this despite the fact that today's Lutheran Church claims to have grown out of his teachings."*

And Luciani saw it that way too, as he once told me, *"When Christ said, 'Thou art Peter and upon this rock I will build my Church,' He did not mean a building of stone and granite nor an organization made up of places of worship. He meant that His followers were to practice His principles. And despite what preachers might tell their congregations, Christ's message was twofold, 'love thy neighbor as thyself' and 'sell all that thou hast and give to the poor.' There is no message more explicit in all of the Bible than is Christ's account of His two archenemies - bigotry and greed - which today, in direct defiance of Christ's teachings, are the fundamental driving forces of our Christian society.*

"For those with small minds who cannot comprehend complex theology, we have Christ's simple testimony as He makes clear that the

Church He intended was not to be one of stone nor a place of worship. He tells us that our relationship to God is a private and direct one - that it requires no middleman - and that it should not be the public display that today's Christians and the Pharisees of His time make of it. Matthew 6, 'And when thou prayest, thou shalt not be as hypocrites are; for they love to pray standing in the synagogues and in public places, that they may be seen and heard of men. Verily, I say unto you, They have their reward in hell.[1] *But thou, when thou prayest, enter into thy closet, and when thou hast shut thy door, talk to ye God in secret; and ye reward will be in heaven.*[1] *And when ye pray use not vain repetitions as the heathen do; for they think that they shall be heard for their speaking in public places . . .'*

"There is, of course, Matthew 18 which is the only text in the gospels that could possibly be interpreted to mean that Christ required one to go to church and adore Him in order to gain salvation, 'For where two or three are gathered together in my name, there am I in the midst of them.' But, if one reads the surrounding text, Christ makes clear that He is not speaking of temples of gold and granite or of those who sing songs to His name, but rather He is talking of those who gather together to practice His principles, 'Love thy neighbor as thyself' and 'sell all that thou hast and give to the poor.'"

I recall most vividly Luciani's recounting of the first time he missed Sunday mass. *"I had just turned eleven and was as poor as a church mouse and often went hungry myself. Yet, I did have a mama and papa to take care of me and love me. They were away visiting a sick friend on that sub-zero Sunday morning when I made my way to church with my fellow Christians. We passed a dozen or so orphans begging in the streets. Most of them were orphans because they had been born out-of-wedlock - the reason why they were barred from church as it was God the Father's sacred testimony in Deuteronomy 23, 'A bastard child shall not enter into the congregation of the lord.' It was this 'holy' testimony of his 'God' that first made me realize what a monster and a liar Moses was.*

"It may have been the intense cold that inspired me, but nevertheless I turned around and went back to my house and quickly cooked up a caldron of soup with all the vegetables I could find and although it meant that we would go without them ourselves for several days, I took it to the orphans and placed it in the snow in the midst of them. For the first time I realized what Christ had meant when He said, 'Where two or three are gathered together in my name, there am I in the midst of them.'

[1] *Some modern Bibles published after 1900AD have deleted the words 'hell' and 'heaven' in order to capitalize on churchgoers. This deletion is quite obvious in the surviving text, itself.*

"By that time church was over, so I had missed mass - a mortal sin in those days. I decided to go into the church to ask forgiveness. But I forgot that they locked the doors outside of service hours to keep the orphans from coming in to get warm. It was then - at that very moment - when those doors would not open - that I realized what Christ had meant by the word, 'Church.' It was then - at that very moment - when those doors would not open - that I decided to become a priest; I would change the word 'Church' back to what Christ had intended. It was then - at that very moment - when those doors would not open - that I first realized that my devout mama was a sheep; and my socialist revolutionary papa was a lion. It was then - at that very moment - when those doors would not open - that I began to shed my wool; and groom my mane.

"I hoped that the scolding I would receive when I got home would not be too harsh - that is, when my parents would find the cupboard empty. But, I didn't get a scolding at all. When they realized what I had done, they both hugged me, as if I were the Christ child, Himself. Although my stomach was empty for a few days, I slept like a baby, for my heart was full."

In Luther's time, the Catholic Church had convinced the populace that the Church was instrumental to one's salvation. The implementation of Luther's plan was to be threefold: 1) to abolish the belief that only a priest could forgive one's sins; 2) the Bible would be printed in modern languages so that laymen could read the Bible themselves; and 3) there was no need for a middleman or a building or a preacher between a man and his God - that the relationship was a direct and sacred one and not for public display.

Although he succeeded to a certain extent in accomplishing these things, Luther did not foresee that ruthless and greedy men - including today's evangelists - would seize upon the opportunity and begin to form their own churches in order to spread their hatred of those who appear to be different. That they would capitalize upon the ignorance and weakness of the minds of men to spread their bigotry - the slavery of blacks - the subordination of women - the persecution and annihilation of homosexuals, Muslims, Jews and other ethnic peoples. Thus, we have a history in which Christianity has been a cesspool of hatred of ones fellowman which continues to go on today.

a brief papacy,

As he died before ever making a formal public address his comments were limited to a few casual remarks. When he said ". . . *God is more our Mother than She is our Father,*" the press inquired whether this was a change in the Church's doctrine, that possibly a fourth person was being added to the Holy Trinity? In retrospect, in that it was publicly announced to the press, this was the only official papal decree that he made during his brief pontificate, one that the Church chooses to ignore today. On another occasion, during an audience, he took a microphone out of a cardinal's hands and handed it to a little boy as if to suggest that what the youngster had to say was more important than what his prince of the Church had to say.

He had a particular knack for explaining complex issues in a simple and understanding way. On one occasion he was asked by a rather frustrated eight-year-old boy,

"*What is the difference between the left and the right? Why are they always fighting with each other? Is it because one believes in God and the other doesn't?*"

"*No,*" the Pope answered, "*They both believe in God. It is just that those on the right want to guide their lives according to scripture, what someone is said to have said to someone else thousands of years ago.*"

"*Oh,*" replied the child who seemed puzzled by the Pope's answer and then asked, "*Then what do those on the left use to guide their lives?*"

"*This,*" replied the Pope, "*This, their conscience.*" and the Pope pointed to his temple.[1]

Once, when interviewing an old peasant woman, who had described 'Piccolo' as the greatest Pope, a reporter asked her the reason for her appraisal. She replied, "*Because I understand what he says. I have known the rules all my life, but never before have I known why.*" [2]

[1] *L'Osservatore Romano 5 Sep '78*
[2] *L'Osservatore Romano 9 Sep '78*

Religious News Service Photo

John Paul explains the *pillars of society* to a young boy

When he shook hands with the communist mayor of Rome, the Vatican cardinals shot vicious glances and when he hugged him they shrugged in despair. On one occasion John Paul was reported in the tabloids as being seen in St. Peter's Square, walking among the people wearing shorts and sandals. But regardless of the validity of this reporting, he asked, he listened, he learned. He talked, he told, he taught. He grinned, he smiled, he laughed. And above all he hugged. And what's best of all is that they learned to hug him back. He made few friends among those of rank in the Church and nations, but he quickly won the friendship of the common man.

caught in a lie or two,

Thirty-three days after his installation he died mysteriously in the Vatican. He was found dead in his bed early on the morning of September 29, 1978. Strangely, although death was determined to have occurred at about midnight, he was wearing his daytime clothes and was in a sitting up position. The bed lamp was still on and the windows were wide open. Still upright in his hands were some notes that he had written while he had been Bishop of Vittorio Veneto. He seemed to be preparing for his first public address, scheduled for the following week.

At seven-thirty on the morning he was found dead, the Vatican issued an official release, "*Pope John Paul died just before midnight September 28, 1978 of a blood clot to his heart. The Pope was discovered by his secretary John Magee about six thirty this morning when he went to look for the Pope when John Paul did not show up for his morning chapel service. He was found to be sitting up in his bed and wearing his daytime clothes with the bed lamp still on. John Paul died while he was reading the "Imitation of Christ" which book was still held upright in his hands. Father Magee, on discovering that the Pope was dead, immediately summoned Cardinal Villot who performed the last rites of the Church.*

*The Vatican**

The first official release from the Vatican stated that he was reading the *Imitation of Christ* when he died. However, when asked by the press, the embalmers who took the papers from his hands, not thinking it to be an important issue, related that they were some notes written on the stationary of the Diocese of Vittorio Veneto, and a few old newspaper clippings. The embalmers, the Signoracci brothers from a nearby school of medicine, told the press that they were picked up by a Vatican car at a little after five-thirty in the morning, -which was an hour before the Vatican release announced that the body was found. They also told the press they had been told by Swiss guards that it was a nun who had discovered the Pontiff early in the morning. In addition, it was their opinion that the Pope had not been dead for more than an hour or two, as it was a rather chilly morning and the windows were wide open and the body was still warm.

The official Vatican release confirmed that the pope had died in the early morning hours and not before midnight in that it had specifically stated that Cardinal Villot had performed the last rites. No priest, let alone a cardinal, would perform the last rites over a cold corpse, as Church doctrine decrees that the soul leaves the body when rigor mortis sets in. Yes, he might say some prayers over a cold corpse, but never the last rites.

The press was quick to follow up on the discrepancy as to who discovered the body and interviewed Mother Vincenza who was the nun that the embalmers claimed had found the body. She told them that the Pope normally rose between four and four-thirty in the morning and that she routinely delivered coffee each morning promptly at four thirty. When she first knocked on the door there was no answer. She waited a minute or so and knocked again, this time a bit louder. It seemed obvious to her that the Pope was still in the bathroom; perhaps he may have risen a bit late. So she opened the door and began to enter the room, intending to leave the tray on his nightstand. It was then that she saw that the bed lamp was on and that he was in his daytime clothes. He was in a sitting up position with the bedspread pulled partway over his legs, reading some papers that

**world press*

he held in his hands. Her testimony confirmed that of the embalmers; the Pope was in fact holding stationary of some sort and not a book in his hands. It also pointed to a discrepancy in time, as the Vatican release had said that the Pope had been found at six-thirty in the morning.

She greeted him with "good morning" and he did not respond. He held to what she described as a mime position as if he was too deeply involved in what he was reading. It was not unusual for him once dressed for the day to be sitting up in his bed reading when she delivered breakfast. Sister Vincenza, who had served Luciani for twenty years, had come to know this man as a jovial one, always smiling, often laughing and sometimes joking. So at first she thought that this was some kind of a joke. Particularly, since he had a kind of a leering grin on his face. So she entered the room and approaching the bed she placed the tray on the nightstand. It was then that she realized that something was wrong. She immediately went out of his room and down the hallway and fetched John Magee who came to the room and found that the Pope was dead.

These contradictions of the official release of the Vatican gave birth to a rumor that the notes held in the Pope's hands at the time of his death were listings of cardinals to be replaced - that John Paul was planning a shakeup of the Church's hierarchy. Although it certainly would not make very much sense for him to be using outdated stationary for such a purpose, the rumor spread like wildfire.

It would make more sense, at least to this author, that John Paul was in fact reviewing a draft of one of the many controversial letters he had written while he was Bishop of Vittorio Veneto. It would seem most likely to be a draft of his famous letter to Paul VI requesting that revisions be made to the doctrine of *Humanae Vitae,* the Church's strict policy prohibiting the use of contraceptives that it was rumored at the time he would repeal. His letter of 1968 to Paul VI specifically recommended *"that some accommodations for artificial birth control must be made within the confines of the Church.*"

It would seem that since it had been a public letter, that in his proclamation, which was scheduled for the following week, he would say nothing that might contradict what he had said ten years before. This would also explain the newspaper clippings that were found on his bed, as the letter had been widely published in Europe. Then again it could have been a draft of any public letter he had written during his time as Bishop of Vittorio Veneto on a wide range of issues which included divorce and remarriage, equality of women in the Church or even homosexuality; all issues which horrified the *Vatican Curia*, that cluster of Church prelates who shared the Vatican with him, a few of which shared the Papal Palace itself with him.

Also, the official Vatican release had specifically stated that it was John Magee, the Pope's secretary that had found him at six-thirty in the morning. John Magee had been the secretary of his predecessor Paul VI who had been serving in transition. A Pope normally retains the previous pontiff's secretary but early on John Paul had announced that he would name a new secretary and that Magee would be retained at least temporarily, as a second secretary to handle the massive paperwork that surrounded the papacy.

By six-thirty in the morning the Pope's body had already been embalmed. Cardinal Villot, recalling the foul odor that the body of Paul VI had emitted shortly after his death a month earlier, ordered an immediate embalming of John Paul's remains in order to prevent a recurrence of what had happened to Paul, which in his case had delayed the body's viewing in St. Peter's Basilica by a day. This explains why the embalmers were brought to the Vatican so early in the morning.

That the body had been embalmed so quickly gave rise to a rumor that the Pope had been poisoned. In Italy at the time, it was commonly known that this was a practice of the Mafia when slow arsenic poisoning was the instrument of murder; embalming the body shortly after death erased the obvious signs of poisoning. It was for this reason that it was illegal in Italy to embalm a body until twenty-four hours after death. Of course, Italian law did not apply within Vatican walls. It should be pointed out that if arsenic were indeed the instrument of death, being an element it would not have broken down over time and would be present in the Pope's cadaver, specifically in his fingernails and hair, even today.

Dr. Buzzanetti, the doctor who pronounced him dead, said that the Pope had obviously suffered a heart attack. And this supposition seemed to be confirmed by the statement to reporters by Bishop Casaroli, the foreign minister, -that the Pope had complained of chest pains at dinner. However, when reporters questioned several others that had been present at the dinner, none of them could recall such an incident, the Pontiff was laughing and in good spirits at dinner. When all this conflicting testimony was reported in the press, the Vatican finally issued a verbal corrective statement to the press that in the confusion following his death some errors had been made in its original release.

Because the Vatican was caught in what appeared to be a strange combination of lies, rumors surfaced that raised the possibility of foul play in the Pontiff's death. The one rumor that seemed not to go away was that the notes held in the Pope's hands at the time of his death were lists of cardinals to be replaced, and that John Paul was planning a shake up of the Church's hierarchy.

Another question emerged. How, if the Pope retired at nine o'clock, could he still be in his daytime clothes and be reading at midnight? When John Magee answered this question he told the reporters that he had forgotten to wake the Pope from his nap that day; that the Pontiff had slept past six o'clock. This would explain why he could still have been reading at midnight, as he would have had trouble getting to sleep.

This raised even more suspicions as the Pope was never before known to take a nap. And, again, Magee responded that the Pope had started taking naps about two weeks earlier; that perhaps the strain of the workload was too much for him. This caused even more concern, as one of the things that evidences the early stages of slow arsenic poisoning - as well as many other slow poisonings - is tiredness; one might take unusual daytime naps.

It was the combination of the uncharacteristic naps and the immediate embalming, which make possible much of the following investigation. For it was the rumor of possible arsenic poisoning that prompted an army of reporters to interview all those who had been in the Papal Palace that fateful night in September of 1978 and they have left the complete record behind them in the microfilm. As a matter of fact, there is a complete record of all those who entered the Papal Palace where John Paul spent the last day of his life. One even knows who might have had access to the kitchen and who had not, each reporter in his or her investigation, trying to land the scoop of the century. Unlike Mark Furman's *Moxley* case, in which the victim was relatively unknown and the record is scant or nonexistent, n this case one is dealing with overabundance of hard evidence. The record is clearly there as to who had access to the Pope on the last day and night of his life and who did not.

On the third day following the Pope's death the nuns, including the mother nun who had cared for the Papal Apartment, were reassigned to some unknown convent somewhere in Europe. This meant that Mother Vincenza who had served him for twenty years would be unable to attend his funeral. John Magee was also sent to some unknown destination in Ireland. This enraged reporters, as it removed the primary witnesses to the circumstances surrounding the Pope's death from their access. Every newspaper in all of Italy questioned the Vatican's action in this respect. If it had nothing to hide why exile the only known witnesses to the circumstances surrounding the Pope's death?

In an attempt to bring an end to the rumors, the Vatican finally responded with an official release to the press,

"Pope John Paul did not have in mind to make revolutionary changes in the Vatican hierarchy as evidenced by the following facts,

On August 27th, he reconfirmed Cardinal Villot as Secretary of State.

On August 28th, he confirmed all of the existing cardinals for their current five-year terms.

The intention of sudden sweeping change that has been attributed to John Paul would be entirely out of character for him. In his previous assignment he had kept the status quo.

The Pope's secretary and the nuns who cared for the Papal Apartment were particularly saddened by the Pope's passing and were placed on sabbatical leave to help them get through this difficult period.

We wish to correct our statement that the Pope held the 'Imitation of Christ' in his hands at the time of his death. This was a communications error. The Pope at the time of his death was reviewing some old notes that he had written when he had been Bishop of Vittorio Veneto. They had been written on the diocese's stationary. That he was able to retain them upright in his hands in the midst of a massive heart attack is due to the grace of God

It is Canon Law that an autopsy cannot be performed on a pope's body.

We wish to clarify our original release that it was the Pope's secretary John Magee who had discovered the Pope's body. It was the Pope's secretary who first realized that he was dead. The Pope was first discovered by Sister Vincenza when she delivered the Pope's breakfast at the usual time. When the Pope did not respond she summoned the Pope's secretary as she sensed something was wrong. It is immaterial whether a nun or his secretary found His Holiness. It is also immaterial when he was found dead. And it is also immaterial when he actually died. All that is material is that he was found dead.

*The Vatican**

But the letter simply raised more questions. Reconfirmation of Cardinal Villot was meaningless as the secretary of state is normally appointed for life. Yes, he can choose to retire, in which another cardinal can succeed him, but otherwise he will normally remain in his position until he dies. The reason for this is that the appointment by a pope of a secretary of state is deemed to be an infallible act as if a pope dies the secretary of state becomes the interim Pope with all of the ecclesiastical

*world press

powers of a Pope. A successor Pope cannot remove an incumbent secretary without endangering the infallibility of his own office.

Also, confirmation of the cardinals as cardinals did not necessarily confirm them in their present positions of power. It was widely rumored that several of them would lose their rank. It was widely speculated that a new foreign minister would be named and that several leaders of important councils and congregations would be replaced. Also, several cardinals who held key positions as apostolic delegates to major nations, -including Great Britain and the Soviet Union, would be replaced. One should keep in mind that these speculations were at the very best, leaks to the press. They were not known facts. Just what were John Paul's intentions were known only to himself and in that he died a week before he was to make his first proclamations they will remain forever a mystery. Yes, that they would have been revolutionary was quite certain. But just exactly what changes he would have made had he lived remain unknown.

The claim that radical change was not characteristic of Luciani came under attack. Although it was true that he had made very few changes during his time as Patriarch of Venice, it was widely know that when he had become Bishop of Vittorio Veneto ten years before just the opposite had been true. Within a month of his assignment he had replaced both the president and the dean of the great seminary there. And within a year he had replaced more than half of the school's faculty. Actually, it was his record at Vittorio Veneto that had inspired the rumor of probable change in the Church's hierarchy in the first place.

It made no sense that Magee would have been so saddened by the Pope's death that he was placed on sabbatical, as he had served him for only a month. It would seem that the Church would have placed John Paul's secretary Lorenzi on sabbatical instead, as he had been his loyal servant in Venice and had lost all that he had.

Although it was *Canon Law* that an autopsy cannot be performed on a pope's body, it does allow for certain exceptions. Suspicion of murder is one of these; the reason why an autopsy was performed on Pius VIII in 1829.

And strangely the Vatican release made no mention of John Paul's position on *Humanae Vitae,* -the Church's doctrine prohibiting contraceptive practices. It was commonly expected that John Paul would reverse or at the very least modify the doctrine, in order to bring an end to the abortions and poverty and starvation that it was generating. This certainly was quite obvious in his official acceptance speech in the Sistine Chapel.

And then there were a few other questions that were innocently raised by the Luciani family itself. The Pope's sister-in-law sought to recover a pair of slipper socks that she had knitted for the Pope in honor of his elevation to the papacy. She knew that as a boy he had often gone barefoot in the Italian Alps, and she wanted to make sure that he had something to keep his feet warm. They were white and had the papal coat of arms on them embroidered in gold. And then there were his spectacles. Although the Pope did not require them for reading; which explained the mystery as to why they were not found on his person as he had obviously died while reading, he would have required them just to walk across the room, as he suffered from acute near-sightedness. That these two items were never returned to the Luciani family would probably rouse up the little gray cells of the typical *Hercule Poirot.* But to this author it is logical that one of the nuns or someone else close to the Pope may have confiscated these items, as they would have something to remember this Pope by whom they loved so dearly. Or perhaps the socks were soiled and the glasses were broken and thereby discarded or perhaps just lost in the shuffle. But I suppose, if one wants to add this to the stack of unanswered questions concerning John Paul's death; yes, -these items have never been found. And then there was the fact that his sister Antonia, in response to her request for a lock of his hair, received a clump of jet black hair two weeks after his interment, which she claimed could not have been his, as his hair was graying.

There remained the unanswered question as to how he could have remained in a sitting-up position with the notes still clutched in his hands if he had, in fact, suffered a heart attack? The Vatican decided to change its policy. It took a position of no longer responding to the press.

And there remained the fact that he retired at nine o'clock, and being unable to sleep, decided to review some notes that he had written in Vittorio Veneto. That he died at midnight still wearing his daytime clothes is perhaps the most puzzling happenstance of all for if one decides to read oneself to sleep, one will invariably first dons one's pajamas or other bedclothes.

Also very strange was that something killed him so suddenly that he was unable to reach for the bell cord, which was a half an arm's length away to his right, as this would have summoned in an instant the Swiss guard who sat at his desk just eighty feet away at the entrance to the corridor that led to the Pope's inner chambers. Or that he was unable to press one of the service buttons on the intercom that was located on his bed stand immediately to his left that would have brought to his side any of five other people who resided elsewhere in the Papal Palace that night. No explanation of this very strange combination of events, or lack of events, was ever offered by the Vatican, or by any of those who wrote books about the event later on.

The Vatican newspaper itself had reported an interesting coincidence. On the second morning preceding the Pope's death the Vatican maintenance workers happened to test the bell cord, -something that had not been done for years, as Pope Paul normally used the intercom. The article said that the bell rang so loud that people who were in the palace at the time - including the Pope himself - thought it to be a fire alarm, and headed for the stairs.*

The cause of the death of John Paul I has never been released by the Vatican, other than that it could have resulted possibly from a coronary blood clot, the assumption of the doctor who had pronounced him dead. Except for some unexplained swelling of his feet, which his doctor had diagnosed the week before his death as the onset of arthritis, *John Paul had no known medical condition.* For those of you who have no substantial experience in reading mystery novels, swelling of the extremities is an early symptom of slow arsenic poisoning.

He had been hospitalized as a child for tuberculosis, and as a teenager with a tonsillectomy. Except for the recent swelling in his feet, the only ailment that he had ever had as an adult, -outside of a broken nose that he suffered in a football game when he was fifty, and a gallstone operation in the same year - had been a bout with bronchitis. His physical examination a year earlier which was released to the press at the request of his family, had detected nothing other than he was a man of extraordinarily good health. Being a borderline vegetarian all of his life, he had never had a cholesterol problem, which certainly poked a hole in the heart attack theory. He was only the second pope in history whose death went unwitnessed.

But, nevertheless, the notice that he had died a natural death was accepted by most rank and file Catholics. This was probably because a strong rumor emanated from the Vatican that Luciani had suffered a half-dozen heart attacks during the last year of his life. That aspiring to be Pope, so the story went, Luciani had kept his deteriorating medical condition to himself because it would have affected his candidacy. And there was some credibility to such a rumor - except for the known facts.

There is the fact that Luciani was not considered to be a viable candidate for the papacy. In fact, no liberal - particularly an *extreme* liberal - was considered a viable contender. Certainly, if Luciani had been setting

**Osservatore del Romano 28 Sep '78*

the stage for his election to the pontificate, it would have made no sense for him to have announced to the press his congratulatory letter to Louise Brown, knowing that it would upstage and possibly enrage many cardinals who had publicly condemned the child. Not a very sound political decision if one wanted to become Pope, as each cardinal was a vote.

Here again the reporters followed up on the presumed heart attacks and have left the record behind them in the microfilm. They found that the Luciani family had no knowledge of the alleged heart attacks. His own personal physician in Venice had never known of the attacks. The press interviewed every cardiologist in the entire Venice metropolitan area and none could be found who had treated the cardinal. There was no record of him in any of the area hospitals. It would have been quite a trick to have suffered six successive heart attacks in a very short time and not have required the services of a cardiologist, much less a hospital. And his secretary Lorenzi and the housekeeper who had shared his private apartment in Venice with him had no knowledge of the presumed attacks. And there was the fact that just three months prior to his elevation to the papacy Luciani had set a speed record in his class in climbing one of the most difficult peaks in Italy. And then there was one more fact, that for five hundred and twenty six consecutive Wednesdays and for five hundred and twenty seven consecutive Sundays at precisely seven o'clock in the morning, as reads the face of the clock, Albino Luciani had said mass for his congregation in Venice.

Biographical briefs released by the Church since the time of his death have gone so far as to state that it was widely known that Luciani was in very poor health at the time of his election. This strategy has been quite successful as this remains the misconception of the mass of the rank-and-file today. It is as if to say that the *College of Cardinals* had elected a man who was known to be at death's door to the most responsible job in the Roman Catholic Church.

Nevertheless, the Catholic world today believes that Pope John Paul succumbed to a heart attack of such massive proportions that he was unable to pull the bell cord, which hung a whisker away from his right shoulder as he sat up in his bed that night. They believe that he was the only man in history who ever suffered the immense pain of a massive coronary attack and was still able to retain the exact position he died in, sitting up in bed and still holding his papers upright in his hands. Such is the gullibility of men. They believe the doctor and the official Vatican release that said it was so, though it is an undisputed *fact* that because his death was unwitnessed only an autopsy could have determined the cause of death. Because the Pontiff died within the Vatican walls, not Italian ground, the death was not covered by Italian law and the Luciani family had no authority to demand an autopsy. However, several field cardinals led by Benelli did demand an autopsy, but one was never performed. So today it is a matter of absolute fact that no one knows what killed John Paul I except those who were responsible for his death.

He had come onto the world's stage together with his loyal secretary Lorenzi, in an outdated Lancia 2000. Had the automobile been brand spanking new, and it was not, it would have been totally unbecoming a common priest, much less a cardinal of the Church. Its fenders had been scorched by time and for the most part it had lost its color. So much so that the Swiss guards had stopped it at the Vatican gates and demanded identification. It was a tin box that had been designed and built for paupers. Forty days later he left in a pine box. A pine box designed and built for paupers. Two hundred and sixty two popes and ten thousand cardinals before him interred in grand, ceremonial, jewel encrusted caskets of gold and bronze and he in a wooden box, this *pauper who would be Pope.*

He had made the rounds, -pauper, then altar boy, then priest, then pastor, then bishop, then archbishop, then cardinal, then Pope, and then pauper once more. He left a total estate valued at less than five thousand dollars, a checking account with about eleven hundred dollars in it, his Lancia 2000, some personal items including his personal clothes and two cockatiels. There was a pair of cut class cruets which had been given to him by his mother on the day of his ordination, and a few other gifts and medals and plaques that he had received through the years on various occasions. Strangely, the *Medaglia d'Oro al Valore Militare,* the Italian government's highest military award, was among them. Undoubtedly, it had been given to him by someone who had won the medal and wanted him to have it, as it was known that he himself did not hold the award. He had given everything he had to the needy, this *pauper who would be Pope.*

So there have been many books written about his mysterious death. And most of them have recounted as I have, the many inconsistencies between the official Vatican releases concerning the circumstances of his death versus what the many witnesses had to say. And they have recounted as I have the many corrections that the Vatican made to its original releases. Now, it is our turn. And I say 'our' not 'my' as it will take both of us, perhaps, all of us to bring this now long unsolved mystery to a reasonable conclusion.

As we shall see in what follows, the supposition that the Pope was murdered is strong as one has the body, immense motive and considerable opportunity. This is confirmed by the Vatican, itself, as it never ordered an autopsy performed. For this would have been the prudent thing to do at the time as it would have brought an end to all of the rumors and all of the controversy and all of the speculation that has persisted ever since. Rumors, controversy and speculation fired by its own bundle of lies, that this book and dozens of other books and editorials need never had been written. As a matter of fact, had a head of state of any other nation died under such conflicting circumstances an autopsy would have certainly been performed.

Then there is the additional cover-up which has already been pointed out: since the time of his death the Church has gone out of its way to misrepresent what he was all about. What other motive could there possibly be for these misrepresentations, other than to cover-up the ecclesiastical motives for murder?

Murder in the Vatican would not be something new, for on at least seven other occasions in the past one hundred years the Vatican cardinals have been brought under suspicion. And one knows this because in the case of six cardinals and one pope, the family of the deceased called for an autopsy. In all of these cases poison was thought to be the instrument of death and suspicions generally focused on one or more of the Vatican cardinals who were known to be enemies of the deceased. Of course, since Italian law has no jurisdiction in the Vatican, with one exception no autopsy has ever been performed on the corpse of a cardinal or a pope in the Vatican.

Metropolitan Nicodim,

And, finally, there is the strange visit of Metropolitan Nicodim to the Vatican in September of 1978. Nicodim was the Archbishop of Leningrad and youthful leader of the Russian Orthodox Church. One must keep in mind that Luciani was a firm believer in Christ which meant that he believed that much of the philosophy of Communism, particularly as it pertained to a redistribution of wealth society, could be safely indoctrinated into modern civilization - something that had not happened in Russia. His enemy was Fascism, not Communism. Nicodim had met both Luciani and Cardinal Suenens quite by accident while traveling on a train from Rome to Florence in 1976. He became an important part of the plan to bring the philosophies of Christ into modern civilization. A job that Christ, Himself, had failed to accomplish in His ministry, as His alleged followers chose to embrace His great enemies - greed and bigotry.

Almost immediately, Nicodim became a powerful voice calling for the redemption of the American Christian, *"Here in my part of the world I must take my orders from the Kremlin bosses, certainly, if not at least I am at no necessity to pretend that they and I pursue the same end. For me, it is that which is told me by both my patron saint of state - Marx; and my patron saint of faith - Christ. So there is no inner conflict there for me. There is no originality in the works of Marx. His sole ambition was to make the voice of Christ a reality in a modern world. Yet, on the other side of the world, the American part of the world, the situation is much worse. There 'Christians' foolishly accept the devil's offer of the Kingdom of Heaven on the sole commitment that they fall down on their knees and worship him. Having once bred hatred of Jews and blacks and now having had that taken from them, they breed hatred of homosexuals, Muslims, atheists and others. They spit in the face of Christ and dare call themselves Christians.*

"America claims to be a free nation, yet, it deprives its citizens of the most sacred right of all - the right of privacy - the right to be left alone. It invades the bedrooms of homosexuals and imprisons them in some cases for the rest of their lives for doing nothing more than loving another human being. It invades the private homes of honest citizens and overturns card tables and trots entire families off to prison, while its holier-than-thou Christian brothers, who impose its gambling laws, openly play BINGO in church halls. It invades the private homes of mothers and fathers and takes them away from their children for long terms for doing so little as being caught with a single marijuana cigarette which couldn't kill a fly. Yet, its Christian leaders finance their elections with profits from cigarette companies which kill tens of millions. The ink was not yet dry on the Civil Rights Bill when right wing anti-black fanatics started their drug war which in the end will expand the proliferation of drugs and guns beyond anything civilization has known. The United States is now on a path toward imprisoning millions of innocent people that any other free nation in the world would treat in hospitals. America believes that the solution to social problems is to build churches and prisons rather than building schools and hospitals. And the reason it thinks this way is to keep subordinate peoples down.

"But, perhaps, what demonstrates most of all, that America is not the land that it pretends to be, is its open borders to its rich neighbor to the north versus its closed borders to its poor neighbor to the south. It dares calls itself a Christian nation, as if to say that Christ would slam the door on these poor and starving children. And even today, ignoring the fact that medical science has determined that who one falls in love with

is God's will, the deranged minds of American evangelistic parents cause thousands of homosexual teenagers to take their own lives.

"Americans also falsely claim that other most sacred freedom - freedom of religion. There, freedom of religion means the right to force ones beliefs on others. In Russia we look at it quite differently. Here, freedom of religion is the right to believe or not to believe. Yes, it has its restrictions as we are limited to practice our religion within the privacy of our homes and churches. Both Christian church bells and Muslims prayers on loud speakers that broadcast religion are banned. Also, preachers are often imprisoned for preaching hatred of any kind of people, whether it be a matter of race, creed, gender or even homosexuality.

"In America, on the other hand, church bells ring out at will carrying the message of Christianity; yet, Muslim Prayers over loudspeakers in Muslim neighborhoods are banned and violators are hauled off to prison.

"American tax laws, which grant tax exemption to wealthy churches, in themselves violate the basic concept of freedom of religion, as they impose unfair tax burdens on the non-believers. The non-believer pays in higher taxes for the believer to believe, and in many cases the believer uses his tax advantage to persecute the non-believer. It is his tax exemption that enables the preacher to purchase millions of dollars of radio and television time to spread his hatred of people who don't believe in what he has to say.

"Free? Free? Americans don't have the slightest conception of what the word means. Although we here don't pretend to have it, we at least know what we are striving for - free, to be so free as to not allow the freedom of one to impose on the freedom of another.

*"Although we too, to a far lesser extent, are guilty of some of these kinds of injustices, we being men and women of integrity do not claim to be a free state. American Christians are Pharisees - the Hypocrites that Jesus threw out of His temple - fools among fools."**

At the time, the laws concerning all of what Nicodim spoke of were more lenient in the Soviet Union than they were in the United States. For example, American laws permitted imprisonment of consenting adult homosexuals in private for sentences up to life. Although some homosexual and heterosexual acts were also illegal under Soviet statute, the laws limited imprisonment of offenders to a period of not more than three years, and the infraction had to be proved to be public and not private. In addition,

* *Leningradskaya Vecherny 17 Oct 76*

in Russia, there is no record of a gay teenager having taken his or her life, although it may have happened.

In 2003, sexual acts between consenting adults in private were decriminalized in the United States; a quarter century after Europe had led the way. The action to overturn its laws was made possible by heterosexuals who realized that many acts that they themselves were involved with in the bedroom were prohibited by state sodomy laws. Had President Clinton had his encounter with Monica in the state of Alabama instead of the District of Columbia, he would have been guilty of a felony punishable for a term not to exceed twenty years. Luckily for him the District of Columbia had no sodomy law.

the sacred right of privacy,

The Supreme Court's decision overturning state sodomy laws which legalized sexual acts between consenting adults in private was a milestone event in the history of mankind.

The ***sacred right of privacy*** had been a freedom in post-Christian Russia from the time of Lenin; it had been a freedom in the Mid East until the seventh century when Mohammed incorporated some of what Moses had to say concerning sex into his Koran; it had been a freedom in the pre-Christian Roman Empire; it had been a freedom in the Greek Empire; it had been a freedom in the Egyptian Empire dating back to 3100BC; it had been a freedom in China and India from the beginning of time; it had been a freedom - which had been temporarily taken away from them by Christianity - in all primitive societies that survived unscathed into the twentieth century, including the African tribes to the south and the Eskimos to the north; and it had been a freedom in the days of the Cro-Magnon Man.

Of all the scriptures of the world, only the God of Moses declares sex to be sinful and evil - the most prolific and powerful message of the Old Testament. Of all the men that ever lived only Moses and his mindless followers believed that the way God makes babies is evil - is the work of the devil. All other scriptures of the world including those of the Hindu God Brahma, Buddha, Tao and the various gods of the Egyptians, Greeks and Romans all believed - without exception - that sex is good and beautiful - a gift from God.

Today, no issue divides church from state more decisively. The Christian Bible continues to hold that all sex is sinful and evil - the work of Satan; while the state has made the rounds and has now returned to the days of Pharaoh and Buddha and Tao - back to the days of the caveman - when sex was believed to be a gift from God.

two cups of coffee and few almond cookies,

On the morning of September 5, 1978, Metropolitan Nicodim was led by Mother Vincenza into the Pope's private quarters. This was quite unusual as the Pope normally met with visiting dignitaries in his public offices. Sister Vincenza carried with her a tray bearing two cups of coffee and a few almond cookies. Later the Pope told the press, "*After Sister Vincenza had left the room and closed the door, the Metropolitan reached for one of the cups and lifting it to his lips found it to be too hot and returned it to the table. He then fell forward onto the table dead.*" *

It may be, of course, that the Pope told the press that Nicodim had not tasted the coffee in order to quell rumors. But whether or not the Pope had told the press the truth or not is immaterial for we have yet another man of extraordinarily good health suddenly dropping dead of an alleged heart attack. Nicodim was a marathon runner and had just that past spring completed an event placing third in his class. His body was returned to Leningrad the same day and because of the Pope's testimony the Russians never performed an autopsy.

Despite John Paul's statement to the press, rumors spread throughout Italy that the *poisoned cup* had been intended for the Pope. As we shall see in Part II of this book, if the coffee had indeed been laced with cyanide or a similar lethal toxin and had it been steaming it would have had the same effect as would a cyanide capsule, which vapors result in immediate paralysis and death. On the other hand, had Nicodim actually tasted the coffee, it could not have killed him this quickly as there is no poison when ingested that kills one instantly. Unfortunately, the cups were washed before the rumors had surfaced. Nevertheless, it is a strange coincidence that the Pope, himself, would die just a few days later of identical symptoms, as if he had bitten down on a cyanide capsule.

The Metropolitan had been summoned to Rome to head up a new venture that would be responsible for changing the economic psychology of the western world, which was at the time and still is today driven by Christ's number one enemy - greed. His job would be to change it into a world of helping others. The Metropolitan would work side-by-side with

* *Osservatore del Romano 6 Sep 78*

John Paul to achieve their mutual goal - to bring western civilization away from the greed and bigotry of God the Father of the Old Testament and closer to Christ.

The arrangement was to be twofold. John Paul would set the example by liquidating the Vatican treasures, perhaps going so far as to turn Vatican City over to real estate developers for tens of billions of dollars and moving to modest quarters in the countryside. Then Nicodim would follow with his part of the plan - to change the psychology of the world by converting modern day Christians from the hypocrites they are into more compassionate human beings - into Christ-like human beings. That each time one would come to the fork in the road, one would no longer ask oneself, *"Now, what is in this for me?"* but rather one would ask oneself, *"Now, what is in this for others?* A horror worse than death for today's Christians. A monstrous job, yet one that Nicodim was both physically and mentally equipped to carry out. That is, before he dropped dead.

It was the sudden death of Nicodim that caused some authors who later wrote about the Pope's death to implicate the American and British intelligence agencies in foul play. Certainly, a capitalistic society thrives on greed and it would not be in the best interests of these countries to have the most influential man in the western world preaching a redistribution of wealth society. There are at least two holes in this theory. It is doubtful that these agencies could have acted this quickly as Luciani was only two weeks into his papacy; one that he was not expected to win by even his most loyal *left wing* supporters. But what nails the lid shut on this theory is that Jimmy Carter was president at the time, and he would have welcomed a more compassionate society. Had it happened today, where America has a president who himself is driven by greed - whose every move is to make the rich richer and the poor poorer, any court in the world would have indicted him for the murder of John Paul I.

a few near misses,

Nicodim's demise was closely followed by an announcement by Belgium radio that the closest friend and advisor of John Paul, Cardinal Suenens, had been killed by a falling section of an aging building façade in Brussels. The radio report, which was based on eyewitnesses of the event, was premature.[1] It had, in fact, been a visiting French bishop that had been killed. It had undoubtedly been that it occurred near the cardinal's palace

[1] *Le Soir Brussels 16 Sep 78*

and that the bishop was wearing black garb topped off with a red zucchetto that caused witnesses to mistake him for the cardinal. Of course, if this was true, that witnesses on the ground made such a misjudgment, then it would have been likely that anyone on the roof of the building would have made the same mistake.

Nevertheless, the incident went without much notice until the following month when Cardinal Suenens, himself, barely escaped death in identical fashion when a small section of a frieze fell from a Vatican building narrowly missing him by inches.[2] Although most of the Vatican buildings are aging, this is extremely rare, as the facades are routinely checked for defects to protect the tourists that roam Vatican City. A couple of months following this incident he had another close brush with death when a companion threw him to the ground in avoiding an onrushing car in Brussels. The hospital reported that the cardinal suffered a slight concussion in the mishap.[3]

There is nothing in the record to prove that any or all of these incidents were indeed attempts on the cardinal's life. Yet, it was quite obvious that the cardinal, himself, sensed that he was in danger as he was never seen again in public without two young priests, who could easily be mistaken for football players - clearly serving as bodyguards. He also moved his office from the first floor of the cardinal's palace in Brussels to the third floor. A move that was unnecessary, as just two weeks after the last failed attempt on his life, John Paul II removed him from his position of power as Primate of Belgium. No longer with his pastoral influence, Cardinal Leon Joseph Suenens was as good as dead!

the cause of death,

And there is one other strange thing concerning Luciani's death. There is normally a likely possibility that a pope will eventually be elevated to sainthood as two-thirds of them have already been named saints. Therefore, historically, no pope in the past thousand years has gone to his tomb intact. That is, a part of the body has been removed for use as a possible relic in the event the Pope is declared a saint. The Vatican maintains an inventory of these parts. Traditionally a tongue, jawbone, vocal chords, a hand or a foot was removed, although in more recent history, less grotesque operations were performed. But, nevertheless they have all left something behind. Even John XXIII lost a finger. For some

[2] *Il Messaggero 18 Oct 78*
[3] *Le Soir Brussels 6 Jan 79*

strange reason this was not true of Luciani. Today he lies in one piece in his tomb, unless, of course, his sister was wrong in her evaluation of the lock of hair that she received. Thus no DNA exists today outside of his tomb.

Notwithstanding all of this, there exists proof beyond a shadow of a doubt that this good man was murdered. And there is also sufficient evidence to determine just how he was murdered. For unlike those who have gone before me, I have the proof!

Yet, I leave the prize up to you: the question as to just who murdered him. Yes, I will offer my own conclusions but I leave the door open to you. I will say nothing here that has not been said before, either in the press or in the official writings and biographies of the many players in this strange story of fate. All that is to my credit is that the full record, for the very first time, will have been brought together in one place. I am hopeful only that in bringing these things together that someone else, someone with great analytical abilities will surface as the *Sherlock Holmes* of the case, will take it a step further, will strike upon the solution to this now long unsolved mystery. This strange chain of events which caused three men within the relative short span of forty days to sleep in the great bed in the Papal Apartment in Rome, the mysterious death of John Paul, and as we shall see in what follows, some others.

After several years of research and investigation I have come up with a number of scenarios for you to pick from. Scenarios as to what actually happened that fateful night in September of 1978. Yes, versus all the other authors of intrigue who have come before me I have the great advantage of time. The time it took for other things to happen, that other journalists were not aware of at the time that they wrote their efforts. And I also have the memory of that time now so long ago in Vittorio Veneto that I am about to tell you of. So one can say that this has been unfair of me, that I have withheld some of the pieces of the puzzle from the others these many years. But, nevertheless, I am certain that I have the answer for you here.

And, yes, there is one more thing. I will answer several other questions you might have. For example, how is it possible that the very same *College of Cardinals* who had elected an ultraliberal in one month turned around and elected an ultraconservative in the very next month? And the question is not so much as to how Karol Wojtyla of Poland won the papacy in the second conclave, but rather it is one of how was it possible that Albino Luciani won the election in the first conclave of nineteen hundred and seventy eight, for after all, the *College of Cardinals* was overwhelmingly conservative.

And I will also talk of many other things. For example, consider the baby pigeons. Baby pigeons? Yes, why there are no baby pigeons? One knows that dogs come from puppies and cats come from kittens and cows come from calves and sheep come from lambs and chickens come from chicks and ducks come from ducklings.

But just where do pigeons come from? Or perhaps you have never noticed? You never wondered why in all of your life you have never seen a baby pigeon? Go to Saint Peter's Square in Rome or for that matter any of the grand piazzas in Europe or the great parks of America and you will see tens of thousands of pigeons and not a baby pigeon among them.

What's that? You believe that they must be somewhere else? Well, go and try and find them and you will find that they are not there. And I will prove that they are not there. For pigeons, among all of God's creation, come from somewhere else.

So I have some answers for you here. And among these is the answer to the greatest mystery of all. Something that, like the baby pigeons, you always assumed was somewhere else. Something that from day-to-day you could not see but something that nevertheless you always assumed was there. And, as in the case of the pigeons, I will prove that it is not so.

So let us go back to that time now so very long ago when I had first visited the remote mountain province of Vittorio Veneto. Back to that time when I first met this man called 'Piccolo'.

Chapter 3

THE LUCIANI EXPEDITION INTO EGYPT

the spring of 1969,

It was an exact point in time, the first day of spring; that day on which the sun rests directly over the equator; that day on which all over creation the sun rises due east and sets due west and day and night end in a dead heat in time.

The Boeing 707 rose slowly out of Kennedy and started out over the New York harbor before banking to the left and heading in its intended direction. As it made its turn, I looked down at that grand lady *who lifts her lamp by the golden door* and wondered how she ever came about. After all, we were a Christian nation, our forefathers; every one of them was a Christian. Of those who had signed the Declaration of Independence, there wasn't a single black, not a single Jew, not a single gay, not even a woman among them. At least I didn't think so. It seemed to me that a towering figure of Christ would be more appropriate here at these great gates to what was, indeed, the *Promised Land.*

In all of Europe I knew only one person. That is, I probably knew others but I didn't know where they were. But this particular one I had always kept in touch with. He had been one of my rivals back in high school in my run for the roses, one of those people I just had to beat out in life. His name was Jack Champney. He was much smarter than I was. His problem was that he didn't know it. He thought that I was much smarter than he was. He had gathered this opinion from how well I had done in high school; that I could keep pace with him all the way down the stretch only to lose him at the wire. He had no idea how much harder I had to work for what I got than he did. For him winning the race was like Frank Sinatra singing "My Way" -almost effortless.

And he had won the race going away. I was just another student in the crowd of several thousand when I watched him take the stand on graduation day. And on this day fifteen years later I couldn't remember a single thing that he had said. And vainly I thought, "If it had been me, today all that had been privileged to listen would remember everything, every single word I said."

And as the plane started to take down the time zones, I thought back to graduation day...

> *. . . that day they were all wearing blue blazers. Usually it was only me. Day after day, year after year, it had only been me. The*

others in sweaters, blue jeans, sneakers, whatever they laid their hands on when they got up in the morning. They used to call me 'pretty boy' – 'momma's boy.' Then one day one of them called me a 'pansy.' That's the day they found out that my small fists could hit and that my feet could kick. And sooner or later they learned that my help with their homework made the difference between honors and failure. So, although I had made a run for it, I didn't come in first or even second, but, nevertheless, when the wreaths were passed out I took home with me the ones that were labeled Catechism, Mathematics and History. And what's more, the yearbook caption along side my picture read, "most likely to become a cardinal of the Church."

Well, I was never to become a cardinal of the Church, for when the V in the road came up, Jack took the path that said *Christ* and I took the one that said *Money.* I went off to the world of business; where with him out of the way I would have less trouble reaping the roses. He went on to attend Holy Cross where he once again took the honors and then began to work toward becoming a very special kind of priest. He took his doctorate in psychiatry at Johns Hopkins and registered as a licensed psychiatrist. His aim, made clear in his letters to me, was to become a member of the Catholic Church's *Commission on Spiritual Events*. The commission, overseen by a panel of cardinals, was the Vatican's investigative unit for apparitions, exorcisms, miracles, and other spiritual claims or happenings.

In his last letter to me he had mentioned that he had been assigned as a secretary for a bishop who was a member of this commission; a nice stepping stone for him on his way to the Vatican. The little known bishop oversaw a small diocese in the mountains of northern Italy. The cathedral, together with the bishop's residence, was located in the remote town of Vittorio Veneto. And just two weeks later I had found my way across all of Europe to Italy.

Milan,

During that time I witnessed the great splendor of Christianity. As I crossed Europe, I must have set the world record for visiting churches, including most of Europe's largest. Because it was too far out of my way, I had to skip Seville. But the others, all the others, from the majestic dome of St. Paul's; the great stone claws grasping at Notre Dame; the magnificent leaded glass windows of Chartres; the ashen wedding cake towers of Cologne and now finally the great Cathedral of Milan with its threatening weather beaten gargoyles oxidized by time, guarding the great square which lay before it; Milan's playground of princes and paupers.

I marveled at them all. I relished them all. But it wasn't these great edifices that impressed me the most. It was something else, something that I would find here in Milan, something that I would stumble onto quite by accident - something that I would carry with me all of the days of my life.

Besides its great cathedral and its great square, Milan has a third great treasure, something that most tourists never hear about; the city's great park of the dead. There you can see it all, every bit of yesterday.

As I entered the cemetery I sort of became a part of it all. All was quiet. The only sound was my footsteps and, perhaps, the breath of a slight breeze. The sky was foreboding as if it were a good day for a funeral. Had there been a lake, and there was none, it would have held dark waters as there was not a thing in the sky to give it life. It seemed that all of the living had forgotten all of the dead. I was alone, alone as one could be.

And it wasn't long before I began to realize that I was wandering in the world's greatest metropolis of the departed. Endless lines of mansions of marble, bronze, glass and some even of gold. Thousands of them. There seemed to be more marble and granite houses in this land of the dead than there seemed to be houses outside in the land of the living, and each one different - so as to command the undivided attention of its own artist, its own architect, its own engineer.

And the sculptures, mostly in marble and granite, but here and there among them, one or two of some precious metal and some even studded with jewels; each arrangement sending a different message, each one befitting *a prince - no, a king – no, a god.* Collectively they echoed of immense wealth. "No wonder they lost the war," I thought, "they had all their money tied up in monuments."

And nowhere could a single flower be found - as if to insure that the beauty of God's creation not overpower these great works of man. There was only the green grass that worked its way like a maze in and out and around and about these great dwellings and monuments of the dead.

And, finally, I turned a corner and proceeded down what appeared to me to be the main boulevard of this great city of death. Flanked on either side by mausoleums of magnificent grandeur, some sealed up like the tombs that they were and many others showing off their merchandise. Through ornate iron grates, one could glimpse the sarcophagi themselves. Some of marble, others of bronze, and a few of gold and yes, -even one of glass. And silence, yes silence all around, as not to wake those that were sleeping there.

As I came to the end of the avenue, I turned the corner and suddenly stopped dead in my tracks. Not *dead* dead, but dead in my tracks. For there just to my left, were a half dozen or so simple, tiny, matching white granite stones. Set in a row on a blanket of green grass, which lay before a matching manicured hedge of green bushes, the power of their simplicity seemed to eclipse the grandeur of all that was about them.

On each stone was carved a heart and within each heart a likeness of George Washington. "The Purple Heart," I thought to myself, and I thought something else, "For here was the real reason why 'they' had lost the war."

Approaching closer with all the solemnity that the moment commanded, I could feel the whir of the breeze; hear the faint sound of the bugle followed by the hallowed roll of the drums and, finally the distant echo of the roar of the cannon. And a spot of light peeked through the overcast sky as if to mark this moment in time. As to give one light to read,

Guy Beene, First Sergeant †
1921-1944
7th Army, 1st Battalion, A Company
Congressional Medal of Honor

Mike Tyminski, Pvt. †
1925-1944
7th Army, 1st Battalion, A Company
Bronze Star

Jerome Rosenberg, 2nd Lt. 3/4
1919-1944
7th Army, 4th Battalion, A Company
Silver Star

Brian Pickering, Pvt. †
1924-1944
7th Army, 3rd Battalion, B Company
Bronze Star

Anthony Jackson, Corporal
1922-1944
7th Army, 1st Battalion, A Company
Bronze Star

Patricia Wilde, 1st Lt.
1919-1944
Army Medical Corps
Bronze Star

It didn't say it, but I clearly heard it, *"That they shall not have died in vain."* And one of those things one calls a tear crept up out of my heart and ran from the corner of my eye and crept toward its lid; and I looked first to the right, and then to the left, and then again to the right, and finally to the left once more. And holding the tear on the edge of my lid, I said to them, speaking as if I were a great orator of some kind, *"Not Thomas Paine with his pen, nor Patrick Henry with his eloquence, nor Paul Revere with his horse, nor Washington and Jefferson with all their courage, not even Lincoln at Gettysburg have spoken louder. For you have made more noise for freedom than all the others who have gone before you or have come after you. And believe me; I pledge to you this day, to each and every one of you, that each and every one of you, will not have died in vain!"*

And I have carried that pledge, that sacred duty with me all of my life. I have carried it every day, every hour, every minute of my life. I have carried it in my mind, and in my heart, and in my being, and in my very soul. And now it is time to carry out that solemn promise, to answer that fervent prayer. Yes, to carry it out for each and every one of them. That what they dreamed of - those things that were to be, will come to be for each of them, and for me, and for you, and for all humanity!"

Vittorio Veneto,

The next morning I took the train to Venice and it was from there that I took the train to Vittorio Veneto.

Exiting the station, I did exactly what Jack had told me to do. I took the first right, and then the first left, and again the first right, and finally the first left once more. And I stood in front of what appeared to be an old southern hotel. A southern hotel surrounded by an aging amber stucco wall eight or nine feet high, -there in the most northern part of Italy. It was of the same light shade of amber as had been most every other building that I passed on the way. And like most of the others, it too and even its wall, was topped with one of those terra cotta tiled roofs that sprawl over so many Italian villages.

I again followed Jack's instructions and pounded with both my fists as loud and as heavy on the great wooden door as I possibly could. Off in the distance I heard footsteps on wooden steps, and then they seemed to have reached firmness for awhile, and then again on wooden steps, and finally firmness once more. Then the juggling and clattering of the unlocking of the door and standing before me was a little old lady who looked as if she had just stepped out of an Italian motion picture of some sort.

And she said, "You must be Lucien. Jack has told me all about you. We have a very special place for you." I followed her into a small reception area where I filled out a registration card and surrendered my passport. I asked her for directions to the bishop's castle and then found my way to my room, which window looked out onto a canal that ran behind the hotel. I freshened up a bit and then headed back out onto the street.

As I made my way from the hotel, I passed over a small ancient stone bridge and found myself channeled down a long, narrow street hemmed in on both sides by stucco houses of all different shapes and sizes. And the stucco was, again, mostly of the same amber color and was in a general state of disrepair. It was as if I was to see a green house or a blue house or a yellow house, I would remember it all of my days. As I looked up I could see the edges of the roofs framing the blue sky, every one of deep orange terra cotta tile. On the edge of the town I entered into a tunnel that had been carved into an ancient fortress, and at the end of the tunnel I stepped out into medieval times, -an ancient twelfth century plaza. I sensed that Romeo and Juliet might be interred nearby.

Unlike the rest of the town, where stucco had been the tradesman's craft, here the buildings were entirely built of large blocks of stone. As a matter of fact all of the ground was stone. And the stone had been bleached through time to almost a stark white. The tatter and wear of the ages had gone unrepaired. As the woman in the hotel had told me, -the cathedral overpowered the scene from the far end of the plaza. Kitty corner to its left, partway up a mountain, was what I presumed to be the bishop's castle, a medieval group of turret-topped towers of which only the tallest had survived intact.

author's collection

the ruins of the bishop's castle (upper left) peers out over Vittorio Veneto

As I made my way toward the cathedral I passed a large fountain on my left, a giant stone trough with lions and gargoyles set into its backdrop wall, strewing water into the pool in front of them. There were a few statues of men and women, here and there set into arched niches in the surrounding buildings. And there were many more arches that through time had lost their inhabitants.

author's collection

arched niches

On three sides of everything I could see rose the Dolomite Mountains. Cliffs engulfed the town like a giant horseshoe; a bit of the medieval ages trapped in a rocky gorge. Midway into the plaza, I noticed a line of large, yellowing stucco buildings of more recent vintage down a street to one side. "Some kind of a college," I thought to myself.

Suddenly, out of nowhere, a man came running toward me wearing a tank top and running shorts and he both smiled and waved as he passed. He wore a large colorful caricature of Minnie Mouse on his chest. I sensed that he must have been about fifty, and I was surprised that the recent jogging fad in the states had reached this remote part of Europe.

At the same instant great bells rang out. Not in a rhythmic sort of way, but in a clanging sort of way, as if they did not want anyone to know what they had to say. The old church was of the identical washed-out color of its surroundings. Its nave was completely out of balance with its tower, as if they had run out of money in the middle ages, when I guessed the building had been built. And the steps told me something else. They started a hundred feet from the church and were as wide as the church itself, and tapered up a flight of forty or so steps to the massive wooden doors of the great edifice. I looked for the wheelchair ramp and saw none. And I thought of Moses' instruction in Leviticus, '*Whosoever he be of thy seed that hath any blemish, a blind man, or a lame man, or anything superfluous shall not approach the altar of his God.*' I thought, "They sure followed his orders in those days."

Then I started along a cobblestone road that was hemmed in by walls on either side. It ran up along side the mountain road toward the castle and I must have climbed for at least an hour or so before I reached the castle gate. Exhausted, I entered through what appeared to be the original castle entrance into a small courtyard. A fountain, not unlike several that I had passed on the way, was set in the center of the courtyard and water was splashing over its edges out onto the courtyard floor, and was running down toward and around me out of the castle gates. Off to one side was an old beat-up car of 40's vintage. The bishop's house itself was of beige stucco and was set within the castle ruins. Its focal point was a grand symmetrical staircase, one set of stairs leading up to a landing from the *left* and another leading up to the same landing from the *right*. Jack stood there and I decided to take the stairs on the *left*.

author's collection

the bishop's castle at Vittorio Veneto hemmed in by castle ruins

We got the usual "hellos" and the "boy, you don't look a day older" out of the way quickly and I said, "I see you don't have an age limit on runners here. I almost got run over down there," and I mentioned the older man who had run past me in the church plaza. And Jack replied, "That was the boss, he turns in a few miles every morning. He was brought up on the other side of the tracks and damn near starved to death as a kid. So, having been a frail child, he developed himself into quite an athlete as a teenager. And he still keeps himself in very good shape. He enters every 10K that comes up and usually wins in his class. If you had showed up a couple of weeks from now instead of today he would take you up a mountain or two with him. He's an accomplished mountain climber and holds the speed record for several peaks in Northern Italy. When he comes back, I'll introduce you to him, but you won't see much of him until dinnertime, as he has to go into Venice today. Let's go inside. I'll show you my little corner of the world."

He pulled back the large wooden door; the heavy leaded glass panels protected by iron lattice work required the strength of both arms. We entered a large open area, the reception area of the house. Definitive paths had been worn into the ancient stone floor and one could make out just exactly where people had walked through the ages. There was nothing there at all. That is, there wasn't a single piece of furniture. Just open space leading to a great, colorless, leaded glass widow at its end that I correctly guessed overlooked the town.

Today, this room is an impressive introduction to the house; its walls are now lined with beautifully framed life sized oil portraits of the more than a dozen bishops who have lived there in the twentieth century. At the far end of the room, the portrait of Albino Luciani, the only bishop of the Veneto country to have risen to the papacy, is hidden behind a door that leads to a small chapel on the left - what is probably better described as a prayer station. Actually, the hand painted arched ceiling contains the record of more than eighty bishops who have served in Vittorio Veneto since the 8th century, each one represented by his coat of arms and period of reign.

author's collection

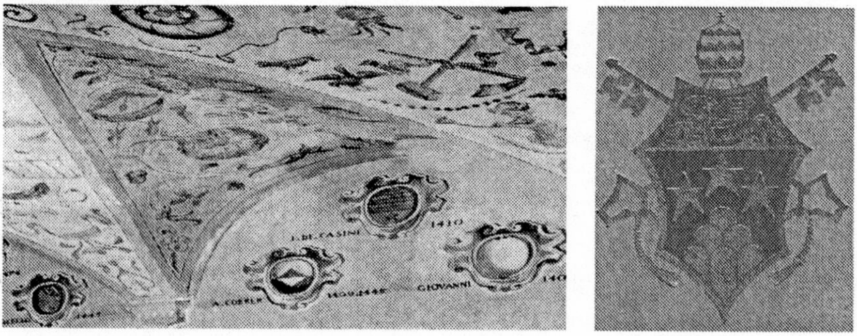

left: the arched ceiling in the bishop's castle. right: Luciani's coat of arms: the foreground represents the six Dolomite mountain peaks for which he held the speed record; the three stars represent faith, hope and charity; the lion represents courage; when the hyena pack comes, the lioness will defend her cubs to the end although it means certain death. The sheep on the other hand will run for her life and leave her lambs behind. "Don't fool yourself, Christ is a God for Lions," he once told his congregation, "He has no room for sheep."

The trappings of the room I speak of herein as the bishop's office have since been moved to a monastery. Today, off to the right is a succession of four large rooms of equal size, each one leading to the next. The ceilings of these rooms today are covered with richly carved mahogany panels that have the appearance of upside down parquet flooring. And the flooring itself is now a mottled marble. The modernization has left the walls a stark white.

The first of these rooms is a large reception room furnished in rich Italian provincial furniture with conversation areas at each end. This reception room leads in turn to the secretary's office, which today is quite modern in appearance, including a copy machine off to one side and a computer set on a modern desk. This room in turn leads to another reception room, again overloaded with Italian provincial furniture, which in turn leads to the bishop's office.

There is one piece of furniture in the house that today is a focal point of history, a small glass fronted curio cabinet that contains a few of the Pope's personal items, the only record of his life other than his tomb that remains in the Church today; a small prayer book, his rosary beads, his red bishop's cap, and a few other items. All in all today, the bishop's castle is a house of magnificent splendor, but at the time of my first visit just thirty-five years ago, except for the arched painted ceiling in the main reception area, things were quite different.

Jack took me to the far end of the entrance hall and we entered what can best be described as an alcove, -his little corner of the world. And a very little corner it was. The office was tiny. I visualized my own office back in the states overlooking the marina at the corporate headquarters of the company in which I was rapidly making my way up the ladder. "I was certainly winning this race," I thought to myself.

The windowless room was as bare as it was small and clashed with the rich green, black and white marble terrazzo flooring, which instead of giving it the feeling of the wealth which it reflected, gave it a feeling of coldness. It was quite obvious that the flooring here was not original, that it had been added to the house in more recent times. Most of the opposite wall was made up by the room's centerpiece, a finely carved mahogany door set in an archway, which I presumed to be the door to the bishop's office. The unbroken line of the yellowing wall was interrupted only by this door and a small bargain basement crucifix above it and a cheaply framed photograph of Pope John XXIII on the wall behind the desk, which was more of an old wooden slab on legs than it was a desk. And yes, one of those cheap souvenir alpine clocks on the opposite wall. A message seemed to be written on the photograph, and approaching it, I read,

"*Albino Luciani,*

Christ has asked me to express His very personal congratulations on this very important day in your life."

The message had been signed by John XXIII and was dated 28 Dec '58.

"It's a copy," Jack offered. "The original is in his bedroom drawer. It was given to the man who occupies the adjoining cell," glancing at the richly carved mahogany door, "when he was raised to the rank of bishop. Piccolo was the first bishop installed by John XXIII and the ceremony took place in St. Peter's." I was struck by Jack's reference to the bishop as 'Piccolo' and, at the same time, by the yodeling of a little nun who ran out of the alpine clock on the opposite wall. Sensing my shock at the sparseness of his *little corner of the world* he offered, "Blessed are the poor, for theirs is the Kingdom of Heaven," and he laughed.

"Shortly after becoming Pope, John XXIII, attracted by Piccolo's many editorials attacking his predecessor Pius XII, visited Belluno where Piccolo was serving as Vicar-General, and recognized his potential. When John indicated that he intended to elevate him to the rank of bishop, Piccolo objected quite vigorously, citing the fact that he was a poor speaker and would be an embarrassment to *Mother Church.* Actually, he told me that the real reason he objected to the appointment was that he was scared to death to speak before large or important congregations. He thought for sure that he would freeze up.

"And although Piccolo did not tell him this, John surmised it. Not letting on that he was aware of this great hurdle which Piccolo felt that in his shyness he could never jump, John started secretly working on his training program. Working through intermediaries, he set Piccolo up on a series of increasingly important speaking assignments in small parishes, and finally he tricked him into his big test."

"His big test?" I repeated his statement in a question.

"Yes, his big test," he replied. "Cardinal Colombo, the Archbishop of Milan at the time, was to address members of the *College of Cardinals* and other Church dignitaries in the Sistine Chapel in Rome. The cardinal called Piccolo to Milan, where he had him write a speech for him. The address was to be heavily steeped in nineteenth century theology, something in which Piccolo excelled.

"Cardinal Colombo then asked Piccolo to accompany him to Rome to help guide him in his rehearsals for his upcoming address. On the day on which he was to speak, the cardinal suddenly fell ill - at least that's what Piccolo was told, and Piccolo being the only logical understudy, was faced with three options: he could resign the priesthood; he could feign illness; or he could try. The boss tells me it was the most difficult decision he was to make up to that point in his life.

"He told me that he realized that he had been set up when halfway through his address he saw the Pope, who was sitting in a darkened corner of the chamber, wink his approval to the cardinal who sat beside him, -Cardinal Colombo, the one he had presumably replaced. '*John was the angel who took me to the pinnacle and taught me to fly. I remember, clearly,*' Piccolo recalls, '*as if it were just yesterday . . .*

. . .and, the angel took me to the pinnacle of the mountain, and like a father condor teaching his baby chick to fly commanded that I COME TO THE EDGE OF THE CLIFF, and I refused saying "I'll fall"; and then he repeated his command in a louder voice COME TO THE EDGE and I again responding in a weaker voice "no, I'll fall"; and finally in a roar of thunder he repeated COME TO THE EDGE, and with all the courage I could possible muster, I went to the edge, and he pushed me, and I flew!'

"After Piccolo came down from the podium, John XXIII approached him and asked him, '*Do I now have your permission to elevate you to your ecclesiastical destiny? Do I now have your permission to make it possible that you can better make the contribution that Christ requires of you?*" And Albino Luciani was installed as Bishop of Vittorio Veneto the following week. His first words to his newly acquired congregation recalled his impoverished days as a child, '*Christ picked me up from the mud in the street and gave me to you.*' His will requires that these words be carved on the plain pine box in which he will someday be interred.

"Actually, Piccolo told me that he didn't give the speech that he had written for the cardinal at all. Instead he told them, '*Our great enemy is the bigot who lives within each one of us. His ally is scripture. Our ally is conscience . . .*'"

And I quickly cut him off, "'*His ally is Moses. Our ally is Christ. And as long as he exists no man is truly free. . . And believe me all the bigot has are words, flimsy words, Flimsy arrows that he thinks will win for him. Flimsy arrows built in an ancient factory.*'"

Jack who had been stopped dead in his tracks by my dissertation exclaimed, "Good, you've done your homework. It will help you in your mission."

"My mission?" I questioned.

"We will get to that later," he replied. We continued to chat for awhile and he had just mentioned that the bishop must have run off to Venice already, ". . . but you will meet him at dinner tonight. He has been looking forward to meeting you," when suddenly, at the outer doorway stood a man of about fifty, the man who had run past me in the park. This time he was clad in an Hawaiian shirt, shorts and sandals. His wet hair evidenced that he had just come out of the shower. Two things struck me, his smiling countenance, and the other was his toes. I never thought of bishops as having toes, especially toes that were as perfectly pedicured as these were. I wondered if the nearby convent provided this service for free to bishops, a service that when I splurged for it cost me fifty bucks a throw back in the states. And yes, a third thing struck me - his voice, as he introduced himself as the man next door.

The voice was a piping, rasping voice. Not as if he was talking through his nose, but as if the pipe was built into his throat. It was a one-of-a-kind voice. And it was this that made it relatively easy for me to follow what otherwise would have been his heavily Italian-accented and somewhat broken English. Realizing that I had been caught off guard, I had forgotten the title that one uses when one addresses a bishop of the Church and I said, "I apologize, I forget what I'm supposed to call you?" And the bishop replied, "Just call me the same thing everyone else calls me, 'Piccolo'." And to this day I have never forgotten Piccolo, partially because of his one-of-a-kind voice and unrelenting and charismatic smile, but mostly because of his toes.

After a very brief chat he said, "I must go, for the thief of the ages is knocking at my door."

And turning toward Jack, I asked quietly, "Did you hear someone knock?"

And the Bishop of Vittorio Veneto laughed and interrupted me,

"*Time. Time is knocking. And time is a thief. For it will rob one of one's childhood, eventually deprive one of one's youth and ultimately take one's life. But it is a good thief. For it provides the span of wonderment for the child, the term of enlightenment while he grows and the age of fulfillment as he gives.*" *

Then he added, "And my time to give is near." And he was off.

"Kind of a piercing voice, huh?" Jack offered, noticing that I had reacted to the bishop's voice with a start. "Actually it was at the ground roots of his fear of public speaking. When he was a teenager Piccolo had a tonsillectomy that went haywire and left him with his uniquely thin, raspy voice; a handicap which John, as I just mentioned, cured with one of his miracles."

blessed are the poor,

"Anyway," he said getting up from his chair, "I might as well show you where the boss spends his time dreaming up the next chapter of events for this sprawling paradise here in the foothills of the great Dolomite

**Luciani originally said this in a eulogy to John XXIII in the Basilica de San Marco in Venice in 1963*

Alps." Rising, he moved toward the great mahogany door and opening it, we proceeded in.

The office could not have been more impressive and my heart sank a little as I thought of my relatively modest surroundings back in the states. I also thought of the tax-free exemption status of the Roman Catholic Church. Yes, the rich marble terrazzo flooring continued into the room, but here it was not out of place. The walls were mahogany; that is, ornately carved mahogany edged in gold. In each of what must have been thirty or forty panels that surrounded the room stood a life-sized beautifully painted angel in Byzantine fashion. Each one was different in both color and dress and each one was embroidered in silver and gold, and each one was armed, and each one sported a halo of golden leaf.

In addition to their protective presence they seemed to be listening, as if all that would be said within these walls would be related to the one above; kind of doing the same job here, as the tapes were doing in the Oval Office some four thousand miles away. Two more life-sized angels, these in three dimensions and of white marble, guarded the huge walk-in fireplace. Just above the mantel was mounted what was obviously meant to be the focal point of the room - an old well weathered oil painting of Christ driving the moneylenders out of His Father's temple. Its dark tones were accented by the brilliance of the golden coins as they cascaded from the tables and seemed to be splashing out of the painting itself - out beyond its overdone, heavily encrusted, golden frame. It seemed reminiscent of Rembrandt himself.

And Jack, noticing that I was appraising the painting, offered, "No, not Rembrandt. It's by Titian. This is Titian country. Some of his best works are in Vittorio Veneto. His masterpiece is the altarpiece in the cathedral you passed on the way. Piccolo put this one here to remind us that Christ too had to deal with the *republicans*. He says this is proof, proof in the scriptures themselves, that the *republicans* trace their roots back to Christ; that is to the time of Christ."

The room was divided down the middle by a low altar railing with twisted golden columns built into a mahogany framework. On one side of the room was kind of a boardroom with a huge coffin shaped mahogany table edged with gargoyles and cherubs. Two rather wide Persian carpet runners lay along each side of the table. They were of a kind so plush that if one didn't take notice one would easily trip over them. On them sat a dozen richly embroidered chairs with matching mahogany gargoyles shooting out of their arms. There were six on each side of the table. There were no chairs at the table's ends, as if one end were reserved for the invisible presence of Christ and the other end reserved for God the Father.

And as I looked up there was a beautifully hand painted ceiling with coat-of arms in its arched niches, the only part of the room that survives today.

On the other side of the great room was the bishop's personal work and reception area with an elegant sofa in Italian provincial, and a low matching coffee table and armchairs. A grand kidney-shaped and ornately carved desk with neatly arranged writing and blotting instruments sat before a stark red heavily brocaded wall. I took particular notice that there were no papers on the desk. As a matter of fact the whole room seemed to be set for display in a museum rather than set up as a workplace.

On the wall just behind the desk, the only break in the perimeter walls of the room other than the door in which angels did not stand, were two relatively recent life-sized oil paintings. The matching simplicity of their relatively inexpensive modern frames clashed with the ornate antiqueness and the wealth that was all about them; one of the reigning pontiff, Paul VI; and the other of his predecessor, John XXIII. Jack walked to the desk and with a kind of athletic curl rolled himself into the large leather chair. Opposite were two pairs of rather large French windows of relatively recent vintage which overlooked the courtyard outside.

Suddenly, the somber setting came to life with the chiming of the quarter-hour. Off to one side was a massive grandfather clock that reached upward toward the ceiling. The ceilings must have approached sixteen feet in height and glancing back at the door and then to the windows I wondered how one ever got a clock of such massive proportions into the room. "It's really a great, great, great, great, great, great grandfather clock," Jack offered. And rising from his chair, he took me to the side of the clock and there, arranged one after another, were four aging brass plates,

Guiseppe Valdini	1621-1639
Medici Palace	1640-1769
Papal Apartment	1770-1879
Vittorio Veneto	1879-

"It was designed and crafted by Valdini, an Italian craftsman living in Switzerland in the seventeenth century. Valdini's clocks normally fetch more than a quarter-million dollars and, on occasion, a half-million.

"It was given to the diocese when Leo XIII visited here late in the nineteenth century to celebrate the establishment of the seminary. The rest of the contents of the room including its paneling, its ceiling and mantelpiece came out of an old monastery that rose on a mountain just north of Naples. It was moved here to Vittorio Veneto as a protective measure when the allies reached Sicily in the Second World War and it had become imminent that they would take Italy. The Pope felt that the allies might destroy it. And he was right as they bombed the hell out of it, mistakenly thinking that it was being used as an Axis headquarters."

Summing up what I had just witnessed, I thought, "*Blessed are the poor for theirs is the Kingdom of Heaven,*" but I thought it would be best to keep the remark to myself.

And as if he could read my mind he offered, "'*Blessed are the poor for theirs is the Kingdom of Heaven.*' Actually," he corrected himself, "'*Blessed are the poor in sprit for theirs is the Kingdom of Heaven,*' are Christ's actual words, the only time Christ is known to have selected a particular population group other than children and guarantee them paradise. Piccolo believes that it refers to those who *reason,* those who don't easily believe, the poor in spirit. Those that use this - their conscience," and he pointed to his temple. "Those Piccolo calls the lions, lions as opposed to sheep. But the mass of theology prefers to believe that Christ was talking about the poor. Certainly, that is not what it says. Christ very obviously meant exactly what He said, '*the poor in spirit.*' those lions who believe that their search for the truth requires some effort of their own, rather than those sheep who just assume that it is handed to them on a silver platter in their scriptures when they are born, that their birthright is their ticket to salvation."

"Actually," he went on, "Piccolo rarely uses the office. He's never been a fan of the pomp and splendor of the Church. He just doesn't feel comfortable here. He handles his paperwork on the dining room table.

"Each of us sees in the great clock a work of fine art and scientific achievement. But Piccolo sees something else. He sees in the clock the right to a good and healthy life for a hundred children. Within a week of his arrival Piccolo started to sell all of this and more in order to build an orphanage for children who would otherwise be aborted. But the Vatican intervened and stopped him. He's never said it, but if he ever became Pope I think that his very first act would be to leverage the Vatican treasures and use the money to annihilate poverty in places like Haiti, Africa and India. I am certain that this room will be returned to its prewar era."

the adversary,

He walked to the great table and taking a seat at one end he motioned that I take the one opposite. "A few words about our adversary," he began.

"Adversary?" I questioned.

"Yes, our great adversary, Moses," he replied.

"Moses?" I questioned again.

"Yes, Moses," he repeated. "Moses is the quartermaster of most of the hatred in the world. It is he who supplies the bigot with his *arsenal of weapons.* And it is a bottomless pit, this arsenal that gives the bigot the words he needs to conduct his evil war."

"It is Moses in the Old Testament who tells us '*that it was God the Father's command that woman live in dire servitude to man.*' It is Moses in the Old Testament who tells us *'that it was God the Father's command that slavery be a way of life.*' It is Moses in the *Old Testament* who tells us *'that it was God the Father's command that those with flat noses, those who we call Negroes today, and the handicapped are subordinate peoples and are not worthy to approach the presence of the Lord.*' It is Moses in the *Old Testament* who tells us *'that it was God the Father's command that homosexuals are outcasts and are to be persecuted.*' It is Moses in the *Old Testament* who tells us '*that it is God the Father's command that sex is shameful and sinful.* ' It is Moses in the *Old Testament* who tells us *'that it was God the Father's command that man is to mutilate the sexual organ of all male children.*' It is Moses in the *Old Testament* who tells us *'that it was God the Father's command that the prostitute and the adulteress shall surely be taken outside the city and stoned to death.*' It is Moses in the *Old Testament* who tells us *'that it was God the Father's command that whoever does not seek the Lord God of Israel shall surely be put to death.*' It is Moses in the *Old Testament* who tells us 'that it is God the Father's *command that only the sons of Aaron, the Aryan race, are to serve at His side, that all others are to be annihilated or cast into slavery.*' And it was Moses who, through his commanding general Joshua, carried out God the Father's instruction in th*e Old Testament* in the taking of the *Promised Land* in which hundreds of thousands of helpless men, women children and even infants were slaughtered, '*Put to the sword the unbelievers, every man woman and child, leave not one alive.'* It is Moses in the *Old Testament* who gave birth to all ethnic cleansing atrocities since, including the horrific undertaking of the Crusades, even the bloody American Civil War and most recently the Holocaust in which six million Jews lost their lives.

"Each of these instructions of the Bible and many more like them are prefixed with the words '*and God spoke to Moses*' and it is these words that make the Bible scripture. Without them it would just be another book, just another fairytale. They tell us explicitly what kind of God we are dealing with in the God of Abraham and Moses, -a God of hate and evil." He raised his voice a notch or so to emphasize his final point, "and no preacher can stand on a stage and tell his congregation otherwise for his scripture, itself, is his adversary!"

He paused again to give me time to grasp all the terrible things that he had just said and the conclusion that he had drawn and then he went on, "The validity of Moses of course depends entirely upon whether or not he was telling the truth. Was Moses telling the truth when he told the story of *the four hundred and thirty years that the Israelites spent in Egypt*? Was he telling the truth when he told the story of *Joseph and his brothers*? Was he telling the truth when he told the story of *the ten plagues*? Was he telling the truth when he told the story of *the Exodus*? Was he telling the truth when he told the story of *the forty year wandering in the Sinai Desert*? Was he telling the truth when he told his people that it was God the Father who had appeared to him on Mount Sinai and had given him the *Ten Commandments*? Was he telling the truth when he told his people that God the Father had commanded *that the Israelites were to take the Promised Land from the people who had traditionally lived there*? Was he telling the truth when he told his people that God the Father had commanded *that the Israelites were to murder the men, women and children and infants who lived there*? Was he telling the truth when he told his people that God the Father had commanded *that they were to enslave their neighbors*? Was he telling the truth when he told his people that God the Father had commanded *that the Aryan race, the sons of the sons of the sons of Aaron, would reign at His side forever*? Was he telling the truth when he told his people that God the Father had commanded *that woman live in dire servitude to man*? Was he telling the truth when he told his people that God the Father had commanded *that the prostitute and the adulteress were to be taken outside the city gates and were to be stoned to death?* Was he telling the truth when he told his people that God the Father had commanded *that the handicapped and those with flat noses (Negroes) were unfit to approach the altar of God*. And, finally, was he telling the truth when he told the stories of *Creation* and of *Adam and Eve* and of *Noah's Ark*?

"For if Moses was telling the truth then the bigot is right; bigotry would be a virtue. As a matter of fact it would be the only path to heaven, for to annihilate all the others is the only way that the Aryan race would end up representing all of mankind. It is the only way in which God the Father's dream as told by Moses in the Old Testament could come true. But on the other hand, if Moses was lying, then bigotry is an abomination, the abomination that any man or woman of good conscience today believes it to be. So the bottom line is, was Moses telling the truth, or was he lying when he told his many stories?

"And this is one of the great hurdles we face. The mass of the Christian world perceives Moses to be some kind of saint, a holy man of some sort. This is the great phenomenon of faith. This is because the picture books and the motion pictures influenced by Christian preachers have created the illusion that Moses was a holy man. But anyone short of an imbecile who reads the Old Testament could only come up with the conclusion that Moses was a monster of some kind."

He raised his voice, this time an octave or so with a tinge of frustrated anger, "There was nothing holy about this man at all. He led the world into thirty-five hundred years of hatred and prejudice and persecution and horror and suffering and destruction and death!"

Once again he paused as if to assure himself that I had gotten the point and perhaps to regain his composure. A good five minutes passed before he began to nail down his position, "Whether or not Moses was lying is perhaps best evidenced by his story of the *Ten Commandments*, for Christ's two most important commandments are not among them."

"Christ's commandments?" I questioned with a puzzled look.

Jack started, "Yes, *The Seven Commandments,*" he repeated, "And the contradiction is so severe that if one professes ones belief in God the Father's Ten Commandments one automatically rejects Christ's *Seven Commandments* - for the underlying philosophy of each could not be further apart.

"*The Ten Commandments* set forth in *Exodus 20* are, as you know - - *'I am the Lord thy God; thou shalt have no other gods before thee.- Thou shalt not make unto thee any graven images - Thou shalt not take the name of the Lord thy God in vain – Thou shalt do no work on the Sabbath, to keep it in my name .- Honor thy father and thy mother - Thou shalt not kill - Thou shalt not commit adultery - Thou shalt not steal - Thou shalt not bear false witness against thy neighbor - Thou shalt not covet (desire to take from) thy neighbor his property, including his house, his wife, his slaves, his ox, nor his ass'*

"The first four of these underline the basic philosophy of the God of the Old Testament - a self serving God. It is the combination of these four commandments that determined the fundamental philosophy of Christianity- that all that is necessary is that one fall down on ones knees and adore his God to enter the Kingdom of Heaven. Keep in mind that the loophole of contrition enables one to lead as evil a life as one wants.

"Christ knew that Moses had listed these four as the first and most important commandments because he intended to use them to trick his people into murdering the Canaanites who worshipped false gods and gain for himself the thirty-three cities of the Promised Land together with all its treasures of gold and silver and bronze. Keep in mind that Moses ends up as the richest man in the Mid East, save Pharaoh.

"For this reason, when asked for His commandments in *Matthew 19*, Christ specifically eliminates these four commandments. Not once in his ministry does He ask anyone to fall down on their knees and adore Him. Conversely, many times in His ministry, He tells us just the opposite. Time and time again, He condemns the Pharisees who fall down on their knees before God in the temple while they practice the two great enemies of Christ - greed and bigotry- in their everyday lives; today's Christians. Christ tells us time and time again in His ministry that building great edifices to His honor and falling down on ones knees and adoring Him has absolutely nothing to do with salvation.

"Whereas Christ retains five of His Father's commandments - - *'Honor thy father and thy mother - Thou shalt do no murder - Thou shalt not commit adultery - Thou shalt not steal - Thou shalt not bear false witness against thy neighbor,'* Christ specifically eliminates His father's tenth commandment which as we know has been an abomination for centuries and he replaces it with His sixth and seventh commandments - - *'love thy neighbor as thyself"* and *'sell all that this hast and give to the poor.'*

"There is no testimony in all of the Bible that is more explicit than is Christ's *Seven Commandments* in *Matthew*. And we know that Matthew copied his commandments from Mark (10), which is the only gospel that could have possibly been written by a man who was alive at the time of Christ's ministry. One would wonder why no one has ever heard of Christ's *Seven Commandments*. And the answer is clear, -it would not be good for the preacher's business. What is good for the preacher's business is God the Father's way, *'You can be as evil as you want to be – my tenth commandment protects your right to own your wife and enslave your fellow man and permits you to greed for material wealth while children in third world countries starve to death. You can breed hatred of your fellow man, -Negroes, Hispanics, homosexuals, Jews, Muslims and other ethnic peoples. All you need do is bow down and adore me.'* A much better deal than that offered by Christ.

"As you know, today, only a few brave men and women on the fringes of Christianity preach Christ's commandments. The mainstay of the Christian preacher, who pretends to be Christ's representative on earth, continues to deprive many of these people who are different, particularly women and homosexuals, of equal human rights under the law. And he inspires greed among his congregation, so that he too can get his share.

"Piccolo once told me that he had once taken the time to analyze the four gospels of Christ. Keep in mind that only these four books -

Matthew, Mark, Luke and John, which to a considerable extent vary from one another, are the testimony of Christ. All the other books of the Bible are immaterial because they are the products of men's minds; like Moses, their authors were all men of motive.

"Piccolo found that in all of His ministry Christ never did anything for Himself. Every single action that He took was for others. Piccolo has lived his life in imitation of Christ all these years. He has never had a use for the Ten Commandments, or for that matter, the rest of the Bible. To go a step further, he sees nothing holy about the rest of the Bible at all. As a matter of fact, except for the four gospels he thinks it to be what it *is* - an evil book.

"Piccolo has only one rule. Each time that the fork in the road comes up he asks himself, *'Now, what would Christ have done in this case?' And he has often pondered the possibility as to how much better the world would be if everyone were to do this.'"* Jack looked at me to assure himself that I gotten this message, his solemn instruction on how I was to lead the rest of my life.

And to this day I have tried to follow Piccolo's rule. Each time that the fork in the road has come up, I too have asked myself, *"Now what would Christ do in this case?"* And I too have often pondered the possibility as to how much better the world would be if everyone were to do this. And one of the forks in the road that has come up for me has made this book possible.

the Garden of Eden,

Silence prevailed and I finally broke the stillness, "Well, it is quite clear that no one could ever prove that Moses was not telling the truth in most of what he had to say. After all, none of us were there; we don't really know what God the Father told him."

Then Jack stopped. He peered about the room, taking time to examine the expressions of each of the angels that surrounded us. His action was quite decisive and it gave me the chance to count them - thirty-three in all. And I thought of the thirty-three years that Christ had lived and of the thirty-three months of His ministry and of the thirty-three months that Anne Frank had hid in the attic. And in retrospect today, I could add the thirty-three days of Luciani's papacy. On the other side of the aisle I thought of the thirty-three centuries that Moses had wreaked havoc among mankind. Jack gave me a look of uncertainty. He opened a drawer in the table and withdrew a sheet of paper and said, "Let's go for a walk."

As we went out of the castle gate a light rain was falling. Not enough to justify an umbrella, but nevertheless it was there, a light mist. "I am about to show you our best kept secret," he said and I followed him down along a path which led down around the side of the snow peaked mountain.

Shortly, we found ourselves in the rocky gorge in which the village was trapped. We made our way through some lush underbrush and finally came to an opening, a kind of grotto. Enclosed by a sheer wall on three sides that must have been a couple of hundred feet high, and cascading off its center panel was a waterfall. It was splattering down onto a bed of rock and finally splashed into a small pond. As I stood there I thought of all earth's species, for I could hear the hum of bees, the chirping of birds, the croaking of frogs, and out from under a bush and hesitating, as if to size us up, was a snowshoe rabbit. I could clearly see a number of fish of many different shapes and sizes glistening in a wide range of colors of silver to gold to blue, making their rounds in the crystal clear water.

"Piccolo and I call it our Garden of Eden," Jack said, "We do our best philosophizing, our best thinking, here. And," he added looking about him suspiciously, "we tell or best secrets here."

As I looked around I began to realize that Adam and Eve certainly had been given a lot to work with. A silent wind crept about the tips of the evergreens that were clustered just to the right of the waterfall. They seemed to whisper spring's early return. A huge umbrella palm stood just to the left of the waterfall and under its protection all of the rocks, which edged the pond on the opposite side, were weed-free. Where the weeds should have been, lilies of the valley sprouted here and there. Next came a wide range of small green trees half circling the pond, forming a crescent so as to reflect the moon that was not there. And just behind them was a row of taller, somewhat overpowering, somewhat darker green trees. As the mist had begun to make its exit tiny slivers of the sun's rays pierced through it, as if trying to take out a frog or two that sat on island rocks in the water. Altogether, like a family reunion posing for a picture.

Interspersed here and there, was much undergrowth. Some bushes were flowering. Some with red, some with yellow, some with blue, some with orange, whatever colors the Master happened to have dabbed into with His paintbrush when He executed this breathtaking work of art. And, much of the color was in motion, butterflies and fireflies hovered here and there and everywhere. Just to our left, yes, I couldn't believe it, was a small tree wearing its spring garb, -apple blossoms. Angel winged white petals drifted down to the waiting waters. And I thought, "Could this young tree be a descendent of the one that started it all?"

Seeing that I had noticed the tree, Jack laughed and said, "Piccolo planted it ten years ago when he first came here and just about everyone who sees it thinks the same thing you were just thinking. No," he said, "its parents were American; it is an American apple tree. Piccolo has always been fond of Americans. He's proud of what they have done and are doing. He is particularly proud of the Kennedys and the work they have done for the handicapped, including having introduced the Special Olympics. And just last year Piccolo held the first Special Olympics ever held outside the United States here in Vittorio Veneto.

"Ten years ago when he first got here he attended the local festival and was disturbed that not a single severely handicapped child was to be seen. Shortly after that he established a clinic, a kind of halfway-house, designed to take many of these children out of institutions and allowing them to live together with the general population. And again Moses stood in his way. Many mothers and fathers didn't want their children being exposed to children who were so severely impaired. They even went so far as to picket the workers when they were building the first ramp into a church here in the diocese, actually the first one built in the world. Their picket signs even quoted the words of Moses in the Old Testament.

"And President Johnson is on top of his list for having fought off the *Christian right* to bring about human rights for blacks. Piccolo knows that the future of the world depends largely on what Americans do. That's one reason I'm here. Of course there is another reason why I'm here."

"Another reason?" I asked.

"We'll get to that later," he responded.

Two large rocks sat at the pond's edge a conversation apart. He took one and I took the other. He paused for a moment or two as to give me one last chance to take in all of the wonderment that was about me and then he started, "The angels in the castle most likely do have ears and it is for that reason that I have brought you here. Although we have never been able to find them Piccolo and I believe that the house is bugged."

He continued, "Just before we left the office you remarked, no one could ever prove that Moses lied in most of what he had to say, as none of us were there, we don't really know what God the Father told him.

"But that is not entirely true," he went on. "Piccolo came up with the idea a couple of years ago that if one could prove that Moses was lying when he told his many stories then one could rid the planet of bigotry once and for all, for it would destroy the *arsenal of weapons* from which the bigot draws his ammunition. So Piccolo decided to go after that part of the Bible where the historical benchmark is exact, the time of Moses.

"Piccolo determined that the foundation of all that Moses said was the story of the four hundred and thirty years that the Bible contends that the Israelites were in Egypt, which marked the beginning of the Hebrew nation, the birth of Christianity. Piccolo knew that if the Israelites were actually in Egypt, as Moses claimed they were, then just about everything Moses said would fall into place. It would prove that everything he said was the truth. On the other hand, if he could prove that they were never in Egypt everything that Moses ever said would fall to ruin. For this, -that the Israelites were actually in Egypt for the four hundred and thirty years that Moses claimed they were, - is the very the foundation of the Bible. Piccolo knew that if the Christian world learned that the Israelites had never been in Egypt then it would blow up Moses' *arsenal of hate* which has enabled the Christian preacher to carry on his evil wars of ethnic cleansing and bigotry for what has now been three-and-a-half millennia.

"Of course, Piccolo knew that being a bishop of the Church he couldn't conduct such an investigation without Vatican approval. So he proposed to the commission that if such an investigation were to prove the word of Moses then it would add great credibility to Christianity. And it certainly would, as I have said there is no other known hard evidence that proves Christianity.

"So with Vatican approval, Piccolo and I and Brother Tom Jones, a local monk, set out for Egypt during the summer school break just last year. Our objective was to uncover evidence of the Israelites' presence in Egypt during the Middle Kingdom Period. The Middle Kingdom includes the period 1800BC to 1400BC, the four hundred years that the Bible contends the Israelites were in Egypt. In the terms used by Egyptologists one would be talking about the twelfth through the eighteenth dynasties.

"It had taken us almost two years to prepare for the expedition. We had to become knowledgeable in ancient symbolism and several languages including Egyptian hieroglyphs and hieratics and Hebrew, Nubian, Hyksos and Greek script. For Piccolo the job was much easier as he was already a scholar in most of these languages. He was more of a teacher than he was a student.

"According to the Bible, it was because of their great numbers that the Hebrews were put into slavery during the last forty years of their time in Egypt," and he quoted from memory, "'and *Pharaoh said, Behold the children of the people of Israel are more and mightier than we: Come on, let us deal wisely with them less they turn against us. So with hard bondage of mortar and brick the Israelites built for Pharaoh the treasure cities of Pithom and Ramesses.*'"

"What did you find?" I asked, quite eager to learn of this link between the Bible and reality.

He paused for moment as a great detective often pauses before revealing the solution to his case. "Nothing," he replied. "all we did was confirm the fact that the Israelites had never been in Egypt. We examined literally thousands of the ancient tombs, about four hundred of which have been excavated in the ancient cemeteries of the cities of Pithom and Ramesses. In addition, there were many thousands of ancient grave markers in these cemeteries.

"We couldn't find a single Hebrew marking on any grave. In fact, prior to our investigation, in all of Egypt only two or three Hebrew markings or names have ever been found in all of the Egyptian tombs and palaces and burial grounds, which are otherwise loaded with hieroglyphs. And these few markings have always been accompanied by the *Star of David* which dates them almost a thousand years after the Israelites' presumed time in Egypt, as King David didn't come along until then. There is nothing, not a trace of Hebrew history in Egypt dating back to Moses time."

"Nothing?" I questioned, much more astonished at the revelation than I was surprised. For it was something that the Christian world had always taken for granted. It would be like looking at a photograph of the Empire State Building after all these years and assuming all the time that it had a first, second, third, fourth and fifth floor; floors that although concealed by low-lying buildings around it were very obviously there. It is quite obvious that the Empire State Building has a first, second, third, fourth and fifth floor as otherwise one could have never added the other ninety seven floors. Although no one has ever seen one it is quite obvious that there are baby pigeons. It is quite obvious that Christianity has a first, second, third, fourth and fifth floor, the five books of Moses, as otherwise one could have never added the other sixty two books of the Bible. One doesn't have to see it to believe it. It is quite obvious that the Israelites were in Egypt. No normal mind would question this fact. I shuddered at the magnitude of what Jack was suggesting.

And Jack answered my unasked question. "Yes, nothing at all. We found nothing at all. And there is much more to it than just the graves. There is the great volume of hieroglyphs in all of the tombs and palaces of Egypt, which if reduced to fine print would fill all of the volumes in the New York City Library and then some. There are over sixty thousand rooms in the tombs that have been opened so far, and they are covered from floor to ceiling with hieroglyphs. In addition, there are tens of thousands of clay tablets and many temples and palaces with even more hieroglyphs.

"And about a third of this volume and the most complete record pertains to the time that the Bible claims the Israelites were in Egypt. The hieroglyphics spell out in great detail every major event that occurred during Egyptian dominance; the birth and death of every pharaoh who reigned; every war that was waged; every battle that was fought; every famine; every plague; every invention; every advancement in civilization;

every celebration - but nothing, not a single mention of any of Moses' tales. There is not a single mention of the way of life of the Israelites in Egypt. In fact, no mention of the story of the Red Sea miracle in which Moses claimed that the entire Egyptian army and its pharaoh perished - which if it were true had to be the greatest event in all of Egyptian history. Nothing, nothing at all, not a trace.

"Also, the Cairo and British museums maintain a complete catalogue of the roughly twelve thousand mummies that have been excavated in the nineteenth and twentieth centuries. Included is a complete description of each mummy - its time of interment, its age at death, its cause of death, its race, its nationality and so forth. Although the more important ones are displayed in museums, many of them are stored in warehouses by the Egyptian and British governments and some of them have been returned to their tombs. About a quarter of those that have been categorized are dated to the Middle Kingdom Period, the time the Israelites were said to have been in Egypt. The overwhelming number of them are Egyptian, there are a few Greeks, Hyksos and Nubians, but there is not a single Hebrew among them.

And this is consistent with the tombs themselves. In the tombs that have been uncovered to date there are more than three million human figures depicting the way of life in Egypt, the great majority are Egyptian and there are a few Nubians and Hyksos among them, but there is not a single Hebrew depicted among them despite the fact that the Bible claims that more than half the population was Hebrew.

"Keep in mind that the Bible contends that several Israelites attained royalty status including Joseph, himself, *'So Joseph died being an hundred and ten years old: and they embalmed him, and he was put in a coffin in Egypt.'* None of these tombs has ever been found. Today we know the name, the dates of birth and death and the period of reign of every single queen and pharaoh who reigned in Egypt from 3100BC to Cleopatra, just a generation before Christ's time. We have recovered the mummies of all but a handful of them, including all of those who reigned during the Middle Kingdom Period. This includes the remains of Amenhotep III, the pharaoh who is presumed by the Bible to have drowned in the Red Sea. They have all been Egyptians except for the Hyksos kings who ruled during their time and two who were Nubians. The chain is unbroken."

He reached into his pocket and pulled out the sheet of paper he had taken from the table drawer and handed it to me.

	period of reign	pharaoh
	2130-2120 BC	Akhtoy
	2120-2081	Merykare
time of the great flood	2081-2075	Mentuhotep I
	2075-2065	Inyotef I
	2065-2016	Inyotef II
	2006-1957	Nebhepetre* and Mentuhotep II
	1945-1945	Sankhkare* and Mentuhotep III
	1938-1938	Nebtawyre* and Mentuhotep IV
	1938-1909	Amenemhet I
	1909-1875	Senwosret I
time of Abraham in Syria	1875-1842	Amenemhet II
	1842-1837	Senwosret II
	1837-1818	Senwosret III
	1818-1772	Amenemhet III
Israelites go to Egypt from Syria	1772-1763	Amenemhet IV
	1763-1759	Sobekneferu
Hyksos conquer Northern Egypt	1759-1523	various Hyksos kings
Hyksos driven out of Egypt	1523-1503	Thutmosis I
	1503-1492	Thutmosis II
	1492-1471	Hatshepsut*
birth of Moses	1471-1403	Thutmosis III
	1403-1360	Thutmosis IV
the Exodus	1360-1349	Amenhotep I
	1349-1340	Amenhotep II
40 year wandering in the dessert	1340–1336	Tutankhamen
	1336-1314	Ramesses I
Joshua conquers the Holy Land	1314-1300	Seti I
	1300-1233	Ramesses II

**queen during time that her son was too young to rule*

Biblical time of the Israelites in Egypt

"This is a complete chronology of the pharaohs who reigned from the time of the great flood to the time of the taking of the holy land. The timetable is exact as it is taken from the hieroglyphs in the tombs. You might note that there is no interruption of pharaohs during the period of the great flood in which all of humanity, except those aboard the ark, was said to have perished."

And I stopped him, "These dates of the pharaohs are not etched in stone you know. I understand that the carbon dating analysis method that is used to determine ancient dates has a substantial margin of error."

He looked at me as if I had not yet finished grade school. "You think that the dating of tombstones is a twentieth century practice? The Egyptians invented the calendar based on a 365 day year in 3312BC. These dates are etched in stone. Perhaps not on every cornerstone, but nevertheless they can be deciphered from the hieroglyphs in the tombs. Carbon dating analysis which is normally used to determine the age of a cadaver, is rarely necessary in the case of the mummified pharaohs. The information contained in the tombs themselves gives us far more accurate information. As a matter of fact, we know the approximate birth and death of those few pharaohs who have not yet been found, -this record is in the hieroglyphs of the tombs of their parents and offspring."

Nevertheless, I went after him again, "Well, maybe the Egyptians had a law that only Egyptian symbols and writings could be put on tombs? Also, Jews would not have been mummified so today there would be no remains."

"You are right," he agreed, "the bodies might not remain, but the skeletons would surely be there. Under normal conditions it takes tens of thousands of years for a skeleton to fossilize and even then the fossil would remain. Under desert conditions the deterioration process is much slower.

"Also, concerning markings, there are a substantial number of Nubian and Hyksos markings that have survived. And one is not entirely dependent on the markings of a tomb to know its contents. The skull of a Jew is quite different from that of an Arab or an Egyptian or a Greek or a Nubian for that matter. Even an amateur anthropologist can tell one from another at a glance. We know that there are no Jews buried in Egypt.

"And then we have the wandering in the desert which took place in the forty years immediately following the Hebrews' escape from Egypt. We know this took place on the Sinai Peninsula, which was entirely a desert at the time. Moses took the tablets of the Ten Commandments from God the Father on Mount Sinai during this period.

"Of course, it is fairly well known that the Hebrews were never on the Sinai Peninsula, as a number of well publicized expeditions before us had done that job quite thoroughly. They dug up half of the peninsula in search of some fragment of pottery or some grave marking or some skeleton or anything that would evidence that the Israelites were ever there. And again, not a single trace could be found. The huge excavation of the Suez Canal failed to yield as much as a finger bone despite the fact that most of the two million who had crossed the Red Sea died during the forty-year wandering, as the average life expectancy at the time was less than thirty."

He paused for a moment as if reaching for a thought and then went on, "Actually, I had become somewhat aware of this while I was still in the seminary. A group of us had taken a pilgrimage to the Holy Land to trace our heritage. One day we were in a coffeehouse and I asked our Jewish host, a professor of the Hebrew University, if there were tours into Egypt that afforded the Jews the opportunity to also trace their heritage. After all, the four hundred and thirty years they spent in Egypt marked the birth of the Hebrew nation.

"And he laughed and told me, 'We Jews believe the Old Testament to be mostly just a story. Yes, important to our heritage and our way of life, but it is simply folklore, fairytales. Our origins were in what was known then and still is now the *Fertile Crescent,* that part of the Middle East which is today occupied by lower Syria and eastern Turkey; a land of plenty. Egypt on the other hand, has had a history of perpetual famine and starvation. That's why they built the Aswan High Dam in 1971, to bring an end to what had been an eight thousand year period of frequent starvation. It would have made no sense for the Israelites to have abandoned the most fertile land in the Middle East, the land of Abraham, and travel five hundred miles south to live in a desert. Except for the limited area that borders the Nile, which was available for cultivation and harvesting only four months of the year, Egypt was then and still is a desert you know. Egypt's fertile land was flooded eight months of the year and this is one reason why the great pyramids were built as the people had little to do from July to February. It would have made no sense for the Egyptians to let the Israelites in, as they had limited fertile land and practically no game.'

"'In addition, the crocodile and hippo population of the Nile left very few fish available in the Nile for human consumption. It would make no sense at all to leave the shores of the great Mediterranean Sea with its abundance of sea life and go to live in the desert.

"Then he told me that in the Holy Land itself there are many stone etchings dating back to Moses time. 'But you won't find a single etching that depicts the Exodus or the Red Sea miracle of any of the stories that Moses told. Particularly surprising is that there are no etchings of the Ten Commandments, not even of the Ark of the Covenant which supposedly disappeared.'

"'Of course,' our host added, 'one won't find a single etching of any of Christ's miracles either. Don't you think it strange that no one among the great multitudes that witnessed Christ's miracles thought enough of any of them to have etched a likeness of one of them into stone? Particularly since hundreds of other etchings of other events from Christ's time survive today including more than sixty etchings of Herod's life who was the predominate historical figure in Christ's time.'

"'Let's not get into that,'" I shot back at him.

"And he quickly came back at me, 'Actually, any man with half a brain would know that the Israelites could not have lived side by side with the Egyptians in the same land.'

"'Why do you say that?' I asked him quite puzzled by the thought.

"And he was quick to answer my question, 'Because the Egyptians believed Pharaoh to be in direct intercession with Son of Re, the Sun God, the reason why the Egyptians lived in servitude to Pharaoh. This is why the great pyramids were built and we know the last of the great pyramids and the greatest temples were built during the time that the Old Testament claimed that the Israelites were in Egypt. Yet, there is no mention in the Old Testament that the Israelites built any of the temples or pyramids other than that during the last forty years when they were enslaved that they built the cities of Pithom and Ramesses under bondage.'

"'The Hebrews, as you know, did not believe in the Sun God or for the matter in Pharaoh's intercession with the Sun God. They, like we today, believed in Moses and Abraham and their intercession with God the Father. To conclude that more than half of the population of Egypt lived in freedom for four hundred years, while the Egyptians themselves lived in servitude to their Pharaoh and sacrificed their lives to build the pyramids and the great temples of Egypt makes no sense.'

"Anyway," Jack went on now as if he were the proverbial snowball rolling down the hill, "we now know as a matter of fact that the story of the Israelites in Egypt was a fib. And this if nothing else tells us the story of Joseph and his brothers, and the story of Moses being found floating in a basket in the Nile, and the story of the ten plagues, and the story of the Exodus and the Red Sea, and the story of the Ten Commandments on Mount Sinai, and the story of God's instruction to Moses to take the Promised Land from the Canaanites and all the rest of Moses' tales were simply stories. Actually, they were outright lies. And of course, this confirms the many findings of astronomy, archeology and genetics, which today have proved that the stories of *Creation* and *Adam and Eve* were just folklore. For these stories too were told while Moses was said to have been in Egypt.

"Without the benefit of what I have just told you, it should be common sense to modern man that the Israelites were never in Egypt. For had the Israelite nation originated in Egypt, as the Bible contends, then the Jews would be making pilgrimages there to visit the gravesites and the other Jewish history which is there, to read the hieroglyphs which detail the way of life of the Israelites during the four hundred and thirty years that Moses claimed they were in Egypt. But there are no Jewish pilgrimages to Egypt because there is nothing there!"

Since that time I myself have visited Egypt many times. I too, have visited the great cemeteries that are located in the cities where the Bible claims that the Israelites lived. And I too, have found nothing, no not a single trace of Hebrew history there. And you will find nothing, for they were never in Egypt. Go there sometime if you are a poor believer. Or rather go there if you are a good believer. Go there and search out your heritage as a Christian and you will not find it there. You will find that Moses is very much *a grownup bigot's Santa Claus.*

Actually, to know this today one would not have to go to Egypt because the television history channels have capitalized on the Egyptian tombs and temples. They take the viewer into hundreds of these tombs and temples and never is there any reference to the Israelites who are said to have lived there, not a single trace of the Hebrews which the Bible contends comprised more than half of the population of Egypt for four hundred years. And it is for certain that if there was the slightest trace of such evidence that these entrepreneurs would capitalize on it. After all, their audience is a Judea-Christian world. But they don't because it is not there. Yet, the typical Christian still believes the first five stories of this great building of faith are there, because the low lying buildings that surround it, his belief, will not let him know that in fact they are not there. As a matter of *fact*, this great building of *faith* has not a single *truth* to stand on. If one is searching for the truth he or she should not be listening to what someone of motive has to say, but one should embark on a trip to Egypt where lies the truth.

I sat there for some time thinking of what all this meant as if I could figure out some way around it. And Jack then told me what it meant.

"What this means, what this means," and Jack spoke his conclusion in a series of definitive statements, "is that the Old Testament is simply folklore and is not the word of God, that as a matter if fact it was not even inspired by God, *that Jesus Christ claimed to be the Son of God who was sent to earth to rid the world of Original Sin as was once foretold in a fairytale!"*

I peered around the pond. It was quite apparent to me that every animal, bird and even insect had come to a screeching halt at what Jack had just said. Even the fish in the pond had slowed up a bit. I thought that at any moment they would attack and rid the world of the infidel who sat before me and I feared that they might take care of the witness at the same time. But they did nothing. They just remained there in a state of shock with frozen stares. "They must all be on his side," I thought.

Then Jack wrapped up his conclusion, "The stories of the Israelite's Enslavement in Egypt, of the Exodus, of the Red Sea Miracle, of the Ten Commandments, of Noah's Ark, of the Creation, and of Adam and Eve are for mothers and fathers who want to bring up their children in a world of make-believe. They prefer to continue playing with the minds of children beyond the age of six as their parents have done before them, rather than to bring them up in a world of reality where they could better develop their minds and be able to make their contribution to society."

He sat pensively for a few minutes, anticipating any question that I might have. I peered around the nature that was all about me once more and wondered if there could be a spy or two among the birds or the bees. And finally, lowering my voice to a whisper, I asked Jack the obvious question, "Who knows the results of your investigation?"

And he replied, "Only a small handful of cardinals clustered in the Vatican know. There is the Pope, the secretary of state, the undersecretary of state, the foreign minister, the deputy minister and, of course, the three of us who conducted the survey. That is, two of the three of us who conducted the expedition."

"Why do you say two of the three of you? All three of you must know. After all, you were all there," I corrected him.

He chose for the moment to ignore my question and replied, "And this is where you come in."

"Where I come in?" I questioned.

"Yes, you," he replied, "for now you also know."

I kind of shuddered when he told me. I again peered around the pond. And Jack noticing my diversion remained silent as to permit me time to check out each one of the creatures that might be listening. Then he started up again.

"Piccolo's intention is to bring an end to this kind of injustice once and for all. To take the voice out of the Bible once and for all that tells one to hate one's fellowman. He intends to take the ammunition from the fascist preacher, as Piccolo puts it *'his flimsy arrows built in an ancient factory.'* And he has now struck on the strategy of battle. He intends to pull the rug out from under Moses. To forever annihilate his great *arsenal of hate*. But in pulling the rug out from under Moses one must take care not to also pull the rug out from under Christ.

"And now we have finally arrived at the point at which I can tell you of the seriousness of the problem we face." He paused for a moment as if collecting his thoughts before going on. He glanced around as to be certain that he could trust all of nature's creatures that had gathered about him, as if to assure himself that there was not a spy among them.

a body floating in the canal,

"A few months ago Brother Tom Jones was found floating in the canal that runs beside the cathedral. His real name was not Tom Jones. I can't even begin to pronounce his real name. When inducted into the order he had picked a long entangled name of an ancient philosopher, and because it was tough to remember and almost impossible to pronounce we just called him *Tom Jones.*

"The official pronouncement was that he had drowned; this despite the fact that he was known to have been a good swimmer. Piccolo grew suspicious and secretly had an autopsy performed on the body. As no water was found in the lungs, the results of the autopsy proved that he was already dead when he went into the water. Piccolo's suspicions were well founded, Tom Jones had been murdered.

"Piccolo told me that we ourselves could be in danger. He was particularly concerned about me, as being a member of the council and a ranking prelate of the Church he was far less a risk to the conservative core in the Vatican than was a rank and file member of the clergy who was more likely to stray to the press. After all, if Piccolo, a potential cardinal, were to go to the press, it would destroy his own ability to eventually accomplish the things he wants to accomplish to make this a better world to live in.

author's collection

the canal beside the church in which Tom Jones was found

"Piccolo told me that he had called the Pope and told him of the autopsy findings, and that Paul had instructed him to relocate me from the seminary dormitory here into the bishop's castle. The house has five bedrooms that are normally reserved for visiting prelates. At the time that I moved in, Piccolo had a half dozen unwed mothers living in the house and because of the impending danger he relocated them to the local convent. The Pope evidently told the members of the *Vatican Curia* of the autopsy findings and warned that if there were any more mysterious shortcomings in the Veneto country that he would order a full scale investigation.

"Paul's action obviously gives us some protection as an investigation could lead to disclosure of the findings of the Egyptian survey. It would defeat the purpose of any further murders since such a revelation would bring about the destruction of the twenty or so cardinals that make up the *Vatican Curia*. Of course, if something were to happen to Paul we would surely be in great danger.

"On Piccolo's directive I have told you of the results of our investigation, results that are known to only a small handful of men, results which could imperil Christianity should they become known prematurely, before the Church is able to complete the separation of Christ from Moses. And I have told you of our own possible demise. So I will leave that much with you for now."

And I quickly corrected him, "To separate Christ from Moses is not possible. After all, Christ claimed to be the Son that the God of Moses promised to send to earth to rid the world of Original Sin."

"I think I will leave that one for Piccolo to answer at dinner tonight." He looked suspiciously at a small bird that had landed on a nearby limb that seemed to be listening, as if it might relate what he was saying to the *Curia* cardinals who were housed in the Vatican. Then he went on, "Today, many Christians who want to seal their *faith* make a pilgrimage to the Holy Land sometime during their lifetime. Luckily they don't go a step further and make a pilgrimage to Egypt, which is just south of the border, for it would certainly seal their *fate*.

"If there were any Hebrew tombs in all of Egypt, you can bet that the churches and the synagogues would be capitalizing on them, would be making use of them to prove their point. But you never hear of them. And the reason you never hear of them is because they are not there," and he raised his voice to emphasize his pounding of the final nail into the coffin of the Old Testament, "The Israelites were never in Egypt."

Then as to wrap it all up, Jack finished, "The survival of Christianity, or for that matter any other religion, depends solely on the population's tendency to believe and in the case of Christianity that belief is now in great jeopardy. We must begin now to separate Christ from Moses, to separate Christ from bigotry for all time. And this is where you come in."

And he started to set the stage for his conclusion, "If Piccolo was to announce his findings today, it would annihilate Moses and the bigot but it would also annihilate Christ for we have not yet entirely separated Christ from Original Sin. This is a delicate process and one that will take a few more years. Piccolo feels by the end of the century the job would have been largely accomplished and people will believe in the man in the robes as Christ is portrayed on the motion picture screen and won't care much about His link to Original Sin. The transformation will have been completed and most people will think that Christ, like the god Zagerus before Him, '*is the Son of God who came to earth to die for the sins of mankind.*' The story of the Canaanite god Zagerus is inscribed on an ancient Mesopotamia tablet held by the British National Museum in London. The tablet is dated 2200BC, about the time of the great flood, five hundred years before Moses time.

"The masses will accept this despite the fact that, unlike the god Zagerus before Him, it makes no sense that '*Christ came to earth to die for the sins of mankind.*' Yes, it sounds good and since the general populace never stops to analyze theology, it will accept it. Christ very obviously never died for the sins of mankind, for had He done so we would not be at risk to hell. The people in Zagerus' time had never thought of hell as being a possibility. That came along later in Moses time. So it made sense in those days that Zagerus '*was the Son of God who came to earth to die for the sins of mankind.*' But it makes no sense today. For today we are going to suffer for our own sins, no one else is going to die for them. Also, keep in mind that Christ never really died on the cross."

I gave him a look of apprehension and disbelief.

"Yes," he answered my expression, "the true trauma of death is the great emotional pain of death and not the physical pain of death. And even in the case of physical pain Christ suffered only a few hours whereas most of us will suffer for weeks or months before death comes as a friend and takes us from our misery. And the greatest physical pains we experience in life have nothing to do with death. For those who have experienced all three, the immense pain of a leg cramp or of a toothache is often much higher on the pain-scale and much more enduring than is having a nail driven through one's hand. Anyone who had a choice of suffering burns over half of their body or being nailed to a cross would choose the latter every time.

"It is the fact that we are about to leave our loved ones and not knowing that we will see them again that is the true suffering of death. And in the case of the Christian one knows as a matter of faith that one is never going to ever see their loved ones again, the reason why all Christian marriages end in the phrase 'until death do us part' or its equivalent. But in Christ's case He, being God, *knew* that for Him it was not the end. For Him, His death on the cross was a time of great joy for He *knew* that He was about to join His Father in Heaven that day. For Christ, dying on the cross was just a charade. And what's more, He knew it.

"A god by definition cannot die, and this was also true of the God Zagerus in the days of the Canaanites, for all gods are deemed to be immortal. And what's more they *know* they are immortal, unlike the rest of us who only *think* that we are immortal. So Christ, like the God Zagerus before Him, never died for the sins of mankind. One should not fool oneself.

"But nevertheless, as I just said, believers never stop to analyze theology, so this is the course that we will take. People will no longer care whether or not the story of Adam and Eve is true or not. Original Sin will be history." He thought a moment and then corrected himself, "No, not history, a fairytale someone once told." An awkward moment followed as I tried to rationalize all that Jack had said in an attempt to somehow salvage my faith.

a mission for Christ,

Then he started up again, "In case something was to happen to us, Piccolo feels that someone else should know; someone who is not geographically close to us, yet someone who we could trust. Someone who we could be reasonably certain would be around at the end of the century after the transformation of Christ's purpose is complete; someone who, at that time, could announce the results of the Luciani expedition into Egypt and bring an end to Moses' influence in the western world for all time; someone who will bring an end to bigotry as quickly as one turns off a water faucet. Then Piccolo, perhaps, long after he is gone, would be able to achieve his work, to complete the work started by Christ two thousand years ago to rid the world of the bigot. For as I said, it is Moses who supplies him with his weaponry and without his armament the bigot will perish." He looked at me with as serious a look as if he was one who held the destiny of the world in his hands and added, "You must do this thing for Christ, that what He stood for will not perish with the greed and hatred of men."

And I stopped him, "But me? How could I possibly accomplish such a thing? I will probably be a *nobody* at that time."

And he quickly shot back, "You will do it in the very same way every other 'nobody' has accomplished his or her objectives. The very same way Paul accomplished his objectives."

"Paul?" I questioned.

"Yes, Paul of the New Testament. Like Paul and his contemporaries Matthew, Mark, Luke and John wrote their book fifty years after Christ died," he paused and then raising his voice he told me, "You, too, will write a book."

"But I don't know how to write a book," I told him.

He shot me a look of finality, "You will write a book," he raised his voice to the point of a demand, "for each and every one of them!"

And my mind drifted back to yesterday, that time that I had taken the pledge in the great cemetery of Milan. "*. . . for each and every one of them,*" and I thought, "perhaps, this is what I must have meant?"

Then getting up he patted me on the shoulder and said, "Enough said. You now have your sacred commission. Let's go to lunch. Vittorio Veneto is smack in the middle of Italian wine country. I'll take you to a little sidewalk cafe where the food is terrible but what counts most, the wine is marvelous."

the factory,

We returned to the road and instead of going up the mountain toward the castle we turned right and moseyed our way down into the village. Passing the cathedral we turned right, and began a long walk in front of the seminary complex. As we made our way along the yellowing nineteenth century stucco buildings he told me, "This is our crown jewel. The seminary is what makes Vittorio Veneto such an important post. It wasn't always that way. Piccolo made it that way."

"When he came here ten years ago it was just another priest factory. Today, although it is exceeded in size by the great Gregorian University of Theology in Rome and another large seminary outside Milan and a third one in Southern France, it is probably the most recognized in the Catholic world. All the others put out good products, anything from *Volkswagens* to *BMWs*, we put out a consistent line of *Mercedes.*

"Piccolo recognizes that priests are salesmen of the faith and he believes that they are a chain. He believes in the age-old adage that a chain is only as strong as its weakest link. That is, if one priest screws up, it will do irreparable damage to all the others. So when he came here, he changed the manufacturing philosophy from one of nurturing the quickest and brightest students to one of concentrating on improving those at the bottom, those who were the slowest and those having the greatest difficulties. Every one of them leaves here a qualified *550SEL,* fully equipped to meet anything they encounter on the highway of faith ahead, able to negotiate the most challenging hairpin curves of doubt that they might come upon.

"A very big part of a seminarian's education here is psychology. This is the reason why I went to med school. Unlike most bishops who surround themselves solely with theologists, Piccolo built into the faculty here a well-balanced staff of scientists, historians and most importantly, psychologists and in my case - a psychiatrist. He believes that the main purpose of the priesthood is to help people lead more healthy lives – mental health he calls it. He is less concerned with the afterlife than he is with this life.

"Not too many people go to church to adore God. They usually go for other reasons - they think it is a mortal sin not to go to church; they go as a matter of habit; but mostly they go for therapy. Some of them find redemption in the ranting and raving of evangelist preachers and others find solace in the most soft spoken of priests. But nevertheless this is what they get out of it, –a once-a-week rubdown of the mind.

"Piccolo found it to be irreprehensible that a psychology course was not a requirement of seminaries; that it was rarely offered as an elective. He once told me, *'The state is a coward when its adversary is the church. It requires all practitioners of the human mind, psychologists and psychiatrists, to have accomplished a prescribed curriculum usually to the doctoral level before authorizing them to deal with the human mind. Yet, it looks the other way when men disguise themselves as representatives of God. The ministry is nothing more than an army of men totally unschooled in the way the human mind works that spends most of its time dealing with the minds of men, mostly with the minds of weak men. No wonder the world is so confused.'*

"Piccolo has urged Pope Paul to do the very same thing that he has done here at Vittorio Veneto. To trade in the *Vatican Curia* – a group of mentally deranged theologists - for a team of experts on people problems, so that the Church can better understand its congregation's needs."

Soon we passed a large tower housing what was undoubtedly the town clock and headed down a cobblestone street. Passing one of those Italian ice cream stands one sees all over Europe, Jack said, "There are over five million of these stands in the world, and this one you will find is in first place. We will stop here on the way back."

"Not many people," I thought, but each one that I saw, some walking, some running, and a few on bicycles, had obviously been there all their lives; a hundred, perhaps two hundred Italians and I. As people looked at me, I relished my individuality. And every one of them, every single one of them, said "Hi Jack" in perfect English, despite the fact that he could speak perfect Italian. And each of them seemed to have an expression of great admiration of Jack, as if he were some kind of god.

author's collection

the town clock in Vittorio Veneto

Chapter 4

GENERAL PATTON

two very different kinds of courage,

At one end of the street, where it formed a wedge with its neighbor, we took a table outside a typical Italian village restaurant, one of those they try to duplicate in the big cities with very little success. Heeding Jack's advice, I decided on bread, cheese and fresh fruit, and he doubled the order. Then Jack uttered something to the waiter in Italian, and he was off.

In no time at all he returned. He spread about the table a wide variety of breads and cheeses and fruits. He then placed in the center of the table a crystal clear bottle of wine having a slight amber touch to it. It was set in chopped ice held in by a clear glass container. Little did I know that I was about to get a taste of the afterlife, itself. To this day, although I have experienced a few reds that have equaled it, I have never known another white to approach it. Reaching for the wine, Jack poured our glasses properly half-full of this memory that is still with me today. And like any other close friends who hadn't seen each other for a number of years we started to chat away the hour about the good old times.

Somewhere along the way I asked him, "Boy, you sure are popular. Just being the bishop's secretary gets you that?"

"It has nothing to do with that," he answered, "it is due to something else entirely."

"My uncle was in the military during the world war. He held two purple hearts and a dozen other enviable decorations. In a heroic action he was hit in North Africa and was hospitalized for six months with serious liver damage. He was nominated for the *Congressional Medal of Honor*, but instead received a *Silver Star*."

"Anyway," he continued, "a year later he was hit again and this time he was paralyzed from the waist down. He was hit by friendly fire when he placed himself between his own troops and two dozen or so Italian school children so as to alert his men that they were about to fire on the children. It actually happened near Milan, quite a distance from here. Because it occurred toward the war's end it helped to heal the wounds of war and since the action was witnessed by so many he was awarded the *Congressional Medal of Honor*, the honor that had escaped him in North Africa.

"This is why I am a celebrity in these parts. This is why wherever I go I get a thousand 'hellos'. The people believe that perhaps some of my uncle's courage has rubbed off on me.

"Well, to make a long story short, my uncle was gay and because his life then seemed wasted he felt that he could be a martyr for the gay cause. Foolishly, he announced that he was gay while he was still in the military hospital. He once told my mother that his admission of his homosexuality took much more courage than when he had placed himself before the *firing squad* to protect the children. He hoped that he could attract national attention but he didn't attract a fly. What he overlooked was that at that time there was no gay cause."

And he went on, "Back then, homosexuality was not exactly the type of thing that his family even wanted to talk about, much less see spread across the front page of the local newspaper. In fact, as you know, it still isn't today."

"So, the Army threw him out?" I queried.

"No," he replied, "at that time there was no box to check, no policy. So although they didn't like it, there wasn't much they could do about it. Yes, if it had happened after Eisenhower added the box during his presidency fifteen years later he would have been court-martialed, would have lost all pension and benefit rights and might have been dishonorable discharged.

"When I said that he didn't attract a fly, this was not entirely true, for he did draw Eisenhower's attention. He drew an official reprimand directly from Ike. A reprimand that General Patton, my uncle's commanding officer, tried to block.

"Actually," he continued, "my uncle relished in it. He saw it as a victory that his action was able to draw the attention of Eisenhower, himself."

"So how is he now? Certainly he could do something now. Especially being one who holds the highest military award," I offered.

"He isn't," he replied, "A couple of months after making his declaration he died quite suddenly from a liver infection related to his earlier injury that was brought on by his confinement to bed.

"Only his father flew to Italy for the funeral. His mother was too distraught. His father told my mother that the army provided full military honors for him, that there was some speculation that General Patton himself, who happened to be in the area at the time, would attend. And although several hundred villagers attended the ceremony, he didn't show up. Not a single officer of rank showed up, despite the fact that my uncle held the *Congressional Medal of Honor*. Yet, someone else did show up."

"Someone else?" I queried.

"Yes, Piccolo showed up. It is not a far reaching coincidence that I managed to secure an assignment here as an instructor in this remote Italian seminary a few years ago and eventually grew so close to my patron. Piccolo had officiated at my uncle's interment. Yes, I groomed myself for this assignment, going so far as earn a PhD in Psychiatry and becoming fluent in Italian, but the only reason I got the job was because Piccolo had rendered my uncle's eulogy.

"As it is today, Milan was an ultraconservative diocese and no local priest could be found who was comfortable in officiating at the ceremony. So the Archbishop of Milan reached out into the Veneto country which, as today, was the most liberal part of Italy, and the obvious choice was the revolutionary and outspoken young priest from Belluno.

"As I said, the army provided full military honors for my uncle, a lance corporal showed up heading up a detail of four soldiers, three with rifles and one with a bugle. Piccolo doesn't remember too much of what he said, other than that he had ended up his string of prayers and comments with a single and embittered statement, *"It is the soldier who shed his blood on the field of battle and not the preacher who cowers in his pulpit, who should determine who should or should not be free."** The detail then raised their rifles and fired off the volleys and the man with the bugle did the best he could with the taps.

"Then, as the crowd of several hundred villagers started to move away from the grave, a strange thing happened."

"A strange thing happened?" I repeated his statement as a question.

"Yes, a large olive green military sedan, one of those with the large bubble fenders that one often sees in the movies, entered the cemetery and moved along its outer perimeter and finally came to a stop in the roadside that annexed my uncle's grave. A young soldier got out of the front seat and opened the rear door and an army officer of about sixty stepped out. When Patton reached the gravesite he introduced himself to Piccolo and my uncle's father as if the rows of stars on his shoulders could not have conveyed the message. A light rain was falling from darkened skies and one could imagine hearing the firing of artillery shells in the distance although there was nothing there. And today, a quarter of century later, Piccolo remembers every single thing that the general had to say.

**Albino Luciani Milan Italy 29 Mar '44 Luciani repeated this statement many times during his ministry*

"The great general told them in his low and rasping but powerful voice, speaking decisively, and pausing on every syllable as if he were addressing Congress, 'At West Point, there are many courses; one learns many things; one learns the history of war; one learns the purpose of war; one learns the strategy of war; one learns the struggle of war; one learns the noise of war; one learns the horror of war; one learns the victory of war; and one learns the hopelessness of war. But the most important course one takes is taken on the great battlefield itself, and that course is called *courage*.'

"Then he went on and added, 'As you know there is a great difference between Ike and myself. For Ike has never taken this course. Never once in his lifetime has he carried himself into battle, into the pit. Not once in his lifetime has he pulled the boy out of the mud and searched for where the mud left off and the blood began. Not once has he reached for the final pulse of this thing called life. Never, not once, has he given himself the great opportunity to realize this great prize we know as courage. His only experience in battle has been in his reading and in his textbooks and in his toy soldiers and in his toy tanks and in his toy ships that he moves about on his great table of war. Like the preacher in the pulpit whose only time in battle has been in the atrocities of the ethnic cleansing wars in his scripture.'

"Then with a great tear forming in the corner of his eye, Patton placed his hand on my uncle's father's shoulder and told him, 'I apologize to you for Ike's action. His action does not speak for me; does not speak for those who fought along side your son; does not speak for America; does not speak for freedom.'

"'Your son,' he went on, 'has won for you and all of us, this thing called *courage*. This thing called *courage* that I, too, have sought many times. That I, as a commanding general, would expose myself upon a tank at the very forefront of my ranks in open line of enemy fire and with artillery shells bursting all around me. I too, have craved for the taste of this thing called *courage*, but even I have yet to realize its dream.'

"'Yesterday,' he went on, 'I assigned my highest decorated and most courageous officer to represent your son's fellow soldiers and America here today. Late this afternoon, I learned that this young Lieutenant Colonel had failed in his sacred duty by delegating his responsibility to a subordinate. This, not because he had more important things to do, but because he didn't have the *courage* to be here. For this required a different kind of *courage*. Perhaps, even a greater kind of *courage*. Perhaps, he was afraid of what the press might do to him; of what his fellow soldiers might think of him; of what his family might think of him; of what American might do to him.'

"'Your son had that kind of *courage*. He was not afraid of what the press might do to him. He was not afraid of what the army might do to him. He wasn't even afraid of what his family might do to him. He didn't even care what America might do to him.'

"The general then stepped a few paces to the left and placed his hand on the shoulder of one of the adjoining tombstones - the one labeled *Anthony Jackson, Bronze Star* and continued, 'Even today the *Christian right in the United States* continues to persecute southern blacks, many of whom have also shed their blood on the great battlefields of this war. And it continues to practice its bigotry against Jews and women and homosexuals and many others; all those who appear to be different.'

"He then placed his hand on the shoulder of the adjoining stone, the one marked *Patricia Wilde, Bronze Star* and added, 'The world will never know of her valor; never know of her bravery; .never know of her courage; never know of her gallantry; never know of these things that had won for it its freedom. All that evidences that she had ever been, is this small white granite stone and the marks upon it.'

"The general then turned toward the crowd and raised his voice, *'After this war is won, after the final volleys are fired, after the smoke clears and the tears begin, America must fight a new kind of war and that war will be fired by a new kind of courage.*

"'Yes, this war will win for America and all mankind this thing we call freedom. But that war, the war within, will someday win for America the great prize of equality for all men and women, something that this war cannot do. For freedom without equality is not what it pretends to be. The diamond would be made of paste.

"'It is our differences that have made us into the great nation of one that we are and the day will come when men and women of good conscience will no longer heed the words of those preachers and politicians who choose to use them to divide us.

"'And when that day comes all children will be born into a world of equal opportunity. Only then will America and the world be truly free. Yes, today men and women of great courage are engaged in this great war which will soon crush the enemy from without, but it must take many more men and women of still another kind of courage who must rise up and crush the enemy from within. Only then would these brave men and

*women not have died in vain. Only then will the diamond, this thing one calls freedom, be real.'**

"And as he climbed into his vehicle, Patton told my uncle's father, 'I have been proud to have had your son serve in my army here,' and looking upwards toward the sky, 'and I am certain that He is proud to have him in His army, today,' and letting a tear drop onto his cheek, he nodded to his driver, and they were off."

Jack went on, "It is the great regret of my family, that in order to save themselves some embarrassment, they intentionally kept the whole situation quiet, that is, they intentionally kept it from the press. They intentionally kept him, my uncle, from making his mark. His Mom and Dad still live with this, their inaction, which they now know was an atrocity on their part. But there is now no remedy. It is too late. Their lives are now broken. They have aged two lifetimes in one. Even I, though only a child at the time, have great regrets about it.

"But, you're right. If he were alive today he could do something. Perhaps not much, but something. In fact, all the other homosexuals who hold the *Medal of Honor* and other awards could do something. But they remain in hiding. For even today this is not something one wants one to know about."

"Others?" I questioned.

"Yes," he replied, "others. In the Great War there were over four hundred congressional medals awarded. If one plays the percentages, this would mean that about thirty to forty of them are held by truly homosexual men. But of course, like my uncle most of them did not survive. But if one or two of them who did survive were brave enough to come forward, it would stop much of the preacher's bigotry in its tracks. But, as my uncle said, that would take more bravery today than did his action in 1944 when he stood before the children. Actually, today in Vietnam, there are a disproportional number of gays versus straights serving and giving their lives for this thing we call freedom, as the current draft law exempts men

** Milan Italy 29 March '44. General George S. Patton at the gravesite of a Congressional Medal of Honor hero who had admitted to his homosexuality while he lay dying in a military hospital. Albino Luciani, who had officiated at the same ceremony, quoted Patton's remarks in a sermon October 17, 1973 in the Basilica de San Marco in Venice, Italy. (author's collection). During the World War, although they did not engage in battle, several women were awarded the Bronze Star; most of these were nurses who risked their lives volunteering to stay behind with wounded soldiers who could not be moved in the wake of advancing enemy forces. During the World War, twenty-seven African American men were recommended for the nation's highest award; several of these recommendations had been made by Patton but were blocked by Eisenhower. In 1997, seven of these medals were awarded to these men, six of them posthumously. The unitalicized remarks by Patton are to the best of Albinos Luciani's recollection as related to Jack Champney, who in turn related them to the author.*

who are fathers of young children. And you've done your time in the army. Did you ever meet a WAC who was not a dyke?"

Then with a gesture of almost reverent solemnity, he stretched out his arm toward me and pulled back his sleeve to display his wristwatch. On one side of the watchband was welded a small heart pendant of George Washington on a purple background. And on the opposite side was a gold star. "My mother, his sister, has his congressional medal, and all the others are buried with him. They are in the great cemetery at Milan."

And looking at the gold star, I said, quite confused, "I thought you said it was a silver star?"

"Look closer," he replied, "there's a tiny silver star in its center."

And I looked and sure enough it was there. And suddenly, at the very same instant, a light bulb went on in my mind. "Milan," I exclaimed, "was his name Champney?" I asked, at the very same instant realizing that it couldn't have been, as it was his mother's brother we were talking about.

"No," he said, "Beene. Guy Beene!"

Judging that he had struck a nerve he fell silent. And as I stared out onto the street, I recalled my pledge in the cemetery at Milan; my solemn pledge. I recalled the etchings that read: *Guy Beene, Congressional Medal of Honor; Anthony Jackson, Bronze Star; Patricia Wilde, Bronze Star* and the others, and in that split moment, my whole psychology concerning gays and women and blacks and others changed and it has never wavered since.

Leaving some of the wine in order that we could find our way, I settled up with the waiter and we started back. Stopping in front of the gelato stand, I followed Jack's lead, "one of these, one of these, one of these and one of those." As we walked toward the seminary, I thought in great wonderment of how the finest gelato in the world could have found its way so near to its finest wine.

And as we came to the end of the street he went one way and I the other way, and he called out after me, "Remember, dinner is promptly at seven thirty."

Don't Ask, Don't Tell: *Wars are not won and lost on the battlefield alone. More often than not, the determining factor is effective intelligence. And intelligence is a two-way street: the security of one's own information, and the ability to secure information of the enemy. General Patton was a religious man, but fortunately for the free world today he was one who drew a line between the make-believe world of the preacher and the real world of battle, something that recent presidents and generals have been unable to do. In Patton's time, homosexuals did pose a security threat and this was because of the stigma that existed at the time. For if an enemy was to gain information that could prove that a certain army officer was gay then he would be a sitting duck for blackmail. For this reason, Patton encouraged an open policy for gays, so much so that on several occasions like the one described* *here, he demonstrated to these soldiers that he accepted them as honorable members of his ranks. Had Patton enforced a Don't Ask, Don't Tell policy America may have very well lost the war.*

Security of one's own intelligence: *Today, with the stigma being lifted from homosexuality, gay soldiers would not normally pose a security risk to the nation. Yet, in the wake of 9/11, the Commander in Chief of the Armed Forces has not only failed to lift the Don't Ask, Don't Tell policy, but he strengthened it, thereby seriously weakening the security of our internal information. Long term career officers, who are most likely to have access to hi-security information, have the most to lose; substantial retirement and other benefits as well as their careers; the 'Don't ask, Don't tell' policy makes them sitting ducks for blackmail. It creates a problem where there is no problem to begin with.*

Ability to secure information of the enemy: *One of the most critical elements in the war on terrorism is the maintenance of an army of linguists who are proficient in Middle Eastern languages. Immediately after 9/11, the Pentagon fired almost a third of these linguists under the 'Don't ask, Don't tell' policy. One could ask why the Pentagon took this action after 9/11 when it had no significant history of having fired homosexual linguists. Certainly, it did not suddenly discover that a number of its linguists were homosexual. The information disclosing the sexual orientation of these linguists most likely emanated from the Mid East. Terrorist' intelligence made these detections and passed them on through intermediaries to Pentagon officials who in turn irresponsibly fired the accused thereby seriously weakening its own intelligence base. The 'Don't ask, Don't tell' policy of the United States is imposed by military officers who are unable to distinguish between* ***the make-believe world of the preacher*** *and* ***the real field of battle.***

Chapter 5

"GOD IS MORE OUR MOTHER THAN SHE IS OUR FATHER"

orphanages vs. churches,

I found myself in an ancient room of stone. Its focal point was its large, bottle-bottom leaded glass windows peering out through ornate iron grates. They were flanked on either side by heavy wooden shutters that opened inwardly into the room and were set upon encasements that projected outward from the wall, so that if the shutters were closed one would think one was looking at a wall cabinet of some kind. Although their lead frames obscured the view it was clear what they were looking at - the ruins of the surrounding castle towers.

The old stone flooring with its centuries of wear was as cold as it seemed to be. A beautiful sideboard of mellowed wood that had to be several hundred years old stood along the wall opposite the windows. Just above it an aging, but quite colorful tapestry of princes and paupers blanketed the wall. At one end of the room a large oil painting in a heavy, gold encrusted frame depicted Christ's miracle of the loaves and fishes. I assumed correctly that it was another Titian. At the other end was another walk-in fireplace that had been cut into the stone wall. A giant black iron cauldron hung in front of it exactly as it was the day that it had been forced into retirement by the stove that stood in the kitchen off to one side. In the center of the room was a carpet of what must have been extraordinary value and on it stood four richly carved chairs that clashed with the table they surrounded. As a matter of fact, everything in the room including the room itself clashed with the table. For the table was one of those cheap, browning enameled top tables of the forties. Four chairs that I would guess would very easily draw twenty or thirty thousand dollars at auction, hemmed in a table that would go for five dollars at a yard sale.

Responding to my unasked question, Jack explained, "When I mentioned this afternoon that when he first got here Piccolo had started to sell all this stuff and the Vatican stopped him I wasn't kidding. But they didn't stop him in time. His first visitor from Rome was Bishop Caprio. When we led him into the dining room and he saw that the table was gone, Caprio threw a fit. He walked about the room ranting and raving and thrusting his arms into the air like a man out of his mind. He ordered Luciani to stop this madness, this illness, '*to sell all that thou hast and give to the poor*.' "

And I stopped him, "You mean that he built the orphanage that I passed at the foot of the mountain with the money that he got for a table?"

"No," he responded. "He built that one with money that was originally intended to build a church. A wealthy local man who was terminally ill intended to will his entire fortune to build a church, but Piccolo talked him into building an orphanage instead. Piccolo considers a church a luxury and to a certain extent unnecessary, particularly when children are starving to death as we speak. He once told his congregation here in Vittorio Veneto, *'Nowhere in all of Christ's testimony does Christ ask that we fall down on our knees and adore Him. Rather, Christ spent His ministry helping others less fortunate than Himself and asked us only to live in imitation of His own example. Those of us that think that we can butter Him up by building great edifices to His honor and falling down on our knees and praising Him, as did the Pharisees in the temple that He so often condemned, believe me, are fools among fools.'*

"As I've told you before, Piccolo's authority comes directly from Christ. "*Now, what would Christ have done in this case?"* Piccolo told me that as long as a single child lacks a roof over his or her head and has not enough to eat, that not a single block of stone will be laid in Italy to build a church. And not a single stone has been laid to build a church in all of the Veneto country since he came here, and that is just the way that it is going to be. And should he ever rise to the papacy, not a single block of stone will be laid to the honor and glorification of God in the Catholic world until every single child in the world has a roof over his and her head and enough to eat.

Piccolo once told me, "'*this is the fundamental difference between Christ and His Father. God the Father is a self-serving God, one that requires His subjects to adore Him as the King He sees Himself to be - I am the Lord thy God and thou are to bow down to no other god than I. But, Christ, on the other hand, walks among His children, He wears no crown on His head, He carries no scepter, only compassion in His heart. He tells us, Love thy Neighbor as thyself – for I am thy Neighbor!'*

"The orphanage you passed at the foot of the mountain is a very special one, as it was the first one built in the world that was designed to allow children to be born who otherwise would be aborted by women too young or too poor to afford them. It is equipped with a world-class clinic and nursery which are necessary to convert newborns into healthy three and four year olds, at which time they are placed into the community or transferred to the main orphanage at the other end of town which is equipped with a school and a gymnasium.

"Piccolo used the money he got for the table to break ground for the main orphanage and raised the rest of the money he needed to complete that project via his popularity program; or, perhaps, better stated his unpopularity program."

"His unpopularity program?" I repeated his statement in a question.

"Yes, as I told you he is an enemy of the pomp and splendor of the clergy. When he came here his first *executive order* was to ask the clergy to sell all of their jewelry to build the orphanage. And although most of the priests complied, a few of them sequestered their gold neck chains and rings of diamonds and rubies and emeralds. Nevertheless, you won't find a single solid gold cross hanging from any of their necks today.

"Of course, not only the clergy got the shock of their lives when he first showed up in Vittorio Veneto - the congregation did as well. Before he came here it was commonplace on Sunday morning to see as many as a hundred or so orphans congregating in the street that ran past the steps of the church, many of them emotionally and physically impaired, a few retarded, some missing limbs, others deaf or blind and of other deformities. Their only possessions were the tattered and torn rags that they wore, mostly covered with mud in the spring and fall and frozen with flakes of snow in the wintertime. And then there were the tin cups they held in their hands, that is, those who were lucky enough to have hands. Most of the parishioners would sneak around to the rear entrance of the church in order to avoid them, similar to how Christians often cross the street today to avoid the homeless in the street on their way to and from church.

"When Piccolo was named bishop and the time came for him to say his first mass, an overflowing crowd came from miles around to attend. When they showed up at the church on January 11, 1959, much to their surprise there wasn't an orphan to be seen. Some went so far as to remark that it was about time that "someone cleaned up this mess." For the first time in years many of them were able to ascend the steps and enter through the main entrance of the church. But when they entered the church they got the biggest surprise of all. For there on the end of each of the first few pews hung a small sign, *'riservato ai bambini speciali di Dio' – 'reserved for God's special children.'* There lined up row after row were about two hundred orphans gazing at the magnificent Titian altarpiece. And as I already told you his first words to his newly acquired congregation that day were, *'Christ picked me up from the mud in the street and gave me to you.'* Since that time this good man has picked tens of thousands of children up from the mud in the street and has given them their rightful place in society."

Suddenly a nun came out of the kitchen and Jack introduced me to her. "This is Sister Vincenza, who has been with the bishop for ten years. She will be joining us for dinner," and then he gestured for the two of us to sit down. For Sister Vincenza it seemed to be more of an order than it was a request. As for me he pointed to one end of the table where a high-backed elegantly carved mahogany chair sat. It seemed to be a step up from the other chairs and I recognized it as one of the two chairs that had been set against the wall in the bishop's office.

As I started to take my seat Jack waived me aside, "I thought I would give you the opportunity to sit in the same chair in which several popes have resided in the past. He picked the chair up and turned it upside down. On the bottom was a row of aging brass plates like the ones that had been on the clock in the office. On them were listed,

Leo XIII	11 November 1879
Pius X	2 January 1904
Benedict XV	24 June 1916
Pius XI	22 September 1923
Pius XII	2 February 1941
John XXIII	22 January 1959
Paul VI	22 July 1968

"Note that the date for John XXIII is three days before he announced plans for Vatican II and change in the Church. In the next six months he visited here quite often, sometimes spending as much as a week here with Piccolo. It was difficult to tell who was the prodigy and who was the protégé. For as history tells us in that short time, one of the most conservative men in the history of the Church was converted into one of the most liberal men in the history of the Church. When I first came here I questioned Piccolo as to how he was able to accomplish this transformation in the space of only a few months. He told me that it took him only a few minutes. He told John what his father had told him many years before, *"Each time that the fork in the road comes up, ask yourself, 'Now what would Jesus do in this case?'"* And the rest was history. After all, Christ was a liberal, you know."

He then set the chair upright and as I squirmed into it I wondered how much it might be worth? Certainly, with a history like that six figures would be appropriate. I thought of telling Jack that if he were to add a plate with my name on it that it might double its value. But I decided to keep the thought to myself.

He ran into the kitchen and returned with a bottle of wine, this one red. There seemed to be a touch of amber to it, but it was definitely red. Twisting the cork out of the opening, he proceeded to fill the overblown wineglasses that were a part of each setting about a quarter full.

"Other famous people have sat in your chair including Albert Schweitzer. He spent a week here five years ago. We didn't see either one of them from the minute he arrived until the minute he left. Afterwards, I asked Piccolo what they were doing all that time? *'We have determined that intelligence has nothing to do with genes. We evaluated, at great length, the testimony of God the Father in the Old Testament and determined, from what we know today, that He was a Borderline Idiot. On the other hand'* he added, *"we evaluated the testimony of Jesus in the gospels and determined that neither one of us could begin to shine His shoes. The only other conclusion that we could reach was that one was Satan; and the other was God.'*

I wondered about this man, this Italian cardinal to be who, breaking protocol, would have his housemaid dine with his guests. Did he have no respect at all for tradition? Or was it that he had greater respect for God's children? Then struggling for something to say I asked, "Do you always have dinner together?" And Sister Vincenza answered, "No. I normally go back to the convent after I put it in the oven. I've found that these guys do fairly nicely by themselves after that." And Jack chimed in, "Yes, Piccolo knows how to put it on the table and, of course, I know how to wash the dishes," and glancing sideways and smiling at Sister Vincenza, "At least, I've learned how to wash the dishes."

The footsteps coming down the stairs were obviously those of the man of the house. Momentarily he appeared, dressed again in street clothes unbecoming a bishop of the Church - a bright yellow shirt with ladybugs all over it, conventional slacks, and a pair of white bucks. This time at least, his toes were missing. He glanced at the table and looked at Jack as if he had said mass and had forgotten to serve the Eucharist. He proceeded into the kitchen and returned with a frosted jug of water, which he poured into the water glasses that were spread across the table.

I have always taken the first sip of wine with bread so when the bishop started to pour the water I started to reach for the bread, and from both my right and from my left I felt two quiet kicks which reached my shins simultaneously. Sitting down and bowing his head, the bishop uttered a few inaudible words, and noticing the others, I quickly bowed my head. Although I had no idea what he was saying, I thought of my grandmother who had taught me my first prayer, "Father, Son and the Holy Ghost, he who eats the fastest gets the most!"

When he looked up, noticing that I was staring at his shirt, he glanced down at it and said, "Every shirt I wear has to have some symbol of the so- called weaker sex. This afternoon you might have noticed some hula girls on my shirt. This is to remind me *that although God made men stronger physically, He made women stronger spiritually*. So we are both equal. We are both needed, only together can we advance. Only together," and he glanced upwards, "can we make His dream come true."

Thinking of that afternoon when we had passed by the seminary, I came up with the obvious question, "If He did make them stronger spiritually, then why doesn't the Bible permit them to serve as priests?"

And Piccolo responded, "The Bible doesn't bar them from being ordained. We do. We, Christ's shepherds, are all men. Every one of the books of the Bible was written by men. Not a single one was written by a woman. Because all of Christ's disciples happened to be men, all popes have assumed that He intended that only men could serve. Yet, these very same two-hundred-and-sixty-two popes in a row have assumed that Christ's basic requirement of each of His followers, *'give up all material things and come follow me,'* somehow does not apply to them, for they have all lived in the lap of luxury while half of the world's children have starved to death. Christ never made it clear. Although He never said women could serve, He also never said that they couldn't serve. And it will happen sooner or later. And what *Mother Church* has to face is that when something is inevitable, it is best to bite the bullet now. Why waste time squabbling about it? Get the job done; use the available time of its ministry to help solve the problems of the world." The bishop said this in an embittered voice of considerable frustration, almost as if he were a tiger in a cage unable to get at its prey.

"Yes, someday, should infallibility come to me, I will be able to accomplish this thing. But right now I have neither the power nor the influence one needs to win the game. And yes, if the day ever comes that I have that power, my very first act will be to right this wrong of the past. And I will do it on my own. For in this thing I need no advice. Other than this," and he pointed to his temple once again, quite frustrated that he could not accomplish this thing on the spot.

all of God's creatures great and small,

Then he added, as if he had read my mind, "I have always, from an early age, had a problem with the Holy Trinity, 'The Father, the Son, and the Holy Ghost.' A triad of men. I have always believed that *God is more our Mother than She is our Father*. Only a mother can give birth and God has given birth to everything around us, including you and I. So that She is our Mother is quite obvious. And if one believes in one God then He must also be our Father. Otherwise there would be two Gods, for no living thing could exist no matter how great or how small, without the union of a mother and father. And this is the scientist, not the philosopher in me that is speaking.

"It is what our dear friend Einstein put before us many years ago that so few of us have bothered to heed. He told us better than any before him or after him of the great mystery of creation; that all matter, animate or inanimate, is made up of moving parts called 'energy' - from the air we breathe to the hardest substance known, diamond. And what he told us was that all of these moving parts all the way down to the tiniest one yet to be discovered have both a mother and a father. Otherwise they would not be.

"And one can see this quite readily in nature. Every animal, every fish, every bird, every insect has a brain, a nervous system, a cardiovascular system, a digestive system, a pulmonary system, a purification system and a reproductive system. There are mothers and fathers among all species no matter how large or how small. Let's take lice for example. Barely visible to the human eye, yet they go about their lives in essentially the very same way we do. They eat, they drink, they defecate, they urinate and most important of all they copulate and perpetuate their kind. Every single one of their offspring is the product of a chemical reaction – the union of different forms of energy, in the case of animals, birds, fish and insects an egg that has been fertilized by sperm. And we know that all of God's living things number about twelve million different species. By 'specie' is meant that they can only mother and father offspring of their own kind.

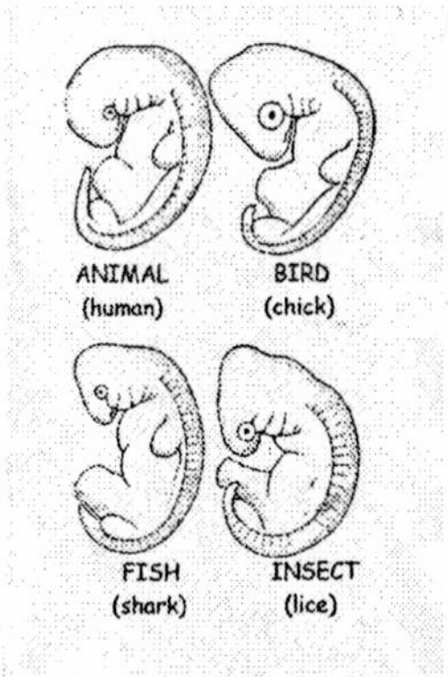

early fetal development; does not reflect relative size

"And beyond the tiniest of insects begins the world of micro-organisms. One might consider a micro-organism to be a living thing that is too small to be seen by the human eye. And the number of species here is unlimited.

"Among the largest of these is the spider mite, up to a half million of which are in the pillow one lays one's head on at night. Although too small to be seen by the human eye, being among the largest of micro-organisms they are easily observed under today's powerful microscopes, going about their daily lives, eating and drinking and defecating and urinating and most important of all perpetuating their kind, mothers and fathers bringing their young into the world. And this can also be seen of body cells, of bacteria, of molecules and basically every tiny bit of this thing Einstein referred to as 'energy' all the way down to the atom. And there are of course, those subatomic particles of energy which are too small to be seen even by present day microscopes. Yet, it is reasonable to believe that there are mothers and fathers among the most infinite of God's creatures. Not that the vehicle of reproduction is limited to the egg and sperm, for many simple organism reproduce by other chemical reactions - other kinds of mothers and fathers.*

"And one knows that the most infinite of all beings is the Creator. And the fact that there had to have been a Creator does not necessarily mean that there is a Supreme Being, a God so to speak. There are three hundred million Buddhists who believe that man is simply an extension of the Creator and that mankind itself is the Supreme Being. And although there can be some question as to whether when we talk of the Creator one is talking of an all-powerful Supreme Being or at the other extreme an infinitesimal being of minute size and power, -one is talking of the Great, Great, Great . . . Grandmother and Grandfather of each and everyone of us."

I stopped him, "How about the *Big Bang* theory, the way scientists say it all started?"

And he was quick to head me off, "The *Big Bang* theory tells us how our universe came about. Whereas it makes scientific sense concerning the formation of the universe, it has nothing to do with explaining the beginning of it all, for there could have never been a beginning of it all.

* *all animal life down to the tiniest known specie of insect has a mother and a father. In some rare instances – as in the case of the duckbilled platypus – is the reproductive process known as parthenogenesis, -the creature has within itself a mother and a father and self-fertilizes. Many simple organisms reproduce asexually, -the interaction of different units of energy producing their offspring.*

Not even the *Big Bang* could have occurred if there was nothing there to begin with. Because nothing can come from nothing and this is not a matter of theology or ideology, it is a scientific fact. It is a scientific fact that something had to be infinite." He paused as if he were a speaker who had come to the end of his address and anticipated questions. And finally one came.

"Then how does one know whether this infinite being is a Supreme Being or is the infinitesimal minute being you speak of?" I asked.

"Purpose," he answered, "purpose." Each one of these creatures no matter how insignificant has purpose. Each one of them knows exactly what he or she is doing.

"For example, one family of these so-called micro-organisms is responsible for building the human body. Literally billions of molecules of protein, over a hundred thousand different kinds; each one going about its daily life in its microcosmic world. And right alongside them are billions of molecules of cholesterol, again thousands of different kinds, also going about their daily lives, building the human brain and nervous system; each one of them knowing exactly what its specific job is in this great factory of creation. And each one of them growing up to be mothers and fathers who will parent children which will enable their population to make their contribution to the epitome of God's creation, a human being."

"You're trying to tell me that an atom has a brain?" I challenged him.

"Of course," he replied, "it knows what to do, probably not as complex a brain as is the human brain but nevertheless, a brain. It moves and it moves in a purposeful manner. If it didn't move in a purposeful manner all of God's creation would be at an end. Only a conscious being can move. As one knows unconscious beings or things cannot move. And the reason they can't move is that they are unable to interact with any other form of energy.

"And it might be that the brain of an atom is much more complex than that of a human being. We know as a matter of fact that relative intelligence has nothing to do with brain size. Science tells us that ants are much smarter than elephants and we all know that we are smarter than elephants.

"For one to say that the Creator is an infinitesimal being of some kind and is not the Supreme Being we speak of is to say that all of these armies of micro-organisms are going about their work without any organization or direction at all. And whereas that is a possibility, it is not a probability. The weight of common sense tells one clearly that one is talking of a Supreme Being of some kind, one that is both our Mother and our Father. Or perhaps two Supreme Beings, one our Mother and one our Father. And the latter is certainly the most logical conclusion one could come to, after all, as we have just discussed, every single living thing no matter how large or how small has both a 'mother' and a 'father'. So it makes all the sense in the world that there are in fact two infinite beings, two Supreme Beings, two infinite sources of energy that at one time came together in a chemical reaction and started it all. Exactly what Einstein tried to tell us many years ago, -that God is both our Mother and our Father." He paused again, this time as if waiting for applause but none came forth, as we were all caught up in deep thought.

"But even if the Creator is an infinitesimal being and not the Supreme Being we think of, there would had to have been two of them to begin with. For a single bit of energy could have never started it all. It is a scientific fact that a chemical reaction requires the interaction of at least two difference sources of energy. Even an atom cannot split without the aid of another form of energy. A single bit of energy would have remained unconscious forever."

"This means that there is a heaven, an afterlife. You have answered my question," I exclaimed, "for now I know and no longer need believe."

But he was quick to correct me, "I have proved to you that there is a God, a Supreme Being or most likely Supreme Beings. But the existence of God does not necessarily mean that there is an afterlife. In fact, the very nature of God's creation itself would dictate that there is no afterlife. For all living things eventually die and if it had been the intention of the Creator that man be immortal it would make no sense that He would cause him to die. There would be no point to it. Also, keep in mind that human beings are made up of many independent entities. They are in fact a composite of billions of tiny beings all going about their daily lives. If one were to say that humans are immortal then it would mean that all of these tiny beings are also immortal, most of which live for only a few minutes in this life.

"No, when one speaks of the afterlife one is talking of the business of religion, of someone who claimed to have had direct intercession with God and that God had promised an afterlife for those who followed the will of the prophet and paved his way with gold."

Chapter 6

THE WINNING CARD

As the bowls were passed around the table, everyone lapsed into silence as if dwelling on what had just been said. Then Jack broke the stillness, "Speaking of religion, Lucien is one of those who wants to make sure that he's playing with a winning ticket."

And Piccolo gave me a look of certainty, "I have a winning ticket for you, every time a winner, *the winning card.* If you promise to use it, I will give it to you. Guaranteed, guaranteed to win. No doubt about it."

Again reaching for the truth, I asked, "What is it? Is it Christ? Is it Allah? Is it Buddha? Is it Brahma?"

And much to my surprise he answered, "None of those," and pointing to his temple, "It's right here. All you have to do is basically do what it tells you to do. Always do what is right. Always do what this," pointing to his temple, "tells you to do. That is enough. Nothing else counts. You do that, and that alone, and you're going to be in the winner's circle. Let there be no doubt about it."

"But how about Christ and the others? Which one is right? How can you tell which one is right? There are so many of them."

"If you are strong enough to do what I just told you to do without any outside help, then that should be enough for you. For in that case you would be dealing directly with your maker. But if you need some help, some more cards, then you need this thing we call religion, the business Jack and I are in. And *the winning card* is not which religion is the true religion; it is what I have just given you, -nothing more, nothing less. The purpose of religion, in fact the sole purpose of religion is to help you play the game, and possibly help you play," again pointing to his temple, "*the winning card.*"

He stopped and paused a bit and said, "I too had a mother and a father and today I know that they are both in heaven. My mother was a believer, a devout Christian who prayed before crucifixes. The first thing I remember ever seeing was a crucifix that she had tacked up over my crib. She saw in the crucifix the image of God and told me that it was good and holy.

"My father on the other hand was a realist, one who sees things as they really are. He saw in the crucifix a near-naked man nailed to a tree, something that a parent should not put in front of a child and tell him or her that it is good and holy. He tore the crucifix off the wall and burned it in the stove.

"This does not mean that my father was an atheist. It was just that he did not believe in the business of religion. He could not accept that God would choose to appear to certain men and not to all of us. And he knew that all of the so-called prophets had great motive to convince others that they had talked to God. He was particularly suspicious of Moses, who profited most of all by his claims that he had talked to God. This made him the leader of the Israelite nation and gained for him '*all the gold and silver and brass vessels of the thirty three cities of the Promised Land.*'

"But nevertheless, since you raised the question: How does one prove that Catholicism, that Protestantism, that Islamism, that Buddhism or that Hinduism is the true religion? And the answer is simple, -one doesn't. It can't be done. It just can't be proved. But what one can do is prove that a certain religion is not the true one.

"Let me give you an example of how this works, that one cannot prove the right religion," and he paused to take a sip of his wine.

the 'expert' said so, it must be so,

"Sometime ago in Paris, where Modigliani had lived and worked, a sculptured marble head was recovered by divers from the canal that ran behind the artist's house. On the assumption that the work may have been executed and discarded by the sculptor, it was brought to the attention of a local museum curator who believed that it could be an original *Modigliani.* The head was subsequently examined by experts in Paris and London who were recognized as the world's foremost authorities on Modigliani and it was found that in fact the work was an original masterpiece by the great artist.

"A local, what one might call a hippie, challenged the find. The experts saw it as an opportunity to gain worldwide publicity for their discovery and arranged a live debate between themselves and the hippie on European television. The upcoming debate was widely publicized throughout Europe and the press made the hippie out to be some kind of a fool.

"The hour long debate allowed for a ten minute summary at its end for each of the debating parties; and although the hippie had disclosed several serious flaws in the experts' analysis, their immense credibility in the field of art enabled them to seal their claim as being a matter of fact in their closing remarks. The great art experts, like the preacher, have the great advantage of immense credibility, which totally eclipses anyone's ability to reason, anyone's ability to think. It was clear to all viewers that the hippie really didn't know what he was talking about.

"Then the hippie got his ten minutes. He started by saying, '*I was hoping that I wouldn't have to go this far but it seems that I have no alternative,'* and he added something that the art world has never since forgotten, *'No one,'* he told them, *'not all the experts on this stage or all the experts in Europe or, for that matter, all the experts in the world can prove that any work of art is an original executed by a particular artist. On the other hand one can prove, beyond a shadow of any doubt, that a particular work is not authentic.'* Then, to the astonishment of all, he proceeded to run a film of he himself designing and sculpting the alleged Modigliani head. He then closed with a single statement, *'The only way that one can tell that one is truly in possession of an original work of art is to watch the artist create it, watch him complete it, have him sign it and to take the work and place it in a safe to which only one knows the combination.'"*

Then the bishop summarized what he had just put before us, "Religions are like great works of art. When you believe one is the true one, as in the case of a great work of art, you are relying entirely on the credibility of the expert. You are relying entirely on the credibility of the preacher, on the credibility of scripture, or, in some cases, on your own gullibility. Nothing more, nothing less. Other than that, it is impossible to tell which one, if any, is the true one.

"The only way you can know that a particular religion is the true one is to have been there. In the case of the Jew, this means to have been there at the burning bush when God the Father spoke His message to Moses. In the case of the Christian, it means to have been there when Christ rose from the dead and ascended into heaven. In the case of the Muslim, it means to have been there upon the winged horse when the Angel Gabriel took Mohammed to visit Abraham and Moses. In the case of the Mormon, it means to have been there at the edge of the pond when God the Father and Christ His Son appeared together to Joseph Smith.

"Otherwise you are relying entirely on what someone said to someone else, who in turn passed it on to someone else, who in turn passed it on to someone else, who in turn passed it on to someone else, for all time. And you have to keep in mind as my father claimed, -that in those days, as in these days, men had great motive to lie in these things; for if they were to convince their fellowman that they had talked directly with God, it would make one a great and wealthy man. And that included Abraham and Moses and Isaiah and Paul and Matthew and Mark and Luke and John and Constantine and Mohammed and Joseph Smith and all the others who claimed to have had talked with God. And it also includes the present day preachers who earn their livelihood that way, -many of whom become wealthy men. Of course, to accept Christ as the true emissary one must go a step further."

"A step further?" I questioned.

"Yes, a step further. As you know in all the other cases we are dealing with historical figures, people who we know as fact once lived. But in Christ's case we are dealing strictly with faith. So in the case of Christianity, one must believe not only that Christ actually lived at one time, but that those who wrote the New Testament were actually Christ's disciple's or associates as they claimed to be. The only historical benchmark we have to make this judgment is that we know the gospels were written after 85AD with the exception of the *Gospel of Mark* which could be dated as early as 69AD. Although it is possible that some of the books could have been written after this time, one knows that they could not have possibly been written before this time and we know this to be a historical fact because some of the things mentioned in these books had not occurred in history until these times. For example, the Book of Revelation talks of the destruction of Jerusalem which occurred in 70AD. Keep in mind that none of the original writings included in the New Testament have survived.

"The oldest partial or substantial copy of the New Testament that has survived is a fourth century text. This artifact, the oldest surviving copy of either testament, is held by the British National Museum in London today. And this is much older than is the oldest surviving substantial copy of the Old Testament which is alleged to be a tenth century text held by the Hebrew University in the Holy Land.*

"One must keep in mind that for the first three centuries after Christ's time there was no organized church at all, just a few Christian cults spread here and there. In 315AD the boy Constantine came to power. Knowing that all of his immediate predecessors had fallen victim to betrayal and were either exiled or murdered, he feared that he too would suffer a similar fate. Shakespeare later capitalized on many of these unfortunate men. Constantine studied those who had lived before them, who had lived out their natural years in power, and found that each of them had convinced the populace that they were in communication with the gods. So one day while leading a detachment of soldiers down a street he suddenly fell down on his knees and claimed to have had a vision of Christ on the cross. Although no one else saw the cross, his men believed him, Nevertheless, this was one of two historical turning points in the history of Christianity that has made it the predominate religion in the Western Hemisphere today. Needless to say, Constantine lived out his natural years in power.

* *Biblical quotations in this book, unless otherwise noted, are taken from these two sources.*

"Constantine's legalization of Christianity in the Roman world would eventually pave the way for Christianity's rise to the world stage; the reason why it is the largest religion in the Western Hemisphere today - religion having been passed down from family to family.

"And we all know that the other major historical pivot point for Christianity occurred a couple of hundred years later when Charles Martel defeated the Moors at Tours. For had Martel lost this battle, then the Moors would have overrun all of Europe and today we would all be Muslims, faith would have very little to do with it, as religion is passed down from family to family. Faith is not based on intelligence or knowledge; it is a result of conditioning. There is an overwhelming chance that a child brought up in a Muslim country will be a Muslim, and one brought up in a Christian country will be a Christian; it has nothing to do with the truth.

"To get back to our point, we preachers believe that the New Testament was written in the last half of the first century. If one goes by the history books it was written much later than that. But for purposes of this discussion let's go by what is taught in the seminaries of the world, when and by whom we preachers believe that the New Testament was written.

"We believe that three of Christ's apostles were involved in writing the New Testament. We must be careful here to distinguish between an apostle who was a disciple of Christ and those apostles who were so- named after Christ's death; the apostle Paul being the most significant of these who is believed to have written the lion's share of the New Testament.

"The twelve disciples were Peter, Andrew, James the son of Zebedee and his brother Phillip; and Bartholomew, Thomas, and Matthew the publican; James the son of Alphaeus, and Thaddaeus, and Simon and Judas. Of these, we believe that Peter wrote the book of Peter. There is some evidence that John the disciple of Christ wrote the three books of John and the Book of Revelation. We know as an absolute fact that Revelation could not have been written before 95AD because, as I said, it talks of things that history knows did not occur until that time. That John wrote the Book of Revelation would seem to be a matter of fact, for its opening verse tells one explicitly that it was *'His servant John: who bear record of the word of God, and of the testimony of Jesus Christ.'*

"The gospels themselves tell us that John was older than Christ and this would place his age when he wrote Revelations, as well as his gospel, at over a hundred. This demonstrates the unreliability of what is expressly stated in the gospels, as it would not have been possible for a first century man to have survived to that age, less write a book. The so-called 'expert' claims John the Disciple of Christ wrote his Gospel and Revelations, but history knows better.

"Then we have the *Gospel of Mark,* which as I mentioned could not have been written before 69AD. There is some evidence that Mark, an associate of Peter, could have, in his late years, written this book, which would make it the most credible book in the Bible. The other gospels, Matthew, Luke and John, clearly plagiarized and embellished what Mark had to say; in many cases using his exact phraseology in describing events. This is quite obvious in their relative descriptions of the crucifixion. We know that these gospels were written much later, and in particular, it is a historical fact that the *Gospel of John* could not have possibly been written before 90AD which is after those in the Mid East first became aware of the eastern belief of a Holy Trinity. And this is important, as the *Gospel of John* contains the only explicit testimony of Christ that He and His Father were one and the same God. John 10, *". . . I and my Father are one . . ."* John is also the only evangelist who describes the Holy Ghost as the Light of Wisdom as the eastern God describes its Third Person. John 14, *"But the Comforter, which is the Holy Ghost, whom the Father will send in my name, shall teach you all things to your remembrance."*

"One might wonder why Mark waited a half-century to record Christ's life. The answer could be in the *Gospel of Thomas* which the history books tell us could have been written as early as the time of Christ. And there seems to be some credence in this, as this gospel, unlike the others, is written in the style of a diary, as if notes were being taken by Thomas during Christ's ministry. Although it includes the ministry and death of Christ, it does not speak of miracles, nor that Christ was born of a virgin, nor of Christ's resurrection. Also, nowhere does it mention the Holy Trinity, and not once does Christ mention His Father, even as He dies on the cross. So although history tells us that this was most likely the first gospel written, it was obviously left out of the New Testament because it had basic ideological conflicts with the others. Yet, it did set forth the basic structure of Christ's life that may have inspired Mark to write his book. The *Gospel of Thomas* is the oldest surviving fragment of the New Testament. Recorded on papyrus rather than parchment, it is dated to the first century.

"Notwithstanding the authenticity of the *Gospel of Thomas,* the *Gospel of Mark* is the only gospel that could have been possibly written by a man who was alive at the time of Christ's ministry. Yet, it is the unanimous conclusion of Biblical scholars that it is most likely that even Mark got his information from Peter long after Christ's death and was not a direct witness of Christ's ministry. And this is important, when one considers the supposition that the evangelists stole the concept of the *Holy Trinity* from the Hindus. That is, the ideology of *Three Persons in One God.*

"To pinpoint a time, those in the Mid East first became aware of the Hindu religion in 85AD – 95AD, a historical fact, precisely the time in which Matthew, Luke and John wrote their books. When Mark wrote his book in 69AD, he was unaware of this concept. In a nutshell, the *Gospel of Mark* includes the short ministry of Christ including a few miracles, the requirement of baptism, the crucifixion and resurrection. So Mark's major contribution in his book versus *Thomas* is that he adds the concept of Christ's resurrection.

"But what is important is not what it contains, but what it does not contain. Mark does not speak of Christ's birth including the theory that it was a 'virgin' birth. That comes along later when Matthew and Luke wrote their books. It is for this reason in modern texts that *Matthew,* and not *Mark,* is the first book of the New Testament - because it begins with the birth of Christ. But, more importantly, is the fact that the *Gospel of Mark* contains no reference to a *Holy Trinity*. As a matter of fact it tells us just the opposite - that Christ and His Father are two separate and distinct beings. Nowhere in the *Gospel of Mark* does Christ claim to be God. As a matter of fact, He repeatedly refers to Himself as the *Son of Man* and not the *Son of God.* And He corrects those who mistake Him for God, *Mark 10, "Good Master, What shall I do that I may inherit eternal life? And Jesus said unto him, Why callest me good? There is none good but one, And that one is God."* He scribbled on his napkin,

Gospel of Thomas - Christ's ministry miracles & crucifixion
Gospel of Mark 69AD - adds baptism and resurrection
Gospel of Matthew 85AD - adds the virgin birth
Gospel of Luke 90AD - a copy of the *Gospel of Matthew*
Gospel of John 95AD - adds the concept of the *Holy Trinity,*

John 14, "Believest thou not that I am in the Father, and the Father in me. The words that I speak not unto me, I speak not of myself; but the Father that dwelleth in me, he doth the works .Believe me that I am in the Father and the Father in me."

So history tells us that those who wrote the gospels were born more than two generations after Christ's time and those who wrote of his birth would have depended entirely upon word of mouth for a century or so for the details of His birth. And this could mean that most of what we perceive to be Christ today is fiction. Exactly what Albert Schweitzer, one the world's most brilliant men, concluded in his, *"Quest for the Historical Jesus."* [1]

"Yet, even if one comes to the conclusion as most of us have that Christ actually lived and performed the miracles attributed to Him, there is still another side to the coin."

"Another side to the coin?" I asked.

"Yes, my father's side to the coin," he replied. "Whereas it is possible that Christ actually lived and that these men wrote about His life many years after His death, it is certainly as reasonable to believe that these men were simply men of good conscience, who recognizing the evilness of the Old Testament, as it had been put together by Moses and the other prophets, decided to right the wrongs of the past and wrote into the record the fictional character of Christ. As you know, the New Testament is a much shorter book than is the Old Testament. Aside from recounting the life of Christ it restricts itself to correcting most of the evils of the Old Testament."

"The evils of the Old Testament?" I stopped him.

"Yes, the evils of the Old Testament. It is Moses in the Old Testament who tells us '*that it was God the Father's command that woman live in dire servitude to man*.' It is Moses in the Old Testament who tells us that it is God the Father's command '*that slavery be a way of life*.' It is . . ."

And Jack stopped him, "I told Lucien all about Moses."

"Good, so much for Moses. But now Christ comes along in the New Testament and He blatantly violates His Father's fourth commandment, '*Honor and obey thy father and mother,*' in just about everything He does. He totally overrules all of the evil things that His Father had commanded in the Old Testament.

"For example, God the Father in the Old Testament commands that the prostitute and the adulteress be taken outside the gates of the city and stoned to death; but in the New Testament Christ tells us, '*He who is without sin cast the first stone*.' And more importantly Christ gives us His commandment, '*Love thy neighbor as thyself,*' which in itself overrules most of the evils of His Father in the Old Testament including the oppression of women and slavery which are the explicit dictates of the third and tenth

[1] *Schweitzer based his analysis on historical data rather than on Roman Catholic doctrine and that of other Christian churches. According to the history books none of the books of the New Testament were written by men who lived at Christ's time and several of them were written in the second century. If this is true, of course, the credibility of the New Testament is severely impaired as it would mean that the stories were passed down through generations subject to embellishment and change. It would be like writing about the life of a common man who lived at the time of Lincoln today, where there is no existing record of his life.*

commandments, as was once presumably given by His Father to Moses. And in almost every other parable in the New Testament Christ overrules His Father's instructions. Not a one of us, including priests, would be permitted to work on Sunday if it were not that Christ, in sowing wheat in the field on the Sabbath, disobeyed His Father's third commandment that expressly forbade it. '*Thou shalt do no work on the Sabbath.*' God the Father felt so strongly of this commandment that he had strengthened it in the Old Testament by decreeing many times that the penalty for working on the Sabbath is death. Certainly, when one professes belief in the Old Testament and the Ten Commandments one is taking the word of Moses over that of Jesus Christ, Himself.

"And Christ Himself, by His very being, violated the most fundamental commandment of His Father. '*There is only one God and thou shalt have no other Gods before thee.*' For if Christ was God, He could not have been the same God as was His Father as just about everything He does in the New Testament contradicts the dictates of His Father in the Old Testament. If He were the same God then He would have been contradicting Himself. And it is these overwhelming contradictions in the New Testament of much of the ideology of the Old Testament that would lead one to conclude that Paul and Matthew and Mark and Luke and John were speaking of a fictional character when they spoke of Christ. Or that Moses was talking of a fictional character when he spoke of God the Father. Otherwise according to the Bible there would obviously be two Gods neither one of which could have sired the human race for a Father cannot be a Father without a Mother. Or perhaps both Moses and Paul were talking of fictional characters?

"Let us put it in a nutshell, the fundamental difference in philosophy between God the Father of the Old Testament and Christ of the New Testament. God the Father commands that we love our neighbor but only those that are like us. He tells us quite explicitly to persecute, annihilate and enslave all those who are different. But Christ in the New Testament tells us something else. He tells us to love our neighbor as ourselves no matter how different he appears to be. He tells us to persecute, annihilate or enslave no one. And this is the fundamental difference between the God of the Old Testament and the God of the New Testament.

"Up until Christ came along people in the Western Hemisphere had only the word of Moses to go by. And for the past two thousand years many of them have continued to ignore what Christ had to say. For if the Christian population of the world believed what Christ had to say, we would have been spared the horrific bloodshed of the Crusades, the Inquisitions, the Civil War, the Holocaust and even the ethnic cleansing wars that persist today. For Christ taught us to love all our neighbors no matter which god they praised, whereas God the Father explicitly commands us to persecute, annihilate or enslave all those who worship false gods, -gods other than the God of Abraham and Moses. And so important is this command of God the Father in the Old Testament that almost half of its volume is dedicated to carrying out His order.

"And you can see this even today. It is this very same Christian preacher who today wages his evil war against women and homosexuals who, just a decade ago, lost his quest to keep the black in his corner through his laws of segregation. It is this very same Christian preacher today who promotes the word 'faggot' who just a few centuries ago introduced the word 'nigger' to American culture. And when the day comes that he finally loses his quest to keep women and homosexuals in their respective corners, he will then turn his hatred toward these so called *realist* or *atheist* children who are beginning to emerge today – children who are taught from an early age that there is nothing healthy about glorifying a near-naked man nailed to a tree; who are being brought up in a world of reality rather than in this world of make-believe in which we find ourselves.

"Nevertheless, that Christ, the Son of God, invalidates His Father's first, second, third, fourth and tenth commandments and adds two of His own has long puzzled Bibliologists. That the teachings of the New Testament are in material conflict with those of the Old Testament seems to make no sense at all. So how could this possibly be?"

east meets west,

He paused for awhile as if to break from the subject and then started up again. "We know from His testimony in the New Testament that Christ at His time was not aware that the Chinese were living on the other side of the world. And this is consistent with the history books which also tell us that the *Silk Road* which had begun in China almost two hundred years before the time of Christ had only reached India at Christ's time. Actually, if one were to go by the history books the people in the Mid East first became aware of the people in the East at just about the time that the *New Testament* was being written, 85AD -- 95 AD.

"We know this to be a fact because history verifies it. For example, we know that paper was invented in China in 105AD and a few documents have survived that are written on paper in western languages that are dated just after that time. The surviving Gospel of Thomas is printed on papryus and not paper, which could date it to the first century. So we know that communications between the Chinese and the Middle East were firmly in place by the turn of the first century or shortly thereafter."

He paused again as to place a period between what he had just said and what he was about to say and then went on. First we should consider the coincidence of the remarkable similarity of the underlying philosophies of Buddha and Christ."

And I interjected, "There is no similarity at all, Buddha introduced the concept of reincarnation and Christ introduced the concept of resurrection of the body, two completely different things."

He corrected me, "I'm not referring to their relative concepts of the afterlife but rather of their philosophy as to how one is to live this life. Christ's philosophy that permeates the New Testament, *'Love thy neighbor as thyself'* is exactly Buddha's message of five hundred years before which has today survived in Buddhist scripture, the Tripitaka, *'Love thy neighbor as thyself'*

"There can only be two possible explanations as to how this remarkable coincidence came about. Either the evangelists stole the idea from the Tripitaka," and every hair on the back of my neck stood straight up, "or Jesus Christ was the reincarnation of Buddha." There can be no other explanation of this strange coincidence.

"But what drives the nail into this coffin is the additional fact that in introducing His philosophy to the Middle East - Buddha's philosophy of five hundred years before - Christ disobeyed the fundamental philosophy of His Father as set forth in the Old Testament. All of the physical evidence we have today, points to the fact that Christ is not the *Son of God the Father* of the Old Testament, but rather that He is the *Son of Buddha.*

"Keep in mind that Christ speaks of 'My Father' dozens of times in the New Testament. Yet, God the Father never once speaks of 'My Son' in all of the Old Testament. The idea that God the Father had a Son is entirely a product of the New Testament. According to the Old Testament, God the Father never had a Son.

the infinite Christ,

"We know that if Christ is God then He had to be infinite. And if He were infinite then Christ had to have been the same God who ordered the murder of hundreds of thousands of men, women and children and infants who did not believe in Him in the horrific taking of the holy land. One can see this more clearly if one were to replace the word *'the Lord'* in the Old Testament with the word *'Christ'* in a typical passage,

"'*And **Christ** said unto Joshua, See, I have given unto thy hand Jericho with all of its vessels of gold and silver and copper and bronze. Take all ye men of war and go around the city seven times, and the priest shall blow with the trumpets. And when ye hear the sound of the trumpets all the people shall shout with a great shout; and the walls of the city shall fall flat; and ye are to enter the city and take to the sword all of the inhabitants thereof, every man, woman and child, leave not one alive!'*

"We know as a matter of fact that Christ was not the same God who ordered the atrocities involved in the taking of the Promised Land because we know that He would have never done such a thing. For Christ's overwhelming message tells us to live in an unselfish society, one of *giving* rather than one of *taking* as was commanded by His Father of the Old Testament. And Christ repeats His instruction on how one is to live one's life in each of His Gospels as if one might miss it in one book, one might run into it in the next book. "'*Sell all that thou hast and give to the poor – lay not treasure up on this earth where moth and rust doth corrupt but lay up treasure in heaven – it is easier for a camel to pass through the eye-of-a-needle than for a rich man to enter the kingdom of heaven – the parable of the widows mite in which she gives her last pence to the poor – and Matthew who says 'if thou be perfect go and sell all that thou hast and give to the poor and thou shalt have treasure in heaven*'. And it goes on and on. There is the additional testimony that Christ required each of his disciples to '*give up all that thou hast and come follow me.*' He so hated the money changers that he threw them out of his Father's Temple. Christ's most powerful and overwhelming message of the New Testament, a message that most Christians choose to believe is not there. They choose to ignore the direct testimony of Christ and rather believe the whims of the preacher who in exchange for a few bucks guarantees them heaven without having to give up a thing.

"And then one must consider the Chinese. And Walla! What do we have there? The fundamental message of Taoism is also *"Love thy neighbor as thyself and sell all that thou hast and give to the poor."* Like Christ of the New Testament and Buddha of the Tripitaka, Tao likewise dictated a redistribution of wealth; a society of *love thy neighbor as thyself* regardless of how different; a society in which all of God's wealth is shared equally by everyone. A society in which a man is judged on what his contribution to others has been, not on how much wealth he accumulates. This is why communism was able to make such inroads into China in the twentieth century; the Chinese were always communists, it's just that they used to call themselves Taoist. For the basic philosophy of communism calls for a redistribution of wealth society - that all of God's wealth is to be shared equally, precisely Christ's message in the New Testament, precisely Buddha's message in the Tripitaka." He stopped for a moment as if thinking and then rose and went to the sideboard and retrieved a sheet of paper. He started writing. He carefully perused what he had written and then set it in front of me,

2500 BC	Hindu stories are first told (Vedas)
1400BC	Hebrew Stories are first told (Moses)
525BC	Buddhism *'Love thy neighbor as thyself'* Tripitaka
479BC	Taoism *'Love thy neighbor as thyself'*
150BC	Silk Road begun in China
4BC-29AD	Christ claims divinity *'Love thy neighbor as thyself'*
85-95AD	*Silk Road* reaches Middle East. For the first time those in the Middle East and those in the Far East become aware of each other's religions.
75-120AD	the New Testament is written (per history)

"There is, of course, a third alternative," he offered.

"A third alternative?" I repeated his statement in a question.

"Yes," he replied, "Coincidence."

"As you know, Christ claimed to be the Son of God that God the Father in the Old Testament promised to send to earth to rid the world of Original Sin and thereby redeem mankind. As promised in the Old Testament? There is nothing in the Five Books of Moses that speaks of such a promise. In all of his testimony Moses accepts the mortality of man. He makes his case quite explicitly in *Genesis* that man had originally been created to be immortal and that as an afterthought God made woman who enticed man to commit Original Sin and forever after that man was destined to return to the dust of the earth. In all of Moses testimony there is no promise that the body will ever rise again. His testimony on the other hand speaks quite explicitly that at death the 'ghost' leaves the body and the body returns to dust. It is the authors of the New Testament who promised that the body would rise again; who gives man back the immortality that had been taken from him by Moses in the Old Testament. It is Christ in the New Testament who gives man back the immortality that had been taken from him by God the Father in the Old Testament. Once again Christ contradicts the will of His Father.

"As a matter of fact, there is no mention of Original Sin in the New Testament either. Christ was baptized by John the Baptist according to Mark *'for the repentance for the remission of sin.'* It had nothing to do with Original Sin. This came along later. That Christ is the Son of God who came to earth to rid the world of Original Sin is a product of a conspiracy of theologians of the middle ages who, realizing that there was no substantial link between Christ and His Father of the Old Testament made one up. That Christ is the *Son of God* is explicit in the New Testament, but that He is the *Son of God the Father* of the Old Testament is just not in the cards.

"We are talking here of what has been for almost a thousand years or so the definition of Christ, *'Christ is the Son of God who was sent earth to rid the world of Original Sin.'* There is absolutely nothing in the Bible that links Christ to Original Sin. Not a word. There is nothing there that links Christ to Adam and Eve. There is nothing there that links Christ to God the Father of the Old Testament. Yes, He speaks of *His Father*, but never of God the Father of the Old Testament. Not once."

Like a boxer landing blow after blow, he had staggered my imagination. I could not think. I certainly could not speak. He started up again.

"Yes, if one wants to reach for a straw one could go back to the *Book of Isaiah* written more than a thousand years after the time of Moses and with an extraordinary imagination could take a part of what he has to say as being a reference to Christ. But even what Isaiah has to say, *'because he had poured out his soul unto death, and he was numbered with the transgressors, and he bare the sin of many; and made intercession for the transgressors,'* and *'Behold a virgin shall conceive, and bear a son, and shall call her son Immanuel.'* would be meaningless to anyone who had not first read the New Testament as Isaiah does not say who he is referring to. Since the oldest scrap of *Isaiah* that has survived postdates the New Testament by a thousand years these phrases could have been added at anytime.

"Yet, it is most probably Isaiah's testimony, which could be interpreted as most anything, that the evangelists used to convince at least a part of the population at His time that Christ was the Son of God the Father of the Old Testament; that convinced some of them to convert to their newly founded religion, which either by the process of reincarnation or plagiarism was a carbon copy of eastern theology.

Christ is not the Son of the God of the Old Testament,

"And one could ask why the evangelists went to the trouble to prove that Christ was the Son of God, whereas they could have just started a new religion from scratch. And the answer is quite clear. At the time most of those in the Middle East believed in God the Father of the Old Testament, so their only logical recourse was to convince the populace that Christ was the Son of this same God.

"But in convincing them that Christ was God, the evangelists were faced with another problem. For if Christ was God then there would be two Gods, a violation of the first commandment, '*There is only one God and thou shalt have no other gods before thee.*' And they also found their answer to this problem in his newly found eastern religion for the Hindu God, the eastern God, had comprised a Holy Trinity for thousands of years before Moses was born. For according to the ancient Hindu scripture, the Vedas, '*there are three people in one God. There is Brahma the Creator, there is Shiva the Redeemer and there is Vishnu the Light of Wisdom who keeps the balance between good and evil, tells one what is right from wrong.*' Three persons in one God, identical in relative function to '*God the Father, the Creator; Christ the Redeemer; and the Holy Ghost, the Light of Wisdom*' in the New Testament. (*The Vedas* are available in most major city libraries)

"Until East met West in 85-95AD the people in the West had never heard of a Holy Trinity. After all, there is no mention of it at all in the Old Testament. Employing the facility of a Holy Trinity was the only way that the evangelists could convince the populace that Christ was God. For otherwise Christ's claim to be God would, as I have said, violate His Father's first commandment '*There is but one God.*' And as we've just discussed, Christ's contradictory testimony clearly tells us otherwise."

There was a long pause now. If I had any doubts I certainly had them now. And then the bishop cleared the whole matter up for me. "But nevertheless, whether one believes in scenario one, that these men actually lived these long lives and wrote of a man who actually lived, or whether one believes, as my father did, that these men influenced by eastern philosophies simply wanted to right the wrongs of the past and created the fictional character of Christ is immaterial. Whether or not Christ ever lived or not is of no consequence. Christianity like any other religion, is a philosophy on how one is to lead one's life and as a philosophy it is very much fact, for we have the New Testament. What is important of any man, even one who proclaimed to be God, is not so much His life on earth but is what He left behind; like Einstein, like Lincoln, like Edison and all the others. What is important of Christ's life is not His link to the Old Testament and not His life on earth, not even His death, but it is what He left behind, His sixth and seventh commandments, *'Love thy Neighbor as thyself"* and *'Sell all that thou hast and give to the poor.'* Christ left us with only one rule in life, *'each time that the fork in the road comes up, we must ask ourselves, 'Now what would Jesus have done in this case?'"* *Then he* stopped as if to read my mind, as if to assure himself that this last and most important phrase was fixed in my mind for all the remaining days of my life.

some other hippies run their films,

"So let us get back to your question. Which religion, which philosophy is the true philosophy? As with great art, it is often possible to tell that a particular religion is not the true one and the most formidable enemy of the prophet is science, - scientific fact and in some cases historical fact. We are seeing this happen each day more and more as we go on. As more and more scientific facts become available, more and more do we question the prophet, more and more is the credibility of the prophet eroded. And this extends to all religions of the world, not just those in the Western Hemisphere

"The credibility of the art expert is similar to the credibility of the religious expert, the preacher. And the lack of credibility of the hippie is similar, for example, to Darwin and Einstein in their day. In the case of the Modigliani scandal there are few people in the art world today who doubt the validity of the hippie's testimony. In fact, there is no one who doubts the hippie's testimony, because today one has the facts. But when he first made his claim, no one believed him, not a soul. For the credibility concerning the issue at hand was entirely with the art expert.

"And likewise, when Darwin and Einstein first made their claims, no one believed them, for the credibility was entirely with the preacher. The populace thought them to be crazy. Darwin proposed that we had evolved from apes before the time of the first excavations of prehistoric bones and the development of modern genetics and DNA. Einstein claimed that all matter is made up of moving parts, energy, including the hardest substance known, diamond; he made his claim before the time that modern microscopes and other advancements of science could prove his point. For them of course, the proof of the pudding was not to come about until after they had gone to the Great House above. But when they first proposed their theories as to how we all came about, no one, not a soul, believed them. What they said contradicted what all the experts were saying, what all the preachers were saying.

"And like the hippie in the case of the supposed *Modigliani*, both these scientists have now had the opportunity to have run their films. Perhaps long after they have been gone, but nevertheless, they have now been run. In the case of Darwin, archeology and more importantly, genetics and DNA have proved his *theory of evolution* beyond a shadow of a doubt. In the case of Einstein, the development of immensely powerful microscopes and other scientific advancements have proved his *theory of relativity*. As compared with microscopes of Einstein's time, which had the capability to magnify up to seventy-five times, the powerful microscopes of today are able to magnify up to a half-million times. So now like the hippie and his *Modigliani* they, Darwin and Einstein too, have had their time on the floor. They too, have had their time before the cameras.

"Yes, what these 'hippies' once proposed as theory is now very much fact. The expert, the preacher, now has only two alternatives. He can admit he is wrong. Or he can avoid further questions. And the only viable alternative he has, obviously, is the latter, -to focus the attention of his followers on something else. He goes so far as to make it immoral, in some cases illegal, for his children to read these books. He takes these works of Darwin and Einstein out of his schools, out of his libraries. He does not want to consider the facts. Yes, more so Darwin than Einstein, as the typical preacher does not have the intelligence to understand the implications of Einstein's work. But, nevertheless, he causes his children to grow up shielded from what these great men had to say. Shielded from what are now known to be the facts, the hippie's film, he brings his children up in a world of make-believe.

"Yes," he continued, "when Darwin and Einstein came along, the preacher would show up in the great arena, call it the courtroom if you wish, to debate the issue. And every time he would win, and this only because of his immense credibility. But where is he today? He is not there. He is not there because he knows that the hippie now has his film, he now has the facts. The preacher now knows that the hippie will make mincemeat of him.

"We see this in the case of Galileo too. Despite the fact that he proved through his *law of falling bodies* that the world was spinning on its axis, people laughed at him for after all they *knew* that the earth was flat, for Moses had told them in his book of *Genesis* that God the Father had told him that it was flat. And God the Father explicitly confirms this on the very first page of the Holy Bible in that He creates the land together with its vegetation on the second and third days and then He hangs the sun and the moon and stars in the sky on the fourth day. Every six year old knows that no form of life including vegetation could exist on earth without its sun. Every six year old knows that it is the sun's process of photosynthesis that makes vegetation possible. And even when Magellan circumnavigated the globe decades after Galileo's time and took from the expert the Bible's story of Creation it made no difference to the believer that the Bible claimed that the world had been created by a God who did not know that the earth was round. That the world had been created by a God who didn't know that vegetation was the product of the sun.

"Religion, as I have said, is like a work of fine art. One might be an expert in religion. And another might be an expert in fine art. The preacher is the expert in religion. It is his job to win the credulity of his parishioners so that they will believe that those teachings are authentic so that they will respond with their faith and ultimately with their dollars. The art dealer, on the other hand, is the expert in fine art, and correspondingly, it is his job to win the credulity of his customers so that, believing the authenticity of the piece, they will respond with their awe and ultimately with their dollars. It's the same game, just being played on two different fields.

"If the preacher is wrong and Christ for example, is not the true emissary, then if the parishioner plays the card, I just told you of," pointing to his temple, "the card that Paul and Matthew and Mark and Luke and John wrote of, he's still in the winner's circle. It makes no difference. And on the other hand, if the artwork is not authentic, and the buyer enjoys it all his life, he's still a winner too.

"To answer your question more directly: No you can't prove which one is the true religion. Believe me, for I and countless others before me have tried. Ask Albert Schweitzer, the most brilliant of all of us, who proved as a matter of historical fact that Christ never lived in his twenty year search for the truth, *The Quest for the Historical Jesus.*

"Faith must remain a product of belief, -a guess at best. The important thing is that one uses the card I talk of, *the winning card*, and that he or she plays it throughout the game, every single day of his or her life.

"Many religions will move you in the right direction. They give you a deck of cards, which will lead you to trump the play every time with your hidden card, *the winning card.* Yet, there are many other religions, beliefs, which, sadly, will hide the card from you. When the time comes to play it you may not even be able to find it here," and he again pointed to his temple; "for *belief* would have blocked your ability to *reason*; for belief would have blocked your ability to tell right from wrong. Christian churches that use their political influence to deny equal human rights to women and gays and others are good examples of this. For a religion to encourage the persecution or subordination of any kind of people is wrong. Although its members might believe otherwise, their chances of winning are seriously diminished for their actions are in direct defiance of the most fundamental command of Jesus Christ, '*Love thy neighbor as thyself.*'

"One looks back just a few years to the time of Hitler and Mussolini and blames these two monsters for it all. Yet, the real culprit in that dreadful war was not its leaders, but it was a weak society that allowed itself to be caught up in a *frenzy of fascism and hatred of others who appear to be different.* And likewise, in the fifties and sixties it was not so much the Christian preachers who preached persecution and segregation of blacks who were to blame, as it was a weak society that allowed itself to be caught up in a *frenzy of fascism and hatred of others who appear to be different.* Today it is not so much the *born again* preachers that are to blame, for the real culprit is again a weak society that allows itself to be caught up in a *frenzy of fascism and hatred of others who appear to be different.* It's the same game, just being played at different points in time."

He paused for a few minutes to afford a time to reload our plates and then went on, "There have been millions of theories on how we came about and most of these have resulted in as many different religions. And most religions including Christianity perpetuate the belief that a magic genie of one sort or another touched with a magic wand and 'puff' there it was, and there we were. These theoretical differences as to how we all came about remain diverse today. This is the nature of belief. One can believe most anything. So the possibilities are enormous. It why fiction books outnumber non-fiction books thousands to one.

"But on the other side, through the years, has been science. Again, originally with as many different proposals. But, today, because of these two men, Darwin and Einstein, unlike the experts - the preachers, all of the 'hippies' of science are in uniform agreement. They all know where we came from and they all know how we got from there to here. For they tell us of that time that the Father and Mother sat in their great factory above and designed the first parts, those infinitesimal bits of energy of which Einstein spoke, those tiny specs of something that started it all. Yes, Einstein provided the parts, and Darwin provided the path. These hippies gave us the facts and fact has no alternatives. One can only know one thing. It is exact. It is a fact!

"So in this respect we come to a sound conclusion. We know that all religions begin as theory and all religions are destined to forever remain theory, -someone's guess. And on the other hand, we know that science too, always begins with theory, -someone's guess. The difference between the two is that in the case of science some of the theories will eventually narrow to fact, and there are no alternatives to fact.

"And science is advancing at such a rapid rate today that it is possible that by the end of the century genetics will prove beyond a shadow of a doubt that man is a direct descendant of the so-called ape man. If that should happen, it will be a scientific fact that we are not descendants of Adam and Eve as Moses had claimed. Of course, the Church is already aware of this fact."*

"It is already aware of it. How can that be?" I questioned.

"The dates. The Old Testament's genealogy is complete and unbroken from Adam and Eve to Christ. The generation length for each of the patriarchs is complete in the Bible except for three of the generations between Noah and Abraham. The 4060BC date one hears about for Adam and Eve assumes that these three men begot their offspring at the average age of the other patriarchs who came between Noah and Abraham. If they, in fact, begot their offspring in the last year of their lives, then the time of Adam and Eve would be 4192BC. So it is a matter of Biblical fact that the earliest time of Adam and Eve could have been 4192BC. Because it is a Biblical fact, every preacher in the world hangs his hat on the fact that Adam and Eve do not predate this time, although it is known as both a matter of scientific and historical fact that the American Indian was running around North America three thousand years before.

"The earliest known hard evidence of a date etched in stone based on a 360 day calendar is 4261BC in Mesopotamia. This artifact is held by the British National Museum in London. The earliest known hard evidence of a date etched in stone based on a 365 day calendar is 3312BC in Egypt. This artifact is held by the Cairo Museum in Cairo. So Adam and Eve are safe by a narrow margin if they in fact came along at the time the Bible claims they came along.

"But then one has to consider the unusually long lives of the early patriarchs. Those between Adam and Noah lived an average of 830 years and those between Noah and Abraham, an average of 447 years, conceiving their offspring relatively late in life. For example, Noah sired his first offspring at the age of five-hundred. Even many of the later patriarchs lived unusually long lives. Moses, for example, died at the age of one-hundred-and-twenty at a time that the average life span was short of thirty.

"The Church believes that when St. Jerome first put together the first Bible* he calculated its genealogy and came up with a date of about

**In 1997 repeated DNA testings proved conclusively that modern man is the direct descendant of the Cro-Magnon man dated 40,000BC. The stories of Creation and Adam and Eve in Catholic catechisms today are footnoted "not a matter of history."*

1000BC for Adam as he used normal life spans for the early patriarchs as they were originally set forth in the five books of Moses. It was common knowledge at his time that the great Egyptian civilization had thrived and the pyramids had been built long before 1000BC; this would have dealt a fatal blow to the validity of Christianity before it really had a chance to get off the ground. So it is believed that Jerome substituted these unbelievable life spans in order to push the date of Adam and Eve back to 4000BC. What Jerome did not know at the time was that it is not biologically possible for a human being to survive past the age of one hundred and fifty. The kidneys filter about seventy-five gallons of blood each day and will fail under ideal conditions between one hundred and forty and one hundred and fifty years. If Adam lived to be 950 years old as the Bible claims then he could not have been the father of the human race for he would have been of another species. So the date of 990BC for Adam and Eve is not a matter of interpretation. It is a matter of Biblical fact."

He shoved his chair backwards got up and went again to the sideboard that stood against the wall and opening a drawer he shuffled through some papers and returning to the table placed in front of me,

Genealogy from Adam and Eve to Christ

↓
Adam 4060 BC
Seth (Cain and Able were Seth's brothers)
Enos
Cainan
Mahalaleel
Jared
Enoch
Methuselah
Lamech
↓
Noah---
↓ ↓

Shem	Hamm
Arphaxad	the father
Salah	of the Canaanites
Eber	who were to be
Peleg	annihilated by Joshua
Reu	*"put to the sword every man, woman and child"*

Serug — in the taking of the promised land
Terah
Abraham — the instruction that all those who
Isaac — appear to be different are to be
Jacob — be annihilated, enslaved or persecuted
Jacob______________
↓ ↓
Judas Levi
↓ ↓
_____Eleazor____
↓ ↓
Phares Moses Aaron (brother of Moses)
↓
Esrom
Aram
Aminadab
Naasson
Sakmon
Booz
Obed
Jesse
King Solomon
King David
Roboam
Abia
Josaphat
Joram
Ozias
Joatham
Achaz
Mahasses
Amon
Josias
Jechonias
Salathiel
Zorobable
Abiud
Eliakim
Azor
Sadoc
Achim

God the Father
decrees to Moses
in the Old Testament
that the sons of Aaron
the Aryan race is
to rule at His side
and that all others are to be
annihilated, enslaved or persecuted
the foundation of all bigotry
and fascism in the western world

Eliud
Mattham
Jacob
Joseph, husband of Mary the mother of Christ

He gave me a few minutes to read over the listing and then said, "The authenticity of the Old Testament depends entirely on the authenticity of its genealogy. After all, that is all that the Old Testament is, -a genealogy of man from Adam to Christ. About three hundred mummies have been found so far that predate Noah's time and the oldest of these approaches Adam's time. Their average life-span is twenty-three and the oldest one lived to be forty-four. Yet, the Bible claims that Noah sired his firstborn at the age of five hundred, which was three hundred years after the great pyramids were built and a thousand years after the Pharaoh Narmer had founded the great Egyptian Empire. Those patriarchs from Adam to Abraham conceived their first offspring at an average age of two-hundred-and-seventy-two. Unless one accepts this as being absolute fact, the *Old Testament* is simply a fairytale. So it is inevitable that we must separate Christ from Moses. The only question is when?"

After pausing for a few more minutes as to partake of the treasures that the good nun Vincenza had set before us, the bishop went on, -this time concentrating entirely on me, "I have told you of *the winning card* because you are delving too deeply into the scriptures, and anyone who takes that journey is certainly to lose one's faith. Most religions, because they are coming more and more into conflict with science and history are more likely to lead one away from God, then lead one to Him. And this includes Christianity"

"Remember," he concluded, "there is only one *winning card.* Only one right religion, the one up here," and he pointed one last time to his temple. He had brought the clatter of knives and forks to an end. He gave us a minute or so to absorb all that he had said and then wiping his chin he asked me, "Where do you go from here?"

"To Rome, where else? To the heart of Christianity, St. Peter's and then I go back to the grind in the States."

And he offered, "I could make arrangements for you to stay in one of the Vatican apartments, but I don't think you would feel very comfortable there. But not far from St. Peter's is a little pensione. You might feel less ecclesiastical there." He took out a business card and wrote an address and phone number on the back of it and handed it to me.

He then took out a second card and wrote something on the back of that card and as he handed it to me he said, "When you visit the Vatican find the office of Bishop Marcinkus. It is in the Government Palace which is the largest building in the Vatican Gardens. Paul Marcinkus. He was here just last week. We were fighting over the branch of the Catholic Bank, which is here in Vittorio Veneto. He runs the Vatican Bank and therefore oversees its affiliate, the Catholic Bank, which operates throughout all of Italy. He intends to turn our branch of the bank over to private interests, something that I don't agree with, but nevertheless something that is going to happen.

"I am sure that he will be happy to arrange to have someone give you a personal tour of the gardens, including a walk-through of the Papal Apartment itself. You will find this quite interesting as it something that the public never sees.

"Thank you," this man with the perpetual smile added, "you have enlightened me. You have given me good substance for my sermon on the mount." And getting up he stopped at the sideboard and picked up a few pieces of stationary headed *Vittorio Veneto. "I will make some notes of what we have talked of today for posterity. Some shot for the cannon. I will see you on the battlefield."* And he headed for the stairs.

And I followed him with a puzzled look.

"The enemy," he told me, "*Christian preachers whose make-believe credibility preys on the ignorance and weakness of the minds of men."*

I smiled and raise my voice, "You can count on me. I will be there."

As the bishop's footsteps faded on the stairs, Jack said, "You'll have to forgive him for leaving so suddenly. He turns in every night at nine and he's up promptly at four. If the Pope himself were here, he would do exactly the same thing."

"Wow, up at four. He must sleep all afternoon."

"Wrong, he has no idea what a nap is. I will walk you to the hotel."

It was sheer silence as we started the long walk along the seminary and it was I who broke the silence, "What does Piccolo mean when he says, 'infallible'?"

"Although he is careful not to advertise it, and he tells others that he has no interest in it, his objective is to accede to the papacy. Because of his work here at the school, as I mentioned, he is a recognized authority on theology. Something he prefers to call 'human theology'. As a matter of fact he has been a chief advisor of both John XXIII and Paul during their papacies. He's well liked, probably a few years from being named a cardinal, an Italian Cardinal. I think he has a shot at it. But he wants this not for the vestments and the pageantry. In fact, he tells me if the day ever comes he will refuse the *Papal Tiara* which has been the focus of papal coronations ever since popes have been elected. He wants to be Pope because he will be able to change things for the better. He wants to complete Patton's dream. He wants to bring about the equality of all God's children. Patton and his armies have given us the diamond and Piccolo with another kind of army of men and women of good conscience will make it real.

"Last year, Paul VI spent the better part of a week here with Piccolo. The very next week he issued the now-famous decree banning birth control practices in the Catholic Church, *Humanae Vitae*. And the very next week Piccolo issued an editorial to the press calling for repeal of the doctrine. In retrospect it seemed to me that this strange order of events had been planned by the two of them. Certainly the ruling was not consistent with Paul's thinking on the subject and ignored the conclusion of the committee that he had appointed two years ago to study the issue. Of course, it made those who surround him in the Vatican extremely happy.

"It was almost as if Paul and Piccolo had some extraordinary motive to have issued such a conservative ruling. Particularly, in that Piccolo went to the press with his letter rather than going direct to Paul, which had until then been his custom. It seems to me that the two of them decided that Paul would issue the proclamation and shortly after that Piccolo would follow with his objection. Perhaps history will someday tell us why they did these confusing things. One thing I do know is that shortly after that Piccolo's attitude changed quite dramatically, from one of *wanting* to be the next Pope, to one of *knowing* that he would be the next Pope.

"Cardinal Suenens, the Archbishop of Brussels and leader of liberalism in the Church continued to speak out publicly against the Church's edict on birth control and went so far as to tell his congregation to ignore it. Cardinal Suenens, who is a close friend of Piccolo, has visited here many times. He told me that in connection with his criticism he was summoned to the Vatican and that in the presence of the Vatican cardinals he was chastised by Pope Paul for his action.

"The cardinal told me that he thought that only public opinion could save him from being removed as a cardinal. However, before he left Rome the Pope called him aside privately and apologized to him for his criticism. '*We must think of the long haul,*' he told Suenens, '*One must not spend one's shot too swiftly. It is better to lose the battle than to lose the war.*'

"As a matter of fact, when Piccolo is deeply troubled by issues that from time to time come onto the table, the first place he goes for advice and counsel is his good friend Cardinal Suenens. Although Piccolo, Pope Paul and others like Willebrands of the Netherlands seem to be driving the train of *righteousness* in the Church, it is Suenens who is often stoking the coals.

"Yet, Paul, recognizing that he is surrounded by fanatics, men who are capable of most any atrocity to preserve their beliefs, is playing his cards wisely. Yes, history will see him as having been a pawn of the *Vatican Curia*; but posterity will know otherwise.

"In Piccolo's words," he added, *"'Paul is a lion, a great lion. But one who wisely conceals his mane in sheep's wool.'"*

And he went on, "As we just discussed, since Paul became Pope he has been appointing nothing but conservatives to the *College of Cardinals* which will of course, elect his successor. It is quite obvious, that since Paul, like John before him, is a liberal, that these appointments have been forced upon him by the *Vatican Curia.* If Paul's successor is a conservative the reforms which he and John XXIII began will come to an abrupt end. But if he is a liberal or a progressive they will go on.

"From time to time there is a consistory, a large block of cardinals that are appointed at a single time. The next of these will be in the mid-seventies. It is Piccolo's belief that if at that time Paul were to load the block with liberals, it would swing the election of his successor back toward the liberal court. Therefore it is important that Paul lives until then, for if he were to die today a conservative would certainly replace him.

"Piccolo has great concern for Paul's safety, as he is surrounded by enemies in the Vatican; men who might resort to anything to protect their interests; to protect what they believe to be the interests of Christianity. In fact, Paul himself hints at this danger in his memoirs, '*my weakness for life has resulted in poor leadership for my flock.*'

As we reached the hotel he hugged me goodbye and that was the last time I ever saw him . . . alive.

And Piccolo? Well that was the last I saw of him too. But I will always remember him. Yes, partially because of his unrelenting, almost Mickey Mouse smile. But mostly because of his toes!

Diocese of Vittorio Veneto Photo

Bishop Albino Luciani

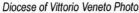

"When I was a teenager my father made me promise that I would live my life in imitation of Christ, and I have kept that solemn promise. Each time that the fork in the road has come up, often only minutes apart, I have asked myself, 'Now, what would Jesus have done in this case?' And I have often pondered the possibility as to how much better the world would be if everyone were to do this."

Chapter 7

. . . AND, YES, SHE WAS STILL THERE

So the next morning I took the train to Rome and I will tell you of that adventure in what follows. But for now I will tell you of my return.

As the plane flew over the great harbor, I looked down to the left and yes, she was still there. Now I knew why she was there. For she knew what she was doing when she cried with silent lips, ***"Give me your tired, your poor, Your huddled masses yearning to breathe free, The wretched refuse of your teeming shore. Send these, the tempest-tost to me, I lift my lamp beside the golden door!"***

She didn't care if they were Christian or Jew, or Muslim, or Hindu, or Shinto, or Buddhist or Tao. For she knew that she must gather from all the ends of the earth the great dispersion of minds that were needed to accomplish the great task that lay before her, to mold America into what it is today. She didn't care whether the men she needed to build and light her cities were Spanish or Dutch; she didn't care whether the men she needed to build her steel and paper mills were Russian or Scandinavian; she didn't care whether the men she needed to build her roads and bridges were Polish or Irish; she didn't care whether the men she needed to establish her communication base of telephone, radio, television and computer technology were Italian or Chinese; she didn't care whether the men she needed to get her airborne were French or English; and she didn't care whether the men she needed to bring her into the nuclear age were Swiss or German. As a matter of fact, she didn't even care if they were men or women. And, above all, she didn't care whether Private John Doe was Christian, Islamic, Jewish, Hindu, Shinto, Buddhist, Tao, agnostic, atheist, black, white, red, yellow, straight or gay, when, in his foxhole he wrote,

"I don't know why this terrible war is being fought,
I don't know what will be its outcome.
But, what I do know, is that I plan to fight this war as if
its entire success or failure depends on me alone!"

Well, believe me Private Doe, you and the others that fought along side you have died in vain, that is until ***"we stamp out what Hitler stood for, once and for all."***① This will only come about on the day that the country for which you gave your life makes good on its founding pledge, ***"This nation is dedicated to the proposition that all men and women are endowed with the inalienable right to Life, Liberty and the Pursuit of Happiness."*** ②

For as General Patton so profoundly vowed at Milan, ***"It is our great differences that have made us into the great nation of one that we are. There should be no room here for those preachers and politicians who would choose to use them to divide us. For freedom without equality is not what it pretends to be. The diamond would be made of paste."***③ And as our hero Albino Luciani so courageously affirmed, ***"Until the day comes that we can guarantee equal human rights to the tiniest minority, we cannot truthfully call ourselves a democracy."***④

These things these great men said are consistent with the current policy of the APA on gay marriage: ***"The American Psychological Association joins its counterparts throughout the free world in supporting the action taken on December 15, 1973, by the American Psychiatric Association removing homosexuality from the official list of mental disorders and adopts the following resolution: "Whereas homosexuality implies no impairment in judgment, stability, reliability, or general social or vocational capabilities . . . Whereas most children are aware of their sexual orientation in early adolescence and are put at risk to severe emotional stress and disorders, including suicide . . . Whereas broad scientific research has not disclosed any significant psychological or emotional differences between children raised in different-sex vs. same-sex families . . . Whereas couples of the same-sex are more likely to share common interests which fosters long term relationships, children of same-sex marriages are less likely to suffer the trauma of divorce . . . Whereas the basic human need to parent children applies to all regardless of sexual orientation: be resolved the state is not justified to deny the legal benefits that the license of marriage offers to same-sex couples in that it deprives them of property rights, health care, social security survivor benefits, estate planning, tax benefits, spousal privileges in medical emergency situations; and most importantly, -it deprives millions of American children in gay families of their constitutional entitlement to equal rights under the laws.***

① *Luciani's response when he was criticized for having defended the gay priest Marc Oraison. 14 Jul 76*
② *Thomas Jefferson, Declaration of Independence, 4 Jul '76*③ *General George S. Patton at the grave of a homosexual Medal of Honor winner, 23 Dec '44*
④ *Bishop Albino Luciani before the Italian Parliament, 16 Jan '67*

"Therefore, be it further resolved, that the American Psychological Association supports the provision to same-sex couples of the legal benefits that can accrue only as a result of marriage." ⑤

Then there is the decision of the United States Supreme Court in its sole historic definition of the word marriage, ***"Marriage is one of those basic human rights of a person fundamental to one's very existence and survival. Under the Constitution of the United States and its Fourteenth Amendment, which guarantees all citizens equal protection under the laws, the freedom to marry, or not to marry, resides with the individual – it is an individual right and therefore cannot be infringed upon by the state nor by any tributary nor by the majority."*** ⑥

Precisely Luciani's definition a decade earlier, ***"The state cannot tell its citizens who they can or cannot marry, less we cease to be a free society. There is no issue more fundamental to freedom than is the right to marry whomever God deems one fall in love with. There is no more fundamental issue that divides democracy from hypocrisy."*** ⑦

"Democracy, which finds its strength in rule by the people, can only find its purpose, its sacred duty to society, in preserving the basic human rights of its loneliest individual." ⑧ It is this issue more than any other that divides those nations that choose to truthfully call themselves democracies and those nations that choose to cease to remain free. It is uniform among these great men and institutions because it is a policy based on fact. The act of *falling in love* is a basic instinct. Fact has no alternatives. Its sole enemy today remains the same one that Jefferson, Lincoln, Patton and Luciani faced many years ago, ***"the hatred of Christian preachers whose make-believe credibility preys on the ignorance and weakness of the minds of men"*** ⑨

This book is dedicated to my patron John Paul I. Yet, I am certain that it would be his wish that he share this spotlight with the untold tens of thousands of homosexual, bisexual and transsexual children and teens, born to parents whose minds deranged by the hatred of Christian preachers, caused them to take their own lives in the twentieth century in the United States. Children who were denied the inalienable right to grow up and *fall*

⑤ *summary of current policy on gay marriage of the American Psychological Association 2004*

⑥ *summary of the high court' decision Loving vs. Virginia, 12 Jun '67 Although the case involved a white man and black woman who had been sentenced to prison for having married, the court's decision protected the sacred right of any individual to marry whomever God deems he or she falls in love with,*

⑦ *Bishop Albino Luciani before the Italian Supreme Court, 22 Jan '59*

⑧ *Bishop Albino Luciani, Christian Democratic Party Convention, 17 Jan '63.*

⑨ *Bishop Albino Luciani, Vittorio Veneto, 9 Apr '69*

in love with whomever God deems they *fall in love* with. And to the more than three million AIDS babies born to date who will never live to the age that they could take their own lives. And one more, *the boy on the fence!*

"Never be afraid to stand up for what is right, whether your adversary be your parent, your teacher, your peer, your politician, your preacher, your constitution, or even your God!"⑩

Note: whereas marriage within the law can grant homosexuals the basic human right of *The Pursuit of Happiness*, it does not exempt them from sin for sexual acts within marriage. For no matter what a homosexual does sexually, it remains sinful according to the Bible. Yet, one must keep in mind that most of what heterosexuals engage in within marriage is also mortal sin as marriage as defined by most Christian churches exempts only copulation. All acts of sodomy, fellatio, masturbation and most acts of foreplay remain mortal sin within marriage as they interfere with God's creation – the sperm's natural access to the egg - as is expressly condemned in the Bible. Copulation within marriage is exempted by a single verse in the Bible, *1st Corinthians 7 Catholic version, "If his passions are strong, and it has to be, then let him marry, and it is no sin."* It should be noted that this verse does not appear in the oldest surviving copy of the New Testament held by the British National Museum in London; that it was most likely added to bring the Bible into compliance with the *Doctrine of the Sacrament of Matrimony* which was introduced in the sixth century. This addition is inconsistence with the *Doctrine of the Immaculate Conception*, –that Christ was born free of the horrific sin of sex; as if copulation within marriage were not sinful all of those born within marriage would be immaculately conceived. According to the Bible and the Sacrament of Matrimony:

sex within marriage

foreplay	*mortal sin*
copulation	*not sinful*
sodomy	*mortal sin*
oral sex (fellatio)	*mortal sin*
masturbation	*mortal sin*

Western (Christian) theology is based on the supposition that sex is driven by *lust* - by Satan - and therefore sex is considered sinful. Conversely, eastern (Hindu) theology is based on the supposition that sex is driven by *love* - by God - and therefore sex is considered to be good and beautiful. Today, those on the *left* believe that sex is good and beautiful and is a great gift from God and no longer think of it as being sinful. Those on the *right* still think of it as a great scourge from Satan and think of it as being sinful as is set forth in the Bible. Regardless of what rules one might make up for oneself, according to the Bible – particularly the Old Testament - all sex is considered mortal sin – no exceptions. So overwhelming and explicit are His condemnations of sex in the Old Testament that it is not possible to accept God the Father as being the Supreme Being on one hand and reject His condemnations of sex as being mortal sin on the other.

⑩ *Archbishop Albino Luciani speaking to a youth organization in Venice, 19 Apr '73*

Chapter 8

THE 'GOD' SATAN

Well, we have pretty much covered the bases. But, this book has failed in its purpose unless it has accomplished Albino Luciani's ecclesiastical goal in life - '*to effectively separate the hatred that permeates the Old Testament from the love that permeates the gospels;*' more specifically - to separate Christ from the 'God' of the Old Testament. Luciani recognized the confusion caused by the misconception of a Holy Trinity - *that Christ and God the Father are one and the same God* - as the fundamental flaw in Christian ideology. So at the risk of some repetitiveness - let's see how well we have done - let's nail the lid on this one. Have we carried out our sacred mission - or have we missed the mark? Perhaps, the best way to begin is to first summarize the sacred message of the 'God' of the Old Testament in a paragraph or two.

the test of human conscience,

In the Old Testament, It is God the Father's 'holy' command, '*sex is shameful and sinful.*' It is God the Father's 'holy' command, '*children born as little girls, like animals, are property and are to live their lives in dire servitude to their male masters.*' It is God the Father's 'holy' command, '*children born into subordinate races are to be held in slavery.*' It is God the Father's 'holy' command, '*children born with flat noses - those we call Negroes today - and children born handicapped; more specifically blind children, deaf children, crippled children, dwarfed children, and children born with other deformities, are not worthy to approach the presence of the Lord.*' It is God the Father's 'holy' command, '*transgender children - those born into bodies of the opposite sex - shall not enter into the congregation of the Lord.*' It is God the Father's 'holy' command, '*artificially inseminated children are not God's children and shall not enter into the congregation of the Lord.*' It is God the Father's 'holy' command, '*children born with the instinct that causes them to fall-in-love only with one of their own sex shall not enter into the congregation of the Lord.*' It is God the Father's 'holy' command, '*children born out-of- wedlock shall not enter into the congregation of the Lord.*' It is God the Father's 'holy' command, '*children of foreign nationalities shall not enter into the congregation of the Lord.*' It is God the Father's 'holy' command, *hermaphrodites - those children born with both sexual organs - and eunuchs - those abused as children and without sexual organs - shall not enter into the congregation of the Lord.'* It is God the Father's 'holy' command, *'children who are molested by pedophile predators shall not enter into the congregation of the Lord.'* It is God the Father's 'holy' command, '*man is to mutilate the sexual organs of all male children.'* It is God the Father's 'holy' command, *'male children who are not circumcised shall not enter into the congregation of the Lord.'* It is God the Father's 'holy' command, '*children who do not seek the Lord God of Israel shall surely be put to death.'*

Yet, Christ threatens His Father in Matthew 18, '*But whosoever shall offend one of my little children; it would be better for Him that a millstone be hanged about His neck, and that He were drowned in the depths of the sea.'* And again in Mathew, He makes clear to His Father that by 'my children' He means all children, no exceptions, '*Blessed are little children, for theirs is the Kingdom of Heaven.'*

In the Old Testament, It is God the Father's 'holy' command, *'a maiden who is in bondage who is raped shall be scourged and her master shall not be punished because she is not free.'* It is God the Father's 'holy' command, '*the young maiden who conceives out-of-wedlock shall be taken outside the city and stoned to death.'* It is God the Father's 'holy' command, '*the adulteress shall be taken outside the city and stoned to death.'* It is God the Father's 'holy' command, *'the prostitute shall be taken outside the city gates and be stoned to death.'* It is God the Father's 'holy' command, '*anyone who does not fall down on their knees and adore Him shall suffer a fiery Hell for all time.'* And it was God the Father who commanded the 'holy' unprovoked attack upon a peaceful people and ordered the murder of hundreds of thousands of helpless men, women, children and even infants in the taking of the Promised Land, ***"Put to the sword the unbelievers, the infidels, every man, woman and child, leave not one alive. Take for thyself the thirty-three cities of the Promised Land together with the copper, brass, silver and gold vessels and treasures thereof."***

the test of common sense,

In addition to passing the test of human conscience, to accept the testimony of God the Father of the Old Testament, one must also pass the test of common sense.

Why did God the Father choose to talk to only two dozen or so men - the so called prophets - and why did He chose to never appear to two or more of them at the same time? Why was this God so fearful of His children that he would not speak to them directly?

Why - as the Biblical record itself tells us - did all of these prophets end up wealthy and powerful men? Most importantly, why were they all men?

Why did God the Father wait thousands of years to appear to the first of these prophets? One would think that He would have given the Ten Commandments and His other rules of how one is to live ones life to Adam - the first man. Why did He wait and give them to Moses who was born almost two thousand years after the great Egyptian Empire had emerged and the great pyramids had been built? Why, did He appear to a man in the Mid East, thousands of years before those in east - the Indians and the Chinese - and those in the west - the American Indian and the Australian Aborigine - would know of Him? Something that is not true in the case of the eastern God, the God Brahma, who can be traced back to the pre-stone age.

prophets for profits,

Nevertheless, it is God the Father who gave birth to all of the ethnic cleansing atrocities in western history, including the horrific undertaking of the Crusades in which millions of Jews and Muslims were given the choice, *"convert or submit to the sword;"* the Civil War in which good and decent men and women rose up against His tenth commandment, *"Thou shalt not take from thy neighbor his slaves;"* and more recently, the Holocaust, in which God the Father gave Hitler the very same 'sacred' command He had given to Joshua three thousand years before, *"kill the infidels, every last man, woman and child, leave not one alive"* which cost six million Jews and other ethnic peoples and homosexuals their lives. And today, *fascism* is once more raising its ugly head; the Christian *born again* movement spreading like a plaque throughout America.

As the child prodigy Albino Lucian once wrote, *"The great enemy of society is not so much these evil men and those preachers driven by greed and bigotry who mimic them, but it is the ignorance and the weakness of the minds of those who are fooled by them"*

The five books of Moses cumulate in the taking of the Promised Land. If one studies these books carefully, one will find that all that he was told in his alleged intercessions with 'God', - *"I am the Lord thy God and thou shall not have false gods before thee; whoever does not seek the Lord God of Israel shall surely be put to death; woman is to live in dire servitude to man; the white Aryan male is to rule the earth; subordinate races are to be enslaved; sex is sinful and evil; etc."* were all designed to motivate the Israelites to take the Promised Land and gain for Moses and

Joshua its vast wealth. For the Canaanites who lived there believed that anyone should be free to worship whatever gods they wished to; like the Egyptians before them, they believed that woman was man's equal and that the black Nubians to the south were also their equal; and they also believed that sex was good and beautiful and a great gift from the gods. It is that Moses convinced his people that the Canaanites in thinking this way were evil people, that inspired the Israelites to slaughtered them, ". . . *every last man, woman and child. Leave not one alive"*

This is the witness of God the Father, a Monster of unparalleled proportions; the 'holy' mentor of all of the tyrants through history and He is the mentor of the *Christian right* who carries on those evil things that Hitler stood for that society has not yet taken from them. \

the infinite Christ,

If Christ is God, then He is infinite and therefore He would have been the same God who excluded from His kingdom all children who were born different including those born physically or emotionally handicapped. He would have been the same God who loved little boys more than He did little girls. He would have been the same God that ordered the unprovoked murder of tens of thousands of children and infants in the horrific taking of the Promised Land. But one knows that Jesus was not the same God who ordered that terrible undertaking. One can see this clearly if one substitutes the word 'Jesus' for 'Lord' in the Old Testament. "*And Jesus said unto Joshua, Put to the sword the unbelievers, the infidels, every man, woman and child, leave not one alive. Take for thyself the thirty-three cities of the Promised Land together with the copper, brass, silver and gold vessels and treasures thereof."* or *"Children born out of wedlock are not to enter the congregation of Jesus,"* or *"Those children born with flat noses and born handicapped are not to approach the altar of Jesus."*

Like other macro-geniuses throughout history, Luciani was what one calls a realist - one who sees things as they really are - rather than as others for personal motive would want one to believe they are. But it wouldn't take a genius of mammoth proportions to recognize that Christ could not possibly have been the same God as was God the Father of the Old Testament; for Christ's two greatest enemies, *greed and bigotry*, are His alleged Father's greatest allies

As Albino Luciani and Albert Schweitzer had once concluded at Vittorio Veneto, *"only an idiot could read the record of God the Father in the Old Testament and the record of Christ in the gospels and conclude that they were one and the same God."* God the Father is clearly a God of *fear and hatred;* whereas Christ is clearly a God of *love and compassion.* One stands on the extreme *right* deeply steeped in *fascism - hatred of those who are different;* while the other stands on the extreme *left* deeply steeped in *socialism - love of all no matter how different.* One dictates a *rich and poor society;* while the other dictates a *redistribution of wealth society.* One threatens His subjects with the fiery depths of Hell if they do not fall down on their knees and adore Him; while the other looks for no adoration but spends His time pulling His children up off their knees and putting them to work helping others. As each fork in the road comes up, one tells you to go to the *right, "Now, what is in this for me?"* while the other tells you to go to the *left, "Now, I wonder what is in this for others?"* One is *Satan;* while the other is *God.*

sell all that thou hast and give to the poor,

We live in a rich and poor society where the assumption is that those with vast wealth will be moved by compassion and take care of those less fortunate. But in reality this is a hypocritical oath. Consider the record.

There are today more than fifty million people infected with AIDS in third world countries. Of these, less than one-half million - less than one-percent - are provided with AIDS medicine. The rest of them, three million of which are children, are suffering horrific lives and will die unspeakable deaths.

Yet, hundreds of thousands of people including the Pope - the man mostly responsible for the spread of this dreadful disease - live in multiple mansions of magnificent splendor, surrounded by priceless works of art and fly around in private jets. Like the money makers that Christ threw out of the temple, the wealthy Christian tosses his leftover pennies into the box and the Vatican treasures remain intact in open defiance of Christ's most prolific teaching – in Matthew, ***"lay not treasure upon this earth where moth and rust doth corrupt but lay up treasure in Heaven" . . . " it is easier for a camel to pass through the eye-of-a-needle than for a rich man to enter the kingdom of Heaven" . . . the parable of the widows mite in which she gives her last pence to the poor . . . "if thou wilt be perfect go and sell all that thou hast and give to the poor and thou shalt have treasure in Heaven."*** And repeated in each of the gospels is the heart of Christ's message, ***"love thy neighbor as thyself"*** and ***"sell all that thou hast and give to the poor."***

And Christ's message which is in stark contrast to His alleged *Father's* instruction to Joshua, *"take from them their lives and for thyself all that they have, their land, their palaces, their vessels of silver and gold,"* is consistent with the fundamental message of Mohammed's *Koran.* ***"Give all that thou hast to your neighbor. For I am your neighbor. If the wealth ye have gained, and merchandise that ye fear may be unsold and dwellings wherein ye delight, be dearer to you than God, dearer to you than your neighbor, then God too will be dearer to others. And you will not reside with Him in His house this day, and for all time!"***

Muslims today claim that there is nothing in the Koran that motivates Islamic terrorists - *kill the infidels, the unbelievers*. And they are right. Like the gospels, the Koran is essentially a good book. Yet, one must keep in mind that like those on the *Christian right,* those on the *Muslim right* take their orders from the 'God' of Moses in the Old Testament, *"Put to the sword the unbelievers, the infidels, every last man, woman and child. Leave not one alive!"*

And on the other side of the world in Hindu scripture - *The Vedas* - is the word of the God Brahma, ***"Care only for others, less I will not care of you. For I am the others. This is all I want of you. For you will not see the brightness that lies beyond the shadow of doom unless you care for others. Unless you care for me."***

And Tao, too, in all of his wisdom, shared this very same fundamental philosophy of Christ, ***"He who profits most in the end, is he who has contributes most to others."***

And Buddha, too, in his *Tripitaka* gave this very same message to his people, ***"When all is done there are only two measurements of life. Oneself and others. The first will lead to treasures in this book of fools. In this book of this life. The other will lead to treasures in the true book. The vast book of eternity."***

The Universal God - Christ - has clearly etched His message in the 'Bibles' of all of the peoples of the world. He has provided them with an equal chance to eternal life. And the rich man who tosses his pennies into the poor box is passing up that chance.

For these reasons and for many others, Luciani knew that Christ was not the Son of God the Father of the Old Testament. He knew that when Christ emerged as the true God in the first century that those that wrote of Him almost a century later had to tie Him to God the Father because at the time the populace believed in the 'God' of the Old Testament. So they had to write into the record that Christ was one and the same God, otherwise Christianity would have never gotten off of the ground to begin with.

Yet, when the evangelists first started out and preached the fabric of Christ's message, ***'sell all that thou hast and give to the poor,'*** they found that they had no customers. It was just too much to give up for what was a long shot at eternity. So the will of Christ was put on the back burners, and it has remained there, ever since.

"Thou art Son of David,"

The link between Christ and God the Father is entirely one way, from the New Testament → to the Old Testament. For example, Christ repeats the phrase *"My Father'* almost a hundred times in the four gospels, yet, in all of the Old Testament, God the Father never once mentions *"My Son."* One would wonder why God the Father did not know that He had a Son? Not once does Christ tell us He is referring to the God of the Old Testament when he says *'My Father.'*

On the other hand, the gospels do specifically tell us who Christ is referring to when he talks of *'My Father,'* Matthew 1, *'Thou art Son of David.'* Yet, we ignore it, and we wrongly take it to imply lineage; not what it says literally, as the lineage from David to Christ is through His stepfather, Joseph, who was not Christ's biological father. Luke 1: *"He shall be great, and shall be called the Son of the Highest; and give unto Him the throne of His Father, David."* Since Christ was not a genetic decedent of David; there is only one other alternative, the gospels refer not to His body but to His soul; Christ's soul was of the House of David - the offspring of David's soul?

There is only one marriage of souls mentioned in all of the Bible, *'And it came to pass, when he had made an end of speaking unto Saul, that the soul of Jonathan was knit with the soul of David. Then Jonathan made a covenant with David, because he loved him as his own soul. . .'* Let that play with your mind a bit.

Nevertheless, the concept of three persons in one God is an ideology of the New Testament - which was written at precisely the same time in history that the Mid-East first became aware of the Hindu religion of the Far East; which hierarchy for thousands of centuries had consisted of three persons in one God: Brahma the *Creator,* Shiva the *Redeemer* and Vishnu the *Light of Wisdom;* exactly the same composition of the *Holy Trinity* the evangelists wrote into the New Testament: God the Father the *Creator* - Christ the *Redeemer* - and the Holy Ghost the *Light of Wisdom*

It is most likely for this reason why the *Gospel of Thomas* - the only gospel that could have conceivably been written at Christ's time, was left out of the New Testament. For not once in the *Gospel of Thomas* does Christ mention His Father. Nowhere in this solely vindicated surviving first century fragment of either Testament is there the slightest hint of a Holy Trinity. And the reason for this is quite obvious. At Christ's time, the Mid East had not yet become aware of the Holy Trinity of the eastern God.

That God the Father of the Old Testament is Satan can most readily be seen in that he dictates sex to be the most horrific sin of all. That sex is dirty and ugly and sinful could have only come from Satan, himself. For today, one knows that sex is good and beautiful and a great gift from God which makes possible His greatest gift of all - a newborn child. Western theology concerning sex is based on the supposition that sex is driven by *lust* - by *Satan*, the reason why it considers it to be sinful; the reason why the act itself in the west is most often driven by *lust*. Eastern theology concerning sex is that sex is driven by *love* - by *God*, the reason why it is idolized in the friezes of eastern temples; the reason why in the east the act itself is most often driven by *love*.

And then there is the fact that Satan relied on his threat of Hell to get the Israelites to murder the Canaanites and employs the very same threat on his present day followers in getting them to carry out his dreadful work - deprivation of equal human rights for others. The threat of Hell is solely the signature of Satan, himself.

One might ask why so many innocent people through the years have carried on Satan's evil work despite the fact that their conscience - as ours does today - must have told them that it was wrong. The only conceivable answer is that when threatened with Hell they were cowards. They were sitting ducks for the hatred of Christian preachers through the years who capitalized on the evilness of the Old Testament - *"Christian preachers who preyed upon the ignorance and weakness of the minds of men."*

Nothing demonstrates this more clearly than does the Tenth Commandment as set forth in all pre-nineteenth century versions of the Bible in Exodus 20,*"Thou shalt not covet thy neighbor his property, including his house, his wife, his slaves, his ox, his ass."* And as modified in modern Catholic and Jewish texts, *"Thou shalt not covet thy neighbor his house, his wife, his slaves, his ox, his ass."* And as modified in the King James Bible, *"Thou shalt not covet thy neighbor his house, his wife, his servants, his ox, his ass."* And as etched in the granite tablets that *born again Christians* demand be placed in public places, *"Thou shalt not covet." Born again Christians* of which fifty percent are women and fifty percent are blacks - *"the ignorance and the weakness of the minds of men!"*

So let us all agree on this one point. Let us place these tablets in every public place in America. But, let us not lie to ourselves. Let us etch on these stones the truth, the hallowed words of the 'God' Satan as they were originally handed down to Moses on Mount Sinai, *"Thou shalt not covet thy neighbor his property, including his house, his wife, his slaves, his ox, his ass."* Let these tablets forever be a reminder that the greatest enemy of a free society is organized religion - which for centuries fooled us into thinking of Negroes and women as property and therefore not entitled to basic human rights.

And let us not forget the youthful leader of the Eastern Orthodox Church, Metropolitan Nicodim, in his redemption of the American Christian, *"In America, 'Christians' foolishly accept the Devil's offer of the Kingdom of Heaven on the sole commitment that they fall down on their knees and worship him."*

Of all the things I remember of Luciani, I remember most clearly his words, *"Christians are by nature cowards. When one prays to God the Father one is clearly praying to Satan himself. It is Satan's threat of Hell that makes these cowards think that he is God and perpetuates his evilness. And his trickery has made civilization into a living Hell for centuries. It is now time for Christ's army of men and women of a new kind of courage to rise up and stamp out what Satan stands for, for all time. That time that Patton once spoke so eloquently of, 'This war will win for America and all mankind this thing we call freedom. But that war, the war within, will someday win for America the great prize of equality for all men and women, something that this war cannot do. For freedom without equality is not what it pretends to be. The diamond would be made of paste.'"*

Luciani recognized that the greatest problem in society was that both those on the *left* who follow Christ's instruction in the gospels -- sacrifice and love of others; and those on the *right* who follow God the Father's instruction in the Old Testament - greed and hatred of others; think that these two deities - who are exact opposites of each other - are one and the same God. That those on the *left* and those on the *right* think that they are allies in this thing called 'God.' The hatred imposed by those on the *right* will reap its evil toll on society, until those on the *left* ignore this incredible misconception on the part of their preachers and pull their heads up out of the sand and realize that Jesus Christ is not the 'God' Satan of the Old Testament.

As Luciani once told the College of Cardinals, *"If one is to be successful in bringing down an enemy, one must know who he is, know where he is coming from ..."* and the enemy of righteousness is clearly the God of the Old Testament and regardless of what his followers might think; he is coming out of the depths of Hell.

On the one side we have overwhelming evidence, both within and without the scriptures, that Christ is the one true God and that His alleged

Father was the imagination of prophets for profits. And what do we have on the other side? The 'expert' - the preacher; the man who says it is; the very same kind of 'expert' who once claimed the authenticity of the Madigliani sculpture. Go and ask him, and he will tell you of his Holy Trinity. Go and ask him, and he will tell you of the four hundred years the Israelites spent in Egypt.

All he has to back him up is that which Albino Luciani once told the graduation class of the seminary at Vittorio Veneto, *"You, as preachers, know no more about the existence of a God, or for that matter which God is the true God, than do your customers. In fact, you will know nothing about the existence of an afterlife until after you are dead; and, then again, you may never know. All you have is your faith and the conviction with which you speak. . . "*

I didn't understand it at the time, but I understand it now. Today, we know the Old Testament to be a work of fiction. It is a world of *make-believe.* And we also know that like those 'holy' men in Rome who impose it upon the western world, it is not the 'holy' book that it pretends to be. It is clearly the work of Satan and it capitalizes on the fears and the weaknesses of the minds of men. It has, as my friend *Jack* once told me, *"led the world into thirty-five hundred years of hatred and prejudice and persecution and horror and suffering and destruction and death!"*

". . . And this evil book will continue to reap its toll, until courageous men and women of the courts rise up and do their sacred duty as required by the copyright laws of nations,

THE OLD TESTAMENT

THIS IS A WORK OF FICTION.
THIS IS A BOOK OF HATRED AND PREJUDICE AND PERSECUTION AND HORROR AND SUFFERING AND DESTRUCTION AND DEATH.
KEEP AWAY FROM CHILDREN." *

* *Parish Bulletin Feltre,* 16 May '21. Eleven year-old Albino Luciani publishes his first of a lifetime of controversial articles as Assistant Editor of his school newspaper

Biblical sources,

Biblical quotations in this book, unless otherwise stated, are taken from the 4th century text of the New Testament held by the British National Museum in London and, whenever possible, from the 10th century text of the Old Testament held by the Hebrew University in Tel Aviv; this, because modern editions have been materially changed from older texts. Since, except possibly for the *Gospel of Thomas*, none of the original works have survived; it is impossible to tell the magnitude of changes that have been made through the centuries to either text. The *Dead Sea Fragments* have never been scientifically vindicated, and it is presumed they are a hoax as they contain verses only from the King James Bible which had not been written until 1621. They do not, for example, contain a single verse from about forty-five books of the Old Testament which are known to have been in existence in Christ's time that did not make it into modern Bibles.

There are thousands of references of sex in the Bible, not all of which are condemnations. Herein, are cited eighty-one explicit condemnations of heterosexual activities and four explicit condemnations of homosexual activities. There are several other ambiguous condemnations of either kind of sex in the Bible. The chapter/verse of each of these condemnations can be found in the combination of the following books which can be obtained from any major bookstore or library,

"Where To Find It In The Bible" - Thomas Nelson Publishers
"What Does the Bible Say About" - Thomas Nelson Publishers
"Find It Fast In The Bible" - Thomas Nelson Publishers

To find chapter/verse of all eighty-five explicit condemnations of sex search the following categories in the above guidebooks: abuse, adultery, copulation; deviate; fellatio; fornication, hedonism; homosexuality; immorality; lust; masturbation; morality; sexual immorality; sodomy.

Specific sources for Chapter 8, not otherwise mentioned in this book:

2 Chronicles 15, '*That whoever does not seek the Lord God of Israel shall be put to death. Great or small. Young or old. Man or woman.*'

Genesis 3, the only time in the Old Testament that God the Father talks to a woman is His scolding of Eve for having enticed Adam into eating the 'Apple.' '*And God spoke to woman, What is this that thou hast done? And the woman said, The serpent beguiled me, and I did eat. And the Lord God said unto Woman, I will greatly multiply thy sorrow and thy conception; In sorrow thou shalt bring forth children; and thy desire will be to thy husband, and he shall rule over thee.* The surrounding text in Genesis clearly defines woman as man's property. Unlike Christ, God the Father loved little boys much more than he did little girls. In fact, He made it clear that the only purpose of little girls was to make more little boys.

Genesis 17, circumcision: The contract was solely between God and man, in exchange for adoration God gives man sole rule over woman and all earthly things, '*And God said unto Abraham, And ye shall circumcise the flesh of your foreskin; and it shall be a token of the covenant betwixt me and you. And the uncircumcised man-child whose flesh of his foreskin is not circumcised, that soul shall be cut off from my people; he hath broken my covenant.'* Today, all medical associations condemn this perverted practice; it causes unnecessary pain and discomfort and often infection to the child; sometimes partial or total loss of function or cancer; at times, loss of the organ; and, on occasion, death. It has no substantial benefit in hygiene. Yet, it goes on.

Deuteronomy 23, bastards: *A child born out of wedlock shall not enter into the congregation of the Lord.* children of other nationalities: *'Ammonite or Moabite children shall not enter into the congregation of the Lord.'*

Deuteronomy 22, transgender: *'The woman shall not wear that which pertaineth to a man; nor should a man wear a woman's garment.'*

Leviticus 21, *'The Lord spoke unto Moses saying, Speak unto Aaron, whatsoever child he be that hath a blemish, whether he be a blind child, or a lame child, or a child with a flat nose, or anything superfluous, or a child that is broken-footed, or broken-handed, or hunched-backed, or a dwarfed child, or a child of scurvy is not worthy to approach the altar of God.'*

Deuteronomy 23, abused children: "*A child that has his privy cut off shall not enter into the congregation of the Lord.*" It was a practice to castrate male children – eunuchs – to serve as servants to royalty and to preserve the voices of soprano boys. There are also several references condemning boy harlots in the Old Testament who were obviously the victims of pedophiles. Although there are many Biblical condemnations of abused children, there is not a single condemnation of pedophile predators including the Ten Commandments. The Law of Moses clearly protects the right of adults to prey on children just as it explicitly protects the right of one man to enslave another. In both cases, it is only the victim that Moses condemns. The pedophile priest is not in violation of the book he lives by.

Leviticus19, rape of enslaved maiden: '*Whosoever shall lie carnally with a woman, that is a bondmaid, and not at all redeemed, not freedom given her; she shall be scourged; he shall not be put to death; because she was not free*

Leviticus 20, adulteress: *'and the man that committeth adultery with another man's wife . . . the adulteress shall surely be put to death.'*

Leviticus 21, prostitutes and out-wedlock-mothers: '*if she profaneth herself by playing the whore; she profaneth her father; and she shall be burned alive.'* There are several other condemnations of prostitutes and out-of-wedlock mothers in the Old Testament. Christ overrules all of them in the gospels, *'He who is without sin, cast the first stone.'*

author's comment,

As Albino Luciani once told me, "Chimpanzees share ninety-nine percent of our genes. They, like us, are inventors and can make and use tools. They, like us, have intelligence that in some cases has been known to exceed that of some presidents. They, like us, have a conscience and know right from wrong. Did you ever wonder why there is no Bible for them? Why they, too, don't have a chance at eternity?"

"They can't write a check," I laughed.

"Right on the money," he shot back seriously, "If chimpanzees could write a check they could satisfy the prophet's greed and dozens of them would have risen up through the ages to take advantage of their imagination and gullibility. And today there would be thousands of chimpanzee churches staffed with preachers to take their money."

"Huh?" I wondered, "I wonder, I wonder if there is a chimpanzee heaven?"

"Actually, they have a much better chance at it than we do." he told me.

"A much better chance than we do?"

"Yes," he replied, "There is a far greater chance that they will do what is right, as like atheists and agnostics, they don't have the greed of prophets of ancient times and the evilness of preachers of today to muddle their conscience."

afterthought,

" . . . 'I still believe that people are good at heart . . . as I look up into the heavens I think that it will all come right . . . that, in time, people will find the courage and strength to overcome the prejudices they were brought into . . . that people will accept one another as the equals God created them to be . . . that their differences will go by the wayside . . . and that, in the end, peace and tranquility will prevail.' "

Albino Luciani, Archbishop of Venice 25 Dec 69. Luciani quotes from *The Diary of Anne Frank* in his first words to his newly acquired congregation in Venice.

PART II

MURDER IN THE VATICAN

He found himself to be sitting in a tailor shop, one of those reserved for kings. There was a large sewing machine of the very latest vintage. A ruffle of white satin flowed from its center as if the bell had rung and the seamstress had gone out to lunch. On a table just off to one side were a half dozen or so rolls of satin, all of the very same shade of white. And then there was the gold. It was wound up on spindles that were lined up at one end of the sewing machine. A dozen or so golden sentinels watchfully guarded a grand catafalque of white.

Then there was the rising vertical mirror with its edges heavily encrusted in gold. A small platform stood just before the mirror. There seemed to be a slight indentation at its center and a haze rising above it as if a ghost were standing there. It was flanked by a half dozen or so breast dummies each wearing a part of some form of dress. And there was one that was all dressed up. That is, all dressed up still short of holding the Eucharist in its hands. For it even wore the papal miter.

The breast dummies were all of a single size. Just a month earlier they had been of another size. And he knew that in just two weeks time they would be of still another size. And only he of all of mankind knew this. For only he could make them change.

Chapter 1

THE SCENE OF THE CRIME

Rome,

I stayed at the little pensione that Piccolo had recommended to me. It was near the Roman Forum, about a fifteen-minute walk from the Vatican.

I spent the first couple of days going through the regular tourist rendition of Vatican City before finding my way to the Government Palace, which is located in the sprawling Vatican gardens. The Government Palace, unlike one might be led to believe, is not where the Pope lives. It houses various administrative offices of the Vatican and a few apartments that are occupied by ranking prelates in the administration. Both the Vicar of Rome, the equivalent of the mayor of Vatican City, and the president of the Vatican Bank have offices and apartments here. At the time, Cardinal Poletti was the Vicar of Rome and, of course, Bishop Paul Marcinkus headed the bank. I presented Piccolo's card to the Swiss guard at the main door and he directed me down a long corridor where I presented it again to a receptionist who sat just to the right of two intricately carved doors featuring angels at their tops and devils at their bottoms.

Much to my surprise Marcinkus himself came out to greet me. Much to my surprise, instead of assigning a subordinate to give me a tour, he took me around the Vatican grounds himself and best of all he took me into the papal palace itself.

The apostolic palace is to say the least huge. Unlike one might think it comprises a great number of attached buildings. There are literally thousands of rooms and hundreds of stairways and dozens of elevators. But in the case of the Pope one has to concentrate on that particular building which houses the papal apartment. And as palaces go it is not a particularly large building. And as palaces go it is not a particularly beautiful building. That is, from the outside. About one hundred and twenty feet square, if it were located in the downtown section of any medium sized city, one could easily mistake it to be an aging department store of some kind. The only ornamentation on its exterior walls is the aging marble cornice-work that adorns its windows.

It is an almost perfectly square freestanding sixteenth century building, which facade faces St. Peter's Square. The building is only four stories high but because of the immense ceiling height, almost thirty feet on each floor; it is as high as is a modern ten-story apartment building.

The ground floor is considered the base of the building and is without ornamentation of any kind. It contains some offices and service quarters and the Vatican bank has offices there. The papal palace itself consists only of the top three floors and these are referred to as the first, second and third floors of the papal palace, whereas in actuality they are the second, third and fourth floors of the building. The reason for this designation is to afford an unobstructed view of St. Peter's Square from all three floors of the palace as the colonnade surrounding the square blocks the view from the first floor of the building. The papal apartment itself occupies the entire top floor.

author's collection

the papal palace peers down over the colonnade surrounding St. Peter's Square

The nineteen rooms of the papal apartment form a U shape on the top floor with the bottom of the U corresponding to the front of the building, which windows overlook St. Peter's Square. In the center of the U is a large courtyard which at one time was used for hanging out laundry to dry and at the time of John Paul's death was vacant space used for outdoor recreation. Bordering the perimeter of the courtyard hemmed in by thirty foot walls are roof gardens and from the top edge of the garden walls a slightly reddish tile roof slopes down outwardly at a slight angle of about fifteen degrees to the perimeter of the building.

On the facade side, which faces St. Peter's Square, the windows are ten across. So when one speaks of a window one is speaking of quite large windows measuring about eight or nine feet in width and over twenty feet in height. At that time there were two framed clear glass paned vertical panels that opened inward within each frame and were protected by two outer wooden louvered shutters that opened outward. Today the old window casings have been completely ripped out and have been replaced by inner and outer sets of windows with double panes of bulletproof glass. The shutters are now lined with steel. When Paul VI lived here he had heavy draperies hung on all of the windows and they were kept closed. This is because he preferred air-conditioning. When John Paul I took over he had all of the draperies removed as they interfered with his opening the windows. He preferred the fresh air.

Of all the places I had the opportunity to visit in Vatican City I remember most vividly my visit to this important building. And the reason for this was because it was quite different from all the others. For the interior of all the others, from St. Peter's itself, to the Sistine Chapel, to the Vatican Library, to the Gallery of Maps and to the Vatican Museum, were very much the same. That is, no matter where you went you were roofed in by an endless array of frescos which were either squared-in or ovaled-in or circled-in by heavily encrusted frames of gilt and gold. If someone were not there to tell you where you were, you would never know. But the papal palace is much different. You knew where you were. For this particular building of the sprawling apostolic palace is much different from all the others.

Two Swiss guards flank the great studded greening bronze door, which marks the papal entrance to the building. They, like the rest of the guards in the palace building, are perpetual. That is, they are always there. A changing of the guards takes place every three hours, as the clock strikes twelve, three, six, nine and then twelve again. And this is true of all of the guards in the papal palace. So a guard has no need to, or for that matter any authority, to ever leave his post no matter what his needs. Not even a trip to the restroom is permitted - one of the reasons the rotation is every three hours.

As one enters through the great bronze door on the ground floor of the palace building there is a long white marble corridor leading to the rear of the building. One might see this corridor as a colonnade of some sort as it is lined with columns on either side. The columns are square and are set directly against the walls that support the arched ceiling. And when I say marble I mean marble. The floor is marble, and the walls are marble, and even the ceiling is marble. The undecorated ceiling is arched and the walls are lined with ancient sconces, which undoubtedly once held gas lamps or candles or other primitive lighting of some sort and have now been outfitted with electric bulbs. The white is kind of an off white, with some ashen remains darkening the marble walls just above the sconces. And although the Vatican contains the largest collection of ancient sculpture in the world, not a single statue is to be seen. There is no carpeting or runners here. One walks on the same marble floors that others have walked on for the past four centuries; one walks through a beautiful white marble tunnel.

In fact, the only piece of furniture other than some simple high-backed mahogany chairs which line the corridor on each side is a rather simple relatively modern mahogany desk as one enters the building. A guard sat there. This one attired in a Swiss uniform of red and blue rather than the yellow and blue which is characteristic of the guards one sees in the postcards. The unique combination of color was undoubtedly representative of rank of some kind. I remember that I was required to sign in at the desk and what's more, I was asked to leave my passport. But Marcinkus was permitted to enter on sight. He explained to me that archbishops and cardinals and other persons of rank and, of course, those who cared for the papal household who had apartments in the building were not required to sign in; they were free to come and go as they pleased. Except, of course, if they were to see the Pope or other resident, and they were not on the list of expected visitors, the guard would get on the intercom and announce their presence.

Religious News photo

the guard inside the entrance to the papal palace

Midway down the corridor there was the only semblance of sculpture, a elaborately carved arched white marble framework which housed a grand staircase of marble which continued up to a landing, -which I guessed led to the anteroom of the papal apartment. A Persian carpet of superlative elegance ran up the stairs. Just beyond the stairs I could see another great bronze door, this one more golden than green. Its arched doorway, again of white marble, had at its pinnacle the papal coat of arms carved into the marble and etched in gold. Two angels of white marble stood at attention on either side of the door, one holding what I guessed must have been the New Testament and the other holding the Old Testament. Later Marcinkus told me that I was right. He told me that Bernini placed them there to remind visitors that they were not only about to meet the Vicar of Christ on earth, but that they also about to meet the Vicar of God the Father. Actually the whole corridor had been designed and executed by Bernini himself. A single Swiss guard stood at the great bronze door at the top of the stairs.

The guard pressed a button on the wall and the door, which I then realized was gold and not bronze, much to my surprise, instead of opening outward, slid open. We followed the guard into what I thought was the small anteroom room of the papal apartment. But as we entered I quickly realized that we were not in an apartment at all. Rather we were in an elevator and if only momentarily, here the marble had come to an end and the gold and the frescos began. I remember looking up at the ceiling and again, if it were not for the size of the elevator I would not know where I was. For there were the frescos of the heavens above, which to the eye of the novice were every bit as magnificent as was those which looked down from the ceiling of the Sistine Chapel. I remember specifically touching its shimmering white marble walls because they were so perfectly pristine I thought them to be an artificial composition of some sort.

I remember asking the bishop jokingly if this elevator also went down and he was quick to respond that this particular elevator only goes up. He joked that there was another one at the other end of the building that went down. He was referring to the elevator on the other side of the building that led to the offices and apartments of some of the ranking members of the *Curia* who occupied the second and third floors of the building. He told me that the other elevator serviced the basement and the first, second and third floors of the building whereas this elevator served the first, second, third and fourth floors of the building and did not extend to the basement. The fourth floor corresponded to the third floor of the papal palace which housed the papal apartment.

We exited the elevator into an open area and, again, marble was the primary backdrop. I could hear water gushing off in the distance somewhere, as if someone had left the water running in a giant tub. Directly above our heads a skylight of blue and golden leaded glass looked down on the elevator which resembled an ornate golden birdcage standing on the floor, with its onion shaped golden dome cleverly concealing its mechanisms. Directly to our left a grand white marble staircase was crowned by a second somewhat larger skylight. We were facing a Swiss guard who sat before two towering windows behind a simple mahogany desk, which was an exact match of the one that was on the first floor. I mentioned to the bishop that they must have gotten two for the price of one at a sale of some kind. And I remember him telling me that they had actually gotten seven for the price of one. The *Curia* entrance at the other end of the palace was set up in the very same way that this side was set up; two guards flanking the main entrance, one just inside at a desk at the entrance to the white marble corridor which like the one we had just passed through on the ground floor led to a flight of stairs that led to a second more golden than bronze door. There was another guard who ran that elevator and two more who were stationed at desks that were located at each of the second and third floor landings. "Thirteen of the one hundred and twenty Swiss guards are stationed here in the palace building," he had told me, "actually thirty nine of them, as they rotate on a three-shift system every three hours. Like clockwork," he had joked.

I noticed that this guard, like the one at the desk on the first floor, was also dressed in red and blue. I supposed that the staircase offered the health nut the option of climbing the stairs in this, what today one might call upwards of a ten-story building. But it was there, I realized, to allow one to go from floor to floor and thereby bypass the elevator, as before the days of elevators it was all that had been there. I was told that before the development of the elevator in the late nineteenth century the papal apartment had been located in the Belvedere Palace, which is now a part of the Vatican Museum. Nevertheless, one using the stairway would have to pass by the same guard. Actually, one using the stairs would also have to pass by the other guards who sat at the desks which were located on the second and third floor landings.

Marcinkus acknowledged the guard and as we turned to our right we looked down toward another all marble corridor that ran back toward the front of the building. It quite obviously ran directly above the one that had led to the elevator on the first floor. It was every bit as high and wide as had been the one on the first floor. I took particular notice that an imposing marble statue of St. Peter stood to the left of its entrance. He was holding one hand out towards us as if he were welcoming us at the golden gates. And he held a large key in the other.

Marcinkus told me that we were in what is commonly known as the papal apartment. "Nineteen rooms in all, it occupies the entire top floor of the building. In all, eight people live here, the Pope's two secretaries, his valet and the four nuns who run the place. And, one more," he added.

"Who's that?" I remember asking.

"The Pope," he answered laughingly.

He opened a beautifully carved door of natural wood with armed angels all over it, which was just to one side of the elevator. The marble archway, which framed the door, had a number of gargoyles carved into it and they seemed to be threatening the angels that were protecting the door; the angels holding swords and spears and the gargoyles holding the proverbial pitchforks. As we entered, although there was no one there, he lowered his voice and told me, "This is the Pope's private chapel. It is open to any cardinal or bishop who resides anywhere in the apostolic palace." I later found out that when Luciani arrived he extended this privilege to anyone who lived in the building including the maids and janitors, a policy that was reversed when John Paul II took over.

Later I learned that Luciani never said Mass here. Rather he would assign the task to young priests and serve as their sacristan. On these occasions, he would kneel before the priest and receive his blessing and communion, a practice which often caused the priest to tremble. He would tell him, *"You must not be afraid, for in the eyes of Christ, all of His children are equal."*

The chapel was small - about the size of one of the side chapels in a large cathedral today. I would say at the most twenty feet wide and fifty feet in length. Its ceiling boasted a magnificent blue, red and golden leaded glass rendering of Christ's resurrection. The rest of the room was built entirely of marble. It was as if we were enclosed in a giant sarcophagus of some kind. Affixed to the length of the walls on either side ran about a dozen golden sculptures. I remember that some of them depicted the way of the cross. Ten rows of four beautifully upholstered chairs, two on each side of the aisle, ran down the length of the chapel. Each of them had a red velvet-topped kneeler set before it and up front, directly in the center of the room and facing the altar, was the Pope's throne. Something quite lengthy was carved in Latin on its leather back and Marcinkus was quick to point out that it was the Lord's Prayer. There was no altar railing. Only the large life sized golden figure of Christ on a wooden crucifix hung before a vertical convex slab of copperish marble that stood just behind the altar and the implements of the sacrifice of the mass broke the color scheme. And, of course, if one were to turn and look to the rear, three beautiful arched stained glass windows through which one could barely make out the sculptured hedges in the gardens outside rose up from the floor. I remember asking Marcinkus if they were by Chagall as, like the leaded glass ceiling, they were predominately blue and reminded me of the ones that I had seen in the great cathedral at Chartres. He told me that they were by someone else, someone of whom I had never heard and no longer recall. I remember Marcinkus taking me to a corner of the chapel where a few golden chalices were set on a small table. "There are almost a thousand of these in Vatican City," he told me, "and many of them are studded with diamonds, rubies, emeralds and pearls."

To the left of the windows was a small door and he took me out onto the garden. "As you can see," he told me, "the chapel is built here on the roof outside of the original context of the building. It was added just recently in 1965." We walked through the garden toward the front of the building and turned right, went a certain distance and passed under an overhead latticework, which held what I surmised to be hanging grape vines and then we turned right again and walked back to the rear of the building. The entire garden was walled in by what I would guess were thirty-foot walls. There were only two doors, the one through which we had entered, and a second one at the end of the garden, which gave access to the center courtyard. At that time the courtyard was filled with wash hung out to dry, but by the time John Paul came along ten years later clothes dryers had changed its function to that of an outdoor recreation area.

As we entered the courtyard, I noticed a small metal box on the wall with what appeared to be a keyhole and asked him what it was. "This gismo is a part of the security system that controls the roving night guard to make sure that he makes his rounds. He carries a key and he must clock in at specified times and places, or an alarm will go off in the main control station, which is located in the Vatican gardens. Not that we don't trust the guard, but if something were to happen to the guard we would know of it and send someone to investigate. There are boxes located throughout Vatican City, including around the ground perimeter of the palace building itself."

Exiting the chapel, he then led me down the marble corridor which led to the rooms of the papal apartment. The sound of the water gushing grew louder as we headed down its length. This corridor, like the one on the first floor, was also roofed in by an arched cathedral ceiling which rose at its pinnacle twenty-five feet above us, but this ceiling, unlike the one on the first floor, boasted frescos of white angels against a stark light blue sky. But similar to the one on the first floor there was not a hint of gilt or gold, only yellowing marble. And I noticed something else that was quite different about this floor - for unlike the first floor, it was air-conditioned.

Marcinkus told me that most of the rooms in most of the buildings that made up the apostolic palace were not air-conditioned and that some of them got unbearably hot in the summertime. Pius XII had a unit put on the roof of this particular building, which at that time cooled only this floor of the building. During the reign of John XXIII a four story service building was added along the rear facade of the palace building and the adjoining building of San Damasus which permitted the addition of large units which cooled all three floors of the papal palace and the corresponding floors of the San Damasus building. Yet, the cooling system still did not extend to the ground floor.

As we proceeded down the corridor we came to a set of white richly carved double doors on the left. "This is the door to the Pope's second secretary's apartment, -a small office, a sitting room, a bedroom and, of course, a bathroom. Its windows look out from the side of the building and overlook the River Tiber. Midway down the corridor we came to a second set of doors, also on the left, -the entrance to the apartment of the first secretary, the layout of which was identical to that of the second secretary's quarters.

And then we came to that point toward the front of the building where the corridor took a right turn. Two mahogany doors, more golden than white, stood there blocking our path. They were intricately carved and rose easily twenty feet, as if they were the doors to some magnificent miniature cathedral. Just above the doors, carved into the white marble that arched the doors, was another rendition of the papal coat of arms - also etched in gold. Two armed angels in white marble, one on either side, guarded the door. "And these doors lead to the Pontiff's inner chambers. If I were to turn the doorknob, the door would open to a small anteroom which is set up as a study in front of a single large window that looks out on St. Peter's Square," he told me, "for there are no locks on any of the doors in the papal apartment and that includes the doors to the private apartments of the others who live on the floor. After all, everyone who lives here lives in a single apartment. Until John XXIII took up residence here in 1958, a ceremonial guard stood at attention just to the right of this door, about twenty feet as the crow flies from where the Pope sleeps. The ceremonial guard became a cost reduction when he was replaced by modern technology and, of course, the two angels by Bernini who stand here now."

"Modern technology?" I queried.

"Yes, at that time a rather sophisticated communication system I will tell you about later was added to the Pope's quarters. Until then, the Pope's only communication with the outside world was a phone and a bell cord that hung over his bed which rang at the guard station at the top of the stairs. Of course, it rang loud enough that the guard stationed here outside of his door would respond to it."

At that point we heard a loud cough coming from the top of the stairs behind us where the guard was stationed. At first, as he was well out of sight, I presumed that it was the guard coughing, but shortly a priest came down the corridor behind us and, acknowledging Marcinkus, he entered the first apartment we had just passed. "That is Paul's second secretary Pasquale Macchi. One of his most trusted friends," Marcinkus told me. I might mention that Paul VI's second secretary Macchi had been relocated elsewhere in the apostolic palace when John Paul arrived and that his quarters had been given over to Lorenzi, the secretary the Pope brought with him from Venice.

We started down the corridor that ran along the front of the building that faced St. Peter's Square. We were halfway down the corridor before we finally came to another set of doors again on our left. "This is the door to the apartment of the Pope's valet and his fitting and storage rooms. By trade he is a tailor, a dress designer, one of the most famous in the world, and is responsible for the design and coordination of all of the Pope's outerwear. If you were to open this door and enter you would find yourself surrounded by silk and satin in a tailor shop of sorts, -one that looks directly out onto St. Peter's Square. These three men, his two secretaries and valet, have the most frequent interaction with the Pope. This is why they are located so close to him," he told me.

As we turned right at the corner of the corridor there appeared a life-sized statue of the Blessed Mother in white marble at its far end. It was set in a fountain, -which explained the water I had heard running when the elevator door had first opened. I took particular notice that this was a dead end, that there was no exit at this end. Marcinkus told me that another revolving guard control box was hidden on the wall behind the statue.

Then he said, "And now we come to where the women of the house live. In Vatican City the men outnumber the women by twenty to one, but here at the very top, they are equal, four to four. I later learned that it was John XXIII in 1958 who had relocated the nuns from the basement of the building as to provide equal representation of God's children here at the top. This first set of doors on the left is to the quarters of the mother nun who runs the place. From her bedroom one can look down at St. Peter's Square and her other windows, like all the others on this side of the building, overlook the San Damasus Courtyard and view the basilica dome. Unlike the formal marble framed windows that run along the façade side of the building, the windows along this side resemble factory widows; that is, if one were to ignore their blue, green and golden glows, for the entire outer walls consist of floor-to-ceiling paneled windows.

"Paul calls her the most important person in the Roman Catholic Church. 'I couldn't get up without her.' Paul once told me," explained

Marcinkus. Later I would learn that, unlike John Paul I who followed him and awoke promptly before four thirty each morning without the aid of an alarm clock, Paul would frequently reach over and turn off his brass alarm clock, the kind with the big brass feet, and go back to sleep.

"The San Damasus Courtyard is the most private garden in Vatican City," he continued, "It is frequently used as a welcoming place for heads of state. And further down here on the left, toward the white marble statue of the Blessed Mother, are the private rooms of the three nuns who care for the papal residence. Each has a small sitting room and bedroom with a private bath and each has windows that look out over the San Damasus Courtyard toward the basilica. They do the cooking, the housekeeping and what have you for all of the men of the cloth who live on the three floors of the papal palace. And these last two doors here on the left lead to the papal nutrition center." He opened the double doors to a modest dining room, which boasted an old wooden boarded up table that had a dozen old chairs sitting around it. There was an old sideboard to one side and a large old rug of some kind hung on the wall at one end. There was nothing that reeked of wealth in this room. At the other end of the room was a door that I was told led to the kitchen.

This remained precisely the layout and the occupants of the papal apartment on the night of John Paul's death. When John Paul II took over he hired a world renowned chef and added a state-of-the-art kitchen. The nuns who do the housework and act as servants were relocated to the basement.

"Directly under the quarters of the mother nun and those of the valet," he added "is the apartment of the Vatican secretary of state and next to that, at the front center façade of the building is the Pope's official office, which, as I mentioned, overlooks St. Peter's Square. Directly under that on the first floor are the offices of the Council for Public Affairs which are overseen by the secretary of state."

As we passed by the Pope's doors again he told me, "Directly under the Pope's quarters is the apartment of the Dean of the College of Cardinals, and directly under the apartments of the Pope's secretaries are the apartments of the deputy secretary of state and the undersecretary of state. And directly under them, on the first floor of the palace, is the apartment of the foreign minister. There are also some important offices on these floors and there is a large conference room where they discuss the problems of the Church or should I say rather - where they figure out how not to discuss the problems of the Church," he laughed, "one might call it the corporate boardroom of the Roman Catholic Church." As we reached the elevator where the guard sat at the top of the stairs, it was clear to me that anyone gaining access to the papal apartment, even if one were to come from the roof garden, would have to pass by this guard.

Although we did not enter the Pope's inner chambers, the bishop did describe the rooms to me in great detail. For later from St. Peter's Square below, he looked up and pointed to the Pope's windows. He read them off to me from left to right, "These three windows which are third, fourth and fifth from the right hand corner of the building, look out from the Pope's private library. It is located directly above the Pope's office, which is on the second floor and occupies the same amount of space. These are the two largest rooms in the building - each measuring about sixty by forty feet, and keep in mind that their ceiling height is about twenty-five feet. As one enters the library there is a desk to the right backed by a line of carved mahogany bookcases, easily twenty feet in height containing a massive collection of richly bound volumes, any one of which a collector would give his right arm for. The artwork in this room has been changed from time to time to suit the tastes of particular popes. In addition to the treasures that the public can view in the Sistine Chapel and Vatican Museum and elsewhere in Vatican City, there are several warehouses filled with artwork and sculptures that a sitting pope can choose from. There is one work of art that has stood the test of time and is a fixture in the Pope's private library, a magnificent painting of Michelangelo's Ascension, housed in a solid gold frame that by itself could very easily feed a thousand children for a year and the carpet on the floor could feed a thousand more. And the painting? Well, easily ten to twenty thousand more. The Pope often holds private audiences in this room.

"Opposite the desk, near the windows, is a mahogany conference table with a dozen or so matching chairs. At the far end of the room is a conversation area where the Pope can view a television set and keep up on world events. There is also, a communications panel on a console next to the desk. It is basically an intercom that connects the Pope with the offices of about two dozen important offices throughout the Vatican. The panel also includes a row of buttons by which he can reach some of the service people in the building - like the kitchen and the guards that are stationed at the desk on the ground floor of the building and the guard stationed at the top of the stairs. There is an identical panel located next to his desk in his official office directly below. The intercom is hardwired to these other offices including to my office which as you know is located in the middle of the Vatican Gardens," Marcinkus told me.

Associate Press Photo

the Pope's private library

"This next window to the right is commonly referred to as the Pope's study. Had we opened the double doors to his chambers we would have entered into this room. The room is set up as a reception area with an overdone ornate antique desk and a half dozen assorted ancient chairs. There is a bathroom off to one side, which is used by those who visit the Pope in his inner chambers. This was originally the Pope's private bath when the papal apartment was relocated to this building late in the nineteenth century. It is quite ornate and the fixtures still have their original solid gold fittings that had been installed at that time.

"The window at the northeast corner of the facade of the palace building, as it faces St. Peter's Square, is the Pope's bedroom window. Just around the corner, on the side of the palace that overlooks the Tiber, are two more bedroom windows and just beyond those is a third window, which fronts his private bath. Although there are nineteen rooms in the papal apartment, it is these three rooms, which is the private domain of the leader of the largest church in the world. Even his private office is located in a more public area on the floor below." At the time I noticed that all of these windows had wooden shutters on them, wooden shutters; that were functional as some of them were open and others were closed, -shutters that were later lined with steel after the attempted assassination of John Paul II in 1981.

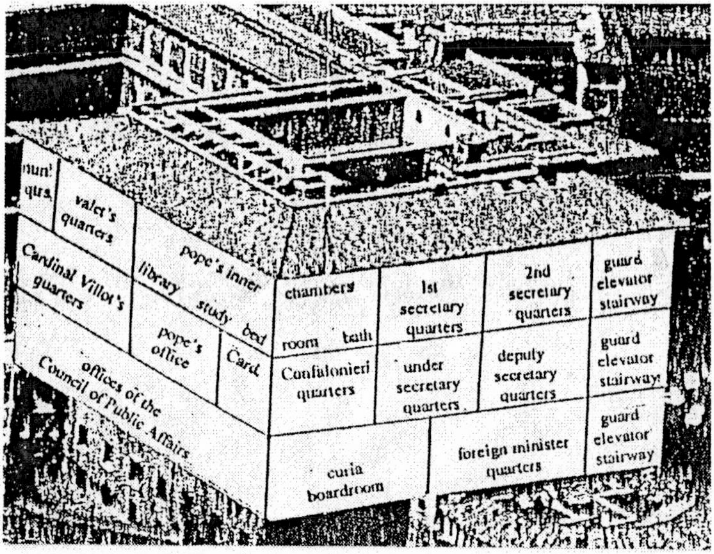

layout and occupants of the papal palace the night of John Paul's death

Marcinkus continued, "Although the bedroom has been described by many as surprisingly small, it is not a small room. Yes, small for a palace bedroom, but not small for a bedroom. Perhaps it is its unusually high ceiling that makes it appear to be much smaller than it is." And he gave me some specifics, "If the bedroom door were open one would have a side view of the bed from the study. As one enters the bedroom and turns right, one would pass in front of a tall, freestanding, dark, carved mahogany wardrobe about eight feet wide. There are no closets of any kind in the papal apartment, as it was built long before the time of closets. The wardrobe contains only the Pope's nightclothes and a few leisure items that he might climb into in the privacy of his chambers. His main outer wardrobe is stored in the fitting room, which is located in his valet's apartment down the hall. Although predominately white and gold, in total composition it would dwarf most wardrobes of kings and queens and Hollywood stars in terms of both extravagance and variation.

"In the corner just to the right of the window that looks out onto the square is a life sized white marble statue of Christ by Bernini. A perpetual red votive candle burns before the statue and there is a red velvet-topped kneeler in front of it. And just to the left of the prayer station is a small sitting area to the left of the window consisting of an eighteenth century love seat in Italian provincial, and two heavily brocaded chairs also in Italian provincial which are joined together by an overly ornate matching coffee table. On a side table there is a small, white antique Italian phone."

Marcinkus went on in his description of the Pope's inner quarters in such great detail that I think if a pencil lay on a table that he would have mentioned it, "On the other side of the room, away from the windows, is the bed. It is dominated by a heavy bronze headboard, which has at its top center a solid gold crucifix that has been welded into the headboard. The headboard is flanked on either side by two imposing, threatening feline gargoyles, which protect the Pope from evil sprits while he sleeps. The bronze headboard has been witness to many a pope's dreams throughout the centuries. Unlike what one might imagine each pope does not bring his own bed. Yes, the mattress and box springs have changed over the years, but the headboard itself has remained as if fixed in time. As a matter of fact it is built into the room.

"The bed itself appears to be much higher than it really is, as it is covered by an unusually thick down comforter and the comforter in turn is topped off with a white, heavily brocaded cover or spread which has the papal coat of arms embroidered in gold on it. As one faces the bed, the only thing obstructing the headboard, which is the focal point of the room, are a triple row of white feather pillows and a white velvet bell cord. The bell cord is wired directly to the guard's desk, which is located just beyond the entrance to the corridor which leads to the Pope's chambers. If pulled it would ring loud enough to wake the dead. At one time this, together with a matching one in his library, were the Pope's only contact with the outside world when he was sequestered in his own little corner of the world but, as I have already pointed out, in the middle of the twentieth century modern technology stepped in.

"Flanking the bed on either side are nightstands. The one on the left serves as a communication center. There is a row of service buttons on a small panel facing the bed that drive an intercom. The intercom does something more than does the bell cord, as it allows the Pope two-way communication with whomever he happens to summon. In addition to the guards, there is also a button to each of his secretaries' offices and bedrooms. And there is one that rings in both the fitting room and the bedroom of his valet, and there is another, which rings both in the kitchen and the bedroom of the mother nun who cares for the apartment. And there is one additional button, which is wired to the secretary of state's office and bedroom on the second floor." At the time this allowed the Pope twenty-four hour access to six separate people. "In addition, just beyond the buttons, on the same nightstand, is a second white antique Italian phone.

"The bed itself, contrary to popular belief, is not a particularly large one by today's standards. That is, it is not the equivalent of a king or even a queen-sized bed. From left to right, confined by its ancient headboard, it spans the width of what is a regular double-sized bed today. Yet, it would be a huge bed by sixteenth century standards."

What we are talking of here is the Pope's bedroom as it was at the time of John Paul's death. I suppose today that the Pope's bedside communication center has been computerized and allows him day and night access to many more people. But at the time of John Paul's death there was only a simple electronic console. It allowed him twenty-four hour instant access to only six people. His two secretaries, his valet, the nun who ran his household, his secretary of state and the guard who sat at a desk just eighty feet from where the Pope sat in his bed reading his papers. Actually, only five of these were in the papal palace on the night that he had died. His valet was away visiting relatives in connection with a death in his family. Nevertheless, not one of the other five heard a ring.

Marcinkus told me that there is a large double rather ornate fifteenth century dresser that is quite imposing standing opposite the bed. And just to the left of the dresser is a small hallway, which runs in front of another huge window and on its left is the door of the papal bathroom.

In stark contrast to the bedroom, the bathroom which is as large as is a typical living room is remarkably modern in appearance and has all of the amenities that one usually associates with marble bathrooms found in the better suites in expensive hotels and this includes whirlpool jets in its oversized tub. Until 1958, when it was built, the space it now occupies was used as a private dining room. It became common knowledge that when John Paul moved in he made only two changes to the chambers. He had all of the draperies removed and he had some exercise equipment installed in the bathroom including a treadmill, which he had brought with him from Venice. And then there was an antique birdcage that housed two cockatiels, which shared the bedroom with him.

Marcinkus also took me on a tour of the second and third floors of the palace. Those floors housed the apartments of the secretary of state and the foreign minister and a few other high ranking dignitaries of the Church. He told me that at one time a proposal was made that the secretary of state's quarters should be moved to a more distant part of Vatican City. After all, the secretary of state is the vice president of the Church. Upon the death of a pope, he dons the Ring of the Fishermen and officially becomes Pope. He has, during the interim period, the full authority, responsibility and power of a pope, although his primary duty is to guide the conclave in the election of a new pope. This means that an interim pope is empowered to make any changes to Church doctrine that he deems fit. One could, for example, eliminate the confessional as a means of forgiving sin.

In actuality, Jean Villot reigned as Pope five days longer than did John Paul I, as he was the interim head of the Church between Paul VI and John Paul I and also between the two John Pauls, -a total of thirty-eight days. If something were to happen to both the Pope and the secretary of state, if they were both killed in an accident, then the next in succession would be the deputy secretary of state who happened at that time to be a common bishop. After the assassination attempt on John Paul in 1981, the secretary of state‘s personal living quarters were relocated to a more remote part of the apostolic palace and the Pope took over the entire top two floors. Also, today, for security purposes, where the Pope sleeps is no longer public knowledge.

While on our tour I found that many of the bathrooms were original on the lower floors. That is, they had been updated with modern antique fixtures to the extent that it is possible to combine the two. Generally these bathrooms were elaborately ornate and one of them even had a ceiling painted by Raphael. The Raphael bathroom in the papal palace with its marble statuary worth millions and golden fixtures and artwork worth millions more, perhaps, more than anything else in Vatican City emphasized to me the contrast of immense wealth of the Church as compared to many people in third world countries who don't have *a pot to piss in.* Thinking back to that time I can understand today where John Paul was coming from when he ordered that appraisals be made of the vast treasures of the Vatican Empire.

I had lunch with Marcinkus in one of the Vatican Garden restaurants; that one that he visited most frequently. I told him of the great white wine that Jack and I had enjoyed that afternoon at the village wedge café in Vittorio Veneto and he told me that he too had been there. "As we priests change common wine into the blood of Christ, so, too, does the little wedge café turn common wine into the blood of gods." Anyway, as I walked him back to the Government Palace and left him at its main entrance, he told me that I probably now knew more about the layout of the papal palace than did the KGB and the CIA combined. And that was the last I ever saw of him.

And to be honest in this thing, I never saw him. That is, Marcinkus himself. For it was only after I got into the investigation of the Pope's death and came upon pictures of him in the press, did I realize that it had not been Marcinkus who had taken me through the papal apartment that morning. Yet, I do know whoever it was who took me on the tour was a bishop, for he wore bishop's garb. I have found that at that time there was a bishop in the Vatican by the name of Paul Masseekoos; with the broken-Italian I had misunderstood the name.

Chapter 2

BEGIN THE INVESTIGATION

Piccolo,

And what became of Piccolo? Well, I've already told you what became of him. Six months after my visit to Vittorio Veneto he was named Patriarch of Venice, and five years after that he was named a cardinal of the Roman Catholic Church, and five years after that he became Pope, and thirty-four days after that he was found dead in his bed.

And I have promised you some scenarios as to what caused three men to sleep in the great bed in the papal apartment in the fall of nineteen hundred and seventy-eight. And here they are for you to choose from, all of the options as to how John Paul could have possibly died and all of those who had motive and opportunity to have killed him.

the known facts,

In order to come up with any reasonable scenarios one must first separate the facts, from the probabilities, from the possibilities, from the rumors. And that we will do now.

To begin with, one knows that John Paul did not die of a heart attack as his doctor had claimed, for we know that he was awake and reading with the light on when he died. And we know this to be fact, as all of the witnesses including the nun and Monsignor Magee who found him, and the embalmers who took the papers from his hands, and the testimony of the cardinals who were brought to his room, and the official Vatican release to the press were all in absolute agreement on this one point, *that he was found to be in a sitting up position on his bed dressed in his daytime clothes reading some papers that he held upright in his hands with the top cover pulled partly over him.* This has to be the starting point of our investigation, for it is the only known absolute fact of all of the circumstances of his death.

Yes, had he been sleeping when the supposed heart attack occurred he might have died in his sleep as he may not have been afforded the opportunity to have reached for the bell cord. But if he was awake, and we know this to be a fact, there is no heart attack, no matter how massive, that would not have allowed him time to pull the bell cord or press a service button to summon help. Or for that matter so painless that it would have left him sitting up in his bed with his papers still held upright in his hands.

It would not take a world renowned cardiologist to tell one that. Any imbecile would understand that. Yet, the great majority of Catholics have believed all this time that John Paul I died of a heart attack. So yes, I will give you all the possible ways in which he could have died. And we will narrow those down to the probabilities. And, believe me, death due to a heart attack will not be among them and if you cannot accept the fact that the Pope did not die of a heart attack, then put this book down now. For you are a sheep. You lack the courage to seek the truth.

So we know two absolute facts. The position in which the body was found; and that the Pope did not die of a heart attack as was previously supposed. The second fact is of course drawn from the first one. And this through the process of elimination gives us quite conclusively a third fact. Something else killed him, something that killed him so suddenly that he was unable to reach for the bell cord which hung a few inches from his shoulder.

And then we have the missing white slipper socks and the spectacles, for they are also known facts. Although they do not seem to be pertinent to the case, we might find that they may have played a role in his death as we make our way.

So in all, we have five facts with which to build our investigation. And we will get to that very shortly. But first, I must lay some groundwork. I must tell you what became of some of the others who were involved either directly or indirectly in this unusual story of fate.

what happened to Jack,

First, there was Jack, my good friend Jack. What became of my good friend Jack after that time in Vittorio Veneto so many years ago?

Six months after the author's visit, John "Jack" Champney was named Acting Vicar General of Vittorio Veneto and served there for a few months as transitional head of the mountain diocese. Not being Italian he was not considered for the post. He was transferred to Milan where he served under Cardinal Pignedoli until 1975 when he was moved to the Vatican and assigned to the *Council on Spiritual Occurrences.* He had no desire to and never attained rank of any significance in the Roman Catholic Church. He three times declined Paul's intent to make him a bishop.

The *Medaglia d'Oro al Valore Militare*, Italy's highest military honor was awarded Jack's uncle thirty years after his rescue of the twenty-seven Italian school children which endeavor ultimately cost him his life. He is the only American ever to be awarded the honor. On March 29, 1975, the medal was presented to Jack in a ceremony at his uncle's grave site with twenty-one of the surviving children looking on. The record of this event together with a likeness of the medal is engraved on the back of his uncle's tombstone. Jack took the medal to Venice where he gave it to Albino Luciani, who was at that time serving as cardinal there. The medal, as it was on the great prelate's person when he was found dead, is today most likely in the possession of the Luciani family in Rome.

When his patron, Albino Luciani, was raised to the papacy, Jack was assigned as an intermediary between the Pope and the *Curia* with the additional duties of quelling the uncertainties of those Vatican based cardinals that represented the core of the *far right* in the Catholic Church. This assignment is documented by his calendar, that much of Jack's time during the thirty-three days of John Paul's reign was involved in meetings with these particular prelates of the Church. This group, led by Cardinal Siri and Bishop Casaroli, feared that this liberal Pope would take the Church's doctrine too far to the *left* and in their minds this could destroy Christianity as was intended by the prophets. Particularly, as was intended by the prophet Moses whom they considered to be the founder of Christianity. They also feared that they themselves would soon be removed from the positions of power that they held in the Church.

Jack's death was coincidental to that of his patron, his holiness John Paul I. On the second day following the Pope's unexpected death, Jack was killed instantly by a hit-and-run driver just outside the Vatican walls. The driver of the car has never been apprehended.

> *It sat there quite silently alongside the aging ivy blanketed wall just outside the Vatican gardens in the early dusk, a large black Mercedes with Vatican license plates, motionless, except for an occasional puff of smoke which shot out of its tailpipe.*
>
> *The silent breathing of the driver and the light drumming of the raindrops on the windshield and the quiet purr of the engine played a quiet sonata of some sort. It was early evening, and the street was deserted as man and machine awaited their prey.*
>
> *Then footsteps on the cobblestones chimed in. And the pedal went flat to the floor. And the purr of the engine turned to roar. And the sonata broke into a crashing crescendo. And then a single thump. No shout. No scream. No cry. Just a single thump. That was all!*

The two friends were interred on the same day four thousand miles apart. The Pope, after lying in state for four days, was put to rest in the papal catacombs below St. Peter's altar. Even in death he imperiled the regency of the papacy. His will required that he, like his predecessor Paul VI, be interred in a plain wooden box. In his case a pine box. No grand marble edifice marks his tomb. Engraved on a simple slab of granite is his name,

IOANNES PAVLUS P. P. I

Hidden from view on the pine box itself are the words,

Don Albino Luciani
1912 - 1978

Christ picked me up from the mud in the street and gave me to you.

As I drove into the funeral home parking lot I thought of my last visit with Jack, the only time I had seen him in the twenty years since that day he had stood at the pinnacle of secondary school life rendering the coveted address on graduation day. Perhaps he should have used the words Lincoln had used so effectively, so modestly, at Gettysburg, "*. . . the world will little note, nor long remember what is said here . . .*" for unlike Lincoln, Jack would have been telling the truth.

I thought of our last phone conversation of just a few days before, when he had told me of those things that I have set forth in the *foreword* of this book. And I thought of his patron, Albino Luciani, who lay in state on a great catafalque at that very moment, partway around the world. I wondered if he was wearing his sandals in his final hours so that all could witness the perfection of his toes. I wondered if his smile was as unrelenting in death, as it had been in life.

"Greatness," I thought, "does not always give notice. Like that of his patron, Jack's was a simple, quiet, silent greatness; one whose words would not long be remembered, and whose deeds would long be forgotten. But nevertheless, one whose purpose would live on for all eternity, live on in his fellowman for all time.

As I stood there before him, I couldn't see him, for the mutilation had been much too terrible to allow the body to be viewed. As I began to realize that he was now still, I recalled what he once was and I prayed that he had had time to complete his work. At the same time, I thought of

Piccolo and I knew that he had not had time to complete his work, -which has caused me to write this book.

As I reached over and lay my hand on the lid of the coffin, just above his heart, to confirm to myself that this was indeed forever goodbye, one of those things one calls tears came up out of my heart and started from the crevice of my eye and crept toward the lid. I glanced first to the right, and then to the left, and again to the right, and finally to the left, once more. And I carefully held it there balanced on the edge of the cliff.

Turning to the audience that sat in grief, I heard the applause move forward in muffled cries; in sighs of desperation and sobs. And I went directly to the one who sat in the front row and introduced myself and at the same time relating a part of my life which had been a part of her son's life. She reached into her purse and brought forward a small package and placing it into my hand she said, "Jack told me that if anything were to happen to him he wanted you to have this." She added, "We gave it to him for his ordination, the most important day of his life."

Later in the funeral home parking lot in the privacy of my car, I looked at the small package which was still wrapped in its brown paper covering. It was postmarked "*Centrale Poste de Roma*" and dated, *September 23, 1978,* -a few days before the Pope's death. As the package had never been opened, Jack had undoubtedly called his mother sometime between then and now. I was puzzled why it was not postmarked "*Poste Citta del Vaticano,*" as had all of Jack's correspondence to me through the years. I unwrapped the package and opened the small box that I found within it and I saw that it was six o'clock, exactly halfway between a Silver Star and a Purple Heart.

a strange coincidence,

A couple of weeks after Jack's funeral, a second package arrived in the mail. It, too, was strangely postmarked from the *Centrale Poste de Roma.* A short note written in Italian was with its contents. It had been scratched out on a small piece of notepaper bearing the letterhead, "*L'ufficio della Segreteria di Stato Vaticana.*" Although I couldn't read Italian it was quite obvious to me that this meant, "*The Office of the Vatican Secretary of State.*" Since the note had been written in Italian I couldn't read the message, other than that it had been signed by Jean Villot. I knew at the time that Jean Villot was the secretary of state. There was a single phrase, "*Il Re del Deserto del Sahara.*" From my Latin days I knew the word "Re" meant "King" and the rest of the phrase obviously referred to the Sahara Desert. Unfortunately, I couldn't read the rest of the note so I discarded it.

The other item in the box was a small booklet. The cover was of black, pockmarked leather and on its face were engraved in gold the words, "The Vatican, 1978." It did not seem to be an official issue, but rather one of those cheap daily reminders one can pick up at one of the many souvenir stands that surround St. Peter's. I still have Jack's daily reminder with me today. So I survive today with only two remembrances of Jack, his calendar and his watch which ticks the hallowed time between a Silver Star and a Purple Heart.

There is nothing of great interest in the booklet, just a simple daily reminder of appointments. I noticed that most of his meetings during the brief reign of John Paul I were with cardinals. Cardinal Baggio, Cardinal Ratzinger, Cardinal Oddi, Cardinal Rossi, Cardinal Samore and several others, all members of the *Vatican Curia.* There was one meeting with Cardinal Carlo Confalonieri, the oldest member and, therefore, dean of the college. Then there were one, two, three, three meetings with Bishop Casaroli. And there had been another with Cardinal Villot, the Vatican secretary of state - the cardinal who had been good enough to have sent me the notebook.

The very next day, Jack had a meeting in Genoa with Cardinal Giuseppe Siri, the leader of the *far right* in the Roman Catholic Church. There was a notation that Bishop Agostino Casaroli and Bishop Giuseppe Caprio had attended the same meeting.

In the conclaves that had elected Paul VI in 1963 and John Paul I in 1978, a substantial block of about twenty votes had remained cast for Siri. This, despite the fact that in both cases once a winner had been determined a motion had been made to make the vote unanimous. As a matter of fact Siri normally controlled about a third of the votes at the start of every conclave, -those on the *right*, just like Cardinal Suenens normally controlled about a third of the votes, -those on the *left*. The strategy of both 'parties' was to somehow capture the third that lie in the middle.

It struck me as odd that two bishops of the Church would travel two hundred miles just to meet with a man of the rank of a simple priest, particularly when they could have met with him at anytime in Rome by just walking down the hall. After all, their offices were located together in the apostolic palace.

But a second notation next to the same date cleared the matter up for me - Jack had run into Cardinal Wojtyla, the Archbishop of Krakow who was just exiting the cardinal's palace as he arrived. It was obvious that Casaroli and Caprio had traveled to Genoa for a meeting with this foreign prelate and their presence had been simply coincidental with Jack's visit. I wondered what could be so important that would cause the Polish cardinal to journey seven hundred miles back to Italy to meet with these men when just two weeks before he had spent ten days with them at the conclave that had elected John Paul I?

I noticed that there was no mention of Cardinal Benelli of nearby Florence as having had attended this meeting. This was because Jack had once told me that Siri, Wojtyla and Benelli were the recognized leaders of the *conservative right* in the Church. Benelli had been the leading conservative candidate in the two most recent elections. In fact, according to the press reports he had taken an early and commanding lead in both elections only to lose at the end. Had Benelli attended, I would assume that they were meeting to plan the strategy as to how the *conservative right* was going to survive under the liberal papacy of John Paul. But that Wojtyla attended who had to travel a great distance, and not Benelli who lived next door, confused me. Nevertheless, at the time it didn't seem to be important to me. Perhaps they were just planning the next conclave.

In retrospect there would be nothing wrong with the leaders of the *conservative right* to meet and plan the strategy for the next conclave to elect a new Pope. Just as there would be nothing wrong for the leaders of the *progressive left* to call a meeting to plan the strategy for the next conclave. What was unusual about this meeting, if it was indeed a meeting called to discuss the strategy of the next conclave, is that the reigning pontiff was still alive. As a matter of fact, no one would have guessed in a million years that John Paul would be dead in just three weeks time.

cause of death,

Since then I have often wondered if there had been foul play in the Pope's death. But I have nothing to support this contention other than that which, as I have recounted above, was released in the press and the fact that I knew for certain that the Pope had not died of a heart attack.

I think I should make it clear, regardless of what was rumored in the press, arsenic poisoning, if it was indeed a factor, was not the cause of John Paul's death. For the most common evidence of slow arsenic poisoning is some soreness of the esophagus or throat. Arsenic also results in some sensitivity and swelling in the extremities in the early stages. In the advanced stages a severe, deteriorating condition is usually marked by infection in the stomach, liver, pancreas, kidneys or bladder culminating in a high fever. At the end there is almost always a bloody discharge. In cases of slow arsenic poisoning these particular organs are likely to become infected, as they are the body's primary organs responsible for filtering arsenic and most other foreign toxins from the blood. Therefore jaundice of the skin and sometimes signs of psoriasis and unexplained coughing are the most visible symptoms of arsenic poisoning throughout the process - which normally cumulates in death in the matter of a few weeks.

John Paul was embalmed within a few hours after death, which like his predecessor Paul VI suspiciously did not include the customary draining of blood and removal of internal organs; suggestive of cover up of poisoning as this leaves neither blood nor tissue to assay for the presence of poisoning.

As I have already mentioned, it was the fact that he was embalmed so soon after death which fired the rumors of possible arsenic poisoning. As a matter of fact, it was Italian law at the time that a body could not be embalmed until twenty four hours after it was declared dead for this reason, that is, to permit the state time to conduct an autopsy if foul play was suspected. Of course, Italian law had no jurisdiction in Vatican City.

Yes, that John Paul presumably died from cardiac arrest would, if one were to ignore the circumstances of his death, make some sense. But that he died of arsenic poisoning is not true, as had arsenic been the sole culprit, in the final days he would have been extremely ill with high fever and possible signs of infection of the urinary or purification system and, of course, would have been jaundiced and confined to bed. And this is not true in John Paul's case. Yes, there were some uncharacteristic naps and unexplained swelling of the feet, but in general he appeared to be in good health and remained on the job and vibrant to the end.

That arsenic poisoning was responsible for the naps and the swelling in his feet is still possible, but it was definitely not the cause of death because it is too slow a process. On the other hand, there is nothing to support the supposition that he died of a heart attack. In truth, none of the facts support such a conclusion. That is, the facts that were reported in the press and what was publicly known of his medical history. No, he was killed by something else - something that killed him so suddenly that he was unable to reach for the bell cord. Something that killed him in such a way that he was able to retain the exact position he died in, still reading his papers. Something that we will, perhaps, never know. But of course, we can come up with some possible scenarios.

anatomy of death,

So just how did John Paul die? Well, we know there are only four possible ways anyone dies. They either die of natural causes. They die as result of an accident. They commit suicide. Or they are murdered. There are no other possibilities. There is no other way one can die.

So just what are the possibilities in John Paul's case? Let's take each of them in order. Let's give each one of them a chance. First, did he die of natural causes? The official release of the Vatican said that he had died before midnight of a massive heart attack. This, as I have said, was the opinion of Doctor Buzzanetti, the attending physician who had pronounced him dead and signed the death certificate stating that he had died at about 11:30PM.

That the Pope did not succumb to a heart attack does not necessarily mean that he could not have died of some other natural cause and here we have very powerful evidence that points to only one other possible natural cause. The position in which the body was found and the fact that he still held his notes in his hands points to a cause of death that was not only instantaneous, but also painless; otherwise he would have reacted to the pain and dropped his notes. And the only known natural death that can result in instantaneous death without the notice of pain is stroke.

John Paul could have died of a stroke. Possible, but not very probable, as the chances of an individual's first stroke resulting in death is about one in forty. This compares to an individual's first heart attack resulting in death being about one in three. So if one were to convert this to chance, John Paul had about a two-and-a-half-percent chance of having died of a stroke.

But had he died of a stroke that would have prevented him from either pulling the bell cord to his right or pressing one of the service buttons to his left, one would be talking about a bilateral stroke. A stroke, even a massive stroke, normally affects only one side of the body. And the chance of a bilateral stroke is far less than one-percent and this possibility would have been further reduced by his relatively young age.

This means of course, that there is much better than a ninety-nine-percent chance that he did not die of a stroke. Yet, it remains a possibility. One should keep in mind that he had no history of stroke or coronary disease at all. The only symptom that preceded his demise was swollen feet, and although this may indicate a pulmonary disorder, it is most often associated with a host of other conditions. And one knows as a matter of fact that his doctor had diagnosed this condition just the week before as the onset of arthritis. But nevertheless, although it is a long shot, it is possible that he could have died of stroke. So let us keep this one in the back of our minds.

We have already outlined the five known facts of the case and now we have arrived at that point at which we are able to come to our first sound conclusion - the fact that the doctor diagnosed his swollen feet as the onset of arthritis and just a week later concluded that his death was due to a heart attack casts considerable suspicions on the doctor himself.

When a man in his mid-sixties, as John Paul was at the time, goes to his doctor and complains of swollen feet, having no history of this condition, the very first thing the doctor will do is rule out the possibility of a pulmonary disorder. This would include a review of the person's medical records to determine whether he is at risk of a heart attack or stroke. He will administer a series of simple tests, -a careful monitoring of the heart with a stethoscope, the taking of blood pressure, and so forth. If any of these exams hints at the slightest possibility of a pulmonary problem then any physician, much less a pope's doctor, would submit the patient to more extensive tests in a hospital.

The Luciani family, after being pestered for weeks by the press, released the details of Luciani's most recent physical examination taken just six months before his death. Several local newspapers pictured an actual photo of the summary sheet of this physical exam, which caused rumors of foul play to reemerge. Luciani's overall cholesterol count on April 15, 1978 was *160* precisely, a perfect count, and his blood pressure in the same physical was *124* over *78,* also a near perfect count.[1] These results and other tests taken at the time prove that Luciani was a man of remarkable health as he approached the time of his papacy.

In addition, a super sleuth reporter engaged the undercover assistance of a young nun and secured the record of Dr. Buzzanetti's examination of just a week before the Pope's death and plastered it on the front page of his newspaper. Again, Luciani's overall cholesterol count was *167* and his blood pressure was *118* over *80,* about what it had been six months before.[2] There are two major medical conditions that drive a heart attack, high cholesterol and high blood pressure. So we now know as a matter of fact that Luciani had scored perfectly in both tests in both physicals and we also know that Dr. Buzzanetti also knew this. And we know something else.

There are two major medical conditions that drive stroke. One is arterial passage and the other is blood thickness. The record secured by the nun in her undercover operation showed that Dr. Buzzanetti did administer a routine external test to check for clear arterial passage of the carotid arteries, those in the neck that control the flow of blood to the

1 *Italia Sera*
2 *Rinascita 19 Oct '78*

brain, and found no blockage. But most important is that he also tested Luciani for blood viscosity and those results showed that Luciani's blood was actually on the thin side, which conclusively rules out the possibility that he could have died of stroke just a week later. A blood thickness test was not administered in his physical examination six months before his death as this kind of testing is only done if it is suspected that a person has a specific related condition.

So one no longer has to surmise, for now one knows as a matter of scientific fact that Luciani did not die of a heart attack or for that matter of a stroke. The evidence is so strong that one no longer needs an autopsy. And we know something else. And that is that Dr. Buzzanetti also knew this. Which raises the question, if Dr. Buzzanetti knew that Luciani had not died of either a heart attack or a stoke, why did he claim that *a blood clot to the heart* was the cause of death in both the Vatican release and Luciani's death certificate?

Now let us consider number two - accident. Again, the position of the body and of the papers at death is the obvious clue. If you can come up with an accident of some kind that could have left the body in the position in which it was found you are much more a *Sherlock Holmes* than am I. So one knows almost for certain that an accident was not involved. Unless of course, he were killed by an accident which was caused by someone else's action and who, in attempting to cover up their involvement, sat him up in the position he was found. This would also be the case if he was murdered in a violent way, with a blow to the head for example. One might try to cover up their tracks and try to make him appear to have died of natural causes. Another very long shot, but nevertheless one to keep in the back of one's mind.

Next we have suicide. The fact that in the process of death John Paul did not pull the bell cord or press a service button could have been intentional on his part. This would be true if suicide had been his intent. There is only one method of suicide that would not have left evidence that would have been discovered by those who found him including the embalmers, and that is poison. Those of you who are masters of the world of mystery know that there exist only two poisons that result in instantaneous or close to instantaneous death, strychnine and cyanide. And strychnine can be eliminated as it results in massive convulsions for a few minutes before death, something that would have never left him in the position he was found in still holding his papers in an upright position.

Concerning cyanide, ingestion of cyanide concealed in food would also take several minutes, perhaps an hour, to kill him. But biting down on a cyanide capsule would kill him instantly, this is because cyanide in a gaseous form is particularly deadly and when one bites down on a capsule it is the gas which is released and inhaled that does the job. But, if this had been the case, he would have required an accomplice, for death occurs so suddenly it is impossible for one to swallow the capsule. And no capsule was found in or among the bedclothes.

But what closes the lid on the suicide theory is motive. Here was a very purposeful man who had worked all of his life to attain the position that he now found himself in. Now he had the power to right the wrongs of the past, to bring an end to bigotry for once and for all. Now he was in a position to bring an end to poverty and starvation in the world. That he would take his own life on the very eve of the realization of his lifelong dreams would make no sense whatsoever.

So to summarize, we have virtually no chance of natural death, practically no chance of accident and certainly no chance of suicide, at the very best a less than one-half-of-one-percent chance of any of these. So we know with reasonable certainty that John Paul was murdered, for there are no other ways in which one can die.

Chapter 3

MOTIVE AND OPPORTUNITY

In trying to determine who murdered John Paul I one would first have to consider motive and opportunity, for these are the two basic requirements of murder, of any murder. As a matter of fact they are the only absolute requirements of murder.

In the case of John Paul's death, motive, to say the least, would be widespread. Any ultraconservative cardinal, bishop or priest who had an intense passion to resist change would be on the list. Those who believed firmly in Moses and knew of John Paul's findings that the Israelites had never been in Egypt would be particularly suspect. After all, it is reasonable to conclude that certain members of the *Curia* had already been motivated to the point of murder by Luciani's discovery, for we know that Brother Tom Jones had been murdered for this reason.

When one is dealing with these kinds of men one is dealing with men of ideology, not men of reality. They live and die for what they believe is right. When John Paul I was elected everything they stood for had come to an end and the handwriting on the wall was telling them quite clearly that even the positions of rank in the Church that many of them held were also about to come to an end.

So when one considers motive, certainly those who aspired to be Pope or to other high positions in the Church would undoubtedly be toward the top of the list. And those who were in high positions and served to lose them would be there also.

Then there are those who might have been bothered by the threat this Pope posed to the regency of Rome; that the Vatican Museum, the Sistine Chapel and the Castel Gandolfo and other royal assets of the Church, including possibly the Vatican itself, might be liquidated to help the poor. It was well known that when he was a cardinal Luciani had obtained a market appraisal on the patriarch's palace in Venice and although it was never released to the press, one would have to surmise that its value would be in the five to ten million dollar range. And as cardinal residences go it certainly would not be at the top of the list. If he were to liquidate these assets and many others to help the poor it might endanger the image of the Church. It certainly would impact the way many of the ranking prelates of the Church including the Pope lived. And it would take from the European cardinals their vacation paradise at the Castel Gandolfo. So there would have been those cardinals who really didn't want to live as Christ and his disciples had lived. Rather they would prefer to live as the princes of the

Church that they saw themselves to be. These of course, would be a little further down the list but nevertheless are there for those of you who wish to consider them.

And then there would be those who believed that the Church could not survive without its regency, something that John Paul was bent on destroying, -that this pauper of a Pope intended to reduce the papacy itself to a Gandhi-like image. There were those who believed that it is the royal image of the papacy that controls the populace and holds the Church together that in regard to spiritual matters the people need a king, in the case of the Church, a dictator, -one who lives in a royal palace. There was considerable consternation among some cardinals, particularly those who shared the Vatican with him, that someone with a Mother Teresa like image would lose the respect of the congregation and would be unable to rule and that the Church would fall into ruin.

Note: early in 2004, as I had done many times before, I traced my patron from the small village of Canale d'Agordo in the Dolomite Alps where he had been born through to Belluno and then on to Vittorio Veneto and finally to Rome. Unlike all of my previous visits, this time I carried in my hand this book, Murder in the Vatican, and no matter where I was, in a park, in a pub, in a store, on the street, or what have you, I was approached by Italians, and each one of them, taking note of the book's title, laughed at me and told me, "You're not telling us anything that we don't already know." Yet, their conformity ended there. For most of those in the liberal north where he had lived and worked his ministry told me that he had been murdered for precisely the ecclesiastical reasons that I have outlined in this book. But in conservative Rome they were of another opinion, for they believed he was murdered solely to protect the regency of the papacy, something that most of them agreed with, for the Roman prefers not to give up his king. Nevertheless, not a single one of them cited the Vatican Bank Scandal which has been the conclusion of all of our predecessors.

And then there would be those bishops and cardinals who were transsexuals drawn into the priesthood by its promise of silk, satin and lace gowns. In that a substantial number of priests are transsexuals it would follow that a substantial number of bishops and cardinals are transsexuals, -women who had been born into men's bodies. We have already mentioned the huge amount of money that John Paul II spends on his costumes and jewelry. One must keep in mind that at the lower end of the Church's hierarchy the most poorly clad bishop spends more on his *dresses* each year than it takes to feed and clothe a family of four.

And then there would also be those who enjoyed spending their Saturday afternoons listening to the sins of the flesh of seven, eight, nine and ten year olds and teenagers. For these sessions were also about to come to an end. Particularly, high up on the list would be those high ranking Vatican bishops and cardinals who heard the confessions of the beautiful Maltese altar boys.

So there are many who may have had a motive to kill this Pope and there are some others we will talk of. But if one considers opportunity the list narrows, for there were a very limited number of people who had access to the Pope's chambers on the evening of September twenty-eighth, nineteen hundred and seventy eight. So let us first concentrate on them.

the last supper,

First of all let's consider the outsiders who lived in the papal palace at the time of the murder. By outsiders I mean those who lived in the papal palace but outside of the papal apartment. There were only five, all residents of either the first or second floors of the papal palace. That is, they did not live on the top floor, which comprised the papal apartment itself. Two were *Curia* cardinals, two others were bishops and the other a monsignor. There were cardinals Villot and Confalonieri and bishop Caprio and Monsignor Fox who lived on the floor directly below the papal apartment. In order of rank these were the secretary of state, the dean of the *College of Cardinals*, the undersecretary of state and the deputy secretary of state. And then there was Bishop Casaroli, the foreign minister, who had an apartment on the floor below that.

All except two of these arrived at about seven-thirty for dinner in the papal apartment on the evening before the Pope's death. Cardinal Confalonieri didn't show up. He had left a message with the guard, that bothered by the painters who had been painting his rooms he wasn't feeling well and would be retiring early. And the deputy secretary of state was in Krakow, Poland visiting Cardinal Wojtyla at the time.

There were ten at dinner in all, -the Pope, Villot, Casaroli, Caprio, the Pope's secretaries Magee and Lorenzi, and four nuns. Although the Pope had overslept from his nap, which caused him to be awakened by Magee, he arrived first and pointed to a chair as each of the others entered the dining room. It was an austere room to say the least. It had poverty written all over it. It had quickly become the new Pope's favorite room in what was otherwise a luxurious palace of feather pillows and silver and gold and priceless works of art. He felt most at home here for it reminded him of when he had grown up in an impoverished village in the Italian Alps.

Its walls were stark white and its two unadorned windows looked out over the San Damasus Courtyard below. There was a long narrow wooden table such as one might find in a workshop. It was made up of some old planks of wood that were set upon two equally old wooden workhorses. Although its surface was well worn from time there was no significant damage except for a few old stains here and there. It was the kind of thing that would be the first thing one would throw out once one would climb out of the cellar of poverty. Twelve rickety matching chairs surrounded it, -that is, to the extent that it is possible to match a few old planks of wood. An old rug hung on one wall.

Everyone in the household had a secret, a secret they were keeping to themselves. John Paul did not know of this secret. For if he knew of it this room, this dining room, would suddenly become much less a home to him. For the table he was about to sit at would easily reap ten million dollars at auction. It was a second century piece of oak taken out of an eighth century monastery. The old rug that hung on the wall could easily garnish a few million more, for it was the carpet that had lain before the main altar in the old church which once stood where St. Peter's stood now. And any one of the chairs could easily be traded in for a new Mercedes.

When they were all seated, Sister Maria Elena sat at the head of the table. Who's she? She was the nun one would often pass scrubbing the floors in the palace building. And at the other end sat Sister Vincenza, the mother nun, the nun who just ten years before had cooked the dinner that I had enjoyed in the bishop's castle at Vittorio Veneto. Nevertheless, none of the others - the *men,* that is - were happy about it. But they had to put up with it.

They did not understand this man who would have a simple maid at the head of his table. But it was not necessary that they understand him. All that was necessary was that he understood himself. For it was a scullery maid who sixty years before had brought him into the world and who had scrubbed many floors and many toilets to bring him to where he was today.

The Pope disappeared into the kitchen and returned with a pitcher of water in one hand and a large bottle of white wine in the other and went around the table reaching over their shoulders and filling the glasses as he went by. In the meantime, his secretaries Magee and Lorenzi were bringing out the breads, the meats and vegetables in a half dozen or so bowls and the other men at the table cringed a bit wondering when it would be their turn to take up the role of servant.

With everyone seated, the Pope gestured to Sister Maria Elena to begin grace. In the fifteen years of Paul VI's reign and in the five years of John XXIII's reign and in the nineteen years of Pius XII's reign and in the fifteen years of Pius XI's reign and in the eight years of Benedict XV's reign and in the eleven years of Pius X's reign and in the fifteen years of Leo XIII's reign only two people had ever said grace in this room, the

Pope, or in his absence, the secretary of state. What kind of pope was this who would have a mere woman, a scullery maid, lead the prayer?

The conversation was light and airy and the Pope was in good spirits. Although he was laughing and joking at times, he was concerned that Cardinal Confalonieri was ill and asked one of the nuns to take him something after dinner. Bishop Casaroli intervened and told him that the cardinal had retired for the night and did not want to be disturbed. Getting up Casaroli added that he himself had an appointment at nine and left. It was most likely that he had no appointment at all, as it was quite apparent he wanted to get out of helping with the dishes; he had done the very same thing the evening before and the one before that. He carried a briefcase with him to cover for his leaving early. He just did not intend to yield to this latest rule of the house. But that he left before nine is probably immaterial to the rest of this story. Or perhaps it might take on some importance as one goes along.

The others lingered at the table, chatting away. At precisely nine o'clock the nuns started clearing the table and the Pope got up to help them. When the Pope disappeared into the kitchen, Bishop Caprio left, as if he couldn't stand it anymore. The Pope came back into the dining room and Villot, who remained chatting with Magee and Lorenzi, joked with them, "that he be must training these nuns to be altar girls." Villot kind of liked the idea that a pope would do these things. What he didn't know was that John Paul was not training these nuns to be altar girls, for he was in fact training them to be priests. And it was quite obvious that both Casaroli and Caprio and possibly Confalonieri who was sleeping on the floor below had already guessed this.

Shortly, the three men followed the Pope down to his chambers and bidding him goodnight, Magee and Lorenzi disappeared into their apartments and Villot went down the corridor hall and past the guard and down the stairs.

So when one considers those who had opportunity, one is limited to only nine people, those who had apartments along the corridor in which the Pope's inner chambers were located and, of course, the guard himself. Anyone coming from a lower floor would have had to have passed by the guard who sat at the top of the stairs opposite the elevator at the entrance to the corridor that led to the papal apartment. Unless a conspiracy is involved, opportunity is necessary to commit the crime of murder. One cannot commit murder and be a thousand miles away, for example. And even if a conspiracy had been involved it would have to have involved at least one of these nine. So let us look at these nine, these nine who shared the papal apartment with the Pope on the night of his death. These nine that we know had the opportunity to commit the crime. Anyone else involved in the crime would have had to conspire with one or more of these nine to have been involved in the murder of John Paul I.

First there was the ceremonial Swiss guard who sat at the entrance to the papal apartment just in front of the windows in full view of the elevator and the grand staircase. And this could be either of two guards or both guards. That is, either of the two guards who rotated the post throughout the night. The three-hour rotation of guards is necessary, as I have already mentioned, to guarantee a perpetual sentinel at the entrance to the corridor leading to the papal apartment. It eliminates the possibility of someone entering when the guard is away momentarily in the restroom, for example. So it is possible that either of these two guards could have entered the apartment at anytime during the Pope's sleeping hours. Of course if anyone chanced by, which would be a long shot in the middle of the night, the guard's absence would have been immediately noticed. That is, unless both guards were involved as one could cover for the other, unless by chance the rotating-guard were to show up on his random rounds which would be unpredictable.

So in the case of the guards one would have to consider motive. And the only motive that I can think of that a guard might have would be promise of rank or money. So although involvement of a guard was possible, it remains somewhat of a long shot.

I think I should mention that if promise of rank to a guard had been the motive, only Bishop Marcinkus could have made such a promise. As in addition to his role as head of the Vatican Bank he was the leader of the *Swiss Guard*. So, when one considers the motive of a guard, the finger points most heavily toward Marcinkus.

This is because to bribe a specific guard to kill the Pope would not be the easiest thing to do. That you could bribe one of the one hundred and twenty guards to do the job is possible. But that you could have bribed the specific guards assigned to protect the Pope's chambers on a particular night would be entirely something else, and that something else could have only been executed by Marcinkus who controlled the Swiss Guard. For he alone had the authority to assign guards to particular posts, particularly that guard assigned to the post closest to the Pope. So he alone could have bribed any guard with money or promise of position and reassigned that particular guard to the post. Something that one should keep in the back of one's mind if something better fails to come up.

I think I should clear up a rumor concerning Marcinkus that is not true. Some books written about the Pope's death claim that Marcinkus was seen walking in the Vatican gardens just behind the papal palace at four o'clock on the morning John Paul was found dead. This is fiction that was created to tie *The Great Vatican Bank Scandal* to the Pope's murder. *The Great Vatican Bank Scandal* had nothing to do with the Pope's murder. Although there was some activity between the Banco Ambrosiano and the Vatican Bank during the reign of Paul VI, the scandal began and ended under the watch of John Paul II. As a matter of fact, the first significant transaction of one hundred and thirty-four million dollars took place one year after the day of his election on October 17, 1979.*

There is nothing in the legitimate press to support these claims that Marcinkus was seen in the Vatican gardens that morning. And since every guard in Vatican City was subjected to a certain amount of scrutiny by the press one can be certain that if he had been seen in the Vatican gardens early on the morning of the Pope's death, that it would have been reported in a newspaper or two. There is the fact that during the days preceding the Pope's death, Marcinkus had the most frequent interaction with John Paul because of the ongoing audit of the Vatican Bank. Yet, although guards did report seeing him in the Vatican Bank offices which are on the first floor of the papal palace building, none of them saw him enter the papal palace itself on the day or evening of the Pope's death. Therefore, one knows that if Marcinkus had been involved in the Pope's death, he would have had to have been involved in a conspiracy of some kind or had to have engaged at least two guards to do the job.

One should keep in mind that Marcinkus was a liberal, an American, and from an ideological point of view he would have welcomed Luciani as Pope. Yet as head of the Vatican Bank he may have been offended by the audit which Luciani had ordered. Perhaps he feared what the audit might disclose. Yes, that he may have been engaged by Karol Wojtyla of Poland before John Paul's death to mastermind what we have come to today as the *Great Vatican Bank Scandal* is almost a given. But that he knew of a conspiracy to kill John Paul at the time is just not in the cards.

On the other hand, Marcinkus craved power. Under Paul VI, although officially only a bishop and president of the Vatican Bank, he had assumed authority over many other functions in Vatican City, including all of its physical properties, -the reason he was head of the *Swiss Guard*. And this made him an enemy of many members of the *Curia* since many of the responsibilities and authorities he absorbed under Paul VI had been taken from members of the *Curia*. There were those who claimed that Marcinkus would do anything for rank or position of power. And one

** Jun-Aug 1982 issues Time-Europe or Keepers of the Keys Wilton Wynn for best summary of facts suggesting foul play in the Pope's death considered him to be the Number 1 suspect.*

knows in retrospect that John Paul II's first official act upon becoming Pope was to name Marcinkus the Vatican head of state. Yet, in that John Paul II eventually fired him and sent him into exile, one knows that Marcinkus had no knowledge of a conspiracy to murder the Pope and this is an absolute fact because he is still alive today. Yet as we shall prove, we know that he collaborated with Karol Wojtyla before the second conclave of 1978 in connection with what we now know as the *Great Vatican Bank Scandal.* So he goes at the bottom of the motive list and only midway up on the opportunity list. This, despite the fact that most of those who wrote books about foul play in the Pope's death considered him the Number One Suspect.

And next we have the four nuns. Keep in mind that it was the mother nun Vincenza who found the body at four-thirty in the morning. So the mother nun certainly had the opportunity, opportunity to have committed the crime at any time during the night and opportunity again in the morning to have cleaned up any evidence of the crime. She, as we know knocked on the Pope's door at four-thirty in the morning, opened the door and discovered the Pope. We know that she entered the room because she had left the tray on the nightstand. How long it was before she roused Magee one does not know, but one has to assume that it was only a matter of a minute or two. To wake the pope or rouse Magee she did not have to pass the guard, as Magee's apartment was immediately adjacent to that of the Pope. The embalmers who arrived less than an hour later claimed that the body had not been dead for much more than an hour or two. This, of course, conflicted with the opinion of the doctor who said that the Pope had died before midnight.

So the mother nun certainly had the opportunity. Could she have had a motive of some kind? One must assume in these things that most anyone could have a motive. Again, there could be promise of rank or of money or something else. Or, perhaps more likely in her case, the threat of harm or death to a loved one if she did not comply.

But the nun Vincenza had served John Paul for twenty years and was probably the very closest person to him in the world. So it is unlikely that anyone would have approached her and threatened her as it would be likely that he would learn of it.

And how about the other nuns? They must have fallen in love with this man who had come to them from Venice, for he was the first pope to demand that they join him in the papal dining room for dinner. Until then, the nuns had been confined to dine in the kitchen. And what's more they could for the first time pray to their God in the Pope's private chapel rather than just scrub its floors for the men to walk on. And they all knew that John Paul was about to bring about the equality of women in the Church. So concerning possible motive, the nuns would certainly be toward the bottom of the list of possible suspects.

Although we have not yet discussed all of them, this is probably as good a place as any to stop and summarize the timetable of events that occurred the evening before and the morning after the Pope's death. For the order in which the events took place could help guide us toward who may have killed John Paul.

the Pope is wakened from his nap by Magee	6:30 PM
dinner	7:30 PM
Pope retires	9:15 PM
Pope dies according to the Vatican release	11:30 PM
police in the square check Pope's windows and note that the window is wide open and the lights are not on	2:00 AM
Pope dies according to the embalmers	3:30-4:30 AM
mother nun discovers that the Pope is immobile	4:35 AM
Magee determines that the Pope is dead	4:45 AM
Magee calls and wakes Villot on the Pope's intercom	4:50 AM
Magee calls embalmers to get ready for pick-up	5:00 AM
Villot arrives on the scene and performs the last rites	5:15 AM
Magee orders a car be sent to pick up the embalmers	5:20 AM
Confalonieri, Casaroli and Caprio arrive	5:25 AM
Doctor Buzzanetti arrives and pronounces him dead	5:35 AM
embalmers arrive. Villot orders them not to drain blood or remove organs from the body to save time	5:45 AM
embalming is completed	6:30 AM
Pope is found dead by Magee according to Vatican release	6:30 AM
official press announcement of his death	7:30 AM
embalmers are interviewed by the press	9:00 AM
mother nun Vincenza is interviewed by the press	1:00 PM
Pope's body is put on display in St Clementine Chapel	6:00PM

Again the original official Vatican press release: "*John Paul died just before midnight last night of a blood clot to the heart. He was discovered by his secretary Magee about six thirty this morning when he went to look for the Pope when the Pope did not show up for his morning chapel service. He was found to be in his daytime clothes and died while he was reading the Imitation of Christ which book was still held upright in his hands when he was found dead. Cardinal Villot was summoned immediately and he performed the last rites of the Church.*"

Of course, much of the press release was corrected as more and more contradictions came to light. And as we said the major differences that surfaced were that the embalmers had told the press that they had arrived at quarter-to-six and that since the body was still warm and the windows were wide open on a chilly morning the Pope could not have been dead for more than an hour or two. In addition, there was the fact that the embalmers insisted that a car had picked them up shortly after five-thirty. This was verified by a suspicious reporter who checked the motor pool records that showed that a driver and a car had been dispatched to the nearby school of medicine that day at five-thirty in the morning. Nevertheless, all of these differences seemed to be immaterial at the time. But now that we are talking about MURDER they become quite important.

There is, of course, the chance that a part of the cleanup operation, if at all necessary, could have included returning the Pope to the position in which he is said to have been found. He may have been killed in some other fashion, which we have not yet considered. Perhaps the killer or killers sat him up in his reading position to make it look like a heart attack had killed him and the murderer(s) may have thought at the time that it would do the trick. There is some credibility to this possibility, as until now the entire world accepted the word of the physician that John Paul died of a heart attack, despite the fact the official Vatican release that had been printed on the front page of every newspaper in the world stated that he had been found sitting up in bed holding a book upright in his hands.

If a struggle had taken place it might explain the missing spectacles and the slipper socks, as the spectacles could have been broken and a sock could have been used to clean up any sign of blood. This would be particularly true if the Pope had been killed by lethal injection. The needle, particularly if administered in a struggle, would have left a trace or two of blood that might otherwise be detected by the embalmers. If the killer had reached down by the side of the bed and picked up one of the white socks to clean a spot or two of blood, he would have been a fool to have left the other behind. But if this had been the case, the killer made the same mistake that the doctor had made. He assumed that a man could suffer a massive heart attack and could still be holding the papers he was reading upright in his hands, and that he could have been awake and reading and been unable to have reached for the bell cord that hung a whisker away from his right shoulder.

So we have covered the guards and the four nuns. And then we have the Pope's valet. We know from the newspaper accounts that the valet was on leave in connection with a death in his family the night John

Paul died and we also know that if he were to have returned that evening, he would have had to have passed by at least four guards, -the two at the entrance to the building, the guard who sat just inside the entrance to the building and the guard who sat at the entrance to papal apartment. We know that this did not happen as all of the guards were scrutinized by the press the very next day in connection with the rumors of foul play that had surfaced.

This is how we know today who was in the papal palace that night and who was not. How one knows today that the valet was on leave and that the Monsignor Fox and Bishop Marcinkus were in Poland visiting Cardinal Wojtyla and that Cardinal Confalonieri did not attend dinner. How one can tell today, thirty years later, just who was at dinner and who was not. And for this information we must give thanks to the many rumors that surfaced after the Pope's death which suggested arsenic poisoning. For every reporter in Italy and his brother was trying to nail down the scoop of the century. At first, because poisoning was considered to have been involved, they concentrated on who might have had access to the dining room and the kitchen and who did not. But, in that the Pope died so suddenly, they soon turned their attention to who had access to the Pope's chambers the night he had died and who did not. For this information they scrutinized the guards who were on duty that night in the papal palace. It is important to note that many of the guards themselves believed the rumors to be true, that foul play had been involved. Particularly, in that they had experienced a laughing, joking, vibrant man one day and a corpse the next. So the record is there today in the microfilm. One knows exactly who was at dinner that night and who was not. And what's more one knows when they arrived at dinner and when they left. And one also knows who else was sleeping in the papal palace and exactly where they were sleeping that fateful night late in September of nineteen hundred and seventy-eight.

Yet, although opportunity is not possible in the case of the valet, one has to consider motive. Was there a motive in his case? Not overwhelming, but it was very decidedly there. Enough perhaps, to justify murder.

The Pope's valet, whom he had inherited from Paul VI, did not like this pauper of a man. He didn't like him from the very beginning. For in the dressing room that annexed the conclave, when he had placed upon John Paul's shoulders the regal, elegantly golden brocaded cloak which he had worked so hard to create for the occasion, the newly elected Pope put it aside. Instead he took a relatively simple cloak from the rack, almost a simple smock, and donning it proceeded toward the balcony. Yes, this Pope who would do away with the pomp and splendor of the papacy would bring an end to his worldwide recognition in the world of fashion. In fact, it would destroy it. It would destroy everything he had worked for all of his life. So when it comes to motive the valet would rank relatively high on the list, perhaps below some of the others, but, nevertheless, he would be there. But if one considers opportunity he would be toward the bottom of the list, for had the valet been seen in the building that day or night it most certainly would have been reported in the press. And in retrospect we know that he did not gain by the Pope's death, as just a month later John Paul II would replace him with a world-renowned dress designer.

Then there was John Magee, who for ten years had served as first secretary under Paul VI and now had been told by the new Pope that Lorenzi, who had served him in Venice, would replace him as first secretary. He might be retained as a second secretary to handle the paperwork or might be considered for pastoral work in his native Ireland. Magee saw it as almost a break in protocol that John Paul would replace him, as it was practically a tradition that a pope retains his predecessor's secretary.

And of course, in Magee's case there was opportunity, the exact same level of opportunity that the mother nun possessed. It was he who on realizing that the Pope was dead, sent the mother nun to fetch Doctor Buzzanetti who lived in another building in a remote part of the apostolic palace. This was somewhat suspicious on his part, as one could ask why he did not call the doctor. After all, there were two phones in the Pope's bedroom although it is reasonable that he did not know the doctor's number and felt that sending the nun was probably the fastest way to summon the doctor. Yet, he must have known that the guard outside at the top of the stairs would have known the doctor's number. Nevertheless, he sent the nun and this gave him the opportunity to be alone with the Pope's body until the all the others arrived almost a half-hour later. Keep in mind that in having the apartment right next to that of the Pope he had free access to the Pope's chambers at anytime during the night.

We know that while the nun had gone to rouse the doctor, Magee had first called Villot on the Pope's intercom. This was protocol, as upon the Pope's death Villot became the leader of the Church during the period of transition. It is known that Magee did not call the motor pool to dispatch a car to pick up the embalmers until after Villot arrived, as the decision to embalm would have had to have been that of Villot. Yet, it is quite obvious that he did call the embalmers before Villot arrived to tell them to get ready, for Villot did not arrive until quarter-after-five and the embalmers were dressed and picked up by the Vatican driver shortly after five-thirty. In that he alerted the embalmers at such an early hour in the morning on his own tells one that he must have so acted because he had experienced a peculiar pungent odor emanating from the body, a body that according to the embalmers testimony could not have been dead for more than an hour. And then there is the possibility that he may have known that arsenic had been involved. It could have been prearranged that he was to call the embalmers immediately upon finding the Pope dead,

It is obvious that he did call the other ranking prelates who resided in the papal palace during this time, as they all came on the scene a few minutes before the doctor showed up. And one also knows that he would have had to have used the phone to call them as the intercom was not wired to their quarters. Bishops Casaroli, Caprio and Cardinal Confalonieri arrived each one of them carrying the small case which contains a standup crucifix and the anointing oils used in the ritual of the last rites. However, Villot was already finishing up the honors by the time they came into the room.

So Magee, from a point of view of opportunity and considering some of the actions he took on his own, must remain high on the list. He would have had the opportunity to commit the evil deed at four o'clock and still have had time to clean up any lingering evidence when the nun went to fetch the doctor between four-thirty and five. To a certain extent he also had somewhat of a motive as history has shown that John Paul's successor retained him as first secretary. Yet certainly not the degree of reward that one might expect if it had been John Magee who had paved the way for Cardinal Wojtyla's rise to the world's stage. Not enough for this author at least to implicate this man in the murder of John Paul I. Yes, if John Magee had been named a cardinal, like some of the others we will talk about, one might think otherwise. In the end John Magee was named a bishop but not until a decade later.

Note: Shortly after John Paul's death, a flood of books were written that charged foul play. Many of these were quite riveting in their detail and caused the rumors to persist into the eighties. Finally late in 1986, Joan Paul II engaged John Cornwell, a noted journalist, to write his book, A Thief of the Night, which purpose was to bring the rumors to an end. Cornwell was invited to the Vatican and permitted to interview some of those who were in the Vatican the night John Paul had died. On the other hand he was not permitted to interview some others that he felt had been more important witnesses, and he was not very happy about this and he tells you this in the first edition of his book (Penguin Books Australia). Despite the fact that his book ignores most of the hard evidence in the press reports, and relies mostly upon these witnesses that were on the Vatican payroll, his best seller brought an end to the rumors for at least a time. And this is a great testimony as to Cornwell's ability as a writer as he convinces his readers in the end that the Pope had in fact died of a heart attack. And today, although one does not know what killed John Paul, it is now known as a matter of scientific fact that it was not a heart attack. Most of the witnesses that Cornwell interviews in his book, including its most important and compelling witness, John Magee, were elevated in rank by John Paul II as a reward for their cooperation. John Magee became Bishop of Cloyne Ireland on March 17, 1987.

So although the events of 1978 don't implicate Magee in the murder itself, the events of 1987 do implicate him in the cover up.

Whether or not Villot or Casaroli or Caprio or Confalonieri or any of the others who strolled into the room before the embalmers arrived at six o'clock were ever in the room alone with the Pope's body is not known. Of course if there had been any collusion any combination of these it would not be necessary for any one of them to be alone with the corpse to have performed any necessary clean up operation. But this would seem to be immaterial, as all of these outsiders would have had to pass by the guard at any time before the Pope's death. Yet any one of them except Villot, who performed the last rites, could have been carrying an empty case, an empty case which could have been used to remove the spectacles, the blood stained slipper socks or possibly any kind of a creature that may have been employed in the dreadful deed. That is, if a clean up operation had been necessary at all.

And one must not forget Lorenzi the Pope's loyal secretary, who that night occupied the second secretary's quarters and also had free access to the Pope's quarters that night. He too, could have carried out the dreadful deed for the conspirators. But the problem in his case is motive. If one can think of a motive that Lorenzi might have had it certainly beats me for he had been Luciani's loyal servant for ten years and his patron's demise brought his career to an absolute end. Yet, there is something mysterious about him. For example he, like Magee, was interviewed by Cornwell and contributed to his success, going so far as to claim that the embalmers did not show up until eight o'clock the following evening despite the fact that the embalmers were interviewed by the press at nine o'clock in the morning and the Pope's body had lay-in-state in St. Clementine's Chapel at six o'clock. Unlike most of the others, he has never been made a bishop. Yet, he would do anything to keep John Paul II happy as his sole ambition since John Paul's death has been to secure sainthood for his patron.

conspiracy,

Then of course, one must consider conspiracy. And when one considers conspiracy one is limited to examining motive. We have already considered what type of people would have wanted this Pope dead. This Pope, who as a cardinal had shown his liberal colors so boldly as to have removed his name from the list of candidates for the post he now held. The major political parties in Italy at the time,

far left	left	moderate	right	far right
				Catholic (Fascist) Party (*Curia* controlled)
	Christian Democratic Party (Aldo Moro & Paul VI)			
Communist Party (Rome)			Republican Party (Mafia controlled)	

John Paul was very decidedly on the *left,* the reason why Paul VI was also on the *left.* From a political point of the view, the only group that had a motive to go so far as to commit murder was the *Curia* cardinals, that group of Vatican cardinals who had withheld their twenty-one votes to rob Luciani of a unanimous election. Whether they acted in unison, or in part, or at all, may never be known. But when one considers motive it was certainly there. So let us consider some of the major players in this thing called the *Vatican Curia*, particularly those who lived in the papal palace.

First there was the secretary of state, Jean Villot. Luciani's election had come as a kind of blessing to him as he had thought for certain that an ultraconservative would replace his old friend and confidant Paul VI. Villot himself, being a Frenchman as I have said, was a liberal, -the reason why during his tenure most of the Vatican cardinals had never recognized him as their leader. So from the point of view of ecclesiastical motive he would not be on the list. And from the standpoint of opportunity he would have had to have passed by at least two guards, those at the head of the stairs of both the second and third floors, to have reached John Paul's bedroom as he lived on the second floor of the papal palace. And he would have had to have done this twice as he would have had to return to his quarters. Normally when one considers succession as a motive in a Pope's death, the secretary of state would be at the top of the list as in modern history the secretary of state has often succeeded to the papacy. However, in Villot's case, he was a liberal, and unlike Luciani was not a very popular liberal, and the *College of Cardinals* was overwhelmingly conservative.

When Luciani was elected there had been actually twenty two votes cast by Vatican cardinals, so one vote was cast for him by one of the Vatican cardinals and although it is not known who cast it, one would have to guess that it came from Villot, -as the others were all conservatives. So from the point of view of both motive and opportunity Villot would rank relatively low on the list.

Yet, much suspicion surrounds Cardinal Villot. For he was the one who was directly responsible for all of the misleading information, including the initial press release that cause the rumors of foul play to flourish in the first place. Particularly suspicious is that he ordered the embalmers not to drain blood or remove organs to save time when the body would not be viewed for more than twelve hours. Since he was the transition Pope it would have been his decision to send Magee and the nuns, the only direct witnesses of the circumstances of the Pope's death, into seclusion. He also composed and approved the first Vatican press release concerning the Pope's death. So we must keep this in mind as we go along.

Then there was Cardinal Confalonieri, the aging dean of the *College of Cardinals*. He slept directly under the Pope's inner chambers. The layout of his rooms was practically identical to that of the Pope's rooms above, except that he did not occupy the huge space beneath the Pope's library. Instead Confalonieri had a small library directly under the Pope's bathroom. He slept thirty feet below where the Pope sat up dead in his bed that fateful night.

We know that Confalonieri had not shown up for dinner the night of the Pope's death, as he himself was ill. Too ill to even have something served in his room. Yet we know that he recovered by early morning, as he showed up early the next morning as soon as he heard that the Pope had died, even before the doctor had pronounced the Pope dead. So these actions on his part cast some suspicion on him.

It would be an understatement to claim that Confalonieri was an ultraconservative. Everything John Paul stood for was his enemy. He was Cardinal Siri's closest confidant and Bishop Casaroli had been his protégé, two of the most conservative men in the history of the Church. It had been principally Confalonieri's influence that had prevented a unanimous vote in Luciani's election on the final recount in his election. Keep in mind that Luciani was an Italian and the twenty-one votes that remained cast against him on the final vote were entirely those of Italian cardinals, so bitter was their hate of what this man stood for that they would do this. So from a point of view of motive one would have to put him toward the very top of the list.

But when one considers opportunity, he too like Villot would have had to have passed by at least two guards to have reached the Pope's bedroom that night. So normally he would rank toward the bottom of the opportunity ladder with all of the others who lived on the lower floors. That is, except for one possibility.

His bedroom was located directly beneath that of the Pope. He, unlike the others, could have possibly thrown something from his open window thirty feet upwards into the Pope's bedroom window, which he knew was always open. And if he were to have mounted a small ladder he could have thrown something from the top of his bedroom window into the lower part of the Pope's open window, a distance of less than eight feet. We know that there was most likely a ladder in his quarters that night as the painters were painting his rooms. And there are, as you readers who are experts in mystery books know, some poisonous creatures - scorpions and the deadly coral snake among others - that are attracted by the warmth of the human body under covers.

From this point of view, Confalonieri had somewhat greater access than most of the others who lived on the lower floors of the palace building. So he would rank partway up the ladder of opportunity. Yet near the top of the ladder when one considers motive. Although we know he was in the Pope's bedroom before the embalmers arrived, we don't know if he was ever alone with the body. But that he was alone with the body is possible. And as I have said, if collusion had been involved that he had ever been alone with the body would be immaterial. If some kind of a cleanup operation were not necessary, having been alone with the body would also be immaterial. But certainly, had he in fact thrown something into the Pope's bedroom from his own bedroom, then he would have had to have recovered whatever it was that he had thrown. And he could not have made this recovery anytime during the night, as he would have had to pass by two guards twice.

And then there was Bishop Casaroli. He is also high on the motive list. Perhaps at the very top of this list. A little bit here about his dreams, his ambitions, his hopes and his aspirations.

It was not Casaroli's objective to rise to the papacy. Sure, as was true of any cardinal, the desire was there, but he knew that being recognized as the extreme ultraconservative that he was, he would never muster the vote of any of the moderates or liberals that would be necessary to win him the papacy. His lifelong ambition lay in locking down the number two spot, secretary of state. But in recent years his hopes had dwindled into a dream more than a realistic ambition.

During the first half of Paul's fifteen year reign Casaroli had held the Pope's ear in the palm of his hand. But now he was glad that Paul was dead. For midway through his time Paul began to ignore Casaroli, Casaroli whose influence on Paul at one time had made many men into cardinals. Now he knew that as long as Paul lived he himself would never be named a cardinal. He would never succeed Villot as secretary of state.

And he knew why the change had come about. At least he thought he knew why.

He believed that it had been his influence on Paul in 1968 that had caused the Pope to put aside the advice of most of his advisors and had caused him to issue the papal decree of *Humanae Vitae*, the Church's doctrine prohibiting any kind of artificial contraception. Something that Paul in time regretted, for Paul had lost the support of many of the cardinals in the field who would have favored a more lenient policy.

When Paul died, Casaroli's dream once again became an ambition to someday be named a cardinal and eventually succeed to the secretary of state position, the vice president of the Roman Catholic Church. No, not that he thought that he would be the upfront choice of a conservative Pope if elected, after all he was just a bishop, but perhaps somewhere down the road if the post happened to open he might be a viable candidate.

The election of a conservative in the first conclave of 1978 was practically a given. If one were to rely on the predictions that were spread across the world's newspapers as to the leading candidates, there was hardly a liberal among them. No newspaper in the world even did so much as to list Luciani as a candidate, despite the fact that although he rarely traveled outside of Italy he was the most widely known cardinal in the world. On the other hand, his successor Karol Wojtyla was scarcely known outside of Poland though he was the most widely traveled cardinal in the history of the Church. During his ten years as a cardinal he visited more than seventy countries and four hundred cities. Wojtyla, being an ultraconservative, brought nothing new, and never made the headlines. Conversely, as an outspoken ultraliberal, Luciani was constantly in the press. Today few of us can name many cardinals as they are mostly conservatives and rarely make the press.

Of course, in Casaroli's case, had eventual advancement to the position of secretary of state been the motive for murder, it would have had to involve two murders, -as Villot the incumbent secretary was still alive, and although aging, had no health problems. Actually, he was full of energy and very much on the job. If one considers Casaroli as a suspect, it would have involved three murders, as three men had to die in rapid succession to have allowed him to succeed to the secretary of state position, Paul VI, John Paul I and Villot. In retrospect today, one knows that this is exactly what happened.

Then there was a nasty rumor that Casaroli might be replaced as foreign minister with a more moderate personality, one who would be less of an adversary to communism, someone who could better work with the communists to work out solutions. If John Paul were to live another week or two Casaroli would not only be blocked forever from going up the ladder, he might very well go down the ladder.

So he, like Confalonieri, would have had reason to hate the new Pope with a passion and this would put him at the top of the motive list. But the problem was opportunity as he lived on the first floor of the papal palace and he would have had to have passed by at least three guards to have reached the Pope's bedroom that evening. And again, he would have to pass by them twice as he would have had to have returned to his quarters. So he remains toward the bottom of the opportunity ladder. Below Confalonieri, as he did not occupy the apartment directly under that of the Pope.*

Note: A bishop who had read the preliminary edition of Murder in the Vatican called me and told me that he was a young seminarian in the Vatican the night the Pope died. He asked me how long I had known Casaroli as he had been impressed by my vivid and remarkably accurate description of the man. He told me that Casaroli, although only a bishop, treated everyone beneath him as if they were dirt, that he considered himself to be a prince among princes of the Church and that he was always dressed in elaborate and rich attire and had a particular fondness for lace. I told him that I had never met Casaroli, that I had constructed his personality from the many biting remarks that he had made from time to time in the press.

He told that on the morning of the murder, "On hearing the news, all us peons gathered together in a cafeteria together with a few Swiss guards, a few nuns and some maintenance workers. At the time there was no reason to believe that anything else had been involved other than murder. The conversation centered on Casaroli and if those present had been a jury that he would have been put away for life. But some of this was probably because we hated him so much. Yet, we knew his ambitions and they certainly fit in well with murder. But we were confused because we knew that he wanted to be secretary of state and we also knew that Jean Villot was in outstanding health and none of us would have guessed that he too would be dead in a few months time." Nevertheless, this bishop was surprised that I even considered Casaroli as suspect, as all those who had written about the Pope's death before me had completely ignored him. And to be honest, as I will point out, I didn't consider him a viable candidate for the electric chair until I was more than two years into my investigation.

Note: most of the press reporting discussed in this chapter can be found in the September 28-October 5 1978 issues of IL Messaggero; IL Manifesto; La Repubblica; L'Osservatore Romano; Secolo d'Italia and most other Italian newspapers

Prince Casaroli with his court

Then there was Bishop Caprio. He would have had a similar motive as had Casaroli, for as undersecretary of state he would most likely be named foreign minister and possibly be made an archbishop if his cousin Casaroli were to go up the ladder. Both Casaroli and Caprio were related to the Gambino family, which was the most powerful Mafia family in Italy and the largest private contributor to the Church, the reason why they had had risen to the bishop level to begin with.

Since he occupied the apartment directly below that of the Pope's first secretary he was the closest to the Pope other than Confalonieri and those who shared the top floor with him. Yet he would have had to have passed by at least two guards. Yes, close enough to the guard on his floor to have possibly waited for an opportunity to somehow elude him, but he would certainly be greeted by the guard on the Pope's floor a moment later. And he would have to have passed by them twice, as like the others he would have had to have returned to his quarters. So he remains high, perhaps at the top of the motive ladder but relatively low on the ladder of opportunity.

And finally we come to the other *Curia* cardinals, those who lived outside the papal palace. Again these would have opportunity only through an accomplice. But from the point of view of motive all of them would be toward the top of the list and two of them would be at the very top of the list.

There would be Cardinal Siri, co-leader of the *far right* in the Roman Catholic Church. He was also the man who retained the twenty one *Curia* votes in the final count of the election that named John Paul Pope. And then there was Cardinal Benelli of Florence. Benelli believed that had

Luciani not been a factor in the election that he would have become Pope. This gave him some reason to believe that in a successive election Siri would yield up his block of votes in a more timely fashion to allow him to carry the tide. So these two would be high on the motive list but would have required an accomplice or two inside the papal palace to get the job done, particularly as they were both comfortably in their beds in their respective cities of Genoa and Florence the night of the Pope's death.

So let's rank these suspects by how they size up as to the two necessary ingredients in the recipe for murder, *motive* and *opportunity.*

	motive	opportunity
absolute	Casaroli and Confalonieri	either of two guards
	Caprio	John Paul himself (suicide)
	Siri and Benelli	any of the four nuns
		Magee and Lorenzi
possible	the guard(s)	Confalonieri
	the valet	Marcinkus*
	Magee	
not likely	the nuns	the valet*
	Lorenzi	Casaroli and Caprio
	Villot	Villot
	the Pope himself (suicide)	Siri and Benelli *
	Marcinkus	

So there are five people who would be high on the motive list and nine that are high on the opportunity list. We know that of the nine people -including the Pope himself - who could have killed the Pope, only one had a possible motive, Magee. Yet we have ruled him out of a possible conspiracy because we know in retrospect that he did not gain in rank; at least on the heels of John Paul's death.

Of the others, only Confalonieri who had the bedroom directly below that of the Pope could have possibly committed the crime without collusion of some sort. So that leaves five people who had substantial motive to see the Pope dead, but who would have to had involved someone else

** only if a conspiracy or an accomplice was involved as these men were not in the papal palace on the fateful night.*

in order to get the job done - Benelli, Casaroli, Caprio, Siri and possibly Confalonieri.

And although I have not put him on the list of suspects one must not rule out Dr. Buzzanetti. As we have already discussed, he performed extensive and adequate tests to exclude the possibility of a pulmonary condition in connection with the Pope's swollen feet and just a week later concluded that he died of a heart attack. We will come back to Dr. Buzzanetti now and then, as we go along.

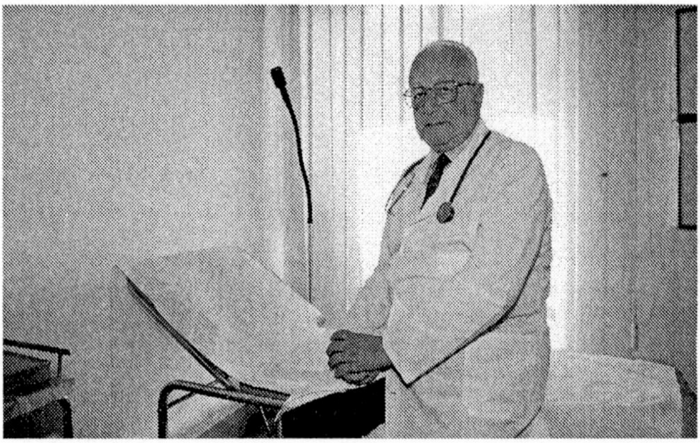

Dr. Buzzanetti

one more suspect,

And finally, there would be one more suspect and his name at that time was Karol Wojtyla. For in retrospect it was he who benefited the most by John Paul's death, for it was he who two weeks later became John Paul II.

Although it is an unpopular thing to say, to ignore him as a suspect in this case would be a little like eliminating the husband as a suspect when a woman is murdered and he is the beneficiary of a one-hundred-million-dollar insurance policy.

There is something missing in the intellect of the general public when it comes to evaluating motive in the commission of an autocratic crime. Any criminal investigator knows that nineteen out of twenty times the person having the greatest motive is usually found to be guilty of the crime of murder. And this is why he concentrates his efforts on those who have the greatest motive.

But when a crime is committed in the public forum not many consider motive in their speculations. Take John Kennedy, for example.

It was common knowledge that Lyndon Johnson, who had lost the nomination to Kennedy, wanted to be president. As a matter of fact, anyone who had followed his career would know that he had an intense craving to be president. He had prepared himself all of his life for the job only to have the prize taken from him at the wire by the upstart senator from Massachusetts. And Lyndon Johnson knew then that he would never be president. He knew this because the more successful that he was in his job the more successful would John Kennedy be in his job. And if John Kennedy was successful, Lyndon Johnson knew that the nation was looking at a quarter century of Kennedys, for Bobby who was Attorney General and Teddy who was a senator were coming up right behind JFK. Keep in mind that in 1963 Chappaquiddick had not yet occurred.

So in the case of the Kennedy murder, no one ever considered the man who had the most to gain to be suspect despite the fact that out of fifty states the murder happened to have occurred by some kind of strange coincidence in Lyndon Johnson's home state of Texas, -where he knew just about everybody from every government official to every business magnate to every mob boss to every shoeshine boy on the corner. And this included Jack Ruby, the man who killed Oswald. With a simple phone call he could have set the whole thing up. The public accepts the fact that it was some kind of an unusual coincidence that the murder took place in the only state in which the vice president had any likelihood at all of pulling such a thing off. The public assumes it was matter of far reaching coincidence that Oswald, who was the only person who could have ever led investigators to the truth, was killed by a man who knew that he himself was dying of cancer and had only a few months to live. If Jack Ruby had not followed Oswald so quickly to the grave we would probably all know today who killed Kennedy. A dying man certainly doesn't profit from a payoff for being a hit man, but it may be that Ruby wanted to provide for the security of a third party, a loved one, and of course he himself had nothing to lose as he knew that he was already a dead man.

On top of it all everyone believed that Oswald acted alone. A man whose military record told us he had qualified with a rifle as a *Marksman*, the lowest qualifying level in the U.S. Army. Yet he was able to fire three rounds within twelve seconds with a rifle that had considerable recoil and he had hit a moving target more than a football field length away, and that he hit it three times, -a target half the size of the bull's eye of a conventional field target. A bull's eye that just a few years earlier, after considerable practice, he had been unable to hit in twenty tries, or he would have been classified as a *Sharpshooter*. Actually, three hits in row of a bull's eye at the same distance would have classified him as an *Expert*, the highest rank of marksmanship in the service. And in that case the target would not have been a moving one.

The public believed that Oswald acted alone because that is what it was told by the government, in the very same way that the mass of Catholicism accepted the claim that John Paul had died of a heart attack when there was no other way to have determined the cause of his death other than autopsy. And the most ridiculous part of it all was that they believed a doctor who claimed that the Pope had died at midnight, -a supposition that was contradicted by the very next sentence in the very same official Vatican release, "*that Cardinal Villot had performed the last rites,*" which action was confirmed by the embalmers who "*were certain that the body had not been dead for much more than an hour*."

And likewise John Paul II benefited by this phenomenon, -the public's great tendency not to consider the man who has the greatest motive. Unlike President Johnson, whose motive would have been limited to personal gain, the motive in the Polish cardinal's case would have been one of principle, that kind of motive which causes great men to kill great men.

There was no gain in principle in Johnson's case as he shared the very same ideologies as did Kennedy, they were both liberals. Johnson could have achieved his ideological goals in life even if Kennedy had remained president and if his brothers had succeeded him. As a matter of fact it was Johnson who eventually brought Kennedy's dreams and aspirations to fruition. Certainly, if one were to take the time to evaluate who had the greatest motive, as any detective would have done in a much lesser case, one would not come up with Johnson at all. And neither would one come up with Castro, the Soviet Union, or even the Mafia.

It is quite obvious that the *Republican Party* had the greatest motive to kill Kennedy, actually to kill both Kennedys. To be more specific the *Christian right* who at the time were in a desperate struggle to keep the last remnants of fascism alive in the United States would have to top the list. And in retrospect we know who benefited the most from the deaths of the Kennedy brothers. It seems inconceivable with all the ongoing investigations into the Kennedy assassination that no one ever gave a thought as to where the *G. Gordon Liddys* of the world were in the two weeks leading up to the assassination of John Kennedy. No one ever gave a thought as to where the leaders of the *Christian right* were in the two weeks leading up to the assassination of John Kennedy. The Republican Party and the leaders of the *Christian right,* those who had the greatest motive to have killed Kennedy,

For had the Kennedy brothers survived, the *Democratic Party* would have dominated the last half of the twentieth century and today we would be the kind of a society those who died on the great battlefields of war intended us to be; that kind of society that Lincoln and Jefferson intended us to be, *'that this nation be one nation under God, conceived in Liberty, and dedicated to the proposition that all men are created equal . . . and that they are endowed with certain inalienable rights including Life, Liberty and the Pursuit of Happiness"*

When Hitler had lost the war Karol Wojtyla lost much of what he dreamed of, and now that Luciani had risen to power the rest of his ambitions were about to come to an end. Again, during the war both Wojtyla and Hitler had the same objectives; both nurtured hatred of people who were different. Hitler would achieve his ends by annihilation and Wojtyla would achieve his ends by political means; the results being identical. Hitler murdered a quarter-million young homosexuals in death camps and Wojtyla is responsible today for more than a quarter-million suicides of gay teenagers. Despite the fact that he accepts the fact that homosexuality is a matter of instinct and will not respond to therapy, he continues to persecute these unfortunate children of God.

If one considers the assassination history of world leaders, the great weight of them have been ideologically, not personally, motivated. Great men do not kill other great men for personal gain. They kill them for reasons of principle, to permit the enactment into society of their own philosophical ideologies. That great men tend to give their lives and even go so far as to risk their very souls for the cause and if one believes literally in what the Old Testament has to say, then the murder of John Paul I was a holy thing to do. It is quite clear from his record that John Paul I did not believe in much of what the Old Testament has to say at all. As a matter of fact it is quite clear that he believed Moses to have been a monster among monsters.

So anyone who believed in the Old Testament and who may have conspired to have murdered John Paul could have a clear conscience in this thing as they went about their holy day-to-day life. That is, if he had in fact been murdered. For there would be nothing unconscionable about killing a pope who, if permitted to live, was about to allow a billion Catholics to use condoms in the bedroom, which according to Church doctrine and the Old Testament would condemn them to eternal damnation in hell. It would be the same age-old game of sacrificing the few for the many. In this case one for a billion and here one is talking much more than lives, one is talking of souls. One life for a billion souls, one just can't get a better deal than that.

So John Paul II and others surrounding him on the *right* did have a very clear motive since Luciani threatened their ecclesiastical destiny. And unlike Lyndon Johnson their motive would have been oriented by principle, that kind of motive that causes great men to kill great men. So unlike Johnson who would have had very slight motive to have killed Kennedy, Cardinal Wojtyla, like most of the others that are high on our motive list, would have seen it as his ecclesiastical duty to conspire to murder his predecessor. For in his mind he would have saved countless souls from eternal damnation.

Then one must consider personal ambition. As we have we already discussed, although you would never get any one of them to admit it, all cardinals aspire to be Pope. And as we know this was true of Albino Luciani. Yet few of them go so far as to embark on the campaign trail, so to speak. Although Wojtyla was never considered to be a viable candidate by the press, he never concealed his personal ambition to accede to the papacy. For in the decade before his election he had traveled the globe and had visited literally more than nine out of ten of the Church's field cardinals, including his well publicized trips to the United States in 1969 and 1977 in which he visited every city in North America where a cardinal was in residence. Although a few of these trips included attendance at Church conferences, there is no record in the press that any of these rather expensive trips had anything to do with fund raising, so one might ask what other purpose could he have had to have spent so much money from the poor box for so many expensive vacations? What could they have possibly have had to do with his responsibilities as Archbishop of Krakow? And the only logical answer to this is that he was lining up the votes.

Philadelphia Enquirer Photo

ON THE CAMPAIGN TRAIL IN 1969

Karol Wojtyla with Cardinal Krol in Philadelphia

Yet there is a much more telling reason than just ecclesiastical motive to include Cardinal Wojtyla among the suspects. And to understand this, one must first understand how a pope is elected.

how a pope is elected,

To begin with, voting conclaves normally last several days and often weeks and in one case exceeded two years. This is because the process is a secret one. As successive ballots are cast none of the cardinals know how the vote is going.

The reason for this is that according to Church doctrine the decision as to who becomes Pope must be Christ's decision and not the decision of a group of men who are collaborating or politicking among each other. This is why after a candidate achieves the minimum margin of victory a revote is taken to make the vote unanimous - that Christ has spoken, so to speak. There have been only two exceptions in which an elected pontiff failed to secure a unanimous vote on the final count and those two were Paul VI in 1963 and John Paul I in 1978. So bitter and so far to the *right* were the twenty-one cardinals who made up the *Vatican Curia*, the cardinals who would share the sprawling apostolic palace with these popes, that they could not bring themselves to accept Christ's decision in these cases. As a matter of fact, to have been so blatant as to have withheld their votes in the final count they must have believed both Paul's and John Paul's elections to have been the work of the Devil himself, that Satan had slipped one or two in on them.

Yes, there are some alleged leaks to the press, which are prohibited by doctrine. In those cases in which I have cited interim counts it is these I refer to; the interim press reports, not the actual conclave results. Keep in mind that the interim press reports have a hole in them a mile wide, as cardinals are sworn by sacred oath not to reveal their choice during the conclave proceedings. Yes, a cardinal might indicate to the press who he is inclined to vote for before the conclave begins, but once the conclave has gone into session he is sworn to secrecy.

This is why the many authors who have recounted the progress of the election of a pope, often in dramatic fashion, have all reported different numbers. Such as, *"On the first ballot Pignedoli led with forty-one votes, Siri had twenty-five, Suenens had thirteen,. . . Then on the second ballot Luciani had come into the pack with fourteen, and Suenens had advanced to twenty-seven, and Pignedoli had all but dropped out of the race."*[1] While another reporter would report, *"Suenens and Siri came out of the gate with thirty votes each with Pignedoli close behind with twenty-two. Things remained relative stable for the next two ballots and then on the fourth ballot Luciani suddenly came from behind to take the roses."*[2] One author, in one of the leading best sellers, had Wojtyla with seventy-three votes and Benelli with thirty-eight on the second to last vote in the conclave that elected John Paul II; a conclave that it is known to have consisted of one-third liberals, one-third moderates and one-third conservatives, as if to say that the two conservative candidates had gathered all of the votes and not a single liberal had voted his issues.

And the issues do count. In fact, as in any election they are all that count. A cardinal does not cast his vote for another cardinal because he thinks he will look impressive in a white satin gown. He casts his vote for the individual who most closely shares his own ecclesiastical thinking.

So as the vote proceeds one can make some judgment as to who a certain cardinal or cardinals might vote for, but until someone wins no one knows how the vote is proceeding.

[1] 27 Aug 78, London Times
[2] 27 Aug 78 La Stampa

the politicking involved in electing a pope,

Of course, someone has to know. That is, someone has to know what the actual counts are at each stage, as someone has to count the votes. And when one considers Cardinal Wojtyla's possible involvement in the death of John Paul I, this is a very critical point.

Generally, two of the cardinals are chosen as counters. There have been occasions in which four counters have been involved, but in the case of the election that chose John Paul I, two were chosen. Only they and the secretary of state are allowed to enter the inner room where the counting takes place. The counters are selected by a vote of the conclave cardinals before the election begins and they normally represent both sides of the aisle, -liberals and conservatives, and they themselves usually have relatively extreme positions on their respective side, one coming from the *far left* and the other coming from the *far right*. There is substantial lobbying that goes on in connection with this vote, as each side concentrates its votes on a single candidate to guarantee that their voting strength is not diluted, which would risk giving the other side the opportunity to secure both counters. So in the case of this vote, the vote for the counters, the cardinals already know who they are going to vote for and the two cardinals getting the most amount of votes become the counters. This makes them the most influential members of the conclave. As these two are the only two who, knowing how the interim voting is going, can effectively steer either side to victory.

Cardinal Leon Suenens, an ultraliberal, and Cardinal Karol Wojtyla, an ultraconservative, were the two counters in the conclave that elected John Paul I. They were the only ones who knew the results of each ballot and this includes the secretary of state who, although present, is not permitted to know the results of individual ballots until the two counters have come up with a winner. At that point, the secretary recounts the ballots and a winner is declared. It should be pointed out that the counters take a solemn oath of secrecy; that is, they are not permitted at anytime during the conclave, no matter how many days or weeks or months it might go on, to reveal to any other cardinal how the vote is proceeding. Ballots are burned immediately after each count is taken and no record is permitted to be retained.

This is important if a conspiracy had been involved in the case of John Paul's death, for either of these two cardinals would have had to have knowingly or unknowingly participated in it. For these were the only two persons who were in a position to tell what would happen in a successive election. They were the only two who knew what the interim counts had been in the first election and therefore were the only two who would know who would have likely been elected had Cardinal Luciani not been a part of the equation. And this of course would be the cardinal who would win the second election. After all, it would make no sense whatsoever to take the great risk involved in killing a liberal pope if his successor was going to be another liberal. At the time, that another liberal would succeed him would be the only logical conclusion one could imagine, as the very same *College of Cardinals* would be involved in the second election.

So the conspirators, if there were any in the death of John Paul I, and no one knows this to be an absolute fact, would have had to assure themselves that another liberal would not win in a successive election. Otherwise they might be as well off with Luciani. And the only way that they could have been assured of this was to have consulted with Cardinal Wojtyla, as Suenens was a liberal and they would have had to have consulted with him while his predecessor was still alive.

Although the interim counts in the conclave that elected Luciani were never made public, the general consensus of the press releases - which relied largely on evaluations of where individual cardinals stood on ecclesiastical issues - seemed to point to the fact that Suenens on the *far left* controlled slightly less than a third of the votes, that Siri on the *far right* controlled slightly less than a third and that the middle third was up for grabs. This seems to be a reasonable conclusion as it is known that Siri had retained twenty-one votes on the recount in Luciani's election and Suenens had none, -which confirms the fact he had yielded up his block of votes to Luciani. Both Suenens and Siri knew that being extremists neither one of them could ever gain the votes of those on the center aisle; that neither one of them would ever become Pope. That for each of them the strategy was to wait his chance until one of the acceptable candidates on his side of the aisle had gained enough votes that combined with the block of votes that he himself controlled would put that candidate over the top.

And this is precisely how Luciani had won the first election. For in his conclave Suenens, being one of the selected counters, knew exactly how the vote was going, and he knew exactly when to make his move and shift his block of votes to Luciani to enable him to win. That Luciani won by the exact number of votes required to win, two-thirds plus one vote, was not a far reaching coincidence of some kind. As a counter, Suenens knew exactly how many additional votes his candidate needed to win the election and he knew where and when to get them. Because he himself controlled the balancing block of votes, he could make his move without breaking his oath of secrecy.

If one accepted the press reports at the time, Siri's candidate would most likely have been Cardinal Benelli, the man who had been a thorn in the side of Paul VI throughout his pontificate. But history, on the other hand, tells us quite clearly that Wojtyla, who happened to be one of the counters, was Siri's choice in the first election because we know as a matter of fact that he was his choice in the second election, -as Karol Wojtyla would never had won that election without Siri's block of votes. In the first election Siri, not being a counter, would not have known when to make his move. He would have to depend on Wojtyla to give him the word to make his move and Wojtyla's word would come one step behind Suenens' move and too late to capture the papacy; this because Suenens being both a counter and the one who controlled a block of votes could make his move at will. But Siri would have had to have waited until the conclave broke for the day in order to 'chat' with Wojtyla and if Wojtyla were to conspire in this way he would break his oath of secrecy.

This points to why Wojtyla, if he had indeed been the leading conservative vote getter in the first election, did not win the first election. For Luciani won on the first day. The conclave never broke for the day. Yet in the second election the conclave did break for the day, which allowed Wojtyla to politick into the night to pick up the few votes he needed to seal his bid for the papacy. And a part of that politicking could have been the eighteen-percent pay raise he gave to the Vatican cardinals immediately after his election despite that fact the Vatican was operating at a huge deficit, which as we have already mentioned drew bitter comment from a *leftwing* cardinal, *"It is almost as it had been part of the deal."*

Even though the rules are firm concerning secrecy one knows that such 'chatting' does go on because popes in modern history have been elected in a few weeks and in the case of these two popes, in a day or two. Common sense would tell one that if the vote was held in complete secrecy as doctrine requires, it would take years before by chance someone came up with two-thirds of the votes.

But there is another more basic reason why Luciani won the election and that was that his rival conservative would have been less attractive to those in the *middle*, and would have had less success in capturing enough of the moderate votes that, combined with Siri's block of votes, would have put him over the top. Actually, in the Church a conservative has nothing to offer a moderate for a moderate, by definition has broken with his conservative past on at least one major issue and it is normally on that particular issue that the moderate casts his vote.

It should be noted that there was no material change in the voters in the two elections. Luciani and one other cardinal, a conservative, had died in the meantime. However, the other cardinal having been terminally ill had not voted in the first election. Also Cardinal Wright, who had been confined during the first election and was therefore unable to vote, showed up in a wheelchair for the second election. So the total number in the conclave remained the same at one hundred and eleven with Wright replacing Luciani. Since a cardinal cannot vote for himself, chances are that the balance may have tilted a slight degree to the *left,* toward another liberal, but one knows at the very least that it remained the same as it had been in the first election. So the cardinal who would be elected in the second conclave of 1978 would normally have been the very same cardinal that would have been elected in the first conclave of 1978 had Albino Luciani not been a factor in the first election, someone who would be fairly close to Luciani in his thinkings. One might put a man like Cardinal Willebrands of the Netherlands at the very top of the list. Someone who like Luciani could attract most of those on the center aisle.

party platforms in a papal election,

But this was not the case. Instead, a man who turned out to be an ultraconservative won the successive election. And one knows that an ultraconservative could have never mustered the moderate vote, those in the *middle*. And this as a matter of fact as one knows that although a liberal could make substantial headway in the moderate ranks, that the *middle* is not normally fertile ground for the conservative.

One can see this more clearly when considering the major issues of that time which, because an ultraconservative was elected in the second election of 1978, remain the major issues today, as a conservative by his very nature does not believe in change. I will list these in order of relative importance to the cardinals who would vote at that time,

Humanae Vitae (the contraception issue)
divorce and remarriage
woman equality in the Church
priest celibacy
homosexuality
embryonic research (artificial insemination)
abortion
priest pedophilia

A moderate, as we have just said, is probably best defined as a cardinal who has broken from his ecclesiastical past concerning only one major issue. That is, he remains steadfast in his ecclesiastical thinkings on all other issues. By contrast, a liberal is probably best defined as one who has broken with his ecclesiastical past on several issues. The vote of a moderate can be gained by a liberal if the voting cardinal is willing to accept some of the other issues that the liberal cardinal stands for in order to win whatever is most important to himself. For example, a moderate who wanted a repeal of *Humanae Vitae* and stood steadfast on all other issues might vote for a man like Luciani, who also had strong feelings about women equality and leniency toward homosexuals. The voting cardinal would accept the changes in what he felt were lesser issues in order to gain for himself what he felt was the major issue. But a moderate would never vote for an ultraconservative, for he would know that if an ultraconservative were elected the change in doctrine that he himself sought would never come about.

So how could this possibly happen? How could the same constituency of cardinals elect at one time an extreme liberal and just a month later elect a man who was an extreme conservative? The only possible explanation of this is that some kind of deal was struck before the second election conclave began. And this deal had to have involved at the very least cardinals Siri and Wojtyla on the *right* and those that controlled the balancing block of votes in the *middle.* The *conservative right* had to win back more than half of the votes which in the first election had been cast for Luciani, about thirty of the one hundred and eleven votes.

Now let's assume that the press releases were wrong, that in fact the Polish cardinal had been a factor in the first election. If this had been true, and history seems to verify it as having been true, then only Cardinal Wojtyla and Cardinal Suenens, the two counters, would have known this. That is, Cardinal Siri and the other conservatives would not have known this - they would be relying on the press releases. Let's say that Wojtyla had gained fifteen votes on his own on the final ballot in the first election. And we know that he could not have gained more than fifteen on the final count because Luciani had won the election with seventy five and Siri had retained twenty-one on the recount.

Luciani on the fourth ballot	75 (two-thirds plus one vote)
Luciani on the final ballot	90
Siri on the final ballot	21
all others on the fourth ballot	15
Total votes cast	111

According to the press reports one, would be led to believe that Benelli held the fifteen votes on the second to last ballot as he had been the leading conservative candidate before the election began and that he had yielded them up to Luciani on the recount. But if Wojtyla had in fact secured these fifteen votes and he knew that Cardinal Siri had locked in twenty-one votes, then he alone knew that together in a successive election they would have a minimum of thirty-six, about half of the votes needed to win.

In retrospect it makes a lot of sense that the press was wrong and that Benelli was never actually in the running to begin with, although almost all newspapers in the world listed him as the favorite in both elections. This is clear because no newspaper in the world listed either Luciani or Wojtyla as being a formidable candidate in either election.

Although one does not take a population poll in the election of a pope, as the people don't have a say in the matter, it is quite certain that had one been taken before the first election Luciani would have been the frontrunner with no other cardinal running a distant second; if for no other reason than at the time he was the most well-known of the cardinals. As we have already discussed ten years before when the archbishop post had opened in Venice, and the people of the Veneto country realized that a cardinal might be moved from Rome, tens of thousands of them marched in the streets of Venice demanding that Luciani be appointed. Likewise, a small group of protestors bused-in from Venice showed up at the Vatican on the morning of the first conclave demanding that Luciani be considered as the newspapers had eliminated him as a candidate. The Swiss guards threw them out and they were restricted to walk the streets that are lined with souvenir shops today.

Nevertheless, Cardinal Wojtyla would have known that he already had so many votes in his pocket, a minimum of thirty-six, almost half of the seventy-five needed to win the election. So his first recourse would have to have been to approach Cardinals Siri and Bishop Casaroli, the leaders of the *far right* in the Church and lock down his position.

Then again it may have been that Wojtyla had gained many more votes in the earlier balloting than the fifteen he held on the final ballot in the first election and had lost some of them as the voting went on. After all, he had campaigned for them. He may have known that had Luciani not been a candidate in the first election and had Suenens not been a counter that he would have won. And what's more this would tell him that he would be a shoe-in a successive election.

So we have the following photo of an article in a Genoa newspaper,

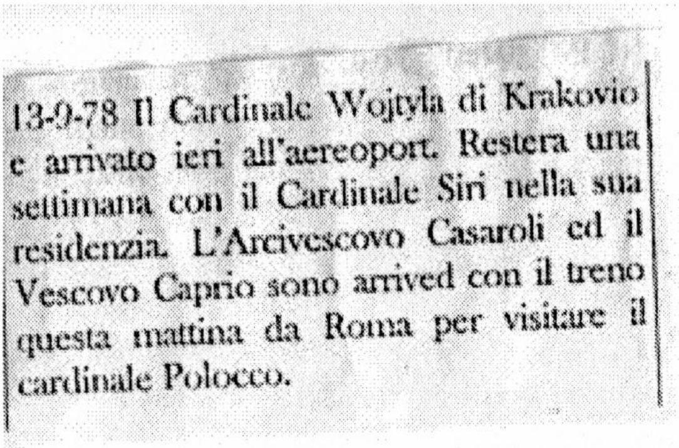

13-9-78 Il Cardinale Wojtyla di Krakovio e arrivato ieri all'aereoport. Restera una settimana con il Cardinale Siri nella sua residenzia. L'Arcivescovo Casaroli ed il Vescovo Caprio sono arrived con il treno questa mattina da Roma per visitare il cardinale Polocco.

*"September 13 1978, Cardinal Wojtyla arrived last night at the airport. He will spend the week with Cardinal Siri at his residence. Bishops Casaroli and Caprio arrived by train this morning from Rome to visit with the Polish cardinal."**

Cardinal Benelli, in nearby Florence, who was recognized by the press as the leading conservative candidate in the successive elections that had chosen both Luciani and Wojtyla did not attend this meeting. At least there is no mention in the press of his having attended.

No one knows what these men talked about in Genoa. But if it did in fact involve the strategy of a second conclave they would have known that Wojtyla, being the ultraconservative that he was, could never attract any of those on the liberal side of the aisle. So their strategy had to have involved those in the *middle*, which was the largest block of votes, certainly enough votes to put Wojtyla over the top, by best estimates at least forty votes and possibly as many as fifty which combined with their thirty-six would give him more than needed.

Today it is quite obvious that the election was impartial in the conclave that elected John Paul II. In retrospect, it would seem that both Suenens and Wojtyla should have been eliminated as possible candidates, since both of them were in a position to have lobbied the second election in their own favor as they both knew how the voting had gone in the first

* *13 Sept 78 Secolo XIX*

election. For they were the only two people in the world who knew who was going to win the second election, -that cardinal who would have won the first election had Luciani not been a factor in that election. Both or either one of them knew exactly how to determine the winner of the next election. To think otherwise would be to think that the very same group of cardinals who in one month elected an ultraliberal turned around the next month and elected an ultraconservative. This does not pass the IQ test. Neither Suenens nor Wojtyla were counters in the second election.

This does not mean that the counters in one election should be automatically disqualified as candidates in a successive election. Just that this measure should be taken where one is dealing with the same constituency of cardinals in two successive elections, -such as was the case in the fall of nineteen hundred and seventy-eight. John Paul II was elected in a tainted process; having been one of the counters in the previous election just a month earlier, he had an unfair advantage over the other candidates. But one also knows that it is a little late to demand a recount.

Nevertheless, putting all of this aside, if a conspiracy was involved in the death of John Paul I either Wojtyla or Suenens or possibly both had to have been consulted concerning this issue: Who would be elected if Luciani were not in the picture? And of all we know of these two cardinals, the finger points only to Wojtyla. This does not mean that Wojtyla would have to have been involved in a conspiracy to murder John Paul I, as the conspirators could have drawn this kind of information out of him without him being aware of just why the conspirators were asking such questions. But if a conspiracy had been involved in the murder of John Paul I, such a conversation did take place. And it must have taken place before John Paul was murdered. For it would make no sense whatsoever to take the great risk of murdering a liberal pope if there was any likelihood that another liberal would take his place. Since the same constituency of cardinals was involved common sense would tell us another liberal would most certainly be elected.

a Muslim is running the Roman Catholic Church

At the time of his election, Karol Wojtyla was widely known to be an ultraconservative. After all, he had led many of the campaigns against change in the Church, particularly where liberals were trying to free Mother Church from her fascists roots, like allowing woman ordination or permitting marriage between blacks and whites. And it was for this reason that he was selected as one of the counters in the election that had elected

Luciani. But did he have any liberal tendencies at all, anything that would attract those in the middle?

Cardinal Wojtyla, for those who knew him then, and as the world sees him today, had then and has today only one liberal tendency. One that is so far to the *left* that even Cardinal Suenens could not accept it at the time. And this position has since become the mainstay of his pontificate.

In 1952, a housekeeper of a wealthy Jewish family secretly took a newborn infant to the local parish priest in the interest of having the infant baptized and thereby permit it to go to heaven. But the parish priest refused telling the woman that "*this baby should be brought up a Jew.*" The parish priest was Karol Wojtyla and this story is recounted in many of his memoirs and biographies and he himself has retold this story on world television.

Although he has never been put on the spot to speak to it, John Paul II believes in the salvation of most of the world's major religions. He does not believe that Christ, in the last and most fundamental testimony of His ministry, actually said, "*Unless one believeth in me and be baptized one cannot enter the Kingdom of Heaven.*" Otherwise he would have been a monster not to have baptized the Jewish infant. John Paul II, the leader of the largest Christian church in the world today, does not believe in the most fundamental doctrine of Christianity. But rather that he is of the conviction that one's salvation depends entirely on how God comes to each and every one of His children which is a basic ideology of Islamism.

One difference between a Muslim and Christian is that the Muslim believes in the salvation of all religions while the Christian believes solely in the salvation of his own religion. This is why Christian preachers through the ages have tried to impose their own beliefs on everyone else. This is why when the Muslims occupied the Holy Land they permitted the Jews to continue to practice their own religion. It is also why when the Christian Crusaders came along both the Jews and the Muslims were given a choice to either convert or succumb to the sword, men, women and children.

Nevertheless, this is not news. Anyone with an intelligence quotient of seventy-five or better who has followed the many travels of this Pope knows this, -that John Paul II believes in the salvation of other religions. That, as a matter of fact, a Muslim is running the Roman Catholic Church today. And although he did not live long enough to let the world know it, this was precisely the philosophy of his predecessor, John Paul I. So here we have a remarkable phenomenon - these two popes who disagreed throughout their ministries on just about every other issue, defy the most fundamental premise of the religion they claim to be a part of, "*Unless one believeth in me and be baptized one cannot enter the Kingdom of Heaven.*" From the point of view of this author this is very much to the credit of both of these popes who have now been caught up on either side of this thing called murder and intrigue.

the moderates in the middle,

So at the time, what kind of cardinals made up the moderate block of votes in the *middle*? Yes, there were a few here and there who wanted *Mother Church* to loosen its ropes on celibacy, homosexuality or remarriage or the suppression of the role of women in the Church. But none of these were the major campaign issue at the time. As a matter of fact, just what was the major campaign issue of the day? And the answer points overwhelming to *Humanae Vitae*, the Church's edict prohibiting the use of contraceptives. It was this issue, and this issue alone that marked the difference between a moderate and a conservative in the election of 1978. The moderate sought repeal of, or at the very least modification of this doctrine, and the conservative did not.

In the time before his election Wojtyla's position concerning this most important issue had been made clear. It had been spread across the newspapers in Europe that were published between 1965 and 1968 when the proclamation was finally etched into stone. Wojtyla had been one of the most outspoken men of the Church on the issue and his position is law in the Church today, "*no use of contraceptives even to prevent disease including the spread of AIDS,*" and the penalty for not abiding by his law is the everlasting fires of Hell.

This is precisely how Luciani had gained the moderate vote in the first election of 1978. Publicly, Luciani had been the loudest voice against the doctrine even after it had become a papal decree. Even going so far as to reach the press with a public letter in which he pleaded with Paul VI in the spring of 1968, "*that some accommodations for artificial birth control must be made within the confines of the Church.*"

So now we have come to a most remarkable conclusion. Not only does an ultraconservative win the successive election, but one who held stark ideological differences from those in the *middle* and on the *left* concerning the most important campaign issue of the time. To two-thirds of the cardinals in the election this meant that if Wojtyla were elected the great majority of the members of their congregations who practiced contraception would be condemned to live in a perpetual state of mortal sin for the rest of their lives. And for those who represented third world countries they were looking forward to decades of poverty and starvation and disease and death.

As I have already indicated, those in the *middle* were conservatives who had differences with the Church on the single issue of *Humanae Vitae*; those who suffered from the results of overpopulation that the Church's anti-birth control policy promoted. Those cardinals who were faced with the day-to-day poverty and starvation that lack of *Planned Parenthood* brought about in the poor countries of India, Latin America and North Africa; although conservative in every other respect, sought relief from the cruel and unusual punishment that this doctrine imposed on their people. Since he won the election it is clear that Wojtyla gained the lion's share of these votes in the *middle* as he certainly could have never gained those on the *left*. It is quite certain that he did not gain the moderate vote on his promise to repeal the doctrine prohibiting birth control practices for this was at the very core of his ecclesiastical existence. So just how did Wojtyla muster the votes of those in the *middle*? We will answer that question, but first let's review what we have determined thus far.

All we have, as I have already mentioned, is the report in the Italian press of the visit of Cardinal Wojtyla to Genoa just two weeks after the election of John Paul I, which was three weeks before his death. Cardinal Siri was the Archbishop of Genoa. But there is nothing in the press to indicate that this meeting of these *far right* prelates had anything to do with a conspiracy to murder John Paul I.

We also know that Bishop Casaroli came up from Rome the following day. Casaroli who three weeks later upon the death of John Paul I, had released the following statement to the press, "*Although there is much room for grief here, had John Paul's pontificate continued it would have resulted in the loss of hundreds of millions of souls*." [1]

a matter of coincidence,

Regardless of all of these speculations and possibilities, it is certainly something more than a remarkable coincidence that one of the two cardinals - of one hundred and eleven cardinals in the conclave - who had counted the votes in the previous election, won the next election. Then there is the most remarkable coincidence of all - the very same *College of Cardinals* that had elected an ultraliberal in one election elected an ultraconservative in the very next election just forty days later. In the first place they had elected a man who just a month before had given his blessing

[1] *2 Oct 78 IL Tempo*

to the world's first artificially created human being and provided a place for her in heaven, and then just a few days later elected another man who, outraged by the birth of Louise Brown, had issued a stern statement to the press condemning the newborn child as "*a child of the devil.*" They had, on the one hand, elected a man who had publicly objected to the doctrine of *Human Vitae*, -the major ecclesiastical issue at the time, and on the other hand had elected another man whose efforts had made it possible. They had chosen a man in the first election who believed woman to be man's equal, and just a month later had elected a man who today requires the solemn oath of all of his candidates for the red hat, *"I promise to oppose the elevation of women in the Church for the rest of my days."*

It would be reasonable that the cardinal who would have been elected in the first conclave, had Luciani not been a factor, would have won the second election. And this would point to a candidate who held similar views as did Luciani. But this did not happen. Instead a cardinal from the other side of the aisle won the second election and that he won it in near record time of just a few ballots certainly adds much credence to the fact that he would have had to have been consulted by the conspirators before the election took place.

We know now that most press reports concerning what went on in a conclave are mere speculation on the part of newspapers as cardinals are prohibited by doctrine to discuss what goes on in a conclave. To be specific only three facts are permitted to leave the conclave and they are: who won the election; the number of votes by which he won; and whether or not the recount was unanimous. Outside of these, no cardinal is permitted to whisper a thing that took place in a conclave.

Yet the press did release its speculations as to how Wojtyla had won the second conclave, *"The cardinals, unable to agree on an Italian cardinal on the first day, decided to look elsewhere on the second day."*[2] The press would have us believe that Wojtyla had not been considered at all on the first day, gained no votes, and on the second day, despite the fact that cardinals are not permitted to discuss their choice during the conclave, day or night, somehow made an about-face and with seventy non-Italian cardinals to choose from, by chance cast two-thirds of their votes for one of them. This would be to say, that after the conclave broke on the first day all of the cardinals assembled that evening in a secret conclave and made the decision as to who was going to be Pope.

Yet, we do know that some chatting does go on between conclave sessions, and that this kind chatting can garnish a few votes for a candidate,

[2] *17 Oct 78 IL Messaggero*

but certainly never a gain of two-thirds of the votes in a single windfall. So we know that the press reporting as to how Wojtyla won the election is a fairytale. It is obvious that when the conclave broke at the end of the first day that Wojtyla was already on the brink of victory. He and his supporters had only to chat with the counter who represented their side of the aisle to determine where they could get the few votes they needed to put him over the top.

It is quite apparent that the conclave of cardinals already knew *who* they were going to vote for before the election process began on the first day of the second conclave of 1978. And what's more they knew *what* they were going to vote for. So John Paul II was not chosen by Christ or for that matter by Satan, but like his predecessor, was chosen by the politicking and collaboration of men. Perhaps in his case, even the murdering of men..

Cardinal Wojtyla deeply disturbed by Luciani's election contemplates his future

Chapter 4

THE PEOPLE'S SACRED RESPONSIBILITY TO ELECT THE NEXT POPE

This gives us an interesting possibility for future papal elections. Since one now knows that Christ has nothing to do with the choice of His representative on earth, why not allow the election process to be the will of the people? All of the people are God's children, so one would think that they should all have a voice in this very important choice. Is this not what God would want? Is it not what Christ would want? After all, in free nations today the people choose who will lead them in this life. Why shouldn't the people have the right to choose their leader who will guide them into the next life? Why should one leave such an important decision up to the collaboration and politicking of men? Why can't one at the very least leave it up to the collaboration and politicking of men and women? But best of all let's let God's children choose who is to be His representative on earth. Let's take the politics out of this most sacred duty of choosing a pope, that with the whole world moving toward democracy for the benefit of mankind it makes no sense that the Church should remain the anarchy that it has become. And when I say that it has become an anarchy, it wasn't always that way.

The *Church* was once a church of the people. Christ appointed the first Pope and for the first three centuries each pope is said to have chosen his successor. One must understand that for the first three centuries there was no organized *Church* per se so one could say that the people cast their *silent votes* in being practitioners of the faith. After the time of Constantine, from the 4th through the 10th centuries, the clergy of Rome elected the Bishop of Rome who was by doctrine Pope. In the 11th century, in an effort to internationalize the papal election, the *College of Cardinals* was formed. This was intended to bring about broader representation by the people. At the time, the clergy of each parish, who were *elected* by the people, elected bishops and cardinals; in some cases by *actual* vote of the people and in many others simply by the *silent* vote of the people. Then, in a series of changes along the way the appointment of cardinals and bishops became solely a papal decision and democracy came to an end in the Church.

Today the *College* represents only half the world, that half of the world whose minds weakened by circumstances or conditioning has allowed itself to be brainwashed into thinking that it is somehow holy to breed hatred toward other kinds of people. The other half, those men and women of good conscience, those who know right from wrong, have lost its representation.

So the time has come for the people to stand up and be heard; for the people to take back the Church. And believe it or not, this is quite possible today. This would be a great tribute to the memory of our hero Albino Luciani, who was the first man in the modern history of the Church to so inspire his followers to think that they could have a say in the election of not only an archbishop but of a pope as well. Their efforts would not have been in vain, those men and women who had the great courage to march through the streets of Venice in 1969 and who were stopped at the Vatican gates in 1978. And one must remember that in both cases, their candidate won. Yes, let's do that, let's give it a try.

Today, the Catholic world thinks that it is inevitable that the successor of John Paul II will be another ultraconservative. After all, he has loaded the voting membership of the *College of Cardinals* with conservatives, actually ultraconservatives. But there is an alternative to this fate and as long reaching as it might appear to be, it is a realistic one. But the job must be done now before John Paul II passes into eternity.

The people should have a say in who will be their next Pope. As a matter of fact they have the sacred responsibility to elect the next Pope. They will do this in the very same way they elect a president: first determine who would be the candidates from either side of the aisle, then run a few polls, and then elect the Pope through one's representative cardinals. And the polls, believe me, will have a profound affect on how a cardinal votes. One should not be foolish enough to think that this kind of thing is not a realistic possibility, for cardinals are also human beings and if they fail to cast their votes in representation of their followers they will eventually have no followers.

When one considers the great havoc that Rome has brought about in the world, -being the driving force behind the spread of disease, poverty and starvation in many countries, and its continuing deprivation of equal human rights for women and homosexuals and the remarried and others throughout the world, the people have not only the right, but the sacred duty to rise up and elect the next Pope.

Let us consider a hypothetical situation. Suppose Albino Luciani were still living today and was offered as the liberal candidate against, let us say, Cardinal Lopez, the Vatican's authority on family values, who most likely would be the choice of the conservative ranks. In first world countries, the polls would clearly show Luciani in a landslide lead with as much as eighty or even ninety-percent of the vote. There is much to support this supposition as the composition of polls taken in Catholic first world countries have shown that upwards of 95% of Catholics do not believe that using a condom is immoral, despite the fact that the man in Rome insists that it is a mortal sin. It stands to reason that if the people don't believe such acts to be sinful that they are not confessing them in the confessional box and therefore they are, as the man who lives in the palace in Rome says, *"destined for hell."* And although they have not been so one sided, most of these same polls generally support things like women ordination, remarriage, priest marriage and homosexuality. So Luciani would carry these countries in a landslide.

But we must be realistic in this, as half of the Catholic vote is in the third world countries of Latin America, Africa and India and the vote there is most likely to go for Lopez, -probably very heavily for him and this because people in these countries who are weakened physically are far more likely to cling to their faith in desperation despite the fact that it is killing their children. But one has to consider how many of these people would vote for a cardinal who would lift the Church's ban on contraception; how many would vote for as cardinal who would permit them to use condoms to prevent the spread of AIDS; how many would vote for a cardinal that would allow their children to be born free of AIDS. So Luciani might also carry a majority here despite the fact that they are controlled by ultraconservative cardinals.

Also, it is the first world countries that in the end will pay for the cost of the poverty, starvation and disease caused by the irresponsible policies of Rome. For example, the American Congress very recently approved fifteen billion dollars to fight the AIDS epidemic in Africa and the only response that came from the driving force behind the AIDS epidemic in Rome was, *"no use of contraceptives to prevent the spread of AIDS for the penalty for using condoms is the everlasting fires of hell. The answer to this problem must remain abstinence even between married couples."* The official voice of the Vatican in this response was Cardinal Lopez, who we speculate might win a good share of votes in these suffering countries, the populace, so blinded by faith, would elect a man to the papacy who already has caused three million AIDS babies to be born only to suffer unspeakable deaths and many more millions of adults to suffer the same fate.

But we must face the fact that Luciani is dead and that there are no liberal cardinals remaining in the Church. Not entirely true. There remain a few moderate-liberals that are still active and one outright liberal, -Cardinal Martini, the retired Archbishop of Milan, who today is on *death row* in the Holy Land. Yet there are others, some of whom are rising up as men of great courage and are standing up for what is right and speaking out against the wickedness of Rome.

One of the most obvious of these is the valiant Archbishop of Brussels Cardinal Godfried Danneels, who is on the current list of candidates that newspapers have already speculated might succeed John Paul II despite the fact that an imbecile would know that with a conclave of ultraconservative voting cardinals he has no chance at all. But maybe men and women of good conscience, Catholics who know the difference between right and wrong, can give him a chance.

Most recently, Cardinal Danneels attacked Cardinal Alfonzo Lopez, John Paul's top advisor on family values on the use of contraceptives in third world countries. Referring to the fact that there is a two-thirds chance that a baby conceived of natural conception in certain African countries would be born of AIDS, he told Lopez and the Catholic world, *"for someone to engage in sex in any AIDS ridden country without knowing the medical condition of oneself and one's mate and not to use a condom is a mortal sin."* And his record doesn't stop there. The Archbishop has from time to time drawn the wrath of Rome on many other issues. He is a stern advocate to permit Catholics who divorce to remarry without obtaining Church-sanctioned annulments, and he is also a strong proponent for the elevation of women in the Church. In his book, *Six Discussions with the Cardinal,* he calls for Pope John Paul II to stand down. He recommends that a change be made in doctrine that would limit the terms of popes, - that popes should no longer be elected for life, as aging popes tend to lose touch with reality and as is the case of this particular Pope could become dangerous to society.

Consider the huge death toll for which John Paul II is responsible today. Three million AIDS babies is three times the number of children murdered by Hitler in the concentration camps of World War II. In addition, from time-to-time, the Belgium cardinal has defended homosexuals. It is largely due to the compassion and intellect of this good man that Belgium was among the first countries in the world to recognize *gay marriage*. And more recently when the Catholic Church and most of the Christian world was finally forced to accept the fact that homosexuality is a basic instinct and cannot be changed by therapy - as has been known in the psychiatric world for thirty years - he distanced himself from his fellow Belgium Cardinal Gustaaf's remark to the press, "*most gays and lesbians are not really gay at all, they are perverts."* In responding to Gustaaf's remark, Danneels did not stop to blink. He sent the following message to the Belgium Community, *"Cardinal Gustaaf's opinion does not reflect the views of Belgium bishops and priests, it is merely a personal and a prejudicial remark. Ignore it."*

There are a few others, like Cardinal Keith O'Brien of Scotland who believes that Mother Church must begin to discuss and debate issues like contraception, celibacy and homosexuality. And then one might even reach outside of the Church and pick out one of those who have the great conviction and courage to move into the fringes of the dark shadows of Mother Church to minister the sacraments to those who have been exiled by the Church in their everyday lives. Most of these men who seem to be operating outside of the Church remain technically monks, priests or bishops in the Church despite the fact that Rome continues to suppress their orders, so they too would also be qualified candidates.

Remember that a candidate for Pope need only be a male and not necessarily a Catholic or a bishop until after the election. Unfortunately, this would exclude women for this round; the rules of a papal election remain the sole power of the existing Pope. But if a liberal or even a moderate is elected this time, women will most likely have their chance next time.

We have reached that point in the history of Catholicism, that change is inevitable. It is clear to the most casual of observers that Mother Church no longer knows right from wrong and it is time for Catholics all over the world to tell her this. If nothing more than to tell her that her irresponsible ban on the use of contraceptives in Africa is nothing short of MURDER.

The Catholic Community has the sacred responsibility to protect its children and this means that its people have the sacred responsibility to voice their opinion as to who should be the next Pope. If they fail in that sacred responsibility the blood of all of the future AIDS babies will be on their hands, as a matter of fact the blood of all AIDS victims and millions of others whose deaths are owed to the fascist whims of Rome will be on their hands. The time has come for Catholics all over the world to cast their votes and have their voices heard. And the vehicle of accomplishment will be the polls.

"that this Church be one Church under God, conceived in Liberty, and dedicated to the proposition that all men and women are created equal . . . and that they are endowed with certain inalienable rights including Life, Liberty and the Pursuit of Happiness"

note: all of the information and events cited in the foregoing chapter can be found by putting the names of the subject or individual involved into various search engines operating on the Internet. Coming soon: voteforpope.org or contact author: 410 625 9741 or vatican@att.net

Chapter 5

PAYOFFS FOR THE HIT MEN

But let's get back to those who may have been responsible for John Paul's death. As we have already pointed out, -tried criminal trials tell us quite conclusively that there is better than a ninety-percent chance that the person having the greatest motive is found to be guilty of the crime of murder. This means that if a husband is the beneficiary of a one hundred million dollar policy there is a ninety-percent chance that the courts with due process of law will in the end convict him of the murder of his wife. So if we can determine who had the greatest motive to kill John Paul, there is better than a ninety-percent chance that we have found our killer or killers.

And this is why we must include John Paul II as a suspect in the conspiracy that masterminded the murder of his predecessor. The great weight of evidence points in his direction, for it was he who collected the *one-hundred-million-dollar insurance policy*. That he was a participant in the scheme that led to his own election is quite obvious to all but the most gullible observer. Whether or not he was directly involved in the murder of his predecessor would be strictly a guess. Yet we know that according to the results of tried criminal cases, it is a ninety-percent guess. So yes, we must add him to the list of suspects - as a matter of fact, at the very top of the list.

Nevertheless, other than motive, if one considers the possibility of John Paul II having been directly involved in the murder of his predecessor, one would be dealing with very slight evidence. One would be limited to the lone fact that two of the nine people who happened to have shared the palace with John Paul the night that he died were elevated in rank by John Paul II shortly after he became Pope, and by coincidence these happened to be the two bishops that he had met with in Genoa just three weeks before the Pope's death. And neither one of these promotions was an everyday occurrence.

Less than six months after the death of John Paul I, Bishop Agostino Casaroli was made a cardinal and raised past more than two hundred others that outranked him to the post of *Vatican Secretary of State*, the second ranking office in the Roman Catholic Church. So as not to draw the wrath of certain cardinals who felt they were in line for the post, or perhaps to avoid arousing suspicion, it was announced that Casaroli's appointment was a temporary role only, to give the Pope time to decide who was best qualified for the job. Three months later John

Paul II made the appointment of Casaroli permanent and at the same time he elevated Giuseppe Caprio, a common bishop, past five hundred others who outranked him, to the rank of cardinal and eventually to the position of *Prefecture of Economic Affairs of the Holy See*, in layman's language *Chief Financial and Administrative Officer of the Roman Catholic Church,* at the time the third ranking position in the Church.

Yet, it is the very strange unprecedented promotion of these two men which is the only record that has survived in the press that could possibly link John Paul II to the murder of his predecessor. And perhaps the fact that Karol Wojtyla had been one of the two counters of one hundred and eleven cardinals in the conclave that elected John Paul I. Then there was the strange circumstance that he happened to have met with these men just three weeks before the Pope died; a meeting which required that he travel seven hundred miles back to Italy, when he had just spent two weeks with them in the conclave that had elected John Paul I. That they met is probably not too important to conspiracy, as such a matter could have been handled by phone.

Yes, one more thing. Immediately on becoming Pope in his first organizational move, Karol Wojtyla made Paul Marcinkus an archbishop and promoted him past four hundred others to the position President of the Vatican State, the Pope's civil position. In all, not enough for an indictment but we will keep Cardinal Wojtyla on the list just in case something else comes our way as we go along.

That John Paul II happened to pick up the proceeds of the one-*hundred-million-dollar insurance policy*; and that Casaroli picked up the proceeds of the *seventy-five-million-dollar policy* and that Caprio, the only person to have been present at the unexplained deaths of the three men whose deaths in rapid consecutive order had made it all possible, picked up the proceeds of the *fifty-million dollar insurance policy*; and that Marcinkus, the man who most likely provided the finances - as we shall see - required to buy the election for Karol Wojtyla, picked up the proceeds of the *twenty-five-million-dollar insurance policy* is enough by itself to keep all of these on our list of suspects. If, of course, John Paul I was murdered. No one knows this to be a fact, just that the death of this Pope has never been satisfactorily explained to the public and all of the facts that have survived point to murder. And then there is the possibility that all of these strange happenstances could, as I have said, have been coincidence, just another string of coincidences in the strange chain of coincidences that caused three men to sleep in the great bed in the papal apartment in the fall of nineteen hundred and seventy-eight.

So we have some answers here. But we have left open some questions as to the strange occurrence that the very same *College of Cardinals* elected an ultraconservative whereas just the previous month they had given the prize to an ultraliberal. Just how did Cardinal Wojtyla muster the forty or some odd votes that lie in the *middle*? For we know he did not waiver on the issue of *Humanae Vitae* either before or after his election; the doctrine that most of those in the *middle* and all of those on the *left* wanted repealed or at the very least modified. So we know he did not buy the votes of those in the *middle* with some kind of a tradeoff of ecclesiastical doctrine. And this tells us that he must have bought them with the only other thing that buys votes,

And unbelievable as it might seem to be, we will see that this is exactly what he did do.

Photo by Tom Drape

a pauper's pine box surrounded by princes of the Church

Chapter 6

THE STRANGE WAYS OF THE VATICAN CURIA

the evidence,

Now let us get to the meat of the problem. Let us review the evidence. Perhaps someone has left behind some footprints here? Better yet, perhaps, some fingerprints? Or better still, some DNA? But let us first clear up some of the loose ends. Like the time of the Pope's death, for example. Yes, let us first close the lid on that one.

All of the witnesses agree without exception that the Pope retired at his normal time at about nine o'clock. And if one believes the doctor's guess as reported in the Vatican release, the Pope died just before midnight. If one believes the embalmers, he died somewhere between three-thirty and four- thirty in the morning. And if one believes the Vatican release that Cardinal Villot performed the last rites at five-thirty in the morning we know that he had not been dead for much more than an hour or two.

That the Pope died at midnight was the guess of the physician, Doctor Buzzanetti, who had pronounced him dead of the alleged heart attack. On the other hand, it was the opinion of the embalmers that the Pope could not have been dead for more than an hour or two when they took charge of the body at a quarter-to-six in the morning. This difference in testimony as to when the Pope had died - the doctor versus the undertakers - was widely reported in the press. Initially, the discrepancies seemed immaterial to the possibility of foul play, so the press dropped it as an issue.

Today we know that the time of the Pope's death is quite material, as it answers many questions including the most puzzling of all. How the Pope, retiring shortly after nine o'clock, would still be sitting up reading and dressed in his daytime clothes at midnight with only the bedspread pulled partway over him? For as we have said before, if one intends to read oneself to sleep, one will first don bedclothes and climb in between the sheets.

If the embalmers were right and embalmers have far more experience than do doctors in examining recently expired corpses, this would mean that the Pope may have died as late as four-thirty in the morning, anytime before the nun discovered him dead.

But to nail this one down once and for all, one can consider motive. Would the embalmers have had any reason to lie and would they have held to their position when the question was put to them a second time, when it was realized that their opinion as to when the Pope had died was in conflict with the Vatican release? At least to this author, the embalmers would have had no motive to lie, particularly as telling the truth caused some problems for the Vatican who was their employer.

And one could ask, would the doctor have had a motive to lie? Would Cardinal Villot, who issued the press release that the Pope died before midnight, also have had a motive to lie? And the answer in this case would be a resounding "yes." As a matter of fact they would have had considerable motive to have lied and their motive would have been to remove any suspicion that the Pope had died under suspicious circumstances. There would be nothing unusual about a pope being embalmed seven or eight hours after death, because Italian law which prohibited embalming earlier than twenty-four hours after death did not apply within the Vatican walls. But it would be highly unusual and suspicious to have embalmed a Pope almost immediately after death; particularly, to have roused the embalmers from their beds at five o'clock in the morning when the body would not lie in state until twelve hours later. So it makes all the sense in the world that Villot and the doctor lied about the time that the Pope died in order to place considerable time between his death and the time of the embalming in order not to arouse suspicion of arsenic poisoning.

Where Villot made his mistake was in announcing to the world that he had performed the last rites over the body, when it was known that no prelate of the Church would do such a thing over a cold corpse.

The corrected Vatican release confirmed this in its statement that implied the time of death was unimportant, "*that it is immaterial when the Pope died; all that matters is that he was found dead.*" The Vatican obviously made this statement because it knew that the time of death was material to the determination that foul play had been involved in the Pope's death; that had the Pope died before midnight as the doctor claimed then foul play was unlikely, but if he had died early in the morning as the embalmers had claimed - the likelihood of foul play was almost certain.

If the Pope died early in the morning it would lead one in an entirely different direction. If the Pope had died early in the morning rather than late the evening before, then it would answer many questions. It would be possible that the Pope had risen at his regular time - around four o'clock - and having completed his toilet he could have donned his daytime clothes and his slipper socks and then sat back in the bed to go over some notes, just as the nun who found him had assumed when she first saw him sitting up in bed. This would explain how he could have been "reading at midnight" and still be in his daytime clothes when it was known that he had retired just after nine o'clock in the evening. For it would mean that he was in fact sound asleep at midnight, -and if he was sound asleep at midnight it would also clear up the conflicting testimony of the police in St. Peter's Square who told reporters that although his windows were wide open they were absolutely certain that his light was not on at two o'clock in the morning. We know this to be a fact, as had the Pope's lights been on all night it would not only have been reported to the guard station in Vatican gardens, but would have been reported in every Roman newspaper the next day as it is a rare night in September that a reporter would not be in St. Peter's Square.

There was the possibility that being quite a chilly morning he may have pulled the top bedspread up over his legs. And the very fact that the night had been chilly and the windows were open would further substantiate the embalmers claim that the Pope could not have been dead for much more than an hour or two as the body was still warm. For the chilly air would have certainly accelerated the cooling of the body.

The preponderance of evidence tells us with a reasonable degree of certainty that the Pope did as *fact* die early in the morning, sometime between the time he awoke and the time at which he was discovered by the nun. This allows us to pinpoint the time of death with some slight margin of error between quarter-to-four and quarter-after-four in the morning and for the history books this means that he was the *thirty-four day Pope* and not the *thirty-three-day Pope* that the Church claims.

the method of murder,

So far so good. Now let us consider all of the possibilities, the possible methods of murder. A killer can kill in any one of three ways. Either he performs the deed himself as in the case of using weaponry or poison or sheer force. Or he can kill by employing another creature, a poisonous creature of some kind, for example. And of course, he can employ someone else to carry out the evil deed. So let's take the second one first. Just to get it out of the way so to speak.

One could speculate that a poisonous creature of some kind was caught between the bedspread and the comforter all night and therefore the Pope could have been protected from the critter during the night by the extra thick down comforter. That in the morning when the Pope pulled the bedspread over his legs the creature was able to carry out its intended duty. This would mean that such a creature could have been placed there anytime after the Pope woke from his nap at six-thirty the evening before.

How could a creature have gotten into the room to begin with? We would have to consider those who were in the papal apartment that night. Again there were only the guard, the nuns and the two secretaries Magee and Lorenzi. We have already considered the motive each of these may have had.

Yet, when one considers that a creature may have been involved then the list grows. For there would be two and possibly three others who could have placed a creature in the Pope's bedroom, for we must keep in mind that both Bishop Casaroli and Bishop Caprio left dinner early, Casaroli leaving a few minutes before nine and Caprio leaving a few minutes after nine. Casaroli had also left dinner before nine o'clock the evening before the *last supper.* So considering this supposition one would have to move these two up the ladder of opportunity as either one of them could have entered the Pope's inner chambers briefly before going on past the guard and down the stairs to their apartments. Villot left the dining room with the Pope and walked him down the corridor to his chambers before going down the stairs to his quarters. So we know that Villot did not have this kind of opportunity.

But we know that a creature concealed in the bedclothes is not too plausible a possibility. It would make no sense to put the creature between the bedspread and the comforter knowing that the Pope was about to get in between the sheets, which would leave the ultra thick comforter between himself and the creature. This is plausible only if one assumes that the killer would have made such a blunder. Not much chance, but something to keep in the back of one's mind together with the other things we have put there.

Of course Confalonieri who had the room directly under the Pope could have possibly thrown a coral snake or a similar creature into the room and although it would naturally gravitate under the warm covers toward a human body, it may have climbed between the bedspread and the down comforter.

There is one set of circumstances that could support the use of a creature in the dreadful deed and that is if the doctor had known of the dreadful deed and Cardinal Villot had not. If this were true it would explain the Vatican release that the Pope had died before midnight versus its contradictory statement that Villot had performed the last rites. If the doctor himself had been involved in the conspiracy he may have assumed that the Pope would had been killed before midnight, since he would have known that the creature had been placed there before the Pope retired and this would lead him to believe that the Pope had been killed much earlier, most likely when he had climbed into bed. On the other hand Cardinal Villot, not knowing of the foul deed, may have felt the body and finding it to be warm would have performed the last rites. He may have thought the time of death to be immaterial and therefore never questioned the doctor's statement. After all, Villot, being a cardinal and not a doctor or embalmer would have not normally known how long a body remains warm after death.

those outside the papal palace,

We have already pretty well determined who within the papal palace could have committed the foul deed. But in doing so we did not consider those outside of the papal palace who might have gained access to the Pope's bedroom without passing by the guard. We have already mentioned that Cardinal Confalonieri had some access through the Pope's windows. Could anyone else have had access through the windows?

On the night of the Pope's death all of his bedroom windows were open and we know this because in an interview with the press four of the policemen assigned to watch St. Peter's Square told reporters that this Pope had always slept with his bedroom windows wide open.

They had taken particular note of this, as the first few evenings of his time in the papal palace were quite hot and uncomfortable. Pope Paul before him on hot nights would have all the windows closed; he preferred to sleep in air conditioning. But John Paul had appeared to be a fresh air fiend. As a matter of fact, the policemen in the square had a betting pool going, -that with the nights growing colder as to when the Pope was going to close his windows. This is why they were certain, beyond a shadow of a doubt, that the Pope's light was not on at two o'clock in the morning - for it was at that time that the changing of the police in the square took place. And it was at that time that they would check the Pope's windows to see if anyone had won the pool.

The papal apartment, as I have already pointed out, is not on the ground floor. It is on the building's fourth floor and it is at a height that might be equivalent to the tenth floor of a modern apartment house. Having been there thirty years ago and again just six months ago, I can think of only two possible ways that one could have gained access to the apartment by way of the windows. And those possibilities we will consider now.

For my knowledge of the interior of the papal palace I must draw entirely upon my visit thirty ago, as they certainly wouldn't let me in there today. But the balance of my recollection of its exterior and its grounds is much more recent. For it was on this visit just six months ago that I scoured the possibilities; thirty years ago there was no need for any possibilities.

First of all, there are no trees at all anywhere near the papal palace. So like any other super sleuth I checked out the roof, particularly since the papal apartment is on the top floor and its roof adjoins the roof of the next building and the roof of that building adjoins the roof of the next building and so forth. Had the roof been used to gain access to the Pope's quarters our list of suspects would grow to several hundred, -all those who lived elsewhere in the apostolic palace.

I took one of those tourist helicopter rides over the Vatican grounds and as we passed over the roof of the papal palace I saw nothing unusual. The roof was slanted outward toward the perimeter of the building. Its angle is not that sharp; a man could have moved about it without risk of falling off. That is, it is possible for someone to have climbed down to the edge of the roof and to have thrown something into one of the Pope's windows. But it is not reasonable to believe that someone could have done this as the roof over the Pope's quarters is in full view of the square. As we have just said four policemen were assigned to the square and off and on they would check to see if he had closed his windows. Also many others, tourists and what have you, roam the square at night and the Pope's residence is often a focal point. Although there was no full moon that night it was not a particularly dark night. So I think one can eliminate the roof as a point of access. And this is important as it greatly limits the number of people who could have been involved in the direct commission of the crime. So once again, a very slight possibility, but nevertheless something to keep in the back of one's mind, -that someone could have come from one of the surrounding buildings and have used the roof to gain access to the papal bedroom.

But as the helicopter passed over the rear of the building I thought I noticed something else. I struck on what I believed was much more than just a possibility. I slipped the pilot twenty dollars and asked him if he could make a closer pass. He told me he would not go closer but that he would go around once again. He pointed to two guards who were stationed atop the flat roof of the service building that adjoined the rear of the palace. He told me that the tripods that sat outside the guard shack were not exactly telescopes and that they could take down a helicopter in a few seconds. He was right, for as we made the second pass both guards stood up and moved toward the tripods. I asked him if the guards had been there when the Pope died and he told me they were placed there when the Vatican beefed up security in 1982 after the assassination attempt on John Paul II.

When we again came out over the side of the building I saw quite clearly that there were some iron fixtures, couplings of some sort, running from the fourth floor toward the ground at the rear corner of the building. There were a few more that ran along the outside of the top floor all the way to the Pope's bedroom. A similar set of couplings ran along the sides of the second and third floors of the building.

This told me that at one time a catwalk extended from these windows to a fire escape which then ran down the backside of the building. They had been painted the exact shade of the building to make them less visible to the eye. But, they were very much there. When I had been there thirty years before I wasn't looking for a fire escape, but it made sense to me that the building would had to have been equipped with a fire escape particularly at that height, as no ladder could reach that high. Also when the building was built fire escapes hadn't been thought of so no internal provisions for escape would have made. This was something that I should have known all along. But I had to be sure that the fire escape was there in 1978 when the Pope died, as I knew that it wasn't there now.

The postcards in the Vatican bookstores and souvenir shops had only recent photographs of the building, so for a day and a half I toured what must have been fifty or so bookshops in Rome. And finally, in a little shop on the Via Pomezia I found an old picture book of the papal palace. The date of the book was 1947, or about thirty years before the Pope's death. Although one would have to look for it in order to see it, as it blended into the building, the catwalk was definitely there. And what's more it ran right up to the Pope's bedroom window. I had a momentary rush of adrenaline and despair, for I realized that if the catwalk had been there the night the Pope died, almost anyone could have had the opportunity to commit the evil deed.

If the crime had been committed by someone using the catwalk, the perpetrator would most likely not have entered the room as the Pope would have been disturbed and he would certainly not ignore an intruder and go on reading his notes. If this was the case, I can think of only one possible murder weapon that would not have left signs of a struggle and or obvious markings on the body. And that would be a poisoned dart.

The only reliable lethal darts in the world bear tips soaked in cobra venom. This is because only the toxicity of cobra venom will survive the dilution process necessary to make such a dart. These darts, which have been used by natives of Africa and India, are certain to result in death of the victim. The problem is that death is not instantaneous, the cobra allows its victim considerable time to seek help. All other known animal and plant toxins lose most of their potency when they undergo the dilution process necessary to make a poisoned dart.

And there is, of course, the possibility that someone could have entered the room when the Pope was in the bathroom before he got into bed. Someone could have gone quietly into the bedroom, slipped a creature of some kind under the covers and crept back out of the window onto the fire escape. This could have taken place anytime after he had risen from his nap the evening before, or as late as when he was in the bathroom after he had risen in the morning.

If the killer employed a small bomb of some kind, there is only one type of bomb that I can think of which would result in instantaneous death; that is, without causing severe damage to the room, and that would be a toxic bomb of some type. Although these types of weapons are not normally available to the general public, someone in the military could have possibly secured a nerve gas grenade or similar weapon which could have done the job quite effectively. In that case, death is instantaneous and John Paul would not have been able to pull the bell cord. And in many ways this meets the criteria of the case, except that John Paul's two cockatiels which he had brought with him from Venice were found alive the next day, safely in the corner of his bedroom. So that pokes a hole in this theory a mile wide.

a creature of some kind,

If the assassin used an animal as a murder weapon, the first creature to consider would be a poisonous snake. Certainly, the embalmers would have noticed the fang marks of any large snake, particularly since there would have been considerable swelling, discoloration and some bleeding. However, it might be that a snake could have bitten the Pope on one of his feet, already swollen from what the doctor had diagnosed as the onset of arthritis, but which we know can also be a symptom of arsenic poisoning.

But this is not possible for quite another reason. John Paul was found in the exact position in which he died – sitting up in bed, still clutching the notes he'd been reading. There is only one snake in the world, which venom is so lethal that it results in immediate paralysis that would be consistent with John Paul's death. And that snake is of the viper family, the puff adder. However, it is a fairly large snake, one that would have been immediately noticed had it been lurking beneath the bedcovers. There are some smaller snakes like the coral snake, which are also fatal to human beings which presence would have been less noticeable. However, all of these allow their victim considerable time to seek help.

A puff adder's incisors are so fine and its movements so quick that many people who see the snake strike them assume that the snake missed them until it is too late. Of all the world's snakes only the bite of the puff adder allows one no recourse if the victim is unaware of having been bitten.

And this is because the venom of all other poisonous snakes attacks the blood whereas the venom of the puff adder attacks the nervous system, in particular the vagus nerve that controls the heart. Yet, there is the fact that a few minutes usually lapse before paralysis sets in, the time it takes for the venom to reach the vagus nerve. This normally would give the victim time to react. Certainly enough time to pull the bell cord or press a service button. But as I have said, so swift and fine is the bite of the puff adder, that unless the victim actually sees the snake, he is often unaware that he has been bitten; unless, of course, the snake's fangs strike a bone. Yes, the victim will feel some tightening of the area, which is owed to the clamp of the jaws on the foot or the hand or what have you. He will normally pass off the slight tinge of the bite as an insect or a nervous twitch and might even attempt to brush it off in some cases. But once the serum reaches the nervous system total paralysis of the entire body is instantaneous. Yes, he could have been killed by a puff adder.

So the only mystery that is left to solve if a puff adder was involved is how a snake of considerable size could have gone unnoticed by the Pope, that he could have slept all night with only the thickness of a comforter between himself and death and not have felt the presence of a fairly large snake.

A puff adder has one other unique characteristic versus all other snake species. It is the only specie of snake that is known to be an aggressive predator of man. Although many tens of thousands of people are killed each year by snakes they most often fall victim to their own carelessness. One either steps on the snake or accidentally invades its habitat. Only the puff adder will make an unprovoked attack on a human being. And this gives us one more flaw in this theory. A puff adder is the least likely of any snake to have sought refuge under the blankets.

Yet there remains the fact that the embalmers did not notice any marks. If a snake had been involved this would give considerable credence to the puff adder theory. A puff adder's incisors, although quite long, are extremely thin and they would normally leave two small dots on the skin, smaller than is a small 'o' in this writing. This is why there is only a tinge of pain in its bite. The incisor marks could have gone unnoticed by the embalmers but only if they had been cleaned of blood. All snakebites, no matter how fine, result in some bleeding, not profuse bleeding, but enough that one could hardly overlook it. Had the embalmers noticed any blood it is certain that the press would have learned of it, for they underwent the most intense interviewing of all. And one knows that they told the press everything else they knew, so this was not the case.

So, because the fire escape had once been there, I thought that I had a possible solution of some kind until I came across another picture in a travel book dated 1968 - about the time I had been there - which was ten years before the Pope's death. In this picture the fire escape was not there. It was then that I remembered Marcinkus talking about the air-conditioning system, -that in 1958 a service building was built along the rear façade of the papal palace which housed a freight elevator and the air-conditioning system. It would make sense that at that time internal fire escape stairways were added permitting the removal of the unsightly fire escape from the building.

Since I certainly could not gain access to the papal apartment itself, I found my way to a pub that I had visited a couple of years back when I had started my investigation into the Pope's death. It was frequented by Swiss guards. On different occasions, I spoke to separate guards, remarking that I had noticed that there were no fire escapes on the papal palace and asking how, in the case of fire, would the Pope ever get out? And in every case they told me that at one time there had been fire escapes, but that they had been replaced several years ago when the service building was added to the rear of the palace and that the service building contains two internal fire stairways, -one that services the second and third floors of the *Curia* side of the building and a second one that services only the papal apartment on the top floor. They told me that the one that services the papal apartment is quite cleverly concealed behind the altar in the Pope's private chapel. And this is an important point, as it means that no one could have gained access to the papal apartment using this stairway without having passed by the guard, as the door to the chapel is in full view of the guard at the top of the stairs.

Well, so much for the roof and the fire escape. Of course, that some kind of a creature could have been involved in the murder remains a possibility. It is just that it would have had to have gained access to the Pope's room only by way of his door. And yes, possibly from Cardinal Confalonieri's bedroom below.

If a creature of some kind was indeed involved, the answer is not so much one of how it could have gotten in his room, but rather how it could have gotten out of his room, and here the list of suspects narrows. Any one of the seven people who were in the papal apartment that night could have entered the room at anytime during the night and cleaned up the evidence, -the guard, Magee, Lorenzi or any one of the four nuns. But if one accepts the fact that the death occurred around four o'clock in the morning, which we have now added to our list of known facts, the list narrows. Three of the nuns come off of the list, as they were not permitted in the room after the Pope was found dead. So we have the mother nun and Magee, which we know were alone with the body at some time, and then we have the doctor, Villot, Confalonieri, Casaroli and Caprio; any one of which could have been alone in the room with the body before the embalmers arrived at quarter-to-six. And we have the guard who we know could have possibly entered the room anytime between four and four-thirty when the nun had knocked on the door. So any of perhaps a half dozen people had the opportunity to clean up the evidence, to have somehow put the creature in a container and hid it somewhere else in the apartment for pick up at a later time. We know that Confalonieri, Casaroli and Caprio all carried cases into the room that may or may not have contained the implements of the last rites. That is, that might have been empty.

And one might ask, -why concentrate on a creature of some kind at all? After all, one has only the very same access to the press reports as anyone else. And it is just that, the press reports, the missing socks. The missing white slipper socks would be quite an unusual memento of the occasion for someone to have collected for himself, a pair of smelly socks. It would more sense that someone might take his rosary beads, a small prayer book, or for the matter, his personal copy of *The Imitation of Christ*, which although not found in his hands was sitting on his dresser across the room.

If the murder involved the use of a deadly animal, then besides removing it from the scene, one would have to clean the wound. The amount of blood, of course, would depend upon the size of the animal involved. Even a large insect, for example, would leave at least a speck of blood, in addition to some swelling and discoloration. Of course, there is no known insect or spider that has venom so powerful that it could kill a human being that instantly; even the dreaded funnel-web spider of Australia will allow the victim up to an hour or so. Even the pale yellow scorpion, which has the most deadly venom of any creature in the world, secretes so very little of its toxin that its victim has minutes and often hours to seek help.

the missing slipper socks,

However, use of a creature could explain the missing socks. There is the possibility that the Pope could have been bitten on one of his feet and had he been wearing the socks, then anyone who was cleaning up the murder scene would have to had to remove the socks in order to clean away any telltale blood that remained on the wound. And the socks themselves, being white, would show a blotch or at least a speck of blood on them so one would certainly not replace them. We know from the embalmers testimony that the Pope, although wearing his daytime clothes, was not found to be wearing his socks. This came to light when his sister-in-law tried to recover them and the press pestered the embalmers concerning them. The record again, is in the microfilm.

And there is of course, the possibility that the socks may not have been on his feet at the time of his death, that he could have been bitten or injured on any part of his body. The killer, on noticing the traces of blood from the wound may have noticed the socks by the side of the bed and used the socks to wipe the blood clean and then taken them with him. It wouldn't make sense for the killer to have cleaned the blood with a sheet or the bed spread, as he would leave a trace of blood behind. And if he used one sock he would have been a fool to have left the other one behind as it certainly would arouse suspicions if one sock was missing and the other was found alone by the side of his bed.

That the socks were missing is suggestive evidence that most likely some bleeding was involved, and it also would confirm that not very much bleeding was involved, for otherwise the embalmers would have noticed the wound. Nevertheless, we know that if the socks were involved, then either a small creature or lethal injection was involved, something that would leave a trace of blood, but not a large amount of blood,

But let's be fair about this. This is all simply guesswork, speculation. The only known fact concerning the socks is that they were missing and never found. Why they were missing and never found could be anyone's guess. It could be that they had nothing at all to do with the Pope's death. And it could be that they had very much to do with the Pope's death.

the missing spectacles,

The missing spectacles are suggestive evidence that a struggle was involved. The Pope's sister-in-law was quite upset that the slipper socks and spectacles were not returned to her, so much so that she complained in the press on several different occasions. In John Cornwell's *cover-up* novel *A Thief in the Night,* a credible witness provided by John Paul II testifies that the spectacles had been returned to the Pope's sister-in-law. *"In fact,"* Cornwell's witness swears, *"I saw her wearing the spectacles on a number of occasions."* Had reading glasses been involved, Cornwell's rendition might stand up in court. However, the Pope suffered from a rare form of near-sightedness. The Pope's sister-in-law was not alive when Cornwell wrote his book in 1987.

poison,

There remains one other possibility; John Paul may have been poisoned at dinner earlier that very night. But this does not seem at all plausible, for if one were to go from A to Z in the alphabet of poisons that one can conceal in food or drink there would not be a single one which allows the victim to go unscathed for three to eight hours and suddenly result in instant death. This includes everything from cyanide to strychnine to the deadly Barbados nut.

why the hurry?

One might ask, if John Paul was being poisoned with arsenic right along, why not wait for the arsenic to take its toll? Why go through all that is said here to speed up his death by a few weeks? What difference would it make? And as we have said earlier it would make quite a bit of difference.

There is the fact that John Paul had just earlier in the week scheduled his first public address for the following week; quite unusual for a pope, as popes normally are in office for a few months before addressing a worldwide audience. It was clear to all but the most passive of observers that he intended to announce major changes in dogma concerning the role of women in the Church and the use of contraceptives. And although many rumors varied as to what he was actually going to say, most agreed that one of his announcements would concern itself with ordination of women. As a matter of fact, just the day before his death he had proclaimed to an audience in the Sistine Chapel, *"God is more our Mother than She is our Father."*

Because a pope's decisions concerning ecclesiastical matters cannot be reversed very easily by a successor pope, lest one threaten the infallibility of the office, this would have caused a murderer having an ecclesiastical motive to switch from slow arsenic poisoning to a quicker method of murder.

Also, he had had a four-hour closed-door session the day before his death with Jean Villot. Since John Paul had always practiced an open door policy this would infer that he was discussing with his secretary of state those *Curia* cardinals who would get to stay and those who would be let go.

So let us review the absolute facts before we go on.

- He was found to be in his daytime clothes in a sitting up position in his bed with a light on, reading some notes that had been written on the stationary of Vittorio Veneto, and not a book as had been reported in the official Vatican release.

- He did not die of a heart attack as had been reported in the official Vatican release, which has until this day remained the official position of the Vatican.

- He died in the early morning hours and not at midnight as had been reported in the official Vatican release.

- He was found by a nun at four-thirty in the morning and not by his secretary at six thirty in the morning.

- Something killed him so suddenly that he was unable to pull the bell cord, which hung a half an arm's length to his right. And it killed him in such a way that he was able to remain in the fixed position that he had died, still holding his papers upright in his hands.

Beyond that I have given you a list of probabilities. And I have also given you a list of possibilities. The probabilities are based in turn on the facts so they have a good chance, or should I say probability, of representing the facts. The possibilities are simply guesses. Yes, calculated guesses, well thought out guesses, but nevertheless, just guesses. Although I can say with certainty that he did not die of a heart attack, I have nothing, nothing at all, other than the mountain of circumstantial evidence that was reported in the press, to prove that there was foul play in the case of John Paul's death.

Except perhaps, that an autopsy was also not performed on Paul VI, who had died just a month earlier, -also presumably of a heart attack. Although Pope Paul, unlike John Paul, had had some health problems, including having had a prostrate operation ten years earlier, he had no history of heart disease, none at all. One would wonder just what were the circumstances of his death, -the mysterious circumstances of the death of Pope Paul VI? And to best understand the circumstances of Paul's death, one must first understand the circumstances of his best friend's death, Aldo Moro.

Chapter 7

THE MURDER OF ALDO MORO

Paul's friend Aldo Moro,

A short time before the death of Paul VI, in August of 1978, Paul's lifelong friend and leader of the Italian Christian Democratic Party, Aldo Moro, turned up in the trunk of a car on the Via Caetani, an avenue not far from the Vatican. He had been kidnapped and murdered by extremists.

Two months earlier when he had first been kidnapped suspicions focused in two very different directions, the *Curia* cardinals in the Vatican which represented the extreme *far right* in Italy, and the Red Brigade who represented the extreme *far left* in Italy.

On the *right*, Moro was seen as being the greatest enemy of the *Vatican Curia* as he controlled much of the thinking of the Italian population, which at that time was entirely Roman Catholic. He was seen as leading the people away from the Church. That is, not away from membership in the Church but just away from much of its doctrine.

Moro was encouraging citizens to ignore *Humanae Vitae* and to use their judgment as to how many children they can afford. He had become the leading proponent in encouraging the use of contraceptives, not only as a means of birth control but as a means of curbing transmission of disease. Both syphilis and gonorrhea had been running rampant throughout Italy at the time, particularly among teenagers. In fact, it was his lobbying just a year earlier which, much to the consternation of the *Curia*, had made contraceptives legal in Italy in the first place. And he had very recently pushed a bill through Parliament which to the great horror of the *Curia* cardinals, had made them available to teenagers.

And Moro was also lobbying that abortion be made legal in order that it could better be controlled by the state, as it was resulting in unnecessary mutilation of many women and often death. Also, he felt that being illegal, it resulted in many abortions that otherwise might be prevented by the state. Driven by the Church's policy that banned contraceptives, abortions were exceeding six million a year in Italy, a country one-fifth the size of the United States. And much to the chagrin of the *Curia*, Moro was embarrassing the Church by demanding that it make sexual education more explicit and easier to understand in the curriculum of its schools. And perhaps worst of all, he was encouraging homosexuals, even transsexuals, to stand up for their rights. He was riling them up. And then there was the fact that Moro had just ten days before his kidnapping formed an alliance between his party, the Christian Democratic Party, and the Communist Party. In a statement to the press, Bishop Casaroli called the new union "*an engine of destruction of all family values in Italy.*"*

Soon after the kidnapping, however, telephone calls were made in the name of the Red Brigade, which dictated ransom terms. The Red Brigade was a Marxist organization, which shared much of the same ideology as did Aldo Moro, a socialist. It was not a communist organization. That is, it believed that much of Marxist ideology could be incorporated into a democratic society.

But despite this fact, rumors persisted that someone within the Vatican walls had hired the Mafia to do the job and within a week the rumors had spread throughout all of Europe and abroad. Most believed that the alleged calls from the Red Brigade were simply a diversionary tactic. Soon a number of different theories concerning the Vatican's involvement began to appear in the press.

Some of them cited the *Curia's* close links to the Mafia; it was fairly common for *Curia* cardinals to attend the funerals of mob bosses and members of their families. Actually, a half dozen or so of the Vatican clergy were themselves Sicilian, including three of those that we have talked about, Bishops Caprio and Casaroli and Cardinal Confalonieri. As a matter of fact, all three of these were of Mafia families. This is not surprising, as Mafia families were the richest in Italy and the largest contributors to the Church. It makes sense that they would use their influence to get some of their members into the hierarchy of the Church.

Actually, Bishop Casaroli in his role as foreign minister was the Vatican's leader in its struggle against communism, socialism and other *leftist* groups like the Red Brigade. For this reason Casaroli had spent much of his time in Eastern Europe and North Africa working against communist aggression. In 1973, five years before John Paul's death, he had survived the crash of a French Caravelle jet in the Moroccan Desert, which killed one hundred and six people. At the time of the crash there was widespread speculation that Casaroli had been the target of communists who had sabotaged the plane. So there was considerable speculation that Casaroli was somehow involved in the Moro tragedy, as he himself had once been a target of assassination by the Communist Party, with which Moro had very recently allied his own Christian Democratic Party.

The intent of Moro's alliance with the Communist Party was mostly political, as it would lock up the upcoming presidential election for

* *IL Messaggero 10 Mar '78*

him. To see this clearly, we must review the results of the previous election six years earlier,

	%
Christian Democrats	38.8
Communists	27.2
Republicans	9.3
Other	24.7

But getting back to the Mafia, the tabloids had from time to time, gone so far as to speculate that some of the members of the *Curia* were, in fact, active members of the Mafia. Although the articles were substantiated by photographs of various cardinals being wined and dined by mob bosses in restaurants and on occasion vacationing with them at various resorts including the Castel Gandolfo, nothing was ever proved of the allegations. All of these happenstances might arouse suspicions, but one must realize that in Italy at the time, all Mafia families were devoted Catholics and major contributors to the Church; these relationships were a matter of good business. This would explain why a cardinal very often would go so far as to take to the pulpit and render the eulogy of a mob boss.

Nevertheless, the lines of communication were firmly in place between members of the *Curia* and the Mafia, should anyone in the *Curia* require the services of the Mafia.

The idea of Mafia involvement emerged in Moro's case because the kidnapping itself had all the earmarkings of a Mafia job, gangland style.

a quiet morning,

Early on the morning of March 16, 1978, Eleanora Moro sat quite pensively at one end of the breakfast table while her husband scoured through a stack of newspapers at the other end. She thought back a couple years to when she and her husband and four children had lived in freedom, back to those days when their lavish estate was just that a paradise with views as far as the eye could see.

But now she lived in a fortress. For now all she could see when she looked out of her windows were the twelve foot high white stucco walls that enclosed the grounds of the estate. And the razor sharp barbed wire that ran along their tops. There were armed guards occupying the turrets, which jetted out wherever the walls happened to run into each other. It was almost as if her family had moved into the Castel Gandolfo, except that the guards were not dressed in the elaborate garb of the Swiss guards.

She also knew that at that very same moment just outside the gates of the mansion a line of cars was forming, as if a funeral procession was about to begin. But she knew that these cars were not loaded with flowers and dressed up mourners, for they were instead, loaded with more armed guards. And she knew why. For they would guarantee Aldo's safe travel to his office and would guarantee the safety of Giovanni, the last of her live-in children, as he made his way to school.

And speaking of the Castel Gandolfo, it was there that it had all started now almost two years before. When, at the request of Pope Paul, Aldo had spent a week with him at the papal residence located within the ancient fortification. She thought that they would spend the time reminiscing about the good old days. Like the time when she had first told Aldo that his first and only son was on his way. Of that time that Aldo had suggested that they surprise his *uncle* and name the boy after him. And so it was that the infant was baptized Giovanni Montini Moro, by Paul who was at the time Giovanni Montini, Archbishop of Milan.

But she knew in her heart that something must have gone terribly wrong that week. For it was shortly afterwards that Aldo had taken up the leadership of the Christian Democratic Party and began to move the people away from much of the ideology of the Roman Catholic Church, away from Paul. After that time Aldo had never met with Paul again. At least as far as she or anyone else knew.

It was shortly after that time that the letters began; the many anonymous death threats to Aldo and his family. The letters which would eventually give rise to the walls that made up the prison she now found herself living in.

Yet, on the other hand, she knew that Paul and Aldo were constantly in touch with each other, for it was she who approved the household phone bills for payment. She knew that every week Aldo would make calls to Paul as if he were trying to somehow reconcile himself with the Pope. And she knew that he must have been making some headway, as the calls were quite lengthy. That is, she knew for certain that Paul had not been hanging up on him.

There was something strange about the order of the calls. They were always made at exactly 8 o'clock in the evening on consecutive days of the week. That is, if one week's call was made at 8 o'clock on Monday, then the next week's call was made at 8 o'clock on Tuesday and the following week's call would be made at 8 o'clock on Wednesday, and so forth. It was almost as if Aldo knew that at these particular times the calls would go directly to Paul without being routed through one of his secretaries, as if to keep the matter of their possible reconciliation a private one between them. That none of the calls were made by the Pope would not leave any evidence of their communicating with each other in the Vatican records.

So it was that morning that she had decided to ask Aldo - Just what was the story? She had noticed the phone calls and that she wanted to know if he had made any progress with the Pope. So she asked the question.

He looked at her and took her by the hand and led her to an overly stuffed heavily brocaded armchair that sat in front of a large picture window, one that at one time had enclosed a beautiful blue pond which, hedged in with the greenery of weeping willows, had served as a home for a half dozen or so families of swans. But now all one could see on this magnificent spring day, was the sun bouncing off a blank white stucco wall and the barbed wire that peered down from its crest.

And he told her, "Paul also has his walls. He, too, is hemmed in. But in his case the walls are built of flesh and bone and mostly of the minds of men. So unlike concrete it will take much longer to tear them down. And only we here on the outside can help Paul tear down his walls. So it is important that his 'walls' not know that they are being taken down from the outside." That is all he told her. He smiled and kissed her lightly on the cheek and left her there in her chair and headed for the door. That was the last time he saw her.

For it was on this same morning that Moro set out from the sprawling suburban estate with a half dozen security guards in two cars for the last time. As the cars entered the city they moved at a whisker above medium speed along the busy Via Fani. Suddenly, the driver of the car directly in front of Moro's car slammed on his brakes causing his driver to crash into its rear. The car carrying his bodyguards slammed into the rear of Moro's car, pinning it in between the two vehicles.

The incident took place directly in front of the busy Café Randolfo, which was located on the south side of the street. Almost immediately on impact, nine men and one woman dressed in the uniforms of the Italian airline Air Alitalia emerged from behind the bushes which hemmed in the sidewalk section of the café, with automatic weapons. When all was said and done all of his bodyguards were dead and Moro was whisked away in another vehicle. Although the Via Fani was on the edge of the city the cars sped off in the direction of St. Peter's. Moro was never seen alive again.

the missing five million dollars,

If the Mafia had been involved in Moro's murder, it is most likely that it would have required a payoff of some kind. At the time it was rumored that it would have had to have been a substantial sum of money, and that if members of the *Curia* were involved it would have had to have come from the Vatican Bank. Keep in mind that we are talking here of a possibility only, that the Mafia had been involved is not a known fact.

It is a matter of historical fact, however, not rumor, that the week before John Paul's death several months later, the audit that he had commissioned had disclosed that several billion lire - about five million dollars - was missing from the Vatican Bank. The discrepancy had been leaked to the press a few days before John Paul's death from unknown Vatican sources. The news made second page headlines in most Italian newspapers and the tabloids made the several billion lire into several billion dollars despite the fact that it was quite obvious that the Vatican treasury never held that kind of money.

A few days later the Pope's sudden death captivated the headlines so there was no follow up of this story by the press and no explanation concerning the missing money was ever offered by the Vatican. And this was because of certain actions taken by John Paul II immediately after taking office, which we will talk about later.

the Red Brigade,

A few hours after the kidnapping, as I have already mentioned, certain members of the press received telephone calls from various people who said they represented the Red Brigade. Although it was an organization that often relied on terrorism to accomplish its objectives, it made little sense that it would kidnap someone from the *far left*. For after all, the Red Brigade itself was from the far *left*. The only reasoning which could possibly tie the Red Brigade to the Moro kidnapping was that Moro's party, the Christian Democratic Party, had recently established its alliance with the Communist Party. This certainly was something that did not please the Brigade. They would have, of course, preferred that he had allied his party with them.

Actually the ideology of the Red Brigade was much closer to that of Moro than was that of the Communist Party. The problem was that it was not a political party and thereby did not control a block of votes. In fact, if Moro were to ally himself with the Red Brigade the alliance would have obviously eroded much of the block of votes he already controlled.

This alliance of Moro with the Communist Party was also something that did not please the Vatican. It is a well known fact that communism is the enemy of organized religion. It is particularly the enemy of the Roman Catholic Church.

What westerners don't understand is why it is against organized religion. And the answer to this 'why' is that communism believes that if a particular religion becomes strong enough it will try to force its beliefs on everyone else. That is, it will try to make the laws of a nation conform to its scripture. We see this very clearly in the United States today, where the Constitution was originally based almost entirely on Mosaic Law, good for Christian white men but not fair to women, blacks and many others, something that men and women of good conscience have been trying to unravel ever since.

This was precisely the case in postwar Italy. Ninety-nine point nine percent of Italians were Catholics. It was all but illegal for a citizen not to be a Catholic, and a practicing Catholic at that. It was almost as if someone were not to go to church on Sunday and cast their coins into the box that one would be arrested and thrown in prison. And of course, the laws of Italy were largely based on doctrine as dictated by the Church.

Aldo Moro, as I have already said, had on his own taken the law giant steps away from the Church and wanted to take it one last step. He wanted all citizens to be free to practice whatever religion they choose to practice. What most westerners are unaware of is that communism does encourage belief in God but it deems that the relationship between man and his Creator is a private and sacred one and not a public one. It also believes that the relationship is a direct one. And being a direct one, there is no need for an emissary, a middleman, -like Mohammed or Christ or Buddha or Joseph Smith. Communism does not believe that one's relationship with God should be the business it is in the western world. In the western world, people don't accept that they have a personal and sacred relationship with their Creator. Instead they believe that they must have an agent, a businessman, a church to oversee their communications with God, -the reason why Christians believe that they cannot obtain salvation unless they go to church. And the reason they are conditioned to believe this, is that unless they go to church the preacher cannot line his pockets with gold.

So it was widely known that in his campaign for the presidency Moro's platform would include this as one of its objectives, -that people would be free to practice whatever religion they chose to practice. Where his platform would differ from the strict ideology of the Communist Party was that people should be free to practice their religion either privately or publicly. This, together with the overall ideology that Italian law be moved closer to the will of the people and away from the dictates of the Vatican was to be the essence of the Moro platform.

The Christian Democratic Party, which Moro controlled, was the largest of the political parties in Italy and its alliance with the Communist Party was a serious threat to the Church. It was particularly dangerous to Bishop Agostino Casaroli, the Vatican's foreign minister, who headed up the Church's struggle against communism.

another coincidence,

The ransom demands allegedly sought by the Red Brigade were for the release of thirteen political prisoners, five of which were known to be members of the Red Brigade. Three of the others were members of the Mafia and the other five had no known affiliation at all.* Two weeks later a second demand required the payment of three billion lire in ransom money. The exact amount, three billion lire, at the time about five million dollars, was not announced to the press. But, today we know the amount. And today we know something more - this was also the approximate amount of the discrepancy that John Paul's audit of the Vatican Bank would uncover just a few months later. It was as if someone wanted to cover the shortfall in the books of the Vatican Bank with the ransom money before its absence was detected. And that it would have been detected was inevitable, for if John Paul had not ordered his special audit in September, it would have been disclosed in the yearend audit anyway.

At first, the police doubted that it was the Red Brigade who had kidnapped Moro. It made very little sense for the Red Brigade to demand the release of thirteen prisoners when only five of them were known to have any connection with them. In fact, two of the prisoners that they allegedly demanded the release of were Mafia members who were being held on capital charges. The Red Brigade had no greater enemy in Italy than the Mafia and there was also the fact that at the time the state was holding a half dozen other Red Brigade members on capital charges, two of which were leaders in the brigade. It made no sense that the brigade would demand the release of five of its members who would most likely have been released in the near future anyway, and allow the state to retain six others for the rest of their lives and at the same time demand the

* *none of the prisoners for which release was demanded were P-2 members (Masons).*

release of two Mafia members who were being held on capital charges. It appeared that such a demand would more likely have come from the Mafia. It would seem that if the Mafia had made such a demand it would have been disguised with a few Red Brigade members in order to cloud its own involvement.

And then there were the descriptions of the attackers themselves. The fact that the attackers were dressed in the uniforms of the national airline would, of course, have been more characteristic of the Red Brigade than of the Mafia, because the Red Brigade was a youth organization. There was, however, the possibility that this could have been another diversionary tactic on the part of mob, to throw the police off track.

The kidnapping had been witnessed by over two hundred people, several of whom personally knew members of the Red Brigade and none of whom recognized any of the attackers. The only general description of the attackers was that the woman was in her thirties and the nine men were all in their forties or fifties. This part of the description pointed away from the Red Brigade and toward the Mafia, as it was widely known that the overwhelming majority of the Red Brigade members were in their teens and twenties.

But with no other leads to go on other than the ransom demands the police concentrated their efforts almost entirely on the Red Brigade and this was because those who made the phone calls claimed to be from the Red Brigade. Despite the fact that if the motive was money, the leaders of the Red Brigade would have been fools not to have kept the phone calls anonymous.

Paul makes a mistake,

Pope Paul himself, began to raise the ransom money and two months later when it seemed that he had succeeded, suddenly, for some unknown reason, he issued a statement demanding that the kidnappers release Moro without condition. On this same day a leak appeared in the press that the government was about to announce that it had agreed to release eleven of the thirteen prisoners. This included all five of those identified as members of the Red Brigade. It would retain the two associated with the Mafia who were being held on capital charges. Also, it would begin a dialogue with the Red Brigade, something that it had in the past refused to do. Almost immediately public opinion leaned on the side of granting the Red Brigade amnesty for all past transgressions excepting capital crimes.

The following day Moro turned up in the trunk of a car. If the Red Brigade had, indeed, been involved, this made no sense; they had no reason to kill him for alive he was worth the freedom of five of their comrades and possibly billions of lire, and what's more, -a chance to be heard, something that had been denied them in the past. Dead he was worth nothing to them. As a matter of fact, dead he poised a great threat to the five brigade prisoners who had been named in the ransom demand; the courts would react in retaliation.

Nevertheless, four years later its leader Mario Moretti and scores of others were brought to trial, and although nothing was ever proved, twenty two of them, including Moretti, were given life sentences for the Moro murder and a series of other terrorist activities. In its judgment the court relied entirely on the testimony of ten others who had turned state witnesses in exchange for light sentences. Not the slightest link of Moretti and his followers was made to either the kidnapping or the murder despite the fact that the trials spanned a year-and-a-half. Where Moro was held captive was never brought to light.

The results of the Moro trial in Italy were viewed with the same type of skepticism as were the results of the Warren Commission in the United States. In the latter case the single bullet theory, -that the bullet that killed Kennedy went on to strike Governor Connolly three times, simply made no sense to the rank-and-file population. And today we know that this theory does not hold much water and that the Warren Commission was most likely wrong in its conclusion.

In the case of the Moro murder, lack of evidence in the convictions caused most citizens to continue to believe what was logical, that the alleged kidnapping and demand for ransom money and the release of prisoners allegedly sought by the Red Brigade were simply diversionary tactics to place suspicions outside of the Vatican. It made more sense to the common man that someone on the *far right* in the Vatican had involved either the Mafia or some other *right wing* organization like P-2 to do the job and had ordered that the ransom calls be made in the name of the Red Brigade. By casting suspicions on the Red Brigade they would not only get rid of Moro, but also the Red Brigade, another great adversary of the *far right* outside of the papal gates. Perhaps most importantly, they would break the grasp that the Communist Party held on the Christian Democratic Party. And this is precisely what happened, as Moro's death marked the beginning of the end of communism in Italy. As a result its population remains entirely Roman Catholic today and there is not a single mosque or synagogue or even a Protestant church in all of Italy.

On the day following the Moro murder, the press interviewed both Bishop Casaroli and Cardinal Confalonieri as to why they had advised the Pope not to pay the ransom money which might have saved Moro's life. They responded that they had, in fact, advised Paul just the opposite. They had reminded Paul that he was dealing with terrorists who would resort to most anything. They told the press that they were greatly concerned that Paul had changed his mind and that he was adamant that he would never pay the ransom money.

In retrospect, one would wonder why Paul, after having successfully raised the money and knowing that he was dealing with terrorists, refused to pay the ransom. Particularly, in that the Red Brigade did have a track record of kidnapping and murder in those cases in which their demands had not been met. On the other hand, they also had a record of sparing the lives of victims when their demands were met.

The only conceivable rational explanation for Paul's action seems to be that he found out that he was not dealing with terrorists. That Paul, like many other Italians at the time had surmised that he was not dealing with the Red Brigade, but that he was, indeed, dealing with someone within his own ranks. After all, only an imbecile would not understand that the greatest motive for Moro's murder lie among those within the Vatican. So Paul may have guessed that it was someone who he gambled would not take a human life. This seems to be the only explanation why Paul risked his friend's life; although he probably did not know specifically who was responsible for the kidnapping, he must have felt comfortable enough to have taken the chance. And the only likely explanation for this seems to be that he had concluded that one or more of the cardinals were involved, and he felt fairly comfortable that they, being men of God, would release Moro on his demand. That whoever it was would not take a human life.

the hunt,

The two months of Moro's captivity saw the largest manhunt, not only in Italian history, but in the history of the world. The entire Italian army was activated and employed in the effort. Roadblocks were set up in and around the city and all vehicles entering and leaving the city were searched. There were armed soldiers on every street corner in Rome. Every leaf was upturned. Every suspected Red Brigade hideout was raided and many were arrested. Every single household and building in Rome was searched. But Moro was never found.

Coming up empty-handed, the Italian police concluded that Moro was being held in one of the foreign embassies, which they were not permitted to search. There was the fact that the car that Moro's driver had crashed into which had been abandoned at the scene was registered to the Venezuelan embassy. It had been stolen from the embassy the night before the kidnapping. Since the foreign embassies in Rome are small buildings there is no way one could hide someone in one of them without the knowledge of its ambassador and thereby the head of state of the country involved. Except, perhaps, for the United States and the United Kingdom, foreign countries had no motive in his murder.

That a covert operation commissioned by either or both of these two countries may have been involved is a possibility as these countries were great adversaries of communism. It certainly would not be in the best interests of these particular countries to have a communist nation sitting in the middle of Europe. And although this was not a probability, it had become a possibility when Moro allied his party with the Communist Party.

But this was not likely because of the timing. Moro's alliance with the Communist Party came as a surprise to the world, just ten days before his kidnapping. It is not likely that if these two countries had been involved they would have acted this quickly, particularly since they had almost a year before the election to plan and make their move. Yet there was one other foreign country which had the greatest motive of all. And that country was The Sovereign State of the Vatican.

Being a foreign country, the Italian police had no jurisdiction in the Vatican, and its many buildings and grounds were never searched. It would be fairly easy for Moro to have been imprisoned there without the Pope's knowledge. The Vatican is much like a small city. It has just under a thousand live-in citizens, which share about three thousand six hundred rooms spread throughout thirty or so multistory buildings. There are a great many smaller buildings spread throughout the grounds particularly within the perimeter of the Vatican gardens. And, in addition, a seminary is located there.

Then of course, there are the other papal properties outside Vatican City like the Castel Gandolfo, which houses five palaces where one could easily be held without detection, which again have many hundreds of rooms, and because of diplomatic immunity were never searched.

But, if Moro had indeed been held by *right wing* extremists in the Church, it is likely that he was held within Vatican City itself, as his body was found just a few blocks from there. That the body turned up within the city limits of Rome puzzled the police as they had searched not once, but twice, every house and building in all of Rome. In fact, when he finally showed up on the Via Caetani they were in the process of conducting additional searches of houses and buildings on an unannounced rotating basis. This led them to the conclusion that Moro most certainly had been held in a foreign embassy. It made no sense whatsoever that the kidnappers would take an unnecessary chance of returning the body to the city while cars were still being searched entering and leaving the city.

Also, it made no sense that the kidnappers would try to hide him in the city to begin with, as they would have known that a massive manhunt would most certainly follow. After all, Moro was recognized as being the John Kennedy of Italy. If they had retained him in the city they would have had to continually risk moving him. It would be impossible to conceal him for long. On the heels of the kidnapping they could have easily taken him out of the city before roadblocks had been set up. Particularly in that the Via Fani where he was kidnapped was on the outskirts of the city. But instead, witnesses were in agreement that the getaway car had sped off in the direction of St. Peter's. Still, it was possible that this could have been a diversionary tactic, and that the car once out of sight may have turned away from the city.

Of course, had they done this, they would have been fools to attempt to return the corpse to the city. And it is known that the car Moro was found in never cleared a roadblock for records had been kept of the make and license number and contents of every vehicle entering and leaving the city. So it can be concluded with a reasonable amount of certainty is that Aldo Moro was held hostage somewhere in Vatican City, although it is not known who retained him.*

That Moro's body had been returned made little or no sense unless, of course, one wanted to destroy Paul. For it was he, the day before who had demanded his friend's release without condition. The return of the body could have had only one purpose and that was to cause great trauma and consternation to Paul. Even Moro's family, which for many years had been as his own family, bitterly angered by his refusal to pay the ransom money, disowned him.

Moro's family even refused Paul the honor of attending his friend's funeral, a funeral at which he normally would have given the eulogy. They never talked to him again. Moro's wife Eleanora, together with her four children Giovanni, Anna, Agnese and Maria, all were upset with him for having refused to pay the ransom money, money that they, themselves, had

** that Moro may have been held captive within Vatican City itself would possibly point to P-2 (Masons) involvement as at the time there were known to be living in Vatican City more than one hundred freemasons. The Mafia with its links to several cardinals also had access to Vatican City. The Red Brigade, on the other hand, had no access to Vatican City. If the Red Brigade had been involved he would have had to have been retained somewhere else.*

helped raise. These children now entering adulthood, that he himself had once baptized and watched grow up, that he felt were somehow his own. It was crushing to Paul, not only had he lost his best friend but he also lost the only family that he ever really knew.

Many years would pass before Eleanora Moro would come to realize that Aldo and Paul had, in fact, not spent that week at the Castel Gandolfo reminiscing about the past. Rather they had spent it planning for the future, -the future of the Church, the future of Italy, the future of the world. A part of the strategy they had decided upon at the Castel Gandolfo was to make it appear to the *Curia* that they were estranged. Aldo was to start moving away from Church doctrine, to enable Paul to gain public support to facilitate his eventually changing doctrine. Paul knew that he himself was in danger and that if anything were to happen to him at that time, a conservative was certain to replace him and if that were to happen it would bring an end forever to the changes he and John XXIII before him had brought to the Church.

On the day of the funeral Paul made a short statement to the press. Although he had no idea of which extremists he was talking, he spoke quite bitterly of his friend's assassins,

*"The extremist believes that he can halt the carriage of change. But, there are too many wheels. Take one away and another will take its place. His is a futile struggle. He has no purpose and he has no place in time. No place in all of humanity. Not even beyond humanity."**

On the other hand, perhaps, Paul did know exactly which extremists he was talking of.

* *Il Messaggero 19 May '78*

Chapter 8

THE CASTEL GANDOLFO

Bereaved by his friend's death, particularly bothered by the part that he himself had played in it, in July of 1978, Paul VI was worn out and did not look well. He was pale and he lacked any semblance of energy. As in the case of John Paul who would follow him, he too had been taking uncharacteristic naps in the time that preceded his death. They had begun shortly after the Moro funeral. It seemed that the strain of losing his close friend was too much for him. On the urging of bishops Casaroli and Caprio he finally agreed to take a rest at Castel Gandolfo, the equivalent of what Camp David is to the president in the states.

Most people think of the Castel Gandolfo as being a monastery of some sort. It is actually the ruins of part of the embattlement built by Pope Urban VIII in the seventeenth century to protect the city of Rome and St. Peter's. There was Castel Franco to the north, Castel Sant Angelo to the west and Castel Gandolfo to the immediate southeast and the sea. Pope Urban had these forts outfitted with heavy cannon and it was he who in 1624 built the Palazzo Pontifico, the papal residence there, as a retreat for the papacy on the outskirts of Rome.

Actually there are five palaces within the confines of what is known today as the Castel Gandolfo, four that would immediately be recognized as the magnificent palaces that they are. But the papal residence itself might be mistaken for an ancient fortress as it is enclosed by the surviving castle walls and turrets. Sitting high on a hill it keeps a watchful eye over St. Peter's as the basilica's immense dome can be seen in the distance from its northern turrets. To the west can be seen the glistening waters of the Mediterranean, and to the east it overlooks a perfectly oval shaped natural blue lake sitting in a field of green trees. In another direction, one can look down at a fabulous view of wooded slopes that fall swiftly down to the gray murky waters of a volcanic crater.

If one follows a narrow alley which runs along the side of the palace to a terrace, off in the distance in another direction one can see the Appian Way, with its familiar line of towering trees on each side framing an old Roman viaduct. Like soldiers standing at attention awaiting their Emperor on a white horse to proceed down between them. On a clear day it seems that one can follow them all the way down to the southeast to the Adriatic Sea. And off in another direction one can see the low rolling Alban Hills. And if privileged enough to witness the view from the papal rooms themselves one would witness a remarkable view of still another lake edged in by a trace of ruins, once the palace of the Emperor Diocletian, the very court in which Constantine the founder of the Roman Catholic Church had once played as a boy. It appears that the only thing one cannot see, is snow.

Today, the gardens at the Castel Gandolfo are among the most beautiful in the world. It has been said of them that they are an exact replica of the Garden of Eden. Paul himself had once said of the gardens, "*Here is a joint effort of God and man, which through the centuries has been a voice against bigotry. It speaks of all languages and customs of the world and excludes none. That is, except for our friends here about us who stand frozen in time. Don't they know that the world is changing? We must tell them so.* "*

And Paul was right. For the architecture of the gardens is not entirely Italian. Rather they are a mixture of Italian, French, Russian, Chinese, Japanese, Indian, African, Australian and even North and South American architecture. And if observant enough, one will see that not even the Eskimo has been left out, for here and there are hints of tundra and every now and then an Arctic rose. There is even a cactus or two sprouting out of the desert sand here and there. It is almost as if one must watch out for polar bears and scorpions at the very same time.

When he spoke of *"his friends who were frozen in time"* Paul was referring to the marble statuary that appears throughout the park-like setting of the gardens, every one of them was of stark white. During his tenure he did do something about it, for today if one were to walk through the gardens, one will occasionally come upon a black marble *friend* here and a pale, almost yellow one, there.

* *L'Osservatore Romano 17 May 64*

the *Godfather's* last ride,

In the still of the darkness on the evening of July fourteenth nineteen hundred and seventy eight, Paul left the Vatican for the last time. He warded off his second secretary Macchi's offer of assistance as he climbed into the limousine that would take him on the fifteen mile ride to the papal retreat.

Cardinal Carlo Confalonieri, the aging dean of the *College of Cardinals* and oldest member of the *Curia*, did take Macchi up on his offer as he struggled into the car next to the Pope.

The car was a conventional black Mercedes from the pool of vehicles reserved for use by the Vatican cardinals and not the ceremonial white limousine that one usually associated with the Pope at that time. Paul had chosen not to use the helicopter, which usually took him to the castle. He would go incognito this time by ground, as if he knew of his fate, he wanted to be witness to the streets and the people of his beloved Rome for this very last time.

Although somewhat slower than he had been at the time of Moro's death a few weeks earlier, there was little outward change in his appearance. Except that there was a slight mustard-like tinge to his skin, in fact his face looked like it was hewn out of yellow pine. It was as fixed as if it had, indeed, been carved of wood. And the wood seemed to be chapping, a flaking of some kind. Other than this his only ailment in his last months of life had been some numbness and swelling in his hands and feet which his doctors had diagnosed as the onset of arthritis. Then there was a slight stomach disorder, which is common for a man of his age. And yes, a slight throat irritation, a sore throat in August.

Cardinal Jean Villot, his longtime friend and confidant had decided at the last minute to go along for a few days. He climbed into the car from the other side so as to wedge Paul in between the two of them. That Villot chose to go along was a break in protocol, normally the *secretary of state* remains in the Vatican when the Pope is away. Macchi took the jump seat in the rear compartment of the car and John Magee, Paul's first secretary, slid silently into the front seat next to the driver.

Although one was a Pope, and another a dean of the Church, and another a cardinal, and another a bishop, and another a monsignor, all five were dressed in black, entirely in black. Only the chauffeur was properly attired in his garb of black. Five men, in all six with the chauffeur, dressed in black suits with a half dozen black boleros topping them off. Except for the presence of the two Swiss guards in their elaborate attire who stood at attention on either side of the great bronze doors of the papal palace one would assume that the Italian Mafia were taking the Godfather for his last ride. That somewhere between here and there his body would be thrown out from the car, perhaps beneath some viaduct on the way.

Or that possibly a gangland style episode was about to occur somewhere along the way. Particularly, if one were to notice a second black Mercedes follow the first one out of the Vatican gates and along the outward wall. Again, four men dressed in four black suits, also topped off with matching boleros. The Pope's bodyguard, Swiss guards in plain clothes so as not to attract notice.

But nothing happened along the way. As a matter of fact there was complete silence. Except for Paul's offer to share his cough drops with those who were with him, his only words during the half-hour journey were, "Why do I tire so? It is not like me to tire so. There is so very much to do." And, as I have said, no one offered an answer. There was just complete silence. No one took him up on the cough drops either. After all, it was midsummer.

He was bothered with an ecclesiastical problem the following day. Bishop Casaroli showed up at the castle demanding that Paul respond to reporters and condemn Cardinal Luciani's congratulatory message to Louise Brown that had been printed in the world's newspapers that day. Paul had only one reaction, he told the bishop, *"The prince of the Veneto country could not be more right. There is a high place in heaven for this little girl. It is sad that I cannot say the same for those of us who hold high places here on earth."**

And, indeed, it was his last ride. Three weeks later, spiraling steadily downward, he was dead. His daily naps, progressing to all day sleeps, to near coma at the end. In the last week, his growing weakness was accompanied by a high fever, the cause of which his medical team for some reason could not determine and therefore could not bring down. Early in the afternoon of his final day his blood pressure suddenly dropped dramatically. His attending physician diagnosed the change as a heart attack. As the Pope was obviously in his last hours the heart attack was announced to the press. His brother Senator Luigi Montini and his nephew Marco Montini who had learned of the Pope's condition on the news were enroute to the Castel Gandolfo when Paul's pontificate came to its end.

From the time that they had loaded him into the Mercedes limousine until his death he had had only one outside visitor. And that visitor was

* *Italia Sera 12 Aug '78*

Lillian Carter, mother of the American president. She had visited him just two weeks before his death and when reporters pestered her, she told them that although the Pope had seemed tired, she was surprised when she learned that he had died.

In his final moments he was surrounded only by Confalonieri, Macchi, Magee and his personal physician, Mario Fontana. There was one more, Bishop Guiseppe Caprio who had arrived unexpectedly early in the morning just a few hours prior to the presumed heart attack. I might point out that there was nothing unusual about this, as Caprio spent much of his free time at the Castel Gandolfo. He was an amateur botanist and he personally cultivated that small section of the gardens that contained plants that were native to the holy land. Cardinal Villot was not present, he had returned to the Vatican in late July to tend to mounting duties. At the time of Paul's death he was in a helicopter on his way to the retreat.

With the time elapsing between the rising and falling of his chest growing more and more apart, Paul died silently, as if falling asleep and the stillness of his death was broken only by the opening of a door and the low murmuring of prayers coming from the hall just outside his bedroom.

One of the sisters who cared for the household at Castel Gandolfo stood there. She gestured to the phone and addressed Bishop Caprio, "It is Bishop Casaroli," she said. Caprio picked up the phone and mumbled an inaudible greeting and then paused and replied, "Yes, it is done. It is over. The '*thief*' has just now left. Christ will understand the duty of His generals."

"What's that?" he asked as if Casaroli were asking him a question of some sort. And then he answered, "Yes, Paul died under the same star that our Savior was once born. It is certain that he is with Him today. God rest his soul."

In retrospect, one could say that all of the conditions that surrounded the death of Paul VI were the symptoms of slow arsenic poisoning. Actually, they were *precisely* the symptoms of slow arsenic poisoning - from the naps to the swollen hands and feet to the obnoxious odor his body gave off which delayed its viewing at St. Peter's for a day. Of course, in Paul's case there was no reason at the time to suspect foul play. So no tests of any kind were ever performed to detect any foreign substance in the Pope's body either when he was alive or after he was dead. And as I have said before if arsenic and not some other toxin had been involved, it would still be present in the Pope's body today. Arsenic, being an element, does not break down in time. It remains permanently in the hair and fingernails of a corpse.

to die like a cat or a dog,

Popes are not normally hospitalized. This is the privilege of wealth and royalty in Europe where the hospital packs up its bags and comes to them. And this was true of the time that Paul had had his prostrate surgery a decade earlier, when one of the rooms in the papal apartment was converted into a makeshift operating theater of some sort. At the very least, in cases of serious illness, an intensive care mobile unit is usually summoned from a hospital in Rome. For some unknown reason Paul's attending physician Fontana never called for a unit. Not even after he had suffered the heart attack with which he lingered for almost a day. This, despite the fact that, when the news of the heart attack reached Rome, an intensive care unit was offered by a hospital that was less than ten minutes away. Actually, except for a single consultation with an urologist in Rome, Dr. Fontana made no attempt at all to seek outside help although the Pope was critically ill. In fact, no notice of his illness was released to the press or for that matter to the *College of Cardinals* or even to his family until after he had suffered the presumed heart attack on the final day of his life.

Several members of the medical profession greatly criticized this inaction. Specifically, they questioned why the Pope was not returned to the safety of the Vatican once it was known that he was seriously ill for the Vatican clinic, itself, had the necessary equipment and personnel to have saved his life. When a member of the press questioned the Pope's doctor on why this was not done, he responded that the heart attack was sudden and unexpected and by that time it was obvious that the Pope was dying, that until the final day, although very tired, the Pope had not shown any signs of serious illness and there was no reason to take such action.

Unbeknown to him, however, another member of the press was interviewing another witness at the very same time. The mother nun who ran the papal residence at Castel Gandolfo who had told a second reporter "*that the Pope had been bedridden for the past two weeks suffering from a high fever and had been slipping in and out of a coma since Tuesday night*" which was five days prior to the presumed heart attack.

A second nun related that she had been with the Pope when the heart attack occurred, "*He had eaten both his lunch and dinner the night before and cereal and juice that morning and it seemed that he was getting better. Then, just before noon when Cardinal Confalonieri began to say mass by his bedside Paul interrupted him and completed the service himself. We were delighted that he was finally getting better. That he was finally getting something into him and that his illness was over.*

"*In the early afternoon in the kitchen we loaded his soup with lentils and other vegetables and when I brought it to him he gobbled it up like he had been starving to death. He then ate half of his meatloaf and picked up the bowl of butternut pudding. He was halfway through the pudding when he suddenly dropped the bowl onto the sheets and started choking and gasping for breath. At first I thought that it was just that he had been eating too quickly. But then I realized that what I was witnessing were convulsions of some sort and I ran out of the room and down the hallway and fetched Doctor Fontana and he examined Paul and told us that it was just a matter of time now. From that time on Paul gasped for breath as if each one was his last. His chest began rising and falling as much as seven or eight inches with every gasp. With each successive breath growing quieter and less pronounced until the end finally came later that night.*"*

The press asked her if the Pope had experienced any pain and she told them that he did not complain of any and that his expression did not seem to reflect that he was in any pain. "*It was just that he couldn't breathe. He was unable to breathe. He was gasping for breath.*"

It was this nun's comments that led the mass of the medical profession to believe that Doctor Fontana had misdiagnosed the Pope's condition; severe respiratory failure without any acute pain is very definitely not symptomatic of a pulmonary condition or heart attack. The criticism was quite widespread and severe as any common physician would have known this, much less a pope's physician. As a matter if fact, most laymen would have known it.

Also, that the presumed attack had occurred at about one-thirty in the afternoon when the Pope was alone with the nun, raised some eyebrows. The official Vatican release had stated that the attack had occurred while the Pope was saying mass at five-thirty in the afternoon. Later the Vatican, realizing that it was common knowledge that Paul always said mass before noon, did correct its original statement but the newspapers kept to the first rendition. Actually, the Vatican had a motive for this discrepancy in time, as the closer the presumed heart attack occurred to the time of the Pope's death at nine-thirty provided a better excuse as to why an intensive care unit had not been called.

And then there was the nun who had the scullery duty of emptying the Pope's bedpan, who told a third reporter that "*there had been nothing*

* *Rinascita 19 Aug 78*

but blood in the pan for a week," -again, evidence of a very serious illness which had nothing to do with a heart attack. A bloody discharge from the bladder is the most telltale evidence of the final stages of arsenic poisoning.

To make matters worse, an urologist in Rome confirmed the nun's story telling still another reporter that he had been consulted by the Pope's physician earlier in the week concerning a bladder infection.* Worst of all, there was the fact that on Wednesday the papal audience scheduled in the audience hall for Saturday, which was the day before he died, had been cancelled. The reason for the cancellation was simply that the Pope was tired. It was the first time in the fifteen years of his pontificate that a papal audience had been cancelled. It was quite obvious that the Pope was ailing for some time before his 'sudden and unexpected death.' When all of these conflicting testimonies were released the next day, the press made heyday of them. Editorials in Italian, French and even American newspapers followed criticizing this inaction on the part of the Pope's attending physician but neither the doctor nor the Vatican ever responded to the criticism.

The four nuns were removed from the Castel Gandolfo the very next day and nothing was ever heard of them again. The Vatican told reporters that they had been reassigned elsewhere in Europe and refused to tell the press where they were. Its explanation of its action was that the sisters were extremely distraught by the Pope's death and needed a rest.

The president of the Italian Medical Society, Dr. Sebastiano Caffaro, was particularly harsh. "*It is unbelievable*", he said in his statement to the press, "*that a pope could be left to die without the care that one would afford a cat or a dog.*"[1]

Dr. Christian Barnard, the noted South African heart specialist, referring to Doctor Fontana's failure to call for an intensive care unit added his own comment, "*If that had happened in any other country in the world the doctor would have been tried for criminal neglect.*" [2] And he was right, for even under Italian law the doctor would have found himself in court.

When the Montini family was repeatedly pestered as to why they were not kept informed of the Pope's deteriorating condition, it issued an official statement to the press, "*Whereas some errors in judgment may have been made in connection with Paul's illness, we take no issue with the will of God.*" [3]

**IL Messaggero 19 Aug '78 (this comment also reported in the world press.*

[1] *Il Messaggero 20 Aug '78*

[2] *Cape Times 22 Aug '78*

Because of a peculiar pungent odor, which emanated from his body, he lay in state for the first day at the Castel Gandolfo. Despite the fact that mourners were kept at a distance it was quite obvious to them that a strong odor was emanating from the body. After a second embalming he smelled like a flower and he was moved to St. Peter's where he lay in state for three additional days.

When the embalmers were questioned as to why the odor had been so pungent on the first day and had changed to that of a rose garden on the second day they told the press that in order to save time they had been told not to drain the body of blood and remove certain internal organs which are normally removed in an embalming. In order to prepare the Pope for the second showing they had injected the body with perfume. Failure to remove the blood and organs is suggestive of cover up of arsenic poisoning as this was a practice often followed by the Mafia as to leave neither blood nor tissue available to assay for the presence of poisoning.

Over five hundred thousand mourners walked past the catafalque on which his body was displayed. Aldo Moro's wife Eleanora and her four children Anna, Agnese, Maria and Giovanni were not among them. They had chosen to abandon him in death as they had in life. To the great consternation of those who would officiate at his funeral he was interred in a plain wooden box of the kind reserved for paupers. Made of cypress it was a step-up from the pine box that would house the remains of his successor, John Paul I.

Two days before leaving for Castel Gandolfo, Paul had given a note to one of the Vatican staff that this was his wish. He had picked up the idea on one of his visits to Vittorio Veneto ten years earlier. It was as if knowing that he was about to die he wanted to make fools of the *Curia*, the hyenas, as they stood there surrounding the wooden box in their rich and elegant attire of crimson and of gold and of silk and of satin and of velvet, and rings of rubies and gold, as if, in the end, he would have the last laugh.

Pope Paul VI was the second pope in five hundred years to die outside the walls of the Vatican. Pius XII also died at Castel Gandolfo but he was moved there only after his condition was diagnosed as terminal and he was moved there together with the intensive care unit, which had been caring for him while he was in the Vatican.

On the night Paul VI died, there were eighteen people in the papal residence at Castel Gandolfo, this despite the fact that in a stretch it could house one hundred and eighty. It is customary for one to find several

[3] *Leggo 28 Aug '78*

cardinals in residence in the castle as many European cardinals vacation there. This was one of the strangest happenstances surrounding his death, that other than those who were gathered about his bedside, there were no other cardinals in retreat at the Castel Gandolfo that week. Particularly strange, since it was midsummer.

There was only Bishop Guiseppe Caprio and four of the five that had shared his last ride with him, four nuns who cared for the papal residence at the retreat, Emilio Bonomelli, the aging Castel director, and six monks, two who worked inside the residence and four who cared for the gardens. And then there was Doctor Fontana and his assistant Buzzanetti. Except for a single portable oxygen tank, there was no medical equipment at all other than that which Fontana had carried in his bag.

Of course, there were the dozen or so Swiss guards. Two standing frozen at attention at the main gate, two more frozen at the front door and four others stationed motionless in the turrets that shot out of towering walls that hemmed in the Castel Gandolfo. And then there was the ceremonial guard that stood just outside the door of the papal apartment. And yes, there were a few others who were sound asleep in what most people would call a carriage house.

Pope Paul had reigned in the shadow of his predecessor John XXIII. Had it not been for this he would be recognized today as being the greatest Pope of modern civilization for it was he, not John, who had made *Vatican II* a reality, who had brought John's reforms to fruition. Had it not been for the *Vatican Curia* that surrounded him, he would have been the greatest Pope in history. He died feeling that he had failed, a broken man. And this is attested to by the very last statement he gave to the press just a week before his final journey, "*my weakness for life has resulted in poor leadership for my flock*." His only hope was that his successor would do what he had been unable to do for fifteen years. He hoped that his successor would be able to break himself free of the *Curial* chains that would be placed upon him when he donned the white cloak of the papacy in the conclave.

Although it was never an issue with the faithful or for that matter with the press, I have always felt suspicious of Paul's death. Much more so than I was suspicious of John Paul's death which had raised such public concern. Yes, the motive was certainly there in both cases. But it was much more strongly there in Paul's case than in John Paul's case. Yes, although it was not reported to the public that he was ill at the time, it was no surprise to the public that Paul had died, as he was eighty and aging. The focus was mainly on John Paul's death because he was relatively young and appeared to be in vibrant health at the time of his sudden death, and the Vatican had been caught in many lies concerning the circumstances surrounding his passing. But the likelihood of foul play is definitely much more certain in Paul's than in John Paul's case, this strange set of circumstances that caused three men to sleep in the great bed in the papal apartment in the fall of nineteen hundred and seventy eight.

the birth and rise of democracy in the Roman Catholic Church

In the two years before his death there had been a dramatic change in the way Paul VI went about his appointment of cardinals. Since the *College of Cardinals* had been formed in the eleventh century the traditionally approved number of cardinals had remained at seventy. When John XXIII was elected in 1958 only fifty three cardinals were in the voting conclave. Twenty one of these were members of the *Vatican Curia* which represented the largest unbroken block of votes, an ultraconservative block of votes without which a candidate could not be elected Pope. John successfully garnered these votes and he did this only in that he had been all of his years a stanch conservative.

Of the fifty three cardinals at the time of John's election, only two or three were known to have even so much as talked about any of the issues on the other side of the aisle. For the first six months following his election John's rule was one of strict conservatism. Then in the spring of 1959 he returned to Rome from one his visits to Vittorio Veneto and did a strange and confusing thing. He raised the authorized number of cardinals to seventy-five and in making his proclamation he made it clear that he would not be limited to this. He was true to his word, as five years later when he died there were eighty-seven cardinals. Nevertheless the authorized number of cardinals remained at seventy-five.

John's objective, which was in fact Luciani's influence, was to bring about a balance of power in the Church. That is, he felt that the Church could only be managed in changing times by having a more or less equal representation of those from the *right* and those from the *left* in its management. As he was almost eighty when elected he knew that he had only two alternatives of action that could successfully accomplish this goal during his pontificate. He could refuse to reconfirm the appointments of some of the existing conservative cardinals and replace them with progressive candidates or he could raise the number of authorized cardinals and fill the vacancies with progressive candidates in order to bring about a reasonable balance of the parties. It should be noted that John's intention was not to annihilate the *right*, for he believed that only a proper balance between the two opposing forces could lead the Church into the third millennium. If the liberals were to gain overwhelming control it would be as damaging as if the conservatives were to have overwhelming control.

Five years later when Paul was elected, the balance was fifty-five conservatives and the other thirty two were known to have some liberal tendencies, at least enough so as to label them liberals. So John had filled most of the vacancies with progressives. Yes, he had appointed a few very conservative cardinals during his time, old cronies who had been friends of his during his conservative days. Unfortunately for Paul, who would succeed him, almost all of these appointments were made within the *Vatican Curia.* The *Curia* remained an unbalanced seat of power.

And what's more, John gave his newly created liberal party a leader when in 1962 he named Leon Joseph Suenens to the *College of Cardinals*. In making the appointment John released the following statement to the press, *"His job is to open the windows and let in the fresh air."** As we shall see in what is yet to come, a gale soon blew through the Roman Catholic Church.

One would ask how a conservative *College of Cardinals* elected Paul, who was a liberal; after all, he brought *Vatican II* to fruition. Catholicism is by its very nature synonymous with conservatism, the norm is to be a conservative and an outspoken liberal is likely to remove himself from the mainstream and therefore damage his ability to accomplish his objectives. Therefore the chances of there being hidden among the conservatives, a certain number of liberals is substantial, whereas the chance of there being a conservative hidden among the liberals is zero. Paul, unlike his predecessor at the time of his election, was already a liberal, but one that for sixty years had wisely lived his ministry as a *lion disguised in sheep's clothing,* so to speak.

For the first thirteen years of the fifteen years of his reign, pressured by the *Curia*, Paul had appointed predominately conservatives. Two years before his death, the ratio of conservatives versus progressives had risen to about eight to one. And what's more, he had increased the number of cardinals assigned to the *Curia* from the twenty-one, who had declined to vote for him when he was elected in 1963, to twenty-five. The *Curia* then represented a block of twenty-five of seventy-five in the voting conclave.

* *L'Osservatore Romano 1 Oct '62*

one hundred and twenty,

Then in 1976, shortly after his meeting with Aldo Moro at the Castel Gandolfo, Paul did a startling thing. It was startling because other than Aldo Moro, he had not sought counsel for it. No cardinal, or for that matter any member of his ranks, had been consulted concerning it. He started to move the *College of Cardinals* toward the *left*.

He raised the authorized number of cardinals to one hundred and twenty. This dealt a paralyzing blow to the *Curia* as now they represented only another block of votes. Now they would be only twenty-five of one hundred and twenty. There was much more than just this to Paul's plans.

A cardinal has only two duties. He is an advisor to the Pope and he has the sacred duty to elect the Pope. Whether the Pope has seventy-five advisors or one hundred advisors or a thousand advisors is immaterial. Then there is the fact that there are many bishops and priests and others who are closer advisors to the Pope than are many of the cardinals. The only unique duty of a cardinal is his role in electing a Pope. The only logic behind increasing the authorized number of cardinals in Paul's case was exactly what it had been in John's case, to achieve a kind of a reasonable balance between the 'parties' or to possibly to give the minority 'party' the edge.

During the period between the time of his decree that had increased the number of vacancies and the time of his death, Paul appointed thirty-eight cardinals, most of them liberals and the others, -Bernardin Gantin and Hyacinthe Thiandoum of Africa, Paulo Evaristo Arns and Aloisio Lorscheider of Brazil, Eduardo Pironio of Argentina, Jaime Sin of the Philippines, although conservatives, opposed his decree of *Humanae Vitae.* Actually, eighteen of them were appointed on a single day, and although Paul had reviewed the list of eighteen conservatives submitted by Benelli and Confalonieri, he appointed eighteen others, all liberals.

Benelli, as undersecretary of state, had risen as the informal leader of the *Curia* after Paul had brought Jean Villot into the secretary of state position midway in his reign, when the conservative that he had inherited from John XXIII died. The *Curia* cardinals refused to accept the liberal Frenchman as their leader. Shortly after appointing the consistory of liberal cardinals, Paul moved Benelli to Florence as archbishop there in order to remove his influence from the Vatican and thereby weaken the *Curia.*

It was becoming more and more evident with each appointment that Paul VI was trying to tilt the election of his successor in the direction of his and John XXIII reforms and directly against his enemies in the *Curia*, who until then had held him in its grasp, who until then had controlled his every move. Still, the conservatives continued to hold a decisive majority in the *College of Cardinals.* Of the roughly ninety cardinals, about seventy remained conservatives and the other twenty or so were liberals. With his time obviously running out, one could ask why Paul had probably risked his life to appoint a few more liberals, when he knew the college would remain overwhelmingly conservative. And the answer is that he knew something then that became obvious to the world after Luciani was elected, something he had done a few years earlier midway in his pontificate.

a stroke of genius,

The major ecclesiastical issue of his time was the contraceptive issue. In 1966 he appointed a commission of sixty field cardinals and bishops, -those who represented the congregations outside the Vatican, to study the issue before he would make his proclamation. And if one remembers reading the newspapers at the time, the conclusion of this commission was to issue a proclamation that would have permitted artificial contraception under certain conditions. It would have left the door open to permit *Planned Parenthood* in those cases where it was justified and this is what the press had predicted at the time, -that Paul would make the proclamation along these lines. After all, he himself was a liberal.

But the press was in for a surprise. For instead Paul issued an absolute ban on contraception with no exceptions permitted - the doctrine of *Humanae Vitae.* Most surmised that it had to have been the pressure from the *Curia* with whom he shared the Vatican that caused him to do such a thing for it was quite obvious that such a thing contradicted his own ecclesiastical convictions.

It was this action more than any other that caused the populace to believe that it was the *Curia*, and not Paul, who was running the Roman Catholic Church. That Paul was simply a pawn in their hands. This opinion of the populace has persisted even to this day. What I am about to say will forever make clear that it was in fact Paul who ran the Church during his pontificate, not the *Curia;* Paul, issued his ultraconservative proclamation for quite another reason.

Paul knew that when he died, because of the great imbalance in the *College of Cardinals,* that a conservative, most likely an ultraconservative, would replace him. He knew this because he knew that there was not enough time remaining in his papacy to bring about a balance of the parties. He was aging and had just a few years left. Yes, he could make some changes, but he knew that he could never convert the eight-to-one ratio that existed at the time into an even balance of the two sides. And he knew that if a conservative were to replace him it would bring an end to all that he and John had worked for.

So in a stroke of genius Paul, the liberal, issued an ultraconservative ruling on the most important issue of his reign, perhaps the most important issue of the century, *Humanae Vitae*. And the reason he issued this firm policy was to bring about a better balance of the two parties in the *College of Cardinals*. He created a 'third party', those in the middle, to whom we will refer as 'moderates' in what is to follow.

One could ask why he appointed a commission made up of the field cardinals to study the issue of contraception and then totally ignore the recommendations of the commission. The answer is that he wanted to be certain that his strategy to form a 'third party' was sound. He wanted to know exactly where each one of the cardinals stood on the issue, so there would be enough conservative cardinals in the field who would feel so strongly about a restricted policy on contraception that they would vote for a liberal who promised to repeal it.

And he got his answer when the committee voted overwhelmingly to give him a recommendation to issue a lenient policy. And Paul, knowing who had voted for a lenient policy and who had not, knew then that if he were to issue a strict policy banning contraception, he would move about a third of the college to the center aisle, and what's more he knew that they would come from the conservative ranks.

So it was Paul VI who so wisely created the block of the votes in the *middle;* cardinals who, although conservatives in every other way, sought relief from *Humanae Vitae*. Paul knew at the time that his very conservative proclamation on this doctrine would shift at least a third of the votes from the conservative side to the center aisle. Although the move by itself would not bring about an even balance in the college, together with other things we have talked of above and will talk of in what follows made possible the election of Albino Luciani in August of nineteen hundred and seventy-eight.

In retrospect it is quite clear that Paul had chosen the little known Bishop of Vittorio Veneto to be his successor way back in 1967. And furthermore, that Albino Luciani himself, had been a part of the strategy that would one day raise him to the papacy. When Paul visited Vittorio Veneto the week before he made the proclamation he locked up the moderate vote for Luciani, those conservatives who would vote for that cardinal most certain to repeal it, by instructing Luciani to issue his now famous editorial calling for repeal of the doctrine. In 1978, when Paul died and the press issued a listing of the leading candidates without Luciani's name, it was totally unaware that when the election began he already had the third of the votes that lie in the middle in his hip pocket.

We know today that this was precisely Paul's strategy. It would make no sense for him to have appointed a committee that rendered an overwhelming opinion that called for a flexible policy and for him to completely ignore its recommendation and issue a firm and steadfast proclamation. For after all, he already knew where he stood on the issue, he certainly didn't need any advice. He had created the commission solely to enable him to determine who among them would be strong objectors to a locked-in policy. He had to be certain that if he were to issue a policy in conflict with his own ecclesiastical beliefs that his action would create a 'third party'. And that is precisely what happened. The great irony of his action was that Paul knew that the *Curia* would not learn of his intention until after he was dead.

the final piece of the puzzle,

Now, getting back to the two years before his death. Shortly after raising the authorized number of cardinals to one hundred and twenty, Paul started to internationalize the *Curia.* He appointed two non-Italian cardinals to head important committees within the *Curia*, -Willebrands of the Netherlands as *Secretary of Christian Unity* and Bernardin Gantin of Africa as *Secretary of Peace and Justice*.

Actually, this was an attempt to liberalize the *Curia* for these were two of the most liberal cardinals in the Church. Willebrands was one of the most outspoken supporters of Cardinal Suenens in his efforts to abolish celibacy as a necessary condition for the priesthood and Gantin, though listed among the conservatives, was the strongest supporter of Suenens and Luciani in their efforts to reverse *Humanae Vitae,* the Church's proclamation banning the use of contraceptives. Being from Africa he was a day to day observer of what overpopulation can bring and his position was made clear in a letter to Paul VI, "*I pray for a day when all children are brought into a world of good health and happiness and opportunity. But, one must face reality that today we bring many children into a living hell. That we wrongly assume the position of judgment that is reserved for Christ when, on the final day, He will sit on the great white throne, above.*"

But these foreign cardinals remained simply figureheads; as Benelli and Siri clearly retained their grasp on the Vatican, as the remaining members of the *Curia* remained very much their pawns.

That Paul died in August, just weeks before three cardinals were to retire, and two others were terminally ill, and that he intended to name nine others to bring the total number of voting cardinals to one hundred and twenty, has always bothered me. For these appointments would have edged the papal vote clearly into the liberal column, which would have guaranteed that his successor would be a liberal. That he died on the very eve of what would have been the culmination of his political objectives certainly was too much of a coincidence for me to swallow.

Also, just a week before the Moro kidnapping, Paul had overruled the *Curia's* stern objections, and had permitted Cardinal Suenens to speak to the *College of Cardinals* concerning the possibility of marriage within the priesthood. Suenens was also able to voice his opinion that the authority to grant dispensations in the case of marriage should be granted to diocese bishops. This would be the equivalent of the Church accepting the reality of divorce and remarriage. And at this same session he called for a reexamination of the Church's policy concerning contraception, stating that the Church's policy on contraception, sooner or later, would be repealed. Concerning this particular issue Suenens' contention was leaked to the New York Times, "*if the Church delays until that time at which it is forced to reverse its decision it would have another Galileo case on its hands.*"

It was also at this very same session that Cardinal Suenens expressed the possibility that the election of the papacy be transferred to the *Worldwide Conference of Bishops* to better reflect pastoral influence rather than remain the responsibility of the *College of Cardinals* which functioned only as an advisory council to the Pope. This, of course, would have been devastating to the *Curia*, as the closer one gets to the congregation the more liberal is the thinking.

At the same meeting, Paul permitted Cardinal Luciani to present his opinions concerning homosexuality. Luciani supported the growing contention of the psychiatric and medical communities that chronic homosexuality was one's birthright. He argued "*that the Bible's condemnation of heterosexual acts was overwhelming in comparison to its very slight and quite ambiguous condemnation of homosexual acts, and whereas one might continue to consider homosexual acts, like any sexual acts, to be morally wrong, it might be pastorally correct to encourage homosexuals to enter into sustained long term loving relationships with one another, possibly with an aim to provide guardianship for homeless children who might otherwise be aborted. The homosexual community provides society with the only significant willing population that could adequately care for unwanted children, those who suffer from mental and physical impairment.*"

For Paul to permit Suenens, who was considered a radical by the Vatican and Luciani who just a few years earlier had spoken out publicly against his own proclamation banning birth control practices, to bring their revolutionary and evil ideas directly into the sacred halls of the Vatican, was most likely too much for the *Curia* to take. That Paul had forbidden the very same issues to be discussed at the first *Synod of Bishops* just a decade earlier, and that he now allowed them to be discussed among his cardinals is representative of the dramatic change in how he was going about his business. Also, of the one hundred cardinals that he did appoint during his pontificate, the first sixty-three were locked-in conservatives and the last thirty-seven were made up of thirty outspoken liberals and the other seven were strong opponents of his doctrine of *Humanae Vitae*.

Cardinal Luciani was also permitted to present his position on the possibility of admitting women into the ministry. He told his captive audience, "*In the short range, we should with no further delay adopt* (Archbishop) *Jadot's proposal that altar girls be permitted to serve in liturgical functions.*" He added his own recommendation "*And that, in the longer run, Mother Church must permit women to hold the Eucharist.*" The very thought of such a happening horrified the members of the *Curia* to the point that the Vatican chambers, if only for a moment or two, echoed the sounds of the House of Commons in which objectors shout at the very tops of their voices. No! No! No!

Archbishop Jadot had been the force behind much of the Church's liturgical changes in the nineteen sixties, including having the priest face the congregation during mass and having it said in modern languages. These actions on the part of Jadot had so enraged the *Curia* that they brought upon him great character assassination, which resulted in his eventual exile and obscurity. As a result, he was the only apostolic delegate to the United States never to be named a cardinal.

But what these two cardinals, Suenens and Luciani, were proposing were far more perilous measures. It was they who had led this thing called the sexual revolution in the Church. But, until then, they had been confined to the field. It was Paul, who so blatantly allowed them to bring their views into the Vatican. It was Paul who was becoming more and more dangerous each day to the *Curia*, for he, unlike the others, was Pope and the *Curia* knew that if he were to live until the end of the year and fill the existing vacancies with liberals his successor would also be a liberal, possibly an ultraliberal. Perhaps even Cardinal Suenens himself, and if that were to happen it would end in their own demise.

With one exception Paul never publicly approved of any of these proposals, but that one exception took the *College of Cardinals* one final step to the *left* and made possible, just a few months later, the election of Albino Luciani as it, in a single swoop, removed eighteen *right wing*, very conservative cardinals, including Cardinal Carlo Confalonieri, the dean of the *College of Cardinals*, and one of its most influential members, from the voting conclave. The conclave makes up that group of cardinals who elect popes.

Although Cardinal Suenens had lost his battle to move the papal election to the *Conference of Bishops,* he did succeed in convincing Paul that those cardinals over eighty should be excluded from the voting conclave. Aging cardinals tend to lose their touch with the world, are too set in their thinking and should not be allowed to vote. At the time, it was thought that Paul had made the ruling as a negotiation of some sort, that he would make the *Curia* and those on the *right* content by denying the move of the papal vote to the bishop level, and yet, on the other hand, give something to Suenens and Luciani and those on the *left*.

But, in retrospect, this made no sense as Paul, himself, was eighty. To exclude those over eighty from the voting process he would be admitting that he, too, had lost touch with the world. Paul was in fact moving the election of his own successor further to the *left* as all eighteen cardinals who were over eighty at the time, -who just three months later would be excluded from the vote, were conservatives including four members of the *Vatican Curia.* This reduced the *Curia* voting strength in the conclave to only twenty-one of one hundred and twenty votes. At the same time he raised the authorized number of cardinals to one hundred and thirty-eight in order to hold the voting conclave at one hundred and twenty, and to create eighteen voting vacancies, nine of which had, in rapid consecutive order, been filled by liberals by the time of his death. Had Paul not made this ruling, to exclude those over eighty from the voting conclave, his successor would not have been Albino Luciani.

The evolution of democracy in the Church and its return to chaos

College of Cardinals

	liberals	moderates	conservatives
'58 John was elected			53
'63 Paul is elected	32		55
'72 *Curia* influence	11		79
'73 consistory (+18)	22		72
'75 college raised to 120 (+45)	39		78
'78 exclude over age eighty (-18)	38		60
'78 other appointments	47		64
Humane Vitae '68 (Vittorio Veneto)	47*	28*	36
2004	3	7	191

** the 75 of the 111 votes that elected Luciani. At the time of Paul's death there were nine vacancies that he was about to fill. Attrition accounts for discrepancies between numbers*

The *Vatican Curia* sensed this. As a matter of fact, they were infuriated. They and the *Curia* knew that if Paul were to continue in power the survival of the Church was in great danger, particularly if he were to live to appoint the remaining vacancies in the *College of Cardinals.* Of course, what they were not aware of was that they would not only be dealing with liberals in the upcoming election, they would also be dealing with some among their own ranks who Paul had so cleverly ten years before created as *moderates*; he knew that the *Curia* would not learn of his action until after Luciani had won the election.

At the conclusion of the meeting Cardinal Suenens, referring to the restrictions imposed by Rome just a decade earlier which forbade discussion of these same kinds of matters in the first *Synod of Bishops*, mentioned "*that it was sad that it should have taken so many years for Mother Church to have listened to reason.*" Although he had lost most of his case, he expressed his deep appreciation to Paul in having granted both he and Cardinal Luciani the opportunity to be heard and in his closing remarks he referred to Paul "*as the lioness who courageously stood her ground to protect her cubs and fought to the death when the hyena pack came!*" Although he gave them not so much as a glance, every member of the *Curia* present knew exactly who he was referring to as the "*hyena pack.*"

The great irony here is that Paul may have indeed, fought to the death. For the hyena is a born killer.

the carnage,

That two popes, John Paul I, who had been the first bishop appointed by John XXIII, and Paul VI, who had been the first cardinal appointed by John XXIII, neither of whom had a history of heart disease, died within a month of each other, certainly would be of unusual circumstance and coincidence. That they both started to take naps which were not their custom in the period immediately preceding their deaths could be just coincidence. That they both had some swelling of the hands and feet that had been diagnosed as the onset of arthritis could also be coincidence. That they both died of heart failure is reasonable, as there are many toxins that precipitate cardiac arrest. But, that they both died of heart attacks due to natural causes, when neither had a history of heart disease, defies the imagination. But I have no evidence to support the supposition that there was, indeed, foul play in either death; just these things which I have pointed out in the forgoing which are entirely a matter of public record.

And then there is the remarkable coincidence that the co-chairmen of the progressive movement in Italy, Aldo Moro outside the Church, and Paul within the Church, also died within a couple of months of each other. There was the extraordinary circumstance that they both, at the very same time just two years earlier, had made a complete about-face in the way they were going about their business. They both died on the very eve of the attainment of their political objectives, one of outright murder and the other of unexplained mysterious circumstances. Had either survived, or had Paul's successor John Paul I survived, the progressive movement would go on within both Italy and the Church and throughout the world. The loss of the three of them at the very same time had brought the movement to a screeching halt.

Then there was one more coincidence. Just a few months after the deaths of Paul VI and John Paul, Cardinal Villot, Paul's longtime friend and close confidant, who had served him as his secretary of state, also died. What is most remarkable is that he died under almost identical circumstances as had Paul - for a few weeks before his death he too, jaundiced and skin flaking, was loaded into a black Mercedes limousine at the rear gates of the Vatican. He too, had developed swollen hands and feet that had been diagnosed to be the onset of arthritis. He too, was taken for his last ride to Castel Gandolfo. He too, was popping cough drops. He too, was to suffer a sudden "heart attack," when he had no history at all of heart disease. And again, at his bedside were Caprio, Confalonieri, Macchi and Magee. But, unlike Paul, he did not die at Castel Gandolfo.

It was his brother who showed up unexpectedly at the Castel Gandolfo, and realizing that Villot was seriously ill ordered him moved to a Rome hospital, after which stay he was returned to his Vatican apartment. Although the hospital cleared up a serious bladder infection and had released him, a few days later his blood pressure suddenly dropped and similar to Paul, he went into severe respiratory failure. Like Paul he lingered for a few hours and died on March 9, 1979 with his brother and sister and Bishop Caprio at his bedside. At the time of his death John Paul II was napping on the floor above in the papal palace.

And again there was the opening of the door and the murmuring of prayers in the hall just outside. A nun stood there and addressed Bishop Caprio. She pointed to the bedside phone. "It is Bishop Casaroli." And, again, the bishop picked up the phone and told the caller, "Yes, Paul died under the same star as our Savior had been born. He is with Him now. God rest his soul. Christ will understand the duty of His generals."

As in John Paul's case it was Dr. Buzzanetti who pronounced him dead. It was also Dr. Buzzanetti who signed the death certificate, *"death due to myocardial infarction,"* this despite the fact that the hospital had treated him for a severe bladder infection, which had nothing to do with a heart condition. One might recall that in the case of Pope Paul, the doctor had made a single consultation and that consultation had been with an urologist in Rome. This together with the testimony of the nun that "*there had been nothing but blood in the pan,*" confirmed the fact that Paul had also suffered a severe bladder infection, the most telltale evidence of the final stage of slow arsenic poisoning in a living person. And again, as in the case of the two popes there was an immediate embalming without the conventional draining of blood or removal of organs, the most telltale evidence of cover up of arsenic poisoning.

So altogether we have three primates of the Church, Paul VI, John Paul I and Jean Villot who today rest in their tombs with their blood supply and all of their internal organs. This we know is an absolute fact, which in turn gives us the supposition that all three corpses retain traces of arsenic in their fingernails and hair today.

a little more about Jean Villot,

When one considers foul play in the case of the coincidental death of Jean Villot one must consider the role he had played in the confusing circumstances surrounding John Paul's death. For it was he, as the interim Pope, who had released the official statement to the press that claimed that the Pope had died before midnight; and that the Pope had been found dead by his secretary John Magee at six thirty in the morning; and that he held the *Imitation of Christ* in his hands. Whereas, in fact, the Pope had undoubtedly died at about four o'clock in the morning and a nun had found him at four thirty and he held notes in his hands that he had written on the stationary of Vittorio Veneto. That Villot had performed the last rites over the body, something that he would have never done had the body been dead for six hours, confirms the fact that he lied concerning the time of death as explicitly stated n the Vatican release.

It was Villot who knew that John Paul had been dead for less than an hour who had released the statement that he had died before midnight. And it had also been Villot who ordered an immediate embalming of the corpse with instruction not to disturb the internal organs or blood supply most likely because he had experienced the same pungent odor coming from the Pope's body as he had just the month before experienced as coming from the corpse of Paul VI. We know that he lied about the time of death in order to place considerable time between the Pope's death and the embalming, so as not to arouse suspicions of arsenic poisoning. And we also know he specifically included in the Vatican release the conflicting *fact* that he had performed the last rites.

That he knew that there had been foul play in the Pope's death is quite obvious. But he may or may not have known who was responsible. He probably knew that if he were to formally investigate the Pope's death as to seek out the killer or killers that he might not live to tell about it.

And the reason I say this is that Jean Villot was one of the most brilliant men in the Church. It makes no sense that he would have issued such a conflicting report of the Pope's death; in all six out of six mistakes in a relatively short press release is not characteristic of a brilliant man. It is quite obvious that he made all these 'mistakes' intentionally. He knew the press would interview those witnesses of John Paul's death just as they had interviewed those witnesses of Paul's death a month earlier. He knew that the embalmers would tell the press that the blood and internal organs had not been removed and this would arouse suspicions as no trace of blood or tissue would be available for analysis after interment. He also knew that the resulting testimony would be in conflict with the press release, which in turn would ignite rumors of foul play in the Pope's death and hopefully start an investigation, as he knew if he were to call for an investigation on his own he most likely would not live to tell of it. And one can see that this was precisely his intention if one focuses on only two of the statements contained in the official release, -that the Pope had died before midnight and that Villot had performed the last rites.

If Villot had not created all of the confusion that surrounded John Paul's death there would have been no investigation by reporters at the time and all of the books investigating the Pope's death that have been written since, including this one, would have never been written. And I am certain that the killer(s) sensed this, especially when Villot continued to rile up the press. He issued a corrective statement about the Pope's death that was even more confusing than had been the original release that in turn had given the press even more reason to investigate the Pope's death. He placed Magee and the mother nun on sabbatical to remove their access from the press knowing that it would drive the press to expand its investigation. Why remove the only witnesses of the Pope's death if the Vatican had nothing to hide?

And, of course, that he had intentionally lied about the time of death and ordered an immediate embalming and specifically told the embalmers not to drain blood or remove any organs, put him in great danger. For this told the killer or killers quite clearly that Villot knew that the Pope, like Paul before him, had been murdered. As a matter of fact, they would have realized that Villot was intentionally riling up the press and this told them that Villot was very dangerous to them.

Whether or not Villot conducted an internal investigation and discovered who had been responsible for the Pope's death is unknown. All that we know is that he too, may have been murdered. Whether it was because he had become dangerous to the killer(s) or that someone wanted to open up the secretary of state position that he held one, will never know; all one knows is that he was murdered

My predecessors, those authors who investigated the Pope's death, all agreed that Villot was responsible for most of the confusion following John Paul's death that sparked the many rumors of foul play. And their conclusions as to why Villot acted as he did have been unanimous. They have all agreed that Villot; having been the first on the scene, realized that foul play had been involved in John Paul's death and acted to protect *Mother Church* and that he ordered the immediate embalming to cover up what he perceived to be signs of poisoning. He had been at the bedside of Paul VI shortly after he had died, so he knew precisely what the symptoms were.

The peculiar odor that a body gives off if poisoned with arsenic is a distinctly unique one. It is not the obnoxious odor that one will experience, for example, if a body releases its bowels upon death, but quite a different one. It is as different from the latter as is the pungent smell of gasoline as compared to that of a cake baking in the oven. So when Paul stood over the bed he would have known precisely what had transpired and one must remember that Magee had also been at Paul's bedside so he too would have known precisely what he was dealing with, which explains why he notified the embalmers to get ready on his own at five o'clock in the morning, yet held up for Villot's okay before he notified the motor pool to send a car.

Yet, we know Villot would not have ordered an embalming at five o'clock in the morning even if he knew that arsenic poisoning had been involved, for he would have known that in doing so it would cause unnecessary rumors - as it was widely known in Italy that immediate embalming of the body was a cover up for arsenic poisoning. It is most likely that he instructed Magee to send for a car for the embalmers so early in the morning in order to start the rumor of arsenic poisoning. For if he had suspected arsenic poisoning and he wanted to protect *Mother Church,* he would have sealed the room and called the embalmers at a more reasonable time - say eight o'clock in the morning, which would have prevented the rumor.

So it is a reasonable to conclude that the corpse of John Paul I was emitting the peculiar odor symptomatic of arsenic poisoning when

Villot first stood over the bed, and that Villot knew that the Pope had been poisoned, not necessarily the immediate cause of death, but he knew that he had been poisoned. And we also know that he wanted the public to know about it, at the very least strong suppositions.

But these suppositions turn into fact when one considers the papers, the fact that Villot personally retrieved the papers that John Paul had held in his hands from the embalmers. And we also know that Villot, as the interim Pope, destroyed them and that their content has never been released to the public. Content which, if made public at the time, would have brought an end to the most prolific and persisting rumor that John Paul had held in his hands lists of cardinals that were to be replaced. That is, had their content been released to the public, it would have cleared up the rumors once and for all and the case would have been closed. Villot knew that they were notes written while the Pope had been Bishop of Vittorio Veneto just as the embalmers had told reporters. Villot knew that since they were not a roster of cardinals to be replaced, if he were to have released them to the press it would have brought an end to the rumors. That he destroyed them, tells us quite clearly that he wanted the rumors to persist.

One could argue that it was Villot who had killed the Pope. But that he started all the rumors indicates this could not be so. And the track record is also there to say that this could not be so, for Villot had no motive to kill either pope. Paul had made him the first non-Italian secretary of state, and he had remained his closest friend in the Church until his death. And Villot had no ecclesiastical differences with the new Pope that could serve as motive for murder. But common sense tells us that he acted in the way that he did, not to protect *Mother Church*, but to create the rumors that he believed would trigger an investigation into the Pope's death - an investigation that was in fact conducted by just about every reporter in Italy, and which is now being brought to fruition in these pages.

His own mysterious death a short time later suggests that he may have quietly conducted his own investigation into the death of John Paul. Perhaps somewhere along the road he did put it all together. Perhaps he was about to give his report to the new Pope, John Paul II, when he suddenly fell victim to foul play himself. Perhaps he had given his report to the new Pope, which caused him to fall victim to foul play. Or, perhaps, someone just wanted to open up the secretary of state position. No one will ever know.

Cardinal Yu Pin,

Someone we have not talked about is Cardinal Yu Pin, the Archbishop of Taiwan. Yu Pin had a similar role to that of Metropolitan Nicodim in the plan to move Mother Church away from Moses and closer to Christ. Yu Pin would concentrate on the eastern hemisphere; while Nicodim would carry out the plan in the west. Yu Pin had been a close associate of Luciani and had just returned to Taipei from visiting him in Venice, when he learned of Paul's death and had to fly back to Rome for the funeral.

Paul's last official act came the day before he died, August 5, 1978. Realizing that he was dying, in and out of a coma and barely able to speak, Paul elevated Yu Pin to Grand Chancellor, a move that was obviously designed to position him to carry out his charge.

Unfortunately, neither one of these men would live to carry out their missions. For Yu Pin would keel over at the funeral of Paul VI just a few days later. Again, the Vatican cited a heart attack despite the fact that Yu Pin had no history of heart disease. And Nicodim, as we have already said, dropped dead just two weeks later at the feet of John Paul I; also, of a presumed heart attack.

So we have one, two, three, four, five, six men who died within a relatively short span of time, every one of them under mysterious circumstances; all of which shared a common bond in the plan to move civilization away from Moses and closer to Christ. And, as I have said on the cover of this book, this is not fiction, it is absolute fact. Yes, go out onto the Internet and into the libraries and look them up and you will find them there. You will learn that this book is nothing more than a history book.

And then, sadly, there was Jack, my good friend Jack. Unfortunately, you won't be able to look him up. Could he too have been a victim of this happenstance of intrigue that changed not only the direction of life in Italy but the direction of life within the Catholic Church? Indeed, perhaps the direction of life in the entire world?

All we have in his case is that he had been in the process of interviewing members of the *Curia* on John Paul's instruction, and that he happened to have been killed by a hit-and-run driver outside the Vatican walls just two days after the Pope's mysterious death. And yes, we have his body, for I can tell you where he is buried. And I can also show you his notes.

Again, I can only set forth the historical facts. The rest I leave up to you. But for me, all of these things were far too much coincidence, far too much for me to swallow, especially at one time.

So as I have said before, I have said nothing here that has not been said before me, either in the press or in the official writings and biographies of the many players in this strange story of fate. All that is to my credit is that the full record, perhaps for the very first time, has been brought together in one place. I am only hopeful that in bringing these things together, someone else, someone with great analytical abilities, will surface as the *Sherlock Holmes* of the case; will take it a step further and will strike upon the solution to this long unsolved mystery, the strange chain of events which caused three men to sleep in the great bed in the papal apartment in nineteen hundred and seventy eight, the mysterious deaths of Paul VI and John Paul I, and some others.

So I can add nothing more, except perhaps that there was this strange happening that both of the packages I received shortly after Jack's death were not postmarked "*Citta del Vaticano.*" And yes, perhaps one more thing, -that the timing of the mailing of the first package, September 28, 1978, the day prior to John Paul's death, followed by a day, a short notation made the evening before in Jack's calendar, "*These naps? There is something very wrong here?* "

And one last thing, a strange note entered in Jack's notebook on the very next day, October 1, 1978, the day on which Jack was killed, "*The King of the Sahara Desert lay silently under the cover.*"

And I thought of Piccolo upon the great catafalque, lying under the cloth bearing his coat of arms, with the endless lines of those who wished to pay their last respects circling about him. I thought it strange that Jack would refer to his patron as the *King of the Sahara Desert*. This is how I know that it was Piccolo that Jean Villot was referring to when he used the same phrase in his note to me a week later, the note that I had discarded. At the time this reference meant nothing to me, nothing at all, for I had followed Piccolo's travels all through the years, ever since I had met him, and I knew that he had never been to the Sahara Desert.

But perhaps, I thought, he might have been there sometime earlier. Sometime, perhaps many years before I had met him. Or perhaps it was just an affectionate nickname of some sort that his friends had given this man called 'Piccolo' somewhere along the way.

So we have left only one question unanswered. How did John Paul II muster the forty votes in the *middle* in the second conclave of nineteen hundred and seventy eight? And we will answer that question now.

Chapter 9

THE GREAT VATICAN BANK SCANDAL

Immediately upon becoming Pope, John Paul II made Paul Marcinkus an archbishop and promoted him to *President of the Sovereign State of the Vatican* thereby changing his reporting status directly to the papacy.* In that he announced this unprecedented promotion of a man he scarcely knew - the Vatican Bank had no business dealings in Poland - to the highest civil office in the Church on the second day of his administration is powerful evidence that some kind of a *deal* with Marcinkus had been struck before the second conclave got underway. This confirms the fact that Karol Wojtyla knew that he was going to win the election before the second conclave of 1978 began, which moves another one of our *suppositions* into the *fact* column. This meant that the *President of the Vatican Bank* no longer reported to the *Prefecture of Economic Affairs*. From an organizational point of view this made no sense at all as the Pope himself took over the direct responsibility of the Vatican Bank, a financial responsibility.

And now that we have his record before us, one knows that this move was totally uncharacteristic of the new Pope. For today the record tells us that John Paul II has a history of having separated himself from the fiscal management of the Church. The fact that immediately after becoming Pope he personally took over the Vatican Bank is uncharacteristic of him. That he took over direct responsibility for the bank could point to any one or all of several different things.

- He may have wanted to keep quiet the five million dollar shortfall that his predecessor's audit had disclosed that allegedly paid off the Mafia for its rumored role in the Moro murder. This does not mean that he was necessarily involved in the scheme, but just that he may have wanted to protect *Mother Church* and sequester the scandal.

- He may have taken over direct management of the bank to permit him to silently divert funds intended for the poor to other purposes that he considered as being more important at the time: To divert millions to the Solidarity movement in Poland, or perhaps to add the many amenities and improvements to his palaces, things we know as fact today that he did do. The latter would not make much sense as these were visible things. After all, the swimming pool is there for all to see, even today.

* *IL Messaggero 19 Oct 78*

- It is more likely that he wanted to make good on his campaign promises.

In our search for the answer as to how Karol Wojtyla could have possibly gathered the thirty or so *moderate* votes that lie in the *middle,* we had come to the conclusion that he could not possibly have traded off ecclesiastical concessions for them. We know this to be a fact because the contraception doctrine from which those in the middle sought relief has never been repealed, or for that matter, even modified. So this led us to the logical conclusion - the only other way he could have possibly mustered these votes was to have bought them. And we know that he must have bought them, because had he not bought them they would have been cast for that candidate who was most likely to repeal the doctrine of *Humanae Vitae*, just as they had been cast for Luciani the month before. As remarkable as it seems we will prove beyond a shadow of a doubt that John Paul II and his supporters did in fact buy them and they paid a great price for them, in the hundreds of millions of dollars to be exact.

Just why would those in the *middle* sell their votes for cash? First of all, as we have established, those in the *middle* were primarily conservatives that had a problem with a single issue, the contraceptive doctrine. We also noted that they were almost entirely from Latin America, Africa, India and other third world countries that, although as conservatives they believed the doctrine to be philosophically sound, they objected to it because of the mass poverty and starvation and spread of disease that it was generating among their congregations. If they were to be paid hundreds of millions of dollars they could not only eliminate much of the poverty problem but still allow themselves to adhere to a doctrine that they believed to be philosophically sound; they would have their cake and eat it too. Such a deal would have been very attractive to these ranking prelates of the third world countries.

We will prove beyond a shadow of doubt that this is exactly why John Paul II took over direct management of the Vatican Bank. Yes, partially to bring an end to the five million dollar scandal and to cover up the diversion of funds that had been raised for the poor to the Solidarity movement in Poland, but mostly to cover up the transfer of hundreds of millions dollars to these poor countries from unsuspecting investors.

The reader should be aware in these things that are to follow we are not speaking of possibilities or probabilities, but we are speaking of absolute fact, fact that is well documented in the newspapers and magazines of the time.

murder and intrigue,

Roberto Calvi was the president of the Banco Ambrosiano, Italy's largest bank and being the federal bank of Italy, it was the correspondent bank of the Vatican. This means that any funds that would be transferred either into or out of the Vatican into or out of Italy would have to go through this bank; it was a function of the federal bank to control all funds that were transferred between Italy and the Vatican and other countries.

For this reason the five million dollar 'payoff' money, if it had indeed come from the Vatican, had to have been transferred to this bank in order to get it into Italy. Roberto Calvi would have been the only man in the world who knew to which account the money had been credited, and if it had been revealed that it had been the account of a Mafia family, or for that matter even the clandestine organization known as P-2 (the Masons), then Calvi would have been caught up in the middle of the Moro murder.* Calvi would have been tried and put away for life, for he would have been proved to have been an accomplice in the Moro murder. Had Calvi credited five million dollars to a Mafia or P-2 account at the very same time that the kidnappers were demanding a five million dollar ransom for Moro's life, it would be overwhelming incriminating evidence against him. He would have no chance in any court of law. Therefore he was a sitting duck for blackmail.

It is possible that the very same cardinals who were responsible for the death of John Paul had also been responsible for the murder of Aldo Moro. As a matter of fact, if Vatican prelates had been involved, it is the only logical conclusion one can come to, and if they were the same cardinals or bishops who ordered the transfer of the five million dollars they would have known of Calvi's vulnerability.

There is the possibility that it could have been the five million dollar shortfall that had caused the killer(s) to switch from slow arsenic poisoning to a swifter method of murder. We know that the alleged shortfall had been leaked to the press just a couple of days before the Pope's death, and it would stand to reason that John Paul was in the midst of investigating it when he met his end. This has some foundation in that Roberto Calvi had a breakfast appointment on the morning of John Paul's death. It was when Calvi showed up for the appointment that he learned of the Pope's demise.

**some speculate that P-2 (the Masons) and not the Mafia murdered Aldo Moro*

If cardinals had conspired to murder the Pope, as I have said before, they would have had to have assured themselves that another liberal would not take his place. They knew that the balancing vote for the papacy lay in the *middle*, for this had come as a shock to them when they realized that it had been those in the *middle* that had won the papacy for Luciani the month before. Actually, it was because they were not aware of the existence of the *moderate* vote before the first election that they failed to successfully strategize that election and had lost the papacy in the first place.

They also knew that before a conclave begins they are free to discuss whatever they want to discuss with the other cardinals. The *moderates,* as we have defined them, were mostly those cardinals who represented poor countries. So the promise could have been made them that for their votes they would receive hundreds of millions of dollars, and there would be nothing wrong with this as to help annihilate poverty and starvation is a humanitarian thing to do. Those cardinals of the poor countries on the receiving end would have not necessarily been involved in some kind of a conspiracy. And one could say that to a certain extent Luciani had been guilty of this very same kind of strategy the month before, -to buy the votes that lay in the *middle* with cash, as it was nothing short of a known fact that he intended to sell the vast Vatican treasures and these same cardinals of poor countries knew they would have been the benefactors. In fact, they may have already begun to spend the money, which made them easy prey for Karol Wojtyla's proposition a month later. Of course, Luciani offered them a bonus in his promise to repeal *Humane Vitae.*

Let us say Bishop Casaroli had ordered Marcinkus to make the five- million dollar transfer. No one knows this to be a fact, but let us consider the hypothetical case. Of all the prelates in the Vatican, we do know that Casaroli, with the possible exception of Confalonieri, had the closest link to the Mafia. So close that if anyone else in the Vatican had contracted with the Mafia to murder Moro, Casaroli would have had to have known of it. After all, he was a member of the most powerful and influential Mafia family in all of Italy.

We should stop here for a moment to clear up some confusion caused by other books written that implicated the *Great Vatican Bank Scandal* in John Paul's death. The Vatican had for many years dealt with the Banco Ambrosiano, as it was the federal bank of Italy and all funds flowing into and out of Italy had to go through that bank. Most of these dealings flowed through the Banco Ambrosiano to and from the Catholic Bank of Italy which was owned by the Vatican Bank. So throughout the reign of Paul VI there had been ongoing transactions with the Banco

Ambrosiano. Normally, in a given month, these would rarely exceed a million dollars; the Vatican's share of the profits of the Catholic Bank of Italy, which was divided up by the Vatican bishops and cardinals. On an annual basis, a typical Vatican cardinal would receive as much as a hundred thousand dollars, which would almost double his annual income. To get to the point, these transactions had nothing to do with the *Great Vatican Bank Scandal.*

Shortly after Karol Wojtyla rose to power, Roberto Calvi began to raise money from European investors, and one year after the date of the election of John Paul II on October 17, 1979 Roberto Calvi transferred one hundred and thirty-four million dollars to the Vatican Bank. This marked the beginning of the *Great Vatican Bank Scandal*. Eventually, the transactions would cumulate to $1.4 billion. The Pope, on an ongoing basis, transferred the money in turn to a conglomerate in Panama that had subsidiaries operating in Latin America, Africa, India and other third world countries; the impoverished countries of the world where poverty and starvation was being driven by the Church's policy banning contraceptives. There is one more fact - the money disappeared and although there were endless investigations ordered by Italian courts over a period of years no one has ever found out what happened to it.

The arrangement ultimately resulted in the downfall of the Banco Ambrosiano. To put the amount of money in some perspective, $1.4 billion at the time was equivalent to what $8 billion would be today; and the fact that it was pulled out of the country's economy overnight resulted in the greatest financial crisis in Italian history. By relative comparison, it would the equivalent of one hundred billion dollars disappearing in the American economy overnight today; the United States having an economy about twelve times that of Italy.

And the big question is, just why did Roberto Calvi take such a risk? Whatever could have caused him to do such a stupid thing? The only conceivable answer is the threat of blackmail, -someone in the Vatican knew of his involvement in the earlier five million dollar payoff transaction and he lived under threat of life imprisonment.

Again the rumors started up as to what happened to the money. Some Italians believed the money was diverted to cartels and was used to finance opposition to the drug war being waged by the United States; they thought that the Church had involved itself in the transaction as it would benefit indirectly in that the Cartel families in Latin America like their counterparts in the Mafia families in Italy are major supporters of the Church. Actually, they were at the time and remain today, the largest individual contributors to the Church in many of these countries. Many others believed that the money was delivered to the Solidarity movement in Poland to fight communism.

But it is far more likely that John Paul II, in order to secure the votes that the Latin American and African cardinals controlled, which he needed to be elected, was making good on his campaign promise and that in the end the money was used to grow Catholicism and annihilate some of the poverty in these countries.

Keep in mind that we are dealing with several known facts. The remarkable occurrence that the very same *College of Cardinals* elected an ultraliberal in one month and turned around and elected an ultraconservative in the very next month. Then there is the fact that John Paul II took over direct control of the Vatican Bank early in his administration and that Calvi shortly transferred $1.4 billion dollars to the Vatican Bank and that the Pope in turn transferred it to a Panamanian conglomerate and that the money disappeared. And another fact: Karol Wojtyla could have never risen to the papacy without the votes that lay in the *middle.* And finally one last fact: the very same man gave birth to all these happenings, John Paul II, *Supreme Pontiff of the Roman Catholic Church.*

To the rational observer this makes a lot of sense as it explains how the *moderate* vote in the election had swung from the liberal side of the aisle to the conservative side without any concession of the major ecclesiastical issue sought by those in the *middle*. It explains how the very same *College of Cardinals* elected an ultraliberal in one month and turned around and elected an ultraconservative the very next month.

For one knows that the *moderates* were made up of conservatives who were torn between their belief that contraception was wrong but still sought repeal of the doctrine because of the poverty and starvation it was bringing about. They had voted for Luciani in the first election because he promised repeal of the doctrine and some dollars. And they had voted for Wojtyla in the second election because he promised them hundreds of millions of dollars to bring an end to much of the poverty the doctrine was causing; the Latin American and African cardinals could, as I have said, have their cake and eat it too; they could continue to adhere to a doctrine that they believed to be correct and yet bring an end to the poverty and starvation it was bringing about. On top of it all, they could better grow the Church in their part of the world; -a stroke of genius on the part of Cardinal Wojtyla, Paul Marcinkus, Bishop Casaroli, Cardinal Siri and whoever else may have been involved.

If the latter were true, and the author has no proof that it is true, except for these things we have spoken of and perhaps the fact that today Latin American and African countries comprise more than half of the

Roman Catholic Church, then there would have been a minimum of three men who would have had to have been involved. There would be Roberto Calvi president of the Banco Ambrosiano who had made the deposits and John Paul II and Archbishop Paul Marcinkus who transferred the funds to the Panamanian company.

And that the supposition of which I speak of above has some factual foundation, that is, that Roberto Calvi transferred the funds under threat of blackmail that stemmed fròm his alleged involvement in the five million dollar scandal. Three years after the $1.4 billion transaction took place, in 1982, Roberto Calvi, president of the Banco Ambrosiano, was brought to trial for falsifying bank records in connection with the scandal. Calvi was distraught and made no effort to defend himself at the trial and drew a four year suspended sentence. When asked in an interview why he refused to defend himself in the courtroom, he replied, "*I am in the service of someone who is beyond the wall.*"*

His comment was plastered across the front page of every newspaper in all of Italy. In Rome, when someone refers to the other side of the wall, they mean the Vatican. It was obvious that he was referring to someone in the Vatican and that he was quite frustrated about it. He was being made to be the fall guy and that he meant his comment to be a threat to whomever it was beyond the wall who held him is his grasp.

Of course, the person *"beyond the wall"* could have only been either of two men, -Paul Marcinkus or John Paul II or a combination of these two. If one reads the record correctly one knows that it could have only been the Pope himself. I say this with conviction because by the time of Calvi's trial Paul Marcinkus had already become the Vatican's fall guy for the $1.4 billion shortfall.

For when the scandal hit the press earlier that year Marcinkus was riddled with questions as to how this could have possibly happened. On one occasion Marcinkus made a slight slip. He told a reporter, "*I have told John Paul* (II) *that if we continue to sweep things under the rug we will eventually trip over it.*"* The week following Marcinkus' *slip* the Pope placed Cardinal Baggio between himself and Marcinkus, which cut him off from the press. Marcinkus was never heard from again, that is in the press. So Marcinkus had already been removed from power when Calvi went to trial. Calvi by his statement, "*I am in the service of someone beyond the wall,*" could have only been referring to the Pope.

**IL Giorno Milan 10 Jun 82*
**La Repubblica Rome 11 Jan 82*

It is this removal from power and eventual exiling of Marcinkus that tells one quite clearly that although he had masterminded the *Great Vatican Bank Scandal*, he, on the other hand, had nothing to do with a conspiracy to have murdered John Paul, as many authors who have written about foul play in the Pope's death have suggested. Although the banking arrangement may have been linked to a conspiracy to murder John Paul, Marcinkus did not know of its link to such a conspiracy at the time that he had made the deal. We know that the *deal* was struck sometime after the time of John Paul's death and before Karol Wojtyla's election. For if it had been made before the Pope's death Marcinkus would have known of its link to a murder conspiracy as Wojtyla and the others would have had no authority in the Vatican Bank because John Paul was still alive. And one knows this to be a fact because Marcinkus is still alive today. All that has survived in the record, including the impeccable character of the man himself, tells one quite clearly that although Paul Marcinkus may have been partially motivated by promise of position of power and rank, his true motive in the *Great Vatican Bank Scandal* was to annihilate poverty, starvation and disease.

Then there was the fact that the week following his statement to the press Roberto Calvi did a very strange thing. With permission of the court he left his beloved Italy and moved to England as if knowing that he was in danger he might seek refuge there. Just a week later on June 17, 1982 came the scene that one sees in the movies and in the storybooks. He was found hanging by the neck from a worker's scaffold under Blackfriar's Bridge in London. An inquest could not determine whether the cause of death was murder or suicide although it was quite apparent that a man of his weight and age could not have normally accomplished the task by himself, as the hanging would have required considerable athletic maneuvering. It certainly was a far reaching coincidence that he happened to have come upon a gallows that had been set up for him at the exact same moment that he decided to take his life. There remained the question as to why he had gone to the trouble of having moved all of his furnishings and belongings to London only to commit suicide there. Later the police did concede that it had been murder. They came to this conclusion because of what happened to Calvi's personal secretary several hundred miles away in Milan on the very same day. [1]

Teresa Corrocher was found hanging in a closet in her home just outside the city. An inquest also failed in her case to determine whether the cause of death was murder or suicide. [2]

[1] *London Times 18 Jun 82*

Regardless of the outcome of the inquests, the simultaneous "suicides" of both Calvi and his personal secretary hundreds of miles apart certainly added fuel to the fires of rumor that continued to spread across Europe. That the two had chosen to take their lives at precisely the same moment was too much for all except the most gullible to believe. It made all the sense in the world that if they both knew something that would bring someone in the Vatican down, they had to be eliminated at the same time, as if either one had survived, he or she would know the inevitable and would seek the protection of the state.

Sometime after the alleged suicides of Calvi and his secretary, Calvi's assistant at the bank who was the account officer for the Vatican account, Michele Sindona, was also found hanging in a closet. The inquest, however, did in his case determine that he had been an obvious victim of murder. It is reasonable that he also knew who in the Vatican Calvi had been referring to when he had told the press, "*I am in the service of someone on the other side of the wall.*" It is certainly a most remarkable coincidence that the only three people in the world who could have known who Calvi had referred to all died in the very same way, hanging by the neck until dead. [3]

So one can draw from all this that the $1.4 billion deal very well might have been a part of a conspiracy that planned the murder of John Paul I. Keep in mind that the trial proceedings were in Italy, so the details of the Vatican's involvement were never released to the courts. For example, we don't know today whether the money was invested in the Panamanian company or loaned to it. All we do know is that it disappeared.

It was that the Vatican was a foreign country that Marcinkus or John Paul II were never brought to trial in an Italian court of law, although they were the only ones who knew what had happened to the money after Calvi had deposited it in the Vatican Bank. And I say this as a matter of fact because on March 1, 1984 the Vatican made a payment of $241 million to European investors in settlement of its role in the scandal, a settlement to which the Church would never have agreed had John Paul II not have been involved in the deal in the first place. *

While we have these others on the table for discussion, those who fell victim to these circumstances, we might add Cardinal Benelli. Shortly after the murders of Calvi and his secretary in 1982, though in guarded condition in a Florence hospital, an order cane from the Vatican

[2] *IL Giorno 18 Jun 82*
[3] *IL Foglio 12 Sept 82*
* *IL Messaggero 2 Mar 84*

to remove Cardinal Benelli from life support equipment and to return him to his mansion where he died two hours later. When his doctor criticized the order, the Vatican claimed that Benelli himself had requested that he be moved. His personal physician told the press, *"That would have been quite a trick, as although the cardinal was expected to recover, he was comatose at the time he was moved."*

Cardinal Benelli had been the most outspoken of the cardinals calling for an autopsy of the remains of John Paul I, going so far as to issue a press release questioning possible foul play in the Pope's death. Although on different sides of the aisle, Benelli was a close friend and confidant of Cardinal Suenens who had been one of the two counters in the first conclave. Suenens may have told him that Wojtyla had been the runner-up in the election that chose Luciani, and that the Polish cardinal would be a shoe-in in a successive election. When Wojtyla met with Cardinal Siri and Bishops Casaroli and Caprio in Genoa just three weeks before John Paul's death, Benelli may have put two-and-two together and sensed a conspiracy.

Cardinal Benelli had also openly criticized the fact that Cardinal Cody accompanied Cardinal Wojtyla back to Krakow after the first conclave in that the Chicago prelate had no business in Poland. It was this visit by Cody to Krakow that led some authors who wrote about the Pope's death, to include him among the suspects. Had Wojtyla been lining up votes for the second conclave, he knew that he would have to carry a majority of the American cardinals who were mostly moderates who had voted for Luciani in the first conclave – a job that Cody was best positioned to carry out.

Also, Benelli had been caught by the Vatican several times talking out-of-school concerning possible Vatican involvement in the murders of Calvi and his secretary and this may have put pressure on him that brought on the heart attack for which he had been hospitalized. Just what Benelli knew concerning what is set forth in these pages died with him.

So all that is known of the *Great Vatican Bank Scandal* tells us that,

- John Paul I had stumbled upon the five million dollar banking transaction that had financed Aldo Moro's kidnapping and murder and that he was in the process of investigating it when he fell victim to foul play as is evidenced by his scheduled breakfast appointment with Roberto Calvi on the morning of his death.

- That Roberto Calvi was blackmailed by someone in the Vatican which caused him to deposit the $1.4 billion in the Vatican Bank and that John Paul II transferred the money to a Panamanian company that had operations in third world countries.

- Someone in the Vatican ordered the murders of Roberto Calvi, Teresa Corrocher and Michelle Sindona.

- Exactly one year after the election of John Paul II on October 17, 1979, Roberto Calvi made the first of the deposits in the Vatican Bank of one hundred and thirty four million dollars. This pokes a hole a mile wide in those books that have tried to link the *Great Vatican Bank Scandal* to John Paul's murder, as at the time of his death there had been no dealings at all related to the bank scandal.

- Cardinal Wojtyla had been involved in the dealings with Paul Marcinkus that eventually resulted in the *Great Vatican Bank Scandal* before he was elected because immediately after becoming Pope he elevated him to the rank of *President of the Sovereign State of the Vatican* and made him an archbishop. This tells one explicitly that Karol Wojtyla *knew* that he had the election sewed-up *before* the second conclave of 1978 began.

Chapter 10

THE LAST OF THE MONARCHS

On the second day of the conclave following the death of John Paul I, Cardinal Karol Wojtyla of Poland, an autocrat rather than a pastoral type, was elected his successor. Much to the delight of those who surrounded him in the Vatican, Wojtyla took steps to restore the majestic imagery of the papacy, which his predecessor had intended to destroy. John Paul II was of the conviction that a pope could only rule effectively if he were to reflect a royal image, that of a monarch. He was of the conviction that if a pope were to be Christ-like in his practice and in his image and in his appearance as his predecessor was, he would be unable to rule, just as Christ had been unable to control the populace at His time, that eventually ended in His downfall and death. And this is seen quite clear in that John Paul II, unlike his predecessor, in his relentless persecution of women and homosexuals and others does not lead his life in *Imitation of Christ.*

Although his biographies would try to tell one something else, the Polish press that followed him through the years as bishop and as a cardinal, tells us that he had an intense craving to be Pope. And this would not be unusual. Although they would never admit it most cardinals crave to be Pope, although it was taken to be some kind of a joke in Wojtyla's case. On one occasion a Warsaw reporter asked him, *"And by what name will you be called?"* And Wojtyla told him, *"Stanislao."** Yet the new Pope, on the advice of his newly appointed public relations director, took the name *John Paul.* It is quite obvious that he took the name of the three liberal popes of the twentieth century because it was the popular thing to do as his predecessors were so admired by the masses.

In his first act as pontiff, he ordered a costly renovation of the papal palace and of the lavish papal residence at the Castel Gandolfo, going so far as to add a swimming pool for his personal enjoyment. This was a complete about-face from his predecessor who had intended to sell

* *Warsaw Voice 11 Feb '68*

the opulent estate with its five palaces and sprawling gardens overlooking the Mediterranean Sea to provide funds to annihilate poverty in third world countries.

In addition, he started to take expensive vacations in Alpine resorts of the type that are reserved for kings and the very wealthy. Also, in order to portray to his public the majestic imagery of his personal being he added a professional photographer to his staff; his job was to create the illusion for the public of a simple man living in a sumptuous palace against his will. Today, the only pictures of the Pope in his private quarters released by the Vatican consist of him sitting at a simple table in front of a blank wall, sharing a bowl of soup with a peasant and another shot by an open window as to completely mask the richness of his surroundings. John Paul II is the only Pope in history to dine on other than nun's food. Shortly after taking over the top floor he relocated the four nuns who had been living there to a basement apartment and replaced them with a world renowned chef and a state-of-the art kitchen. A great part of the public relations effort has been to commission more than fifty biographies to be written about himself and not permit a single one be written about his predecessor.

To give some idea of how effective the public relations effort has been, most of his biographies tell one that it was he who was the driving force behind *Vatican II* in 1963. And his gullible following accepts this, despite the fact that they know him to be the most conservative Pope in the history of the Church. What his paid biographers would have us believe is that the most conservative bishop of the time (he was not cardinal at the time of *Vatican II*) was the architect of the most liberal step ever undertaken by Mother Church in its two-thousand year history. If one takes the time to read the London Times' and the New York Times' ongoing coverage of Vatican II, one will find that there is no mention whatsoever of the Polish bishop.

It was Cardinal Suenens who was the LBJ of Vatican II, who brought the sides together and got the job done. If it had been up to Karol Wojtyla nothing would have been done. As a matter of fact, he has been trying to unravel much of what was accomplished in *Vatican II* throughout the years of his papacy, trying to bring the Church back to where it was when Albino Luciani had first discussed the of idea of democratizing the Church with John XXIII in the spring of 1959.

Public relations in a single word, is *politics*. So overpowering is his political skillfulness that it is not possible to discern what makes up the rest of the man. That is, if one defines political astuteness as the ability to control the minds of others regardless of how distasteful things might be. And one knows we are talking in John Paul II of a political giant for throughout his papacy he has controlled the admiration of more than a billion followers despite the fact that what he stands for is unconscionable to most of them. The focus of his reign has been on salvaging the last remaining remnants of *fascism,* -the subordination of women and the persecution of homosexuals and other people who appear to be different.

Also, it has been the rule of his papacy to *"avoid scandal at any cost,"* as Archbishop Marcinkus so blatantly told the press, *"I keep telling John Paul* (II) *that if we keep sweeping things under the rug we will eventually trip over it."* And we know today that early in his administration he made the decision to *sweep the children under the rug* as well when he refused to allow priests who were accused of pedophilia to clear their names in a court of law, and instead encouraged bishops to pay off alleged victims of pedophile priests, a *rug* that *Mother Church* today finds herself tripping over, time and time again.

So here we have one who was politically clever enough ten years before the death of Paul VI to begin to pave his way to the papacy. And sadly, unlike his republican counterparts in government whose campaigns are financed by the very rich, one knows that money intended for the poor financed his many travels throughout the world, travels that would one day make him Pope. As I have already mentioned, seventy countries and over four hundred cities in all, the most traveled cardinal in history. He knew that to leave his responsibilities in Krakow behind and be the overnight of guest of voting cardinals in their palaces and mansions was his best bet. That he failed to have gained the notice of the press or of the rank and file made little difference to this man who would one day be Pope. All that counted to him was that he would gain the notice and the friendship of the voters, those cardinals who would one day cast their votes for him.

As we have suggested in our analysis of the election that chose his predecessor, Karol Wojtyla may have indeed been the other vote getter in the early stages of that election and that having been one of the counters he would have known this. He would have known that had Albino Luciani had not been a factor in the first election, then he would have won; which would have told him that if anything was to happen to Luciani, then he would become Pope.

the Pope's new swimming pool,

When Karol Wojtyla inherited the papal throne in 1978, the Vatican Bank had a deficit of twenty million dollars which had been built up over ten years and at the end of his first pontifical year with uncontrolled spending the deficit had risen to forty million in just a single year. Had the Vatican Bank enjoyed a surplus instead of a deficit, then the Pope's extravagant spending would have gone unnoticed. But because a deficit was involved it brought sharp criticism from those in his ranks who were brave enough to speak out against the extravagant spending of the new Pope. And among them was Cardinal Suenens,

"In order for one to see clearly what has happened here one must first understand the function of the Vatican Bank. To begin with it, except for its dealings with the Catholic Bank of Italy, it is not a 'bank' at all in the common sense of the word and one can plainly see this in its official title, 'The Institute for Religious Works.' In reality, it is a clearing house for funds that have been raised for the poor through various charitable orders of the Church. By quite a margin the largest single client of the 'bank' is Mother Teresa, whose religious order ministers to the poor and dying in the slums of Calcutta and numerous other cities of the world. Because the Peter's Pence was insufficient to offset the bank's operating deficit, the money that built the Pope's lavish swimming pool and other improvements to the papal palaces both in Rome and at the Castel Gandolfo had to have come from funds that were raised by Mother Teresa and others like her to help those children suffering from starvation and illness throughout the world. Also, it makes no sense," Cardinal Suenens told the press, *"to pay the Vatican cardinals huge salaries out of these same funds that were intended for the poor."* [1]

Suenens was criticizing John Paul II for his uncontrolled spending, particularly for his having raised Vatican cardinal salaries by eighteen-percent to about one hundred and thirty thousand dollars in today's dollars in spending money. The statement to the press often credited to Suenens that *"John Paul raised the Vatican cardinal salaries so quickly after his election that anyone other than a moron would see it as a part of the deal,"*[2] was actually made by another cardinal who was unhappy with the election results. The statement inferred that Wojtyla had purchased the Vatican cardinal votes on the promise of a raise in pay.

Nevertheless, it was Cardinal Suenens' harsh criticism which caused John Paul II to put pressure upon the rich dioceses of the world to increase their share of 'Peter's Pence.' 'Peter's Pence' is a fund that had been established to provide spending money for the Pope. The strategy behind the fund was in that it came only from rich parishes it would spare the Pope from using funds intended for the poor to support the lavish lifestyle of himself and the others in the Vatican. And although the Peter's Pence was a substantial amount of money when he came into power, a few

[1] *Euobserver 17 Feb 80*
[2] *world press 1-5 Nov 79*

million dollars, it was insufficient to offset the deficit or cover the cost of the swimming pool and the many other amenities John Paul added to his palaces and to pay for his expensive alpine vacations. So as Cardinal Suenens had pointed out, the excess had to have come from monies that had been deposited by Mother Teresa and other charitable organizations. Perhaps, it would be fitting today for the Pope to name the pool after her, *The Mother Teresa Swimming Pool*. After all, as Cardinal Suenens pointed out, she paid for it.

During the same time, the first year of his pontificate, it was widely publicized that John Paul had diverted considerable millions "illegally" from the Vatican Bank to support uprising operations in Slavic countries against communism, the largest amounts going to the Solidarity movement in Poland. How the press could repeatedly describe the transactions as being "illegal" is beyond this author, as Italian law had no jurisdiction within the Vatican and Vatican law is whatever the Pope deems it to be. Unlike most might want to believe, the Roman Catholic Church is not a democracy. It is a dictatorship. And it is a dictatorship of one man. Yes, to the extent that such funds were, in fact, diverted from feeding the poor they were morally wrong. But they were not illegal, as nothing the Pope does within the Vatican walls can possibly be deemed to be illegal for he, himself, is the law. He is the *President*, the *Senate*, the *Congress* and the *Chief Justice of the Supreme Court* of the *Sovereign State of the Vatican.*

And concerning Peter's Pence, John Paul's influence upon the pastors of the rich parishes of the world has since raised it to what it is today, about seventy five million dollars a year, personal spending money for the Pope. Twenty million dollars of this money went to build the sumptuous one hundred and fifty room Palace of Santa Marta in Vatican City which was completed in 1995. The new palace will bring an end to a thousand year history during which cardinals were housed in humble and sparse quarters in the Vatican during the conclaves that elected more than a hundred popes. The new palace rivals the finest ultra-luxury hotels in the world. It was the availability of vacant rooms in this palace at the time a dozen or so American cardinals together with their aids flew first class to meet with the Pope concerning the pedophilia problem that prompted Maureen Dowd of the New York Times to criticize some of them for staying at a five-hundred-dollar-a–night hotel near the Roman Forum.

Aside from the physical surroundings of everyday life, John Paul II has radically changed the way business is carried on in the Vatican. Whereas his predecessors saw the Vatican as a forum where all those with different ideas could voice their opinions in order to make this a better world to live in, John Paul II has closed the Vatican chambers to anything that might suggest a change in ecclesiastical doctrine. For it is the nature of the ultraconservative that the *die has been cast in stone* by scripture and that the purpose of the papacy is not to solve the many problems of the world but rather to force the world to live within the confines of scripture. And his scripture tells him the very same thing that it told Pius XI and Pius XII when they made *fascism* the backbone of the Axis powers during the thirties; *fascism,* which finds its definition in the supremacy of the white Aryan male and the subordination of women and blacks and the persecution of homosexuals and others who are different. For the scripture has not changed. The Roman Catholic Church, like all other Christian churches, has today modified its position concerning these things only to the extent that society has forced changes upon it. And the Roman Catholic Church, like most other Christian churches, continues to cling to whatever bits of *fascism* that society will permit, -for *fascism*, the instruction of God the Father to Moses in the Old Testament, is at the very core of John Paul II's existence.

It has been the express policy of the *Vatican Curia*, since the death of John Paul I, not to permit any controversial issues to be discussed within the Vatican. The only exception to this policy has been priest pedophilia, which has been forced upon the Vatican because of the many child molestation suits that have been brought against the Church. Suits that could have never been brought against the Church had it not been for Suenens' and Luciani's efforts in forcing the sexual revolution within the Church, which today permits sex to be discussed openly within families.

But other than this, the Church's policy has been one of completely ignoring these kinds of issues as problems. The Roman Catholic Church has completely closed its mind to change with the times. It has fixed its thinking in concrete. It has stuffed plugs into its ears. It no longer need listen to the problems of the world, for it has its doctrine.

Just a week after the Polish Pope was installed, Cardinal Suenens started to press for the possibility of ordination of women in the Church. In a private audience at which Suenens was present, John Paul II criticized him for his proposal. Suenens, in a spur of the moment emotional response, *"There is nothing in all of the Bible that prevents women from serving. It is the age-old bigotry of men that any catholic male can accede to the papacy no matter how small his ability and that no catholic female can accede to the role of a common priest no matter how great her ability.* " *

* *L'Opinione 28 Oct 78*

Although it was not his intention, the press reported that Suenens had insinuated that the Pope was a bigot. The tabloids picked up the story and took it a step further saying that Suenens had, indeed, called the Pope a bigot, a male chauvinist. In general, the feminist organizations did not take advantage of the situation. Except for some small American organizations, most of them remained silent.

Later, Suenens apologized in the press for having embarrassed the Pope. He said that he had gone to Rome with some conviction that he could accomplish this lifelong ambition of Luciani; he would make the ordination of women a reality in memory of his longtime friend and confidant. Suenens told the press that John Paul had revealed to him just a week before his death that he was about to make this change in doctrine and that he intended to make the change unilaterally, as there was nothing, not a thing in the scriptures, that stood in his way. But Suenens' apology was to no avail.

In his very first act of realignment of the *College of Cardinals* John Paul II removed Cardinal Suenens, the leader of liberalism in the Church, as the Primate of Belgium. John Paul's intent was obviously to bring an end to Suenens' pastoral influence. His action was seen as a message to all those cardinals who might also be of the school of Lacordaire, *"have an opinion and assert it."*

At the same time the Pope reversed Paul's decision to internationalize the *Curia.* He removed Cardinal Willebrands as *Secretary of Christian Unity* and Cardinal Gantin as *Secretary of Peace and Justice.* The *Curia* was, once again, a cluster of ultraconservative governors. Shortly afterwards, he removed Willebrands as Archbishop of Utrecht in the Netherlands in order to bring an end to his liberal influence on his congregation, influence which had spread throughout Europe.*

Shortly after that John Paul II removed Archbishop Jadot from one of the most powerful positions in the Church as *Apostolic Delegate to the United States* to the position of *Secretariat for Non Christians* in the Vatican, a step just above *janitor*. Bishop Jadot, among other things, was the man who had brought about the most visible changes in the Church in

**although not much is said here in these pages concerning the Dutch cardinal, Willebrands was every bit as much a part of what has made Europe the leader in achieving equality for all of God's children, for he was the third courageous member of this trio of men who let in the fresh air. It was the Holy Trinity of Willebrands in Utrecht and Suenens in Brussels and Luciani in Venice, who taught the people of Europe what they had failed to learn in the world war, -that fascism is wrong; the reason why America lags behind Europe in achieving true democracy - why homosexuals are still struggling to achieve equality in the United States.*

the twentieth century by allowing the mass to be said in local languages so that it would be understandable to members of the congregation. And among many other things he pushed through the doctrine that allows women to participate in the mass. Jadot is the reason why the priest faces the congregation today. Despite all these accomplishments and much more, being the liberal that he was, Jadot would never be named a cardinal, that is, as long as John Paul II remained in power.

A process had begun to replace the most vociferous of liberal prelates in the short term and to rid the Church of the rest of them via attrition in the long term. That is, to replace upon death or retirement, all cardinals who held to liberal positions, no matter how slight, with men who were firm in their support of the conservative positions of the Church, particularly concerning birth control, remarriage, homosexuality and the subordination of women in the Church. At the dawn of the new millennium, the *College of Cardinals,* with the exception of the few brave men who we have talked about, is solidly behind the Pope in these beliefs. They are all of the court of Clemenceau, "*they have no ideas of their own, but defend them with ardor.*"

Today, the *College of Cardinals* has been purged of all but a few sparks of liberalism, of democracy. The fundamental qualification John Paul II requires of a candidate for the celebrated red hat is one's strict unbroken commitment against contraception, remarriage and equal human rights for homosexuals and women. Apart from this, all other qualifications of a cardinal are considered immaterial. The Church today, philosophically, is precisely where it was prior to 1959 when John XXIII first started to walk away from tradition - first started to walk away from *tribalism.* The *College of Cardinals* is now entirely a *Republican Congress* and the *Vatican Curia,* as it always has been, is entirely a *Republican Senate.* For the first time since the reign of Pius XII, the Roman Catholic Church is headed by a *Republican Pope* supported by a *Republican Congress* and a *Republican Senate* and a *Republican Chief Justice.*

In that the Catholic Church, once the most influential organization in the world, has taken an irresponsible position concerning the population problem, the greatest problem that faces modern man today, is of great moral consequence. Yet, what this thoughtless philosophy has brought upon the Church is its loss of influence not only throughout the world, but among most of its congregation as well.

What all this has resulted in has been a separation of the power in the Vatican from its populace. The hierarchy of the Church has chosen to ignore the fact that its flock is wandering off in another direction. Its flock is deciding, more and more each day, to take upon its shoulders the responsibilities that its shepherds have chosen to ignore. And these *sheep*, actually these *lions*, are saying in a very loud voice to Rome, "If you don't think the population explosion is your problem . . . If you don't think that the abortions that are related to the lack of birth control practices are your problem . . . If you don't think that abortions that are owed to the stigma you attach to out-of-wedlock pregnancies is your problem . . . If you don't think that the poverty and starvation that is brought into the world by overpopulation is your problem . . . If you don't think that your position on remarriage that forces divorcees to live in exile outside of long term loving relationships is your problem . . . If you don't think that the trauma and often suicides of homosexual children and teens is your problem. Then we will handle these problems for you."

And they are doing exactly that. In the United States and Europe more than ninety-percent of all Catholics practice birth control of some sort and most do not support the Church's position on banning embryonic research. The overwhelming majority has removed the stigma attached to out-of-wedlock pregnancies and most divorcees are ignoring the Church's threat of excommunication and damnation by living happy and contributory married lives. And that the Church has decided to continue its persecution of the *strange little boy in the playground* has not been met well either, as the great majority is supporting his quest for an equal share of this thing we call *Life, Liberty and the Pursuit of Happiness.*

Men and women of great courage who although they never heard it said to them are following Albino Luciani's solemn instruction,

"Never be afraid to stand up for what is right whether your adversary be your parent, your teacher, your peer, your politician, your preacher, your constitution, or even your God."

This means that the overwhelming majority of Catholics in these countries no longer believe in the infallibility of the papacy, that one of the most well imaged popes in history is also its least respected, that most Catholics don't follow his instructions at all as they do not believe that his instructions come from Christ. In fact, most of them know that they come from his ancient past. To say that John Paul II is unaware of the irreparable damage he has done to the credibility of the Church is to say that he is an imbecile, -that for twenty centuries two hundred and sixty three popes have maintained the infallibility of their sacred office only to have it perish forever under the management of an autocratic leader who prefers to live in the fifteenth century BC.*

And the official numbers tell us something more. Since the death of John Paul I, the number of practicing Catholics, those that regularly attend church services, has declined in the United States and Europe from better than three-quarters at the three quarter mark of the twentieth century to about one-quarter at the start of the new millennium.

On the other hand, in Latin America, Africa and in many other underdeveloped countries, the reverse is true. Influenced by an army of ultraconservative cardinals only a small percentage of the population practice any form of birth control and the Catholic population has more than doubled in these poor countries. And this, of course, has resulted in an explosion of immense poverty and starvation and in the uncontrolled spread of AIDS.

But for at least a part of humanity, men and women of vast courage, the mass of Catholicism, are rising up against what their shepherd *believes* is right, and are doing what they *know* is right.

silent greatness,

And whatever became of the man behind it all?

After being forced into retirement when Karol Wojtyla rose to power, Cardinal Leon Joseph Suenens continued his relentless onslaught from the *left*, but with some minor exceptions concerning the rights of women in the Church, he had very little success.

In 1982, in an interview with a Brussels newspaper, Suenens suggested that Mother Teresa be elevated to the *College of Cardinals*.[1] His suggestion, of course, would have required a change in the doctrine that forbids the elevation of women to higher orders. John Paul II immediately issued a statement to the Italian press through his secretary of state Casaroli "*Cardinal Suenens should be reminded that it was not upon his shoulders that the papal cloak was placed in the conclave of October 1978,*" [2] reminding the cardinal that the appointment of cardinals was a papal decision and not a cardinal decision. Casaroli, in a side comment to the press, added that "*Cardinal Suenens was ignoring the fact*

**the doctrine of infallibility of popes from St. Peter to modern day popes was formally put into the record books in the middle of the nineteenth century by Pius IX.*

[1]*Het Laatste Nieuws 12 Jul 82*

[2]*IL Popolo a4 Jul 82*

that a cardinal requires a certain minimum level of intellectual ability."[2] Although the tabloids tried to make an issue of the comment, it soon died a natural death.

Of course, Suenens could have made it neither a papal nor a cardinal decision for he could have made it a people decision. As he had told the newspaper reporter, "*If a vote of the people were to be taken as to who has made the greatest contribution to society of all the clergy of the twentieth century she would garnish more votes than any of us.*"[3] So Suenens could have used political pressure to force the Pope to make the appointment and had he chosen to do so, it is fairly certain that John Paul II would have made the appointment, an appointment that Suenens knew would eventually lead to the ordination of women. But, nevertheless, he dropped the issue so as not to embarrass Rome. That John Paul II was never to elevate Mother Teresa as a cardinal is fitting testimony to the fact that he is a male chauvinist, a bigot, exactly what tabloids have often suggested.

When one insinuates that someone is a bigot, particularly if that person is a pope, one better be standing on firm ground. And the record is firmly there, for during his reign John Paul II has appointed over two hundred cardinals, all men. All those who aspire to the red hat under his reign must take the solemn pledge, *"I promise to oppose the elevation of women in the Church for all the rest of my days."* But then again, perhaps he has nothing against women, maybe it's just that he believes that none of them are worthy enough or smart enough to be advisors to his papal monarchy.

Later that same year, as his good friend Luciani had done many times before him, Suenens came out in the press against American bishops who were paying substantial amounts of money to victims of alleged pedophile priests in the interests of squashing rumors, -adhering to the Pope's policy of *sweeping things under the rug*. The following week, Suenens was summoned to Rome where he was chastised by John Paul II and was told that he used "*poor judgment*" in his criticism and was ordered to correct his "*mistake.*" There is no record in the press that Suenens ever corrected his *"mistake."* Instead he embarked on a tour of seminaries counseling aspiring priests that they not betray the sacred trust that mothers and fathers of young children place in them.

And the very next year, when medical science proved it was John Paul II's policy banning protective sex that was the driving force behind the AIDS epidemic in Africa, Latin America and other countries, Suenens

[3] *Het Laatste Nieuws 12 Jul 82*

again enlisted the press, *"I appeal to Your Holiness to reconsider, for if you delay a change in policy until that time at which society takes the matter out of your hands, that Mother Church will have another Galileo case on her hands. That sometime in the next century your irresponsible policy would have killed more men, women and children than did the policies of Hitler; in refusing to open your heart to this thing at this time you risk taking your places in history alongside these tyrants of tyrants."* [1]

In the fall of 1983, Ronald Reagan made a commitment to Jerry Falwell on the campaign trail to ban funding of AIDS research and made his now infamous remark, "*they live like that - let them die like that.*"[2] Suenens called Reagan's comment "*barbaric.*" The loss of life driven by the homophobic hatred of this American president would delay federal funding of AIDS research for almost a decade and in the hallowed archives of history these words will one day take their place alongside the name of this president.

Although he was never raised to the papacy, Cardinal Suenens did more than did any other prelate in history to move the Church toward good and just conscience, away from the bigotry of its past. His critics viewed that his thesis dictated that the Church was a *Church of the People*. That it was a democracy; that the Pope must execute his office to the common will of the people. Suenens' proposal that the bishops elect the Pope was just one step in a process that would eventually lead to the people electing the Pope. They claimed that Suenens did not believe in the infallibility of the Pope, that he did not accept that the Pope's proclamations come directly from Christ.

However, in their criticism, they were ignoring the fact that the *College of Cardinals* does by its very existence disclaim the infallibility of the Pope for the *College of Cardinals* serves as the advisory council to the Pope. Christ in His divinity, very obviously, needs no advisors.

the ten-story building of righteousness,

But Suenens, like his good friends Luciani and Willebrands, saw his role as something much more. He saw it as a duty to right the wrongs of the past. To bury forever the bigotry that had been the backbone of Christianity ever since Moses spelled out the difference between *master and slave*, and *black and white*, and *man and woman*, and *Aryan and outcast*, and *believer and unbeliever*, and *normal and handicapped*, and

[1] Liberazione 12 Apr 83 [2] CBS news video tape 12 Sep 83 In 2003, a film was censored by major television channels because it contained the CBS video taped remark. Available in major libraries.

straight and gay, and *us and them*, four thousand years before. In his very own words he meant his statement "*to bring an end forever to the differences between the peoples of the world. Whether they be black or white or brown or yellow or men or women, or men that had been born as women, or women who had been born as men, or what have you.*"[1] And he reminded the world in his dossiers, "*those that choose to persecute the strange little boy in the playground should keep in mind that Christ, Himself, was just that, a strange little boy in the playground for He was born asexual.*[2]

And in his memoirs, "*Let us make the courageous resolution to bring men together instead of dividing them, eliminate from our vocabulary and our conversation and our thoughts all that can hurt or wound our neighbor, so that there might descend on our earth a little of that peace God has promised to men of good will.*" [3]

Suenens' vision for the Church, his vision for the world, was so vast that it would have required *Vatican III* to become reality. *Vatican II*, so often referred to as the equivalent of *World War II* concerning change in the Church, *Vatican III* would require the equivalent of *World War III* concerning change in the Church, concerning change in the world.

Suenens was the man, the force, behind all three popes, John XXIII, Paul VI and John Paul I, the three popes of the twentieth century who allowed their conscience to overrule the evils in their scripture, the three popes who had brought the elevator to the fifth floor of the ten-story building of righteousness. But it has remained there ever since.

For the most part, Suenens was ignored for the rest of his life. That is, until a leak to the press hinted that at an upcoming address he was scheduled to make at John Carroll University in Cleveland he would suggest that the appointment of bishops be removed from the Pope to the *Conference of Bishops*. Suenens, who had once tried to remove the vote for the papacy itself to the *Conference of Bishops* and had failed, would now attempt to remove the appointment of bishops to the *Conference of Bishops*. His position was that a pope who is either an liberal or a conservative would narrow his judgment in his appointments to his own personal convictions, or to the personal convictions of those around him. If a pope reigned long enough, this would eliminate the '*two party*' balance which John XXIII and Paul VI had worked so hard to establish and had become so important to the Church in successfully negotiating its way in a changing world.

[1] [2] [3] *Leon Joseph Suenens wrote a series of books in the 80s which are available in major libraries*

In particular, this was a direct attack on John Paul's policy of loading the Church's hierarchy with ultraconservatives, the Pope in his appointments was loading its ranks with those who were fixed in their ecclesiastical thinking, not only at the cardinal level, but at the bishop level as well, the Pope was irresponsibly ignoring people, finance, and other managerial abilities in appointing his mangers.

After years of silence Suenens had once again become dangerous to the Vatican, this time, perhaps more dangerous than ever before. For rather than making his case within the closed walls of the Vatican, he would make his noise in a public forum that would reach the editorial pages of the world press. Five days after the leak to the press of his intentions, a week before his scheduled address, he was found dead. In its obituary, the New York Times said of him, "*. . . vibrant and on the job to the very end. . . Suenens was the Architect of Twentieth Century Catholicism.*"

A draft of the speech that he never made was found in his typewriter and a housemaid innocently released it to a *Sun Times* reporter. "*. . . One can see what I say here, very vividly,*" it said, "*that if in the case of the United States, the President were allowed to appoint the members of Congress, he would then have the power of a dictator. He could load the Congress entirely with those who share his own convictions, democrats or republicans, and thereby muster the vote to render his own appointment invincible. But believe me in what I have to say here today, a plane with only one wing can fly in only one direction, and that direction is very decidedly down!*"

He died very much as his good friend John Paul had died several years earlier. As the New York Times reported, vibrant and on the job to the end, he too, was found sitting up in his bed in a frozen state of some kind. He was still wearing his reading glasses and in his hands was clutched a book. The bed lamp was still on and the window next to his bed was wide open. The book was his own book, one that he had written many years before. The name of the book was . . .*Day by Day.* It was opened to page fifty-six. His eyes were still open and they seemed to be fixed on a phrase at the bottom of the page, "*Let us all look around us with new eyes. A whole world of discovery will open up before us!*"

It seemed that Suenens was editing his best seller for republishing. For in the margin of the opposite page were scribbled the words, "*always look forward, never look back!*"

The great man had left his mark in time. Six men in all, had left their mark in time; seven with John XXIII. All disciples of Lacordaire *"Have an opinion and assert it!"* And the record is there for all time. It is there for men and women of good conscience to soak up.

the toll,

• May 17, 1978	Aldo Moro	shot to death
• August 6, 1978	Paul VI	death by poison
• August 11, 1978	Cardinal Yu Pin	death by poison
• September 5, 1978	Archbishop Nicodim	death by poison
• September 29, 1978	John Paul I	death by injection
• September 30, 1978	John Champney	hit-and-run driver
• March 13, 1979	Jean Villot	death by poison
• June 17, 1982	Roberto Calvi	death by hanging
• June 17,1982	Teresa Corrocher	death by hanging
• September 12, 1982	Michele Sindona	death by hanging
• October 26, 1982	Giovanni Benelli	Vatican order
• March 18, 1,996	Leon Suenens	sudden/unknown

left: the King rules from his golden throne. right: he receives one his loyal subjects who has taken the oath required of all cardinals, "I promised to oppose the elevation of women in the Church, contraception, remarriage and to continue the persecution of homosexual children and teenagers for all the days of my life." He sells his soul to the devil for a red hat.

In the fall of 2002, a proclamation emanated from the Vatican that after his death the Pope would be known as John Paul the Great, the first time in history that a person has self-proclaimed his or her greatness.

author's comment,

My original objective was to write the first complete biography of Pope John Paul I. At the time that I first began my research in Belluno, Italy where he had spent much of his young life, although I knew that he had not died of a heart attack, I was not of the conviction that there had been foul play in his death; this, despite the fact that I was fairly certain at the time that there had been foul play in his predecessor's death, Paul VI. But of course, in speaking of his life, I could not ignore his death.

And concerning his death, I scoured the Italian press. It was only then that I began to realize that he too may have been murdered. My early suspicions focused on Cardinal Benelli, as according to the press he had been the leading candidate in the election that had chose Luciani, and therefore would most likely become Pope if something were to happen to Luciani. But soon I began to realize that he too may have been murdered. Then I focused on Bishop Marcinkus and Cardinal Villot, those that others who wrote books about the Pope's death had convicted.

When I came up empty handed in their cases, I realized that John Paul had been murdered for ecclesiastical reasons. As his biographer, I knew that Luciani had been a liberal, in terms of Catholicism an ultraliberal. Yet, I knew that since the time of his death, the Catholic Church had painted him out to have been a conservative, in many cases an ultraconservative. There could be only one reason for this misrepresentation and that is to cover up the fact that he had been murdered for reasons of ecclesiastical motive. Certainly, if the populace were to remember him as having been the liberal that he was, then it would make no sense that the very same constituency of cardinals elected an ultraconservative the very next month, as everyone knows that cardinals don't vote for a man because they think that he will look pretty in a white satin gown.

I have offered the possibility that the *Great Vatican Bank Scandal* may have had something to do with this unexplained happening in order to give one an alternative to the only other possibility, -that Karol Wojtyla having been one of the counters in the first election may have known that he had indeed been the other major candidate in that election and therefore knew that if anything were to happen to Luciani, he would become Pope. The unexplained deaths of seven men who enjoyed the wine at the corner wedge café in Vittorio Veneto on the afternoon of March 11, 1978, in rapid consecutive order, made possible the papacy of John Paul II and the elevation of three common bishops to the second, third and fourth most powerful positions in the Roman Catholic Church.

"The National Government must preserve and defend those Christian principles upon which our nation has been built . . . and which define our morality and family values."

Adolph Hitler - Berlin 1 Feb 33. Hitler capitalizes on the wave of terrorism in Germany and convinces the people that he must have dictatorial powers. Above, he accepts as Chancellor of Germany and issues his "*New World Order Proclamation.*" He establishes the Aryan superiority of the German people and sets the stage for World War II, including the annihilation of Jews, gypsies and homosexuals. In his time, *Christianity* was synonymous with the word *Fascism* - hatred of those who are different - something that those on the *religious right* continue to believe today.

"One looks back just a few years to the time of Hitler and Mussolini and blames these two monsters for it all. Yet, the real culprit in that dreadful time was not its leaders, but it was a weak society that allowed itself to be caught up in a *frenzy of fascism and hatred of others who appear to be different.* And likewise, in the fifties and sixties, it was not so much the Christian preachers who preached persecution and segregation of blacks who were to blame, as it was a weak society that allowed itself to be caught up in a *frenzy of fascism and hatred of others who appear to be different.* And today, concerning deprivation of basic human rights for homosexuals, it is not so much the evangelical preachers that are to blame, for the real culprit is, once again, a weak society that allows itself to be caught up in a *frenzy of fascism and hatred of others who appear to be different.* It's the same game, just being played at different points in time. Believe me, we will never be truly free until we stamp out what Hitler stood for, once and for all!"

Albino Lucian - Venice 14 Jul 76. the cardinal defends the French physician priest Mark Oraison who acknowledges his homosexuality and claims that the act of *falling-in-love* is the will of God.

Epilogue

the evening of September 29, 1978,

He found himself to be sitting in a tailor shop, one of those reserved for kings. There was a large sewing machine of the very latest vintage. A ruffle of white satin flowed from its center as if the bell had rung and the seamstress had gone out to lunch. On a table just off to one side were a half dozen or so rolls of satin, all of the very same shade of white. And then there was the gold. It was wound up on spindles that were lined up at one end of the sewing machine. A dozen or so golden sentinels watchfully guarded a grand catafalque of white.

Then there was the rising vertical mirror with its edges heavily encrusted in gold. A small platform stood just before the mirror. There seemed to be a slight indentation at its center and a haze rising above it as if a ghost were standing there. It was flanked by a half dozen or so breast dummies each wearing a part of some form of dress. And there was one that was all dressed up. That is, all dressed up still short of holding the Eucharist in its hands. For it even wore the papal miter.

The breast dummies were all of a single size. Just a month earlier they had been of another size. And he knew that in just two weeks time they would be of still another size. And only he of all of mankind knew this. For only he could make them change.

It had been just seven o'clock in the evening when he had passed by the guard who sat at the desk at the entrance to the short corridor, which led to the papal dining room. So the guard knew when he had come. The advantage he had in this thing was that the guard would not know when he would leave. For the guard would be replaced at promptly nine o'clock. and the new guard would not know that he was still here. In fact, he would not know that he had ever been here. And that was the advantage that he had in this game.

He knew that he would leave at exactly the same time he had come. That is, the same time as reads the face of the clock. Except that the sun would be rising, not falling. For it would be seven o'clock in the morning.

And the guard at seven in the morning would not know when he had arrived. He would assume that he had passed by his predecessor sometime before six in the morning, that time when the clamor had begun. After the mother nun had opened the door. After Magee had discovered the destiny of this pauper who would be Pope.

It would be a long night. But he knew that he must be patient, that he must bide his time. That at precisely three thirty in the morning he would creep into the hallway and steal silently down to the pontiff's bedroom door. That he would wait there until he heard the Vicar of Christ rise and get up and go into the bathroom. He would wait to hear the bladder empty and then the treadmill hum. But only when he heard the shower water running would the coast be clear for him to enter and leave his little friend behind. Only then would the breast dummies change.

January 27, 2023, ***Marrakech Journal***,

Marrakech, Morocco. Deaths due to the sting of the giant golden scorpion have reached an all time high. Last year, one hundred and twenty three people are known to have succumbed to this predator which is commonly referred to as the *"King of the Sahara Desert,"* not to be confused with the *"African Emperor Scorpion"*, which is far less deadly and is more commonly known as the black paradox scorpion.

The venom of the pale yellow scorpion is the most deadly of any predator in the world immensely more potent than is that of the viper, which is the most deadly of snakes. The difference being that because of its small size it injects very little venom. The giant golden scorpion of the Sahara, on the other hand, a mutation of the pale yellow species, injects enough venom to kill twelve men. It is the largest and most deadly of the three dozen or so scorpions in the world whose sting is known to be dangerous to man. In fact, it is the only scorpion whose sting does not permit time for the application of an antidote. Once a rarity, a freak occurrence, the giant golden scorpion has now developed into a separate species of its own. It first appeared in 1973 when a French Caravelle jetliner crashed in the Moroccan dessert and it killed three of the twenty six survivors of the crash before rescuers could reach the site.

Scorpions are the greatest natural predator of man. Although snakes kill more people, scorpions kill immensely more people on a per capita basis as they live only in the desert where very few people live. If they were as prevalent as are snakes or spiders they would kill tens of millions each year.

In that this loathsome creature is particularly attracted to the warmth of the human body when under covers, desert campers are warned not to sleep directly on the ground. Unlike most other scorpions, the venom of the giant golden scorpion results in instantaneous paralysis, rendering its victims rigid, frozen in the position in which they were stricken. This is because like its ally of the snake family, the puff adder, its venom attacks the nervous system and results in instant failure of the vagus nerve which controls the heart. This deadly predator of man allows his victim no last words.

March 12, 2027, *The New York Times*,

Atlanta, Georgia. Infant and child deaths due to ingestion of the plant omithogalum umbellatum have now risen to over a hundred in the south. The plant, which was brought into the country from the Middle East a number of years ago, has also been responsible for the loss of over a thousand household pets in the state of Georgia alone. The flower, more commonly referred to as the *Star of Bethlehem* because of its remarkable white star like design, when ingested causes a sharp drop in pulse rate and severe respiratory convulsions that culminate in death within a very few hours. There is no known antidote for the poison. Although all parts of the plant are poisonous, the bulb, which has a bitter kind of nutty taste is particularly dangerous. It has been tied to a number of homicides, as it is easily concealed in foods that have a nutty flavor, particularly soups and puddings. Homeowners are advised to rid their gardens of the plants, particularly if they have pets or young children who might nibble on them, or have yards that are not enclosed by fences which prevent children or pets access.

December 17, 2043
CNN reporting,

"It is five o'clock in the afternoon here in St. Peter's Square. A light rain has started to fall and umbrellas are beginning to pop up here, there and everywhere. All eyes are on the chimney of the Sistine Chapel which, hopefully, any minute will announce that a new pontiff has been named. We expect our first American Pope."

Within the conclave all remains quiet, each cardinal watching the doors of the inner room where the votes are being tallied. Within that room the count has been completed and the name is known. Almost immediately the white smoke begins to rise from the chimney. A loud roar is heard from the square outside.

The doors of the room open and the Vatican Secretary of State, Cardinal Pasquale Amedore, approaches one of the cardinals in the conclave and asks, "Do you accept your canonical election as Supreme Pontiff?"

And the chosen cardinal replies, "I accept."

The secretary then asks, "By what name do you wish to be called?"

And the cardinal whispers a name to him. Then two cardinals approach with the white papal cloak, and the selected cardinal, donning the robe, moves toward the balcony.

Outside, the rain is falling more heavily now and white smoke is bellowing from the Sistine Chapel. Yet, all eyes are on the balcony.

Then, at last, the doors open, and the new leader of the world's largest congregation appears.

And one in the crowd who is too short to see asks another, "American?"

"No, English." And the other responds, "English?"

"Yes, she's English. Louise Brown, the first *test tube* Pope!"

The Kingdom of Heaven
Office of John Paul I
December 25, 2003

Office of His Holiness
Vatican City, Rome
Attention: Karol Wojtyla, John Paul II

My Dear Karol,

It has been many years since you and Cardinal Suenens placed the white cloak upon my shoulders in the Vatican conclave in the Sistine Chapel. Many years since we have been able to walk and talk in the woods with the cat and the fox and the poodle, Medoro.

I had lunch yesterday with John XXIII and Paul VI, and with our old friend Pinocchio. We had the good fortune to partake of the wine that grows in the little café on the corner wedge in Vittorio Veneto. And we topped it all off with a quadruple helping of gelato at the little stand just down the street. It was pure heaven you see.

But I am writing to you not to discuss the light of the day, but rather the darkness. As you know, all the darkness of the world can be squeezed into a single corner, the growing population problem, this, because it generates all of the other problems. And our good Mother and Father have asked us why the Roman Catholic Church has not stepped forward to do its part to help control this problem? For unless it does, the earth They say will very soon return to darkness, for the light that Their great disciple, Edison, once brought into the world will go out forever. In the short span of a single century the population has exhausted more than half of the world's oil supply, something that it took our good Mother and Father more than two hundred million years to create

Our good Father and Mother tell us that They designed the planet to provide for four billion people, and when John, Paul and I left there, now some twenty or thirty some odd years ago, there were already that many there then. Now we understand there are over six billion.

John is quite concerned about this, as according to his plan, which both Paul and I had endorsed, the population should have gone down, not up. He wondered what was going on down there, that the work he had started had not been completed? He suspected that something had gone wrong in the transition somewhere along the way?

And I told John that when I had received word that the *thief of time* would come and take me in the night, that I hurried and gathered up my notes, and I left them in my hands for you. But our good friend Pinocchio, here, tells us that those little devils Casaroli and Caprio had gotten their fingers on them and that you had never seen them.

You evidently still prohibit birth control practices. This is the number one culprit. What has been happening, however, is that the rich nations in North America and Europe have been ignoring your edict; that the people themselves have taken upon their shoulders this responsibility that the Church has chose to ignore. So the Catholic population, discounting immigration, in these countries has been declining.

On the other hand, the Catholic population in Central and South America, Africa and other less developed countries of the world has been skyrocketing; these parishioners have been following the Church's directive to build large families. So, yes, the overall Catholic population has been growing, but this growth has been generating massive poverty, suffering and starvation in these less developed nations.

A good example of this is that since the time we left the average Catholic family in the United States has sired 1.9 children. Whereas the average Catholic family in Mexico, its poor neighbor to the south, has sired 5.7 children and the great majority of these children are brought into a life of poverty, suffering and starvation. There are now more Catholics in the relatively small country of Mexico than there are in the United States; this, despite the fact that a quarter of the Catholic population in the United States has been born in Mexico. More than one-third of the Mexican population is made up of children who have not yet reached their thirteenth birthday and most of these are living in absolute poverty and many others like them in Africa and India are starving to death. As a matter of fact, there are over one hundred million children in the world today who will never reach their thirteenth birthday.

My good Karol, do you know what it is to starve to death? Even as a little child? The pain and suffering is immensely more excruciating than that experienced by our Mother and Father's Son on the cross. Doesn't this bother you each night when you pray before the marble statue of Bernini, which at auction could buy a healthy life for ten thousand of these children? When the robes and gold you wear could be traded in for a thousand more? Did you not know of the letter of Cardinal Gantin of Africa that he wrote to Paul, *"I pray for a day when all children are brought into a world of good health and happiness and opportunity. But one must face reality that today we bring many children into a living hell. That we wrongly assume the position of judgment that is reserved for Christ when, on the final day, He will sit on the great white throne, above."*

But then again Casaroli and Caprio must have taken it from my hands with all the others. This does not speak very well of *Mother Church.* Also, John, Paul and I were equally disturbed by the growing number of abortions. Our plan was twofold,

First, the sexual revolution would eliminate that half of abortions which were caused by embarrassment, that the young girl, who at one time thought that she had gotten herself into trouble, would realize now that she had, indeed, gotten herself into paradise. It has been reported to us that the Church continues to fight against this effort and this greatly disturbs us. Yet, many courageous men and women who have struggled for what is right, have led the sexual revolution which has successfully reduced this, once the primary cause of abortions, to practically zero.

Secondly, another third of abortions were due to teenage pregnancies, in which the young girl did not want to interrupt her young life or could not afford to support the child. And here it was our intent to leave you with a perfect solution. Clinical homosexuals, as you know, comprise almost ten-percent of the population. And it was the Mother and Father Themselves who told us, in no uncertain terms, that this is not a problem. That it is a solution. That it is a part of Their design to provide economic and loving support for these children who otherwise would not be permitted to come through the tunnel. Before I left, I had conveyed this possibility to the Vatican - that the Church should encourage homosexuals, those who are born with the ability to *fall in love* only with one of their sex, to enter into long term loving lifetime relationships, as to allow for the fulfillment of our Mother and Father's plan. To provide love and guidance for children who otherwise would be aborted. But undoubtedly our mutual *friends* Casaroli and Caprio must have swept this one under rug, also.

So despite the fact that the first part of the plan reduced abortions by more than half, total abortions have gone up, not down.

And then there is that growing number of children who will never reach their sixth birthday, already three million, born only to die unspeakable deaths. These are known as AIDS babies, -a result of your policy on unprotected sex. The risk of a child being born of AIDS is becoming so great in some heavily populated Catholic African nations that governments are moving to take the cards out of your hands; it will longer be your choice to ban protective sex and as our dear friend Cardinals Suenens once warned, *"you will have another Galileo on your hands."* Your irresponsible policy of ban on protective sex will very soon result in a ban on natural conception.

And divorce? Yes, divorce and remarriage. I understand that you still persecute those who were not lucky enough to find their lifelong mate on the first time around, that you exile most of them and treat those you retain in exchange for fees and lies as second class citizens. What kind of monster is this church which would condemn these unfortunate children of God to a life of loneliness and despair? Have you no mercy, Karol?

And I told John and Paul that I am particularly concerned about your ongoing persecution of who our good friend Cardinal Suenens refers to as "*the strange little boy in the playground*" Science has told us beyond a shadow of a doubt that he has a condition that he is born with. This is a fact of life. This strange little boy is as much a work of the Mother and Father as you and I. In fact, They tell us that he is one of Their special children. He has as much a right to live his life as you or I. It is just the way the game is played and, as the good Mother and Father so ardently declare, "*It is just the way it is going to be played!*"

And I asked John and Paul, "Why does Karol persist in persecuting these children? Does he not know of the trauma of the strange little boy when he is taunted by his peers? When he is rejected by his parents? Does he not know of the realization of the young teen when he or she realizes that, for he or for she, it is not to be? That he or she's commitment to another can never be seen in society? That he or she can never be a mama or papa?"

But of course, today our Mother and Father have made it possible for everyone to be a mama and a papa through Their miracle of artificial insemination. Yet, you continue to wage a bitter war against Their will, and deny these unfortunate children of our Mother and Father their inalienable right to "*Life, Liberty and the Pursuit of Happiness*" But men and women of great courage who know right from wrong, are rising up and taking these reins from your hands and soon you will have still "*another Galileo on your hands.*"

And there is the matter of women's equality in the Church. I thought I would have pretty much taken care of this one for you my dear Karol but my friends here tell me that the *thief* came and took me in the night just a whisker in time before I would have made this one history. Do you not know that "*God is more our Mother than She is our Father?*" That She is not happy that this kind of petty bigotry goes on -that the Church continues to deny women the privilege to create the Eucharist? It grieves Her dearly that there are still men who still think this way in these things. I know Karol, because I am with Her now and have witnessed the tears flow. She is quite bitter of this thing. Are you and your followers so gullible as to take the word of Moses, the monster of all monsters, in his testimony that mankind has no Mother. That he so despised women that he made no mention of Her in his evil book, this evil thing you call your Holy Bible. Or is it more reasonable to believe that mankind does as a matter of fact have both a Mother and a Father? After all even Moses admitted this when he referred to God as our Father, for a Father cannot be a Father without a Mother.

And there is one more thing Karol. Since the beginning of your reign local bishops have been encouraged to pay off victims of alleged pedophile priests, a result of your policy to *"avoid scandal at any cost."* Do you not know Karol, that a part of that cost is children? Do you not know that it was your sacred duty not only to have not encouraged this sort of thing but to have stepped in and brought an end to it a quarter of a century ago when these misdeeds were first starting to get out of hand? I understand that you still require children as early as the age of seven to discuss what they do with their sexual bodies with potential predatory priests. Have you gone mad, Karol ?

And I asked John and Paul, "Karol is a good man. He has a good heart. It is almost as if he does not know *right* from *wrong?*"

And John suggested, "Perhaps he's not playing with a full deck?"

And it was then, my dear Karol, that it struck me like a bolt of lightning, or as one says in the states, -a ton of bricks. "My God," I said, "my goodness," I corrected myself. "Go quickly, Karol, go quickly into the bedroom. For the *thief of time* is on his way. Go quickly to the great dresser, which stands against the wall. Go quickly to the lower drawer. Go quickly to the lower left-hand corner. And there you will find it, my good Karol, the card, the *winning card.*

It will win for you, Karol. And if it wins for you, then it will win for him, it will win for her, and it will win for all humanity.

And then Karol, only then, will you and I and John and Paul and Aldo and Jack and all the others be able to walk in the woods with our good friend Pinocchio together with the Cat and the Fox and the Poodle, Medoro. And yes, one more, my dear Karol, our old friend Cardinal Suenens, that one day, now so very long ago, came into our lives!"

Your trusted friend,
Piccolo

Don Albino Luciani, John Paul I

afterthought,

Christianity has given the western world much of its greatest architecture, its greatest art, its greatest music, and most of all, its greatest story - the story of Christmas. It is sad that so many evil men have disguised themselves as representatives of Christ and have preyed upon the ignorance and the weakness of the minds of men; conditioning them into thinking that greed and bigotry are somehow virtuous; cleverly misusing Christianity as an evil cloud to spread their hatred of those who are different, from the persecution of Jews, to the subordination of women, to the enslavement of Negroes and to the ongoing persecution of gay children and teenagers today. And most recently, these so-called *evangelistic* or *born again* preachers - the last remnants of *fascism* – have been imposing their hatred upon America's *realist* children; children who are being brought up in a world of *reality* rather than in a world of *make-believe* as were their parents. Children who believe that one's relationship with one's God is a sacred and personal one and not one that should be the business of greedy men. Through the years these evil preachers have made a mockery of our heritage. As our hero Luciani once so profoundly proclaimed, *"If we are ever to be truly free, we must stamp out what Hitler stood for, once and for all."*

I feel that I have said poorly what Albino Luciani could have said so much better. But the important thing is not that I have written, but that you have listened, and that what this good man had to say is now, forever, a part of you.

Now, take this with you wherever you go: Each time the fork in the road comes up - often only minutes apart - ask yourself, ***"Now, what would Jesus have done in this case?"***

Thank you for having read my book.

George Lucien Gregoire

all comments responded to: **vatican@att.net - 410 625 9741**

sequel to this book: ***A God for Lions***
also published as ***The Reincarnation of Albino Luciani***

The author brings Albino Luciani back to life in the voice of a ten year old boy, 'A God for Lions' demonstrates that Christ etched His fundamental message – 'Love thy neighbor as thyself' - into the scriptures of all of the major religions of the world, so that everyone would have an equal chance at salvation. Like 'Dante's Inferno' in which he takes the reader through the various layers of hell, the reincarnated Luciani takes the reader through the very different heavens of the Christian, the Muslim, the Jew, the Hindu, the Buddhist and the Taoist. The work is based on Luciani's doctoral thesis, 'The Origin of the Human Soul.' in which he defines the human soul as it exists in this life, and as it will survive into the next life.

vatican@att.net
www.murderinthevatican.com.
www.authorhouse.com

Printed in the United States
34740LVS00007B/126